FOR ALL THE SAINTS

FOR ALL THE SAINTS

ST. JOHN THE EVANGELIST EPISCOPAL CHURCH

a history

James E. Frazier

AFTON PRESS

Designed by Mary Susan Oleson
Editorial and Production Assistance
 by Beth Williams
Printed by Pettit Network Inc., Afton, Minnesota

Library of Congress Cataloging-in-Publication Data

Frazier, James E.
For all the saints : a history of St. John the
Evangelist Episcopal
Church / by James E. Frazier.—1st ed.
   p. cm.
Includes footnotes (p. 292) and index.
ISBN 978-1-890434-86-1 (hardcover : alk. paper)
1. St. John the Evangelist Episcopal Church
(Saint Paul, Minn.)—History.
2. Saint Paul (Minn.)—Church history. I. Title.
BX5980.S2155F73 2014
283'.776581--dc23

                                        2012010039

Printed in China

Patricia Condon McDonald
Publisher

🌣 AFTON PRESS
165 Western Avenue N., Ste. 15
St. Paul, MN 55102
651-436-8443
aftonpress@gmail.com
www.aftonpress.com

The publication of

FOR ALL THE SAINTS

ST. JOHN THE EVANGELIST
EPISCOPAL CHURCH

has been made possible by gifts from

James E. Johnson, Dusty Mairs, Betty Myers

and

C. Robert and Camilla Beattie
Louis and Carolyn Benepe
Roger and Roberta Benson
Deborah L. and Phillip A. Bienhoff
Elizabeth Ann Biorn
Patricia D. Brynteson
Carolyn Buser
Marvin and Susan Cadwell
Bradley and Mary-Louise Clary
Edward and Monica Cook
Carol Daniels
Jay and Rebecca Debertin
Judith Parish and
  Richard Diedrich
Karen Dingle
Alden Drew and Mimie Pollard
Richard M. and
  Genevieve Dunlop
Anne L. Elsinger
Silas and Olivia Ford
James E. Frazier
George C. Power Jr. Family Fund
  of The Saint Paul Foundation
Bob and Phyllis Goff
Kathryn Q. Graber
Reynolds W. and Mary D. Guyer
Edward H. Hamm
Gar Hargens and
  Missy Thompson
Robert H. Horn
Barbara J. Johnson
Mary L. Johnson
Lucy Rosenberry Jones
Ron and Judith Josephson
Robert and Beth Kendall

Judge James W. Kerr Jr.
John and Judy Kinkead
Christopher and Leeann Kuhn
James and Nancy Langler
Craig and Elizabeth Lindeke
Gail E. Lorenz
Richard and Susan Lyman
Patrick and Roxanna Markie
Nancy D. Martin
Malcolm and Patricia McDonald
Phyllis Merrill
Thomas and Mary Murakami
Peter and Karla Myers
Fred and Patricia Myers
Catherine A. Napier
Pauline G. O'Brien
Jeffrey J. and Margaret A. Olsen
Lyelle and Mary Frances Palmer
Michael Parish
Virginia B. Parrish
Don Postema and
  Gabrielle Lawrence
Joan Potter
Andrew and Sara Schmitt
Susan Oehler Seltzer and
  Jonathan Seltzer
Jay and Kathryn Severance
Ella C. Slade
Libby Snelson and
  Dr. Brett Gemlo
Judith Southwick
Ann Walton
Jerry and Becky J. Woelfel
Biloine W. Young

Front cover: St. John's church tower. Kevin Matthews, Eugene, Oregon.
Opposite half-title page (p. 2): Wilder memorial baptismal font. Aimee Baxter, St. Paul, Minnesota.
Frontispiece (p. 4): Wood carving of St. John the Evangelist on lectern in front of altar facing the congregation. St. John the Evangelist Episcopal Church, St. Paul, Minnesota.
Copyright page (p. 6): Benedicite stained glass window and organ pipes. St. John the Evangelist Episcopal Church.
Back cover: Easter Sunday, 2011. St. John the Evangelist Episcopal Church.

*For all the saints who for more than 130 years
have made St. John's what it is today.*

CONTENTS _____

foreword

LIKE YOU, DEAR READER, when I was called to St. John's in 2011, I was eager to imbibe the stories and share in the memories contained on the pages that follow. To know a place and a people, and to know them thoroughly, to understand what gives them form and substance, one must examine the soil in which they have grown and found nourishment over the years.

When I arrived at St. John's I likened my first task as a new rector to the work of a historian, asking questions, listening to the stories, and seeking out the collective wisdom of the place to which I have been called as pastor and priest. Little did I know that fine work was already under way in this regard, and that much of this would be collected in a bound volume for me and for all of us to consult morning, noon, or night. Thanks to the careful and meticulous work of Jim Frazier, what you hold in your hands is a well-honed and comprehensive look at the stories, the events, and characters that have made our church home, St. John the Evangelist, the place we have come to cherish and love. Taken at its total—the many musings, remembrances, the vestry minutes and *Evangelist* articles—this is a story about, and *for*, all the saints who have graced our parish across the years.

In times past the term "saint" was reserved for those who had lived virtuous and heroic Christian lives and, in many cases, those who had died for their faith. In recent times the gaze has turned toward recognizing saints as ordinary people just like you and me. Like us, saints have good days and bad. They are imperfect—human, really—composed of the same dust that gives each of us form and substance. Yet, like saints we are also graced with the presence and very breath of God. Through Jim's careful and thorough retelling we hear a story of a place where over the decades, centuries even, folks have gathered, and in all their humbling, stumbling humanity, opened themselves to the possibility that God could be present in and through their lives. I am grateful for his portrayal of this community, both fair and eloquent, and I am grateful to find myself in the midst of saints such as he has described, who are worthy of this history.

The Rev. Jered Weber-Johnson, RECTOR

The Rev. Jered Weber-Johnson.

Organist and Choir Director James E. Frazier.

IT WAS A CHILLY NIGHT on March 23, 1885, when the men of St. John's vestry met at its frame church at Ashland and Mackubin in St. Paul. Among other things, they ordered its clerk, Albert Matheson Eddy, to send letters to Mrs. H. G. White and her sister, Mrs. E. M. Davis Jr., of Philadelphia. These letters were to express the gratitude of the parish for the sisters' gift of "a beautiful solid silver chalice and paten (in a suitable case) with linen cloths to be used with them on the altar as required by the rubrics." The women intended that the communion service, being "used in commemorating our Redeemer's love . . . may also serve to perpetuate the memory of dear ones, who, having served Him faithfully, no longer need such emblems, for they now see Him 'face to face.'"

Being a memorial not for anyone in particular, but for all the saints, and not only for those who lived and died as members of the parish, but indeed for *all* the saints, the gift of these sisters suggested the title for this book: *For All the Saints*. This perception is particularly poignant in a place like St. John's, where the columbarium behind the high altar contains the remains of some of our saints who have preceded us in death.

The sisters' gift reflects the fact that the church in its earthly estate, enjoying life through grace, is one with the church triumphant, with those in glory who see God "face to face." The two women wrote that their gift expresses "a kindly interest in the work of those who are striving to have bound together in Christ those who are in this life with those who have passed from this life to His blessed place of rest."

This first memorial gift to be named in the written records of the parish, the sisters' communion service also launched what would become a long history of generous gifts by members of St. John's to memorialize deceased loved ones and to commemorate important events, reminding us meanwhile that we are surrounded by a cloud of witnesses. It is hard to overlook the ubiquity of plaques sited around the parish buildings or the inscriptions etched on stained glass windows and carved into wood, remembering countless members of the parish, many of them named elsewhere in this book.

A congregation is not a club. Nor is it a party or a bloodline. We do not join it by having the right credentials, by paying dues, or by knowing the right people. Some may be rich while others are destitute. Many of St. John's early members, the families of prominent St. Paul business leaders, employed maids, seamstresses, chauffeurs, and gardeners, while more than one of its boy choristers later recalled that they did not realize how poor their families were at the time. Then, as now, there was more diversity at St. John's than at first met the eye. No one needs to be beautiful or healthy to join in our congregation; indeed all have warts, wrinkles, and painful secrets to bear. Some arrive and stay for generations while others drop by for a moment or a season, virtually unannounced and unnoticed, and slowly disappear.

But all are saints. And together they constitute a congenial mix of ordinary and extraordinary folks who cherish knowing that they all belong. And to what do they belong? Though they may not all be able to articulate it, they belong to a community that seeks the Holy. In worship, in service, and in community they seek the divine. It may invigorate them, it may challenge them, it may baffle them, or it may completely escape them. But they all seek the indefinable, the unfathomable, the inestimable, whatever they believe gives ultimate meaning and sense to their sometimes incomprehensible lives. This book is about all of these people. Those named and those unnamed. The well-remembered and the largely forgotten. All deserve our holy regard.

THIS BOOK WAS FRED'S IDEA. One fine day in October 2010, St. John's historian and longtime archivist Frederick Myers approached me with the audacious suggestion that I should write a new history of the parish, to set the record straight. As the idea grew on me, I finally acquiesced. Fred, by the way, became archivist not by election or appointment but merely by being asked one day if he'd mind "organizing all of those boxes."

I realize that an effort such as this one may draw criticism for bias, ignorance, or even sloppy research, but this was a risk that I thought worth taking. In a very real sense, I am less the author of this book and more its editor. Beginning in 1882, the vestry minutes, and later *The Evangelist* and the *Yearbooks*, among other documents, constitute the congregation's writing of its own history, making this book the church's autobiography. Every historian, of course, must draw lines, lines between the public and the private, for instance, lines between the facts and the imaginings, and in the case of this book, lines between those who are named and those who are not. No offense is intended as this book is for all the saints, but for my errors of fact or omission, I apologize.

The only way to acknowledge and thank my Advisory Committee is through admiring understatement. Six remarkable people agreed to take this fascinating walk with me without any real assurance as to where it might take them. But in their various ways they have helpfully guided, gently chided, and patiently abided my sometimes faltering efforts. In the process I have made of them lasting friends. They have undertaken some of the research themselves and explored the archives, they have shared their memories, they have corrected and otherwise improved upon the manuscript, they have supported the overall project, and they have contributed of their own resources and raised an enormous amount of money in order to bring this book to life. All of them have long connections with the parish, so much so that in some respects this book can be said to be a scrapbook of their own memories. I extend my deepest gratitude to Alden Drew, Jim Johnson, Dusty Mairs, Patricia McDonald, Betty Myers, and Fred Myers, and commend them all for their competence and their commitment to this worthy effort.

The author also acknowledges with gratitude and appreciation the many others who provided information, photographs, and other important contributions to the content of the book. These include Aimee Richcreek Baxter, stellar parish photographer, who gave unstintingly of her time and talent to provide numerous superior images for this book, particularly of the stained glass windows; Sean C. Benjamin, Public Services Librarian, Howard-Tilton Memorial Library, Tulane University; the Rev. David Benson, assistant rector under the Rev. William Mead; Barbara Bezat, Northwest Architectural Archives, University of Minnesota; Marshall Carter, Trinity Church, Bay City, Michigan; Aaron W. Davis, Esq., copyright attorney; Priscilla Farnham, parishioner and former executive director of the Ramsey County Historical Society; Angela Ford, granddaughter of the Rt. Rev. Edward M. Cross; Rhoda R. Gilman, author of *Henry Hastings Sibley: Divided Heart*; Gar Hargens, parishioner and president of Close Associates, Architects; Dennis Harrell, archivist, Christ Church Cathedral, Cincinnati; John M. Lindley, editor of *Ramsey County History*; Randal Loy, historian to the Dean of Grace and Holy Trinity Cathedral, Kansas City, Missouri; the Rev. Dr. Andrew MacBeth, interim rector at Christ Church, Grosse Point Farms, Michigan; Mary Maronde, project specialist, Humphrey School of Public Affairs, University of Minnesota; William McIntosh III, author of "The Spiritual Journey of St. Philip's Church: 1906-2012;" Larry Millett, journalist, former architectural critic for the *St. Paul Pioneer Press*, and author of *Lost Twin Cities*; Chuck Neve, minister of administration, Dayton Avenue Presbyterian Church; Eliza Rosenberg, research center associate, Ramsey County Historical Society; John Schuessler, managing editor, *The Living Church*; Kathy Mead Van Heusen, daughter of the Rt. Rev. William H. and Katherine Mead; the Rev. Frank Wilson, the fifteenth rector of St. John's; and the Rev. Letha Wilson-Barnard, vicar of Holy Apostles Episcopal Church, St. Paul.

And also the many parishioners and friends of St John's, including Kenneth H. Bayliss III, Cammie Beattie, Robert Beattie, Bruce Binger, C. Robert Binger, Tom Binger, Helen Boyer, Kathy Brown, Pat Brynteson, Marvin Cadwell, Sue Cadwell, Robbin Clamons, Bradley Clary, Mary-Louise Clary, Marilyn Conklin, Edward Cook, Jay Debertin, John Edgerton III, Dorothy Ek, Julia Ferguson, Beverly Finley,

Jonathan Frost, Gary Hagstrom, Bob Horn, Phyllis Goff, Robert Goff, Tom Jacobs, Caroline Jaffray, David Jensen, Helen Jensen, Lucy Rosenberry Jones, Judith Pinkerton Josephson, Jennifer Kinkead, Gregory Larsen, Gabrielle Lawrence, Nan Lightner, Mary Lilja, Barbara Lindeke, Craig Lindeke, Richard Lyman, Dorothy MacDonald, Shirley Kartarik Michienzi, Jim Moore, the Rev. Barbara Mraz, Clelia Thompson Mulally, Peter Myers, Catherine Ann Napier, Jeff Olsen, Vikki Peterson, Sona Plummer, William Plummer, Diane Power, George C. Power III, the Rev. Diana Rogers, Shirley Sailors, Jay Severance, Ella Slade, Hank Snyder, Dick Yore, and Kristy Yore.

I am grateful to have found an exceptionally talented publisher among our own parishioners. Patricia Condon McDonald is the founding publisher of Afton Press, which brought this beautiful tome to print. Beth Williams at Afton Press provided copyediting, proofreading, and indexing, and coordinated this book project at every step of the way. Graphic artist Mary Susan Oleson designed with remarkable thought and care the striking cover and each interior page, enveloping this history of our parish in a volume worthy of its content.

Through all of these saints, and through all the saints, may God be glorified.

James E. Frazier,
ORGANIST AND DIRECTOR OF MUSIC
(2004–2013)

AND IN TRIBUTE *to* W. FREDERICK MYERS II

Parish historian and archivist

A life-long student of history and languages nurtured at Macalester College

A member of the Men and Boys Choir

Clerk of the Vestry

A member of the Property and Building Committees

Teacher in the Church School

Convener of the Men's Breakfast on second Saturdays

A member of the Parish History Committee

The lovable curmudgeon who died during the final preparations for this book.

The St. John's History Book Committee, left to right, standing: Jim Johnson, Jim Frazier, Alden Drew, and Fred Myers; seated, Dusty Mairs, Betty Myers, and Patricia McDonald.

Dayton Avenue Presbyterian Church where St. John's congregation held its first services on January 9, 1881. The churchmen are unidentified but may be the Presbyterian church's pastor, Dr. Edwards, and some of its trustees, 1885.

ON MARCH 22, 1981, in celebration of the centennial of St. John the Evangelist Episcopal Church, parishioner Woody Keljik preached the following sermon from its pulpit. Addressing his twentieth-century congregation as if he were speaking to an earlier gathering on the third Sunday in Lent in March 1881, Mr. Keljik described for them the journey on which they were about to embark, amidst their present circumstances, prefacing his remarks with these words of Psalm 127, verses 1-2:

Unless the LORD builds the house,
the builders labor in vain.
Unless the LORD watches over the city,
the guards stand watch in vain.

"THESE WORDS, among the most magnificent in the Psaltery, if not in the whole of the Old Testament, are highly suitable to the occasion upon which we are met this morning. For this is the start of a long and difficult journey, largely upon uncharted seas. We shall be engaged in a frenzy of building—our physical church, and its voluminous furnishings and equipment, our membership rolls, our Church school, our mission, and our outreach.

"If we build with earthly and temporal tools, trusting in our varied skills to guide us, and forget to call upon Him who alone builds with celestial tools, indeed, the tools of the carpenter of Nazareth, then all our dreams shall vanish as at daybreak, and all our hopes turn to ashes and dust. . . .

"It is not the custom in preaching from an Anglican pulpit to take more than formal note of the temporal events of the day in community, state, nation, and in the world at large. Rather we preach from a text taken from one of the lessons appointed for the day or from the Propers—the Collect, Epistle, or Gospel appointed for that Sunday . . . but today shall be an exception as it seems fitting and proper to view the scene near and far to determine whence we came, where we are, and whither we are going.

"I should wish first to define the nature of this meeting this morning, in order to inform those who might have come in off the street to worship with us, that today, the 20th of March is the official launching of the Parish of St. John the Evangelist in the Diocese of Minnesota. And we gain this distinction and privilege by vote of the Standing Committee of our Diocese and the approval of our beloved Bishop, the Rt. Rev. Henry B. Whipple, first Bishop of Minnesota. . . .

"While our own Church will be abuilding this spring and summer on Ashland Avenue, we are grateful to the pastor and congregation of the Dayton Avenue Presbyterian Church for . . . the use of their church. May it please God that this fraternal association between our churches and

Left to Right: 1. Bishop Henry Whipple, the first Episcopal Bishop of Minnesota in 1859, photo ca. 1870. 2. The Catholic Chapel of St. Paul, the nucleus of the city of St. Paul. 3. Father Lucien Galtier, born in France, the first Roman Catholic priest in St. Paul, ca. 1850. 4. James M. Goodhue, Minnesota's first newspaper editor, ca. 1850.

our denominations shall endure while both may last.

"We can look back with pardonable pride upon the enormous progress of our city, less than forty years distant from Father [Lucien] Galtier's construction of his chapel on 3rd Street near Minnesota Street, which he likened in its poverty to the stable of Bethlehem. [That he changed] the name of the settlement from Pig's Eye to St. Paul . . . asking that it be tied to the Apostle to the Nations occasioned an ingenious bit of verse from Mr. James Goodhue, publisher and editor of the *Minnesota Pioneer* [who] found an analogy to the name change in the story of the conversion of Saul on the road to Damascus as told in the Acts of the Apostles: 'Pig's Eye, converted shalt thou be, like Saul; Arise and henceforth be St. Paul.'

"In these forty years we have experienced great events. Our territorial period from 1849 to 1858; the attempt to take the state capital from us and put it down in St. Peter in 1857; the terrible financial panic of 1857 which bankrupted many of our citizens and reduced real estate prices to a half and a quarter of what they were; the Great Rebellion [Civil War] and our important role in its suppression: our state was the first to volunteer our First Minnesota Infantry Regiment on President Lincoln's call . . . ; our internal war in the state in the midst of the war, in the Santee Sioux Outbreak [Dakota War of 1862] in Brown, Nicollet, and Yellow Medicine Counties; the panic of 1873 which almost destroyed Duluth; the successive grasshopper plagues in the late '70's and finally

this terrible and dreadful winter of '81 which continues to rage even now, though by chance today is the Vernal Equinox, the first day of spring. But in spite of all, we now number over 40,000 souls and are growing rapidly. I had occasion to speak to our Mayor, William Dawson, during the week, and he informs me that the character of our immigration has been changing through the '70s and appears headed for more startling changes in the present decade.

"Whereas the original mix of our people through the Rebellion was largely Yankee with some German and Irish admixture, lately the influx has been heavily from Northern and Western Europe almost directly. But, now, for the first time we are seeing men of a more unfamiliar visage, speaking strange tongues, on our city's streets, as the first arrivals from Southern and Eastern Europe reach St. Paul. Poles, Italians, Hungarians, and Greeks, and be certain that the future will witness even greater changes—Father Galtier was inspired when he named us for the Apostle to the Nations. . . .

"Governor John Pillsbury, with whom I also had occasion to speak last week, along with his legislators, appears to be almost in shock over the calamitous fire that destroyed our state capitol ten days ago. The poor legislators, as you no doubt have read, were barely able to get out before the roof collapsed over them, and are today hard-pressed to pursue the work of solons in quarters suited to their dignity. And as we also lost our State Insane Asylum to fire at about the same time, the *Cincinnati Gazette* was unkind enough to

LEFT TO RIGHT: 1. First Minnesota Regiment, Company D, at the corner of Nicollet Avenue and First Street in Minneapolis, 1861. 2. Dacotah House, used as a hospital by Dr. W. W. Mayo during the Dakota War of 1862, New Ulm, ca. 1865. 3. The St. Paul Roller Mill Company on West Kellogg between St. Peter and Market Streets, ca 1881.

write that they are not quite sure which of the two institutions housed the greater number of the mentally ill. But we shall prove them wrong, for the Governor has assured us all that a new and much larger capitol will arise on the same site at 10th and Cedar, very quickly. . . .

"Mr. Garfield's inauguration on the 4th of this month should give us all great satisfaction, not only because in him and in Mr. Arthur, we have an excellent President and Vice-President, but also because it brings to an end all the bitterness and divisiveness caused by the election of '76 and the Tilden-Hayes dispute. Mr. Hayes, though a fine man, was wise not to seek re-election.

"I should be remiss in discussion of the current scene, if I did not say a few words on the fine city that is growing up west of the River. You will recall that a few years ago, St. Anthony was annexed to Minneapolis, which gave the latter a surge in population. It is a beautiful and thriving city and I urge you, if you have not done so recently to pay it a visit. It is less than an hour and a half by horse-drawn car. I say all this in spite of the vain boasts made by some of their leaders recently that they expect someday to exceed in population our own fair city. You laugh and with good reason, but we can be magnanimous and say to them, in the words of the prophet Joel, 'Let their young men see visions, and their old men dream dreams.'

"Those of you who follow such matters are probably familiar with some of the proceedings at our general convention recently concluded in Boston. Rev. Dr. William Huntington submitted a resolution [which] was adopted and calls for the appointment of a Committee to study certain changes in our 1789 *Book of Common Prayer*. The changes, I believe, revolve about the *Nunc dimittis*, the *Benedictus* and the Propers for a number of the Trinity Sundays. I am astonished that a man of the erudition and intelligence of Dr. Huntington would busy himself with the effort to tamper with what is, next only to the authorized Bible itself, the most priceless literary treasure of the English speaking peoples. Our Prayer Book is unchanged since the days of Bishop Seabury and only the war of the Revolution and our dissolution from the British Crown made changes at that time necessary. Otherwise, it stands very much as it was in the reign of Charles II, in 1662. Although we are a new and weak parish, we should summon such resources as we have to oppose these gentlemen. . . .

"But our progress is not only in population and construction, but nearly staggering nationally in industry, invention and transportation. We hear from Mr. Henry Villard in New York, the president of our Northern Pacific Railway, that his line, within two or three years will reach the distance to the great Western Sea and will link our city by twin ribbons of steel to the Pacific. Among our local railroad men, Mr. Kittson and Mr. Hill, together with a group of Canadian financiers have revived the old St. Paul and Pacific and now promise that it, too, will reach the coast within fifteen years.

"More startling is the news from the East during the past two years. Mr. Bell in Boston is now installing miles of lines in New

LEFT TO RIGHT: 1. Minnesota's first state capitol at Tenth and Cedar Streets, ca. 1875. 2. John Sargent Pillsbury, governor of Minnesota, 1876-1882. 3. Garfield Memorial Arch, erected in St. Paul to commemorate the assassination of President James A. Garfield in July 1881.

Haven to carry the human voice over a wire. We are now promised the possibility of speaking to our neighbors in St. Anthony without either of us leaving our parlors. Mr. Edison in New Jersey goes him one better and is now completing experiments which seek to capture and hold the human voice on a cylinder of metal. His invention to provide illumination through an incandescent lamp may result in our streets one day blazing at night with the lighting power of tens of thousands of candles. To each of these we can do nothing but repeat the words of Mr. Samuel Morse, when the first message went across the electric telegraph 'What hath God wrought?' Perhaps we have reached the limits of human ingenuity and in the interests of economy, we may well consider the closing of the Patent Office.

"Dispatches arriving from St. Petersburg inform us that Czar Alexander II was assassinated a few days ago. You will recall that it was this particular Czar who freed the Russian serfs [in 1863]. . . . In Germany we see the rise of a great new empire, under Count Otto Bismarck, and a new Kaiser in Wilhelm Hohenzollern. The older Austro-Hungarian Empire, made up of a babble of tongues and peoples, continues under another Kaiser, Franz Josef. In France, though the latest Napoleon was deposed ten years ago, and a republic now exists, the same grandiose dreams of Empire in Asia and Africa persist. While in Britain, where the temporal head of our own Communion resides, the Queen, The Defender of the Faith, has recently also become Empress of India through the efforts of Mr. Disraeli. Contemplate for a moment this vast array of power: Alexander III, Czar of all the Russias;

Wilhelm Hohenzollern, King of Prussia and Emperor of Germany; Franz Josef, hereditary King of Hungary and Kaiser of the Austro-Hungarian Empire; Victoria, by grace of God, Queen of Great Britain, Ireland and the Dominions beyond the sea, Empress of India; Umberto, King of Italy, who dreams of the Adriatic Sea again becoming an Italian lake, as it was 1400 years ago; and in our own country, our leaders speak of Manifest Destiny as we drive the original inhabitants into ever lessening enclaves. . . . As men and women of the religion of Christ, what must be our view and in what light must we judge this vast assemblage of power, including that of our own country? . . .

"And how can we, a freshly hatched little parish, without a church building, a handful of members, beginning a long, long trail in this terrible and dreadful winter of '81, still raging throughout the state, how must we accommodate? For the road is strewn with obstacles and the way will be steep. We shall experience financial problems, weather problems, sickness, death of our leaders, discouragement, and near despair. We shall be plagued, too, be certain of it, with the normal complement of the shortcomings of human nature. The effects of pride and envy, of greed and anger, and gluttony, lechery, and sloth. We shall be hard pressed again and again. Whence will we turn for strength, sustenance and support? Is it a vain thing, was it without purpose, is it for naught, that we chose for the name of our parish that of the Fourth Evangelist, St. John, whose symbol for centuries has always been that most puissant of birds [the eagle] before whose wings and talons and beak all other creatures of the sky shrink in terror? 'Hast thou

LEFT TO RIGHT: 1. William Dawson Sr., mayor of St. Paul, 1878-1888, with son William Dawson Jr., and grandson William Dawson III, ca. 1895. 2. Snow blockade, Southern Minnesota Division, Chicago, Milwaukee and St. Paul Railway, 1881. 3. West side St. Paul during high water, 1881.

not known, hast thou not heard, that the everlasting God, the Lord, the Creator of the ends of the world, faints not, neither is weary? . . . He giveth power to the faint and to them that have no might, he increaseth strength. Even the youths shall faint and be weary and the young men shall utterly fall, but they that wait upon the Lord shall renew their strength. They shall mount up with wings as eagles. . . .'

"Let us then, so lay our plans, so set our course, so devise our goals, so blaze a trail, and so conceive and prosecute our mission in this state and city, in this Diocese and parish, that men and women, yet long unborn, our successors here as the generations unfold, peering back through the shadows and mists and murky fog of the distant future, in a time and circumstances of which we here today can have but the scantest of knowledge, will say to us, the founding congregation of the Church of St. John the Evangelist, as gathered here on this, the third Sunday in Lent, in the year of our Lord 1881, 'Well done, well done, thou good and faithful servants.'"

WHILE IT MAY BE DIFFICULT TO BELIEVE, because today there are no Episcopal churches in downtown St. Paul, in the early years of the city, there were three. Christ Church was the "mother church" of the Diocese of Minnesota. Organized in 1850 by the Revs. James Lloyd Breck, J. V. Merrick, and Timothy Wilcoxson, the original Christ Church stood at the corner of Cedar and Fourth. A second church erected in 1871 was destroyed by fire shortly thereafter, and a third church was built at the corner of Fourth and Franklin and opened for worship in November 1872. This third Christ Church was razed in late 1930 to accommodate the expansion of the city auditorium. Then when the interstate highway system cut a swath through the downtown area, the congregation abandoned its fourth church building, at Sixth and Pleasant, in December 1973, and moved to the eastern St. Paul suburb of Woodbury.

St. Paul's Episcopal Church was organized in 1856 and celebrated its first service in the newly built Washington Schoolhouse at Eighth and Olive Streets in July 1857. The cornerstone of its first church was laid by Bishop Kemper in July 1878 at the corner of Ninth and Olive, for twenty-six communicants. The congregation held its last service in this downtown church on July 28, 1912, before moving to its present location on Summit Avenue at Saratoga Street, where it is known as St. Paul's-on-the-Hill. Men of prominence served St. Paul's downtown as wardens and vestrymen, including Minnesota Governor Henry Hastings Sibley, who was buried from this church.

The third parish to be established in downtown St. Paul was the Church of the Good Shepherd founded in 1867 by the Rev. William C. Pope. Its first service was held in May of that year at Mackubin's Block on Washington Street, between Third and Fourth Streets. When the Mackubin's Block was destroyed by fire in April 1868, the congregation quickly rebuilt; its new church building on Twelfth and Cedar Streets was dedicated in October 1869.

LEFT TO RIGHT: 1. Christ Church in downtown St. Paul, ca. 1860. 2. The Rev. Mahlon N. Gilbert, bishop coadjutor of the Diocese of Minnesota, 1886-1900. 3. St. Paul's Episcopal Church, ca. 1870. 4. Church of the Good Shepherd, ca. 1880.

A Meeting of the Vestry was held at the Church building the 23d January 1882.

There were present.

Rev. Henry Kittson Dr. Senkler

W. H. Conover J. Schefer

Major C. J. Allen Jos. McKay

Col. J. F. A. Studdart Robt. A. Bethune

The Meeting was called to order, the Rev. Henry Kittson in the Chair.

Robt. A. Bethune was appointed to act as Secretary.

The Rev. Henry Kittson left the Chair, and, on Motion, J. Schefer took it.

It was then moved by Dr. Senkler, seconded by Col. Studdart, that the Rev. Henry Kittson receive the appointment of Rector of this Parish.

chapter one

THE REV. HENRY W. KITTSON 1881-1884
The Birth of St. John's

RAMSEY HILL. All three of the sites on which St. John the Evangelist Episcopal Church would eventually construct its buildings in which to worship, study, and conduct its ministries are located in the area now called Ramsey Hill. Bordered by the Cathedral of St. Paul on the east, Dale Street on the west, Marshall Avenue on the north, and the Grand Avenue bluff on the south, this region was an expanse of mostly fields and scrub oaks when St. John's celebrated its first public worship—a service of evensong— on January 9, the Sunday after Epiphany, in 1881.

Our first congregants gathered in the chapel of the wooden Dayton Avenue Presbyterian Church, with its high-pitched roof, at the corner of Mackubin Street, immediately following Sunday School.[1] St. John's first Sunday School class was comprised of twenty-one enrolled scholars and four teachers—Mr. and Mrs. Horne, Laura Mann, and Frank Barton. Parishioners read from the 1789 *Book of Common Prayer* then in use in American Episcopal churches. There were four boys in the choir, with fifty-four people representing fifteen families, namely: Ward, Schefers, McKee, Larkin, Slater, Senkler, Emerson, Mann, Pain, Horn, Horton, Wagner, Barton, Cartmel, and the Rev. Henry Kittson. Their offering of five dollars went to pay the Presbyterians for the use of their building.

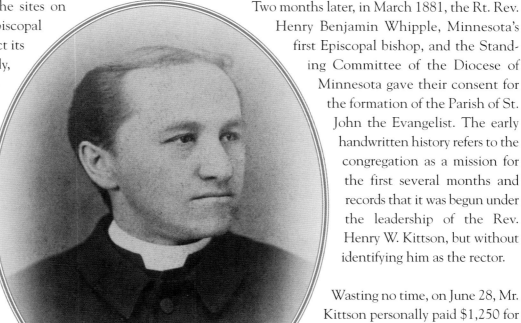

The Rev. Henry Kittson, St. John's first rector.

Two months later, in March 1881, the Rt. Rev. Henry Benjamin Whipple, Minnesota's first Episcopal bishop, and the Standing Committee of the Diocese of Minnesota gave their consent for the formation of the Parish of St. John the Evangelist. The early handwritten history refers to the congregation as a mission for the first several months and records that it was begun under the leadership of the Rev. Henry W. Kittson, but without identifying him as the rector.

Wasting no time, on June 28, Mr. Kittson personally paid $1,250 for two lots on which to construct a church at the northeast corner of Ashland Avenue and Mackubin Street. Mr. Kittson retained ownership of the land. This location fell within the fashionable Woodland Park addition to St. Paul, three blocks due south of the Presbyterian church, and a mere two blocks northeast of St. John's present buildings on Kent Street and Portland Avenue. It was a generous deed on the part of Kittson, and he immediately had the support of parishioners Eugene Ward, W. L. Anderson, Jacob Schefers, and W. H. Mingaye in his efforts to build a frame church. This first St. John the Evangelist Episcopal Church faced west, cost about two thousand dollars, and seated one hundred fifty members.[2] Parishioner Louis Wagner was the builder for this new church in which the congregation held its first service— a service of Holy Communion—on July 28, 1881. The celebrant was the Rev. Theo. Riley; the gospeller, the Rev.

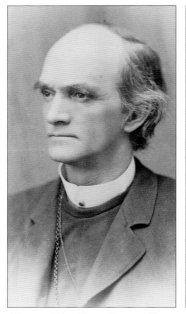

Above: The Rev. George Brayton Whipple, Bishop Whipple's brother. Right: Bishop Henry Benjamin Whipple, Minnesota's first Episcopal bishop (1859-1901).

William C. Pope; the epistler, the Rev. Henry Kittson. The Rev. Mahlon N. Gilbert, rector of Christ Church in downtown St. Paul, addressed the congregation, which was said in number to have been "fair," with about twenty-five people receiving communion. At Choral Evensong at seven o'clock, the clergymen in addition to Mr. Kittson included the Revs. Dr. Knickerbacker, Livermore, Miller, Johnson, W. Pope, and George Brayton Whipple. Bishop Whipple gave the address. There is no known image of this first St. John's church.

The Parish of St. John was formally organized on December 29, 1881, and laymen were elected to positions of leadership. Present at this historic meeting were N. H. Mingaye, Jacob Schefers, I. F. A. Stoddart, Louis Wagner, Joseph McKee, Edward Quinliven, Robert A. Bethune, W. H. Conver, and Dr. A. E. Senkler. Jacob Schefers was elected senior warden, and W. H. Conver, junior warden, with McKee, Senkler, Bethune, Stoddart and Maj. Charles J. Allen elected to the vestry.

At their first meeting, on January 23, 1882, the gentlemen of the vestry named Mr. Kittson their rector and Mr. Conver their treasurer. This meeting was seminal; several items on the agenda bore significance to the legal and canonical sta-

A NEW ORGAN arrived in January 1882 at St. John's, which also prided itself for its surpliced choir of thirteen boys. Young Bryan Ripley Dorr, pictured at right in 1885, would become a chorister in the men and boys choir and later, the

organist at Park Congregational Church in St. Paul. The Rev. Kittson subscribed to certain principles in the catholicizing trend that had its roots in the nineteenth-century Oxford Movement in England. Indeed his advanced tastes were esthetical and ecclesiastical, meaning "high church." Otherwise he would have hired a professional adult quartet that did not vest, then the general norm. One writer, in 1890, objected to "the display of divers colors and fashions often seen in the church choir."[3] Choirs in surplices constituted an innovation, along with the use of candles (often called Eucharistic lights), Eucharistic vestments, and sometimes, incense, were perceived as a progressive movement at the time. Indeed, many churches in the diocese would have surpliced choirs in the coming years.

tus of the congregation. This vestry inaugurated the system of giving by pledges. Prior to this time the congregation's financial support of St. John's came from the rental of "sittings," a widespread practice in those years. A household would pay monthly rent for a particular pew, good for the year, entitling them to sit in that location whenever they attended services. The disadvantage of this system was that it reinforced class distinctions, inasmuch as those who could pay more would have the better seats, while those paying less would sit on the sides or in the rear of the church. The

The residence of vestryman Dr. Senkler at 177 Virginia, 1889.

Some parishioners likely were members of the Delta Lawn Tennis Club at Selby and Mackubin, photo ca. 1888.

Some enjoyed boating and strolling at Lake Como, ca. 1880.

Left: Major Charles A. Allen was named to St. John's first vestry in 1881. Right: Albert Matheson Eddy was elected a warden at the first meeting of the vestry on January 23, 1882. Mr. Eddy lived at 579 Holly Avenue.

new system of pledges entitled everyone to "free" seats, thus blurring class distinctions. Parishes that had free seating in those years were considered progressive. At St. John's, the pledge system was adopted and put into operation on Easter Sunday, April 9, 1882, but was abandoned in 1886 when the pew rental system was restored.[4]

At this same January meeting of the vestry, the gentlemen agreed to take the proper legal steps for the incorporation of the parish in the state of Minnesota, which was accomplished on April 18, 1882.[5] The Articles of Incorporation filed with the Secretary of State were signed and sealed by the Rev. Kittson, along with wardens Jacob Schefers and Albert Matheson Eddy, and vestrymen Bethune, Allen, Conver, McKee, and Wagner.

A day earlier, St. John's parishioners had assembled for their first Annual Meeting on April 17, 1882. The rector reported that services had been held regularly in the church since the vestry was formed the previous December. There were thirty communicants in the parish.[6] During the partial year completed there were two baptisms, one marriage, and one

THE REVEREND HENRY W. KITTSON was born in 1848 at Pembina, now in North Dakota, at the border with Canada, where his father, Norman W. Kittson, had established an American Fur Company trading post. The elder Kittson was the son of a non-commissioned officer in the British Army who had come to Canada in 1776, the year Americans declared their independence. In the mid-1850s Norman Kittson moved to St. Paul where he operated a fur trading and supply business.

Young Henry was meanwhile educated at Bishop's College near Lennoxville in Quebec, then a seminary for the training of Anglican clergy, from which he received his BA and MA degrees. In 1875 he married Flora Macdonald Grant of St. Johns, Quebec, and was canonically received into the Diocese of Minnesota four years later. Before coming to St. John's, he served seven years at the Mission of the Ascension in West St. Paul, where weekly celebrations of the Holy Communion were the rule from the beginning. The seats were free and Henry Kittson established a vested choir.

burial. The second baptism, in November, was baby Mildred Beatrice Kittson, the daughter of the rector and his wife, Flora Kittson. Mildred Beatrice Kittson had been born in Montreal three months earlier, in August 1881. The rector's salary was fixed at $750.

A year later, on Easter Monday, March 26, 1883, the rector reported fifty-three communicants, thirteen baptisms, seven confirmations, two marriages, and four burials. Then on Whitsunday (seven weeks after Easter) the Rev. Henry Kittson baptized one of his own children, his and Flora's first son, Alexander Henry, born April 12, 1883. Little Alexander lived less than a year. His was the second burial service performed by his father at St. John's, on November 22, 1883. The keen grief that the young parents felt at their loss impacted the rector's health.

HENRY KITTSON CONTINUED his generosity to the fledgling parish. At its meeting in October 1882 the vestry accepted the rector's proposal to enlarge the vestry room and place gas fixtures in the church and vestry room—at his own expense. Music was important to the congregation, and the vestry resolved to include the organ in its insurance coverage. In March 1883, it allotted $50 for choir purposes from March through Easter, and a generous $1,200 for the ensuing year—more than the rector's salary. There was also an organ fund, suggesting that the parish had hopes for a better and larger instrument. Vestryman Robert Bethune was filling in as a volunteer organist until a permanent organist could be engaged. As early as June 1884 the parish posted notices of its choral evensongs in the St. Paul Globe, noting that seats were free and that "the St. Anthony cars pass within one block of the church."

As we have seen, the land on which the frame church stood was owned not by the parish but by Mr. Henry Kittson. In April 1882 the vestry agreed to his proposal to sell the lot to the church and reimbursed Kittson for the $25 interest he had paid on the purchase price to June 28, 1881. Nothing was done about reimbursing him for the $1,250 he had spent on the lot.

Roughly a year after the transfer of the land to the parish, Mr. Kittson asked to lease from the parish the rear, or northerly, portion of the lot—a span of twenty-five feet on Mackubin—to erect there, at his own expense, a parish school house. With the understanding that the parish would have the use of the building for the Sunday School as well as for social and other purposes, the vestry leased the property to Mr. Kittson at the rate of one dollar per year, for a term of ten years. Construction on a stone building at 114 Mackubin was begun sometime after April 1883.

The Rev. Mr. Kittson expected to pay for the new stone building from funds promised him by friends, but when these friends proved unable to fulfill their promises, Kittson asked the parish to take the building off his hands. Henry Kittson presented the vestry with a proposition from his father, Norman Kittson, to loan the parish $7,250 ($6,000 for the

"Commodore" Norman Kittson's 1850s residence in St. Paul at 603 Jackson Street, photo ca. 1935.

The stone school built by the Rev. Henry Kittson, pictured here in 2013, is the only extant St. John's building from the 1880s.

A CANADIAN BY BIRTH, Norman Kittson came to Minnesota in 1834 and was employed as the sutler at Fort Snelling until 1839. In 1843 he became a special partner of the American Fur Company in partnership with Henry Sibley. One of Canada's pioneer railway builders, "Commodore" Kittson served in the Minnesota Territorial Legislature from 1851 to 1855. In 1851, with partner William H. Forbes, he established the Old St. Paul Outfit Company for Indian supply trade goods and freighting to the Red River. By 1855 he had moved to St. Paul and was mayor of the city from 1858 to 1859. In 1860 he became an agent of the Hudson's Bay Company, and in partnership with James J. Hill he established a line of steamers and barges on the Red River. With Hill and two other men he helped to finance the Great Northern Railway. Kittson County in northwest Minnesota is named for him. While not himself a religious man, in St. Paul Norman Kittson participated in the building of four churches, including St. John the Evangelist, and was concerned for their welfare.[7]

The welcoming arch for the Villard party, Northern Pacific Railroad. Looking across the intersection of East Fourth and Rosabel, the Chicago, St. Paul, Minneapolis and Omaha Railway Building is seen on the northeast corner, 1883.

building and $1,250 for the lot), payable on or before five years from the date of the loan, with five percent interest, to be secured by a mortgage. The stone school building would be transferred to the parish in completed condition and free from all encumbrances. In connection with this proposal the rector offered to pay the parish a rental of $200 per year for five years for the use of the building for school purposes. The vestry accepted this proposal on November 1, 1883, and the qualified voters of the parish approved it on December 3, 1883, whereupon the stone building became the property of the church.

St. Paul was booming. On September 3, 1883, a grand reception took place in the city honoring Henry Villard, president of the Northern Pacific Railroad, to mark the uniting of the two sections of track, one east from Portland, Oregon, and the other west from St Paul. Villard and about five hundred guests, including General Ulysses S. Grant, and statesmen and capitalists from Europe and America, converged upon St. Paul. The city was adorned with streaming banners and triumphal arches, "while the military and civic parade which took place soon after their arrival has perhaps never been equaled in St. Paul as a brilliant

and imposing pageant."[8] President Chester A. Arthur was among the distinguished guests arriving from the west; St. Paul's own railroad builder, James J. Hill, was among the honored speakers.

The atmosphere at St. John's was often less than celebratory, however, as the young parish struggled with issues of money and personnel. At a meeting on June 26, 1884, the vestry offered the rector a leave of absence for two or three months, at his option, for reasons of poor health and the stresses of his ministry. Two months later, Kittson's physician ordered him not to return to work, for the winter at least. On September 22, he expressed his willingness to resign his position on the grounds of being unable to do the work, "if the vestry thought it advisable and for the good of the parish." The vestry accepted his resignation on October 16, 1884.

All was not settled, though, between the Kittsons, father and son, and the parish, and there would be long years of contention over ties of money and real estate. Almost four years later, at the Annual Parish Meeting, on Easter Monday, April 2, 1888, the treasurer reported that $181.25 interest had been paid to Norman Kittson, up to June 24, 1887, but that the amount of $7,250 on the mortgage would come due on December 24, 1888—in eight months. Moreover, they still owed back salary to Mr. Kittson.

The next month, on May 10, 1888, Norman Kittson died while on a train from Chicago to St. Paul. His estate, including the mortgage on the church property, was bequeathed to a minor heir, Alfred S. Kittson. The trustee and guardian would be the St. Paul Loan and Trust Company, which extended the mortgage by one year.

In 1889, with mortgage again coming due in December, junior warden John Ames and vestryman Emerson Peet met with officers of the St. Paul Trust Company, seeking some arrangement by which the property now mortgaged to the Kittson estate could be transferred to the trust company, releasing the parish from its indebtedness. Ames and Peet believed such an arrangement was possible and also sought terms whereby the vestry could lease the property for parish use for a number of years. The vestry had resolved that the lot now owned by the parish was insufficient in size for its needs and purposes, and that the location was not the proper one for the permanent buildings of the parish.

The St. Paul Trust Company proposed that the parish deed the real estate and buildings to them for the amount of the mortgage and accrued indebtedness on the property, amounting to about $8,750, the trust company to take the property as it stood and to give the parish a lease of the property for three

to five years at $50 per month. The parish agreed to these terms, the lease of the property and buildings, for three years, to begin July 1, 1890. By January 5, 1891, all the necessary documents had been ordered and signed. In March of 1893 the parish renewed the lease for a period of two years.

Then on October 1, 1895, the vestry notified the St. Paul Trust Company of its intention to cancel the lease and to vacate the property at the end of the month, surrendering possession of the premises at Ashland Avenue and Mackubin Street, which had been the parish home for roughly thirteen years.

Norman Kittson built this grand house at the top of Selby Avenue, kitty-corner across Summit Avenue from the fine homes of the Wilder and Hill families, in 1888. It survived until 1905 when it was razed to make way for the Cathedral of St. Paul.

ST. PAUL ICE PALACE
1886.

Lith by H.M.Smyth Print. Co. St.Paul.

chapter two

THE REV. E. JAY COOKE 1884-1888
Pledges to Rents

THREE WEEKS FOLLOWING the Rev. Kittson's departure from St. John's, the vestry at its meeting on November 6, 1884, voted to extend a call to the Rev. Eleutheros Jay Cooke as their second rector. Cooke formally accepted the call in a letter dated November 15, and began his duties on the first of December. His salary was set at $1,500 per year.

Thirty-seven when he came to St. John's, the Rev. E. J. Cooke was born into a prominent family in Sandusky, Ohio. The two-story limestone house of his paternal grandfather, pioneer Sandusky lawyer and congressman Eleutheros Jay Cooke, his namesake, is now a historic site. His father was Pitt Cooke, the brother of Civil War financier Jay Cooke, for whom Minnesota's Jay Cooke State Park is named.[1]

The Rev. E. Jay Cooke.

At the time of his call, the Rev. Jay Cooke, as he was commonly known, was at All Saints Church in Northfield, Minnesota. While there, he was also priest at the Mission of the Holy Cross in nearby Dundas, where he was expected to read a service every Sunday. Finding the work too difficult, as he was responsible for three services and two Sunday Schools, the Rev. Cooke had resigned the post at Dundas in January 1884.[2]

Mr. Cooke was later described by one of his successors at St. John's as "a man of decided opinions, impulsive, warm and sympathetic," who was called to the rectorship when the congregation was weak and struggling, and who earnestly worked to build up and strengthen the parish.[3] Said to be a pious man, but not ecclesiastical, Mr. Cooke was full of good humor. And he was as low-church as Kittson was high-church. Thus was St. John's secured as a low-church congregation.

Like that of his predecessor, the rectorship of the Rev. Mr. Cooke would be preoccupied in part by a building project, and despite all the rigmarole surrounding the church's stone building, it proved to be a useful source of rental income for the parish during Cooke's tenure.

In a letter to Mr. Cooke, dated July 23, 1887, Mr. Robert Arrowsmith, writing from Brooklyn, New York, proposed to rent the building for $450 per year and one half the expenses involved in making alterations necessary for his purposes: the addition of running water, a "neat and healthful closet," a urinal, and four windows in the cellar, also the laying of cement from the door to the present location of the furnace.[4] The vestry accepted his proposal and agreed to a two-year lease from September 1, asking for earnest money of $250 (the estimated cost of the alterations).

Arrowsmith established in the building an educational institution, the Barnard School for boys, named after Frederick A. P. Barnard, the president of Columbia University in New York City.[5] Arrowsmith held a Ph.D. from Columbia and was appointed a Fellow of the College in 1883. He had taught briefly at Racine College in Wisconsin and written a number of foreign language textbooks on life and times in Germany and ancient Rome, which he edited for American schools.[6]

THE BARNARD SCHOOL was a private school that met the aspirations of St. Paul's elite who wished for their sons an education equal to what they might receive in the private schools in the East. It originally had a technical component suitable for a trade school, "a thorough course of instruction fitting [the students] for the Colleges and Scientific Schools, the Military and Naval Academies, and for commercial life."[7] After a while, however, the Barnard School's curriculum focused on English, the classics, mathematics, etymology, declamation, history, and French, Latin, and Greek.[8]

In its first year, Barnard had twenty-two students aged ten and older, most of them members of St. John's parish, some of them "from such prominent St. Paul families as pioneer entrepreneurs Norman W. Kittson[9] and Henry M. Rice and a bevy of more recent transplants from the East who had also made their fortunes in St. Paul."[10] Unfortunately the furnace in the school proved so inadequate that Arrowsmith had to dismiss his classes at the end of November. In its second year the student population had swelled to twenty-nine students, including the scions of local luminaries General Judson Wade Bishop, George R. Finch, and Joseph L. Forepaugh.[11]

The first private school in St. Paul to survive to the present day, the Barnard School eventually became what we know as the St. Paul Academy.[12] St. John's stone building in which it was birthed is still extant, tucked behind the church building at Ashland and Mackubin, which succeeded St. John's first church.

Almost directly across Mackubin Street from the Barnard School was a school for young women, known as the Freeman School, after the president of Wellesley College, with a "similar philosophy and motivation but quite a different character."[13] It would ultimately become the Summit School for girls.

The Barnard School vacated the St. John's building in 1889 and found lodging on Laurel Avenue, before moving into the Blair Flats at Selby and Western. Then from 1894 to 1900 it occupied part of the building across the street that now houses the W. A. Frost restaurant. Later still it occupied a site at the corner of Portland Avenue and Dale Street, across from St. John's future Club House. The school for boys and the school for girls merged in 1969 to be known as St. Paul Academy-Summit School.

St. John's treasurer's report for the Annual Meeting on April 6, 1885, Easter Monday, indicates an increasing interest in parish outreach. Donations are shown for diocesan missions, Jewish missions, Chinese missions, and for the diocesan orphanage Sheltering Arms. The vestry approved a resolution thanking James Blaikie for his services as organist and choir director for the past year and hoped circumstances would permit his continuing relationship with the parish.[14] Blaikie served four brief tenures as parish organist.

Among those elected to the vestry were General Henry S. Sibley and William H. Merrick. Sibley has been thought erroneously to be the Henry Hastings Sibley who was the first governor of the state of Minnesota. In fact, Governor Sibley was an active participant in St. Paul's Episcopal Church, then in downtown St. Paul. He was a vestryman there until at least 1877 and was buried thence in 1891. In any case, it was Henry S. Sibley—the "S" was for "Saxton"—who served as treasurer of St. John's and remained on the vestry until probably 1888.

William H. Merrick, who was elected to the vestry that evening, was the great-grandfather of current parishioner William Howell (Bill) Plummer Jr., making the Merrick-Plummer lineage probably the longest to survive in the parish, over five generations.

Mr. Merrick, of Welsh ancestry, was general manager of the Singer Sewing Machine Company in the Northwest. His wife, Carolina E. Gale, whom he married in 1879, was treasurer and then president of the Parish Aid Society. Their son, Gale Clifford Merrick, served on the Standing Committee, was head usher, served on the Diocesan Council, and was

St. John's representative on the Church Extension Society. His wife, Sadie, was a supervisor of St. John's Red Cross Unit during World War I, and treasurer and secretary of the Altar Guild. Gale and Sadie bore a daughter named Margaret Gale Merrick, a member of the girls choir in her youth, who married William Howell Plummer.[15] The latter served on the vestry, was an usher, and also parish treasurer for many years. William Plummer and his wife Margaret were the parents of parishioner Bill Plummer.

After the vestry and Sunday school, the notable pioneer organization of St. John's was the ladies' Parish Aid Society. Begun as a sewing circle, perhaps in 1885, the guild soon took on a greater significance in the life of the parish.[16] As there was no guild room at the time, the women met at the residences of the members, over afternoon tea, and membership gradually increased. Originally the society raised funds for modest purposes, such as a quartet choir, and "they resorted to every device to raise the required amount"! When one of the charter members of the Parish Aid Society, Mrs. Eugene Ward, died in 1909 it was written that her name was read at roll call ever since the founding of the society.

In the vestry minutes for May 2, 1885, we learn that after only four years, with the congregation now swelled to 250 parishioners, the frame church built by the Rev. Kittson was no longer adequate. The vestry first considered turning the church around lengthwise on the lot and widening it by twelve feet on each side, thus doubling the seating capacity and requiring three aisles instead of one. And this is where architect Cass Gilbert comes into our St. John's story. Gilbert was living with his mother in the house he designed for her at 471 Ashland when the vestry asked him to expand and "beautify" the frame building and in the process reorient it to Ashland Avenue.

That September the Rev. Mr. Cooke appointed a building committee to oversee the addition of a fifty-by-twenty-four-foot addition: wardens Capt. E. C. Bowen and Maj. George Q. White, and vestrymen Victor M. Watkins, Edward Corning, and George C. Squires. The men resolved to carry on with the work as early as possible in the spring of 1886. The other Episcopal churches in St. Paul were full to overflowing,

William and Margaret Plummer, late 1930s.

and there was no Episcopal church within a mile of St. John's. The vestry also now decided to begin renting pews, instead of relying on pledges; it had had trouble during the past year securing enough funds to support the parish.

At a special parish meeting on July 6, 1886, the twenty-two men present, and a number of ladies with them, expressed support for the vestry's decision to enlarge the church and congratulated them "upon the future which we believe awaits this parish and we hereby pledge to them our continued interest and hearty cooperation." Services in the church were discontinued during the construction, but by early August the vestry was attending to the finishing of its modest building project. The church addition must have been more or less completed by early October because the vestry meeting on October 9 took place in the vestry room. At this same meeting, both the junior warden Joseph McKee and senior warden George W. Dellinger resigned their posts, implying there had been a dispute or a difference of opinion on some undisclosed matter. The vestry refused to accept Dellinger's resignation, but McKee's was allowed to stand.

St. Paul's First Ice Palace

IN 1886, countering one Eastern newspaperman's description of St. Paul as "another Siberia, unfit for human habitation in winter," our fair city built its first ice castle—and organized the first winter carnival of its kind in the United States. St. John's vestryman George R. Finch was president of the newly formed St. Paul Ice Palace and Winter Carnival Association that erected this splendiferous palace measuring 140 x 175 feet and comprised of twenty thousand blocks of ice weighing five thousand tons. Its central tower rose to a height of one hundred feet.

Top: The gate entrance to the ice palace. Above: Owls Club float in Winter Carnival parade.

George Finch wears the badges of twenty-four winter clubs on the Winter Carnival uniform of his prosperous wholesale dry-goods company, Auerback, Finch, and Van Slyke.

Alas, there is no known image of St. John's frame church at this juncture, but the congregation was no doubt delighted with its enlarged church as it looked to its promising future.

Its confidence was supported by the prevailing mood of high optimism in St. Paul:

> The improvements in all directions [crowed the *St. Paul Daily Globe*] have fully kept pace with the increase in the number of inhabitants. Magnificent business blocks and public buildings have sprung up on every hand; churches and school houses, which will compare with those in any of the older cities of the East, have been erected in every section of the city; handsome and palatial residences have been built by the thousands; public improvements have been prosecuted with vigor, until St. Paul has become one of the handsomest and solidest looking cities in the United States.

The Rev. Mr. Cooke was barely into his second year at St. John's when St. Paul staged its first winter carnival. St. John's parishioner George R. Finch was the first president of the carnival association, which oversaw in St. Paul's Central Park, just north of downtown, the construction of "the most strangely beautiful structure that had up to that time been erected on any part of the globe."

Such frivolity notwithstanding, there was always a shortage of money at St. John's. In April 1887 Mr. Cooke requested that his salary be increased by $100 but was informed by the vestry that it was not in a position to do so. In July the sexton, John Newlander, also asked for an increase in pay that was likewise turned down. In December 1887, Mr. Cooke asked for and received a four-week leave of absence with a continuance of salary.

In late June 1888, Mr. Cooke was given a two-month leave of absence for health reasons, and he went with his family to the Boston area. He was absent for the July, August, and September vestry meetings. Then, in a brief letter to the vestry, which he presented to them at their meeting on October 1, Mr. Cooke submitted his resignation, effective immediately. His letter closed, "With sincere regard and best wishes for you all and with fervent prayers for God's blessing on you and this Parish, I remain, Affectionally yours, E. Jay Cooke."

Mr. Cooke then retired from the meeting and the vestry accepted his resignation on the spot, ordering the secretary to convey to him their expression of appreciation for his services "and deploring the circumstances necessitating his withdrawal from the Rectorship."

With croquet mallets in hand, the Rev. E. Jay Cooke and his wife, Molly, pose with his cousin Henry Cooke and wife Esther at his uncle Jay Cooke's summer home on Gibraltar Island in Lake Erie, Ohio, in 1894, almost six years after leaving St. John's.

St. Paul's streetcar line began running on Grand Avenue in 1890.

chapter three

THE REV. JOHN HAZEN WHITE 1889-1891
The Second Expansion of the First Church

THE NEXT RECTOR at St. John's was the Rev. John H. White who came to us from Christ Church in Joliet, Illinois. During his tenure at Christ Church, he had received many calls to other parishes, one of them from Christ Church in downtown St. Paul, but he declined all of them until accepting our call in 1889. His wife was Marie Louise Holbrook White. Mr. White's work in Joliet had been:

eminently successful. He found [the parish] in a very depressed condition, weak in membership, and sadly needing a new church building. He left it, after a rectorship of eight years, with about 300 communicants, a handsome stone church, a guild house and rectory, clear of any debt, and a people full of zeal and interest in church work.[1]

The Rev. John Hazen White.

College in Gambier, Ohio, that state's oldest private school, founded by Episcopal Bishop Philander Chase in 1824. White completed his theological training in Middletown, Connecticut, at Berkeley Divinity School, which today is affiliated with the Divinity School at Yale University in New Haven. Ordained a deacon in 1875, and priest in 1876, he served as assistant to the rector at St. Andrew's Church in Meriden, Connecticut, from 1875 to 1877. He was also the vice-rector and instructor in Latin at St. Margaret's Diocesan School in Waterbury, Connecticut, for nearly two years, resigning to accept a call from Grace Church in Old Saybrook, Connecticut. There he remained until 1881, when he accepted the call to Christ Church, in Joliet.

He was also described as:

a man of energy and progress. He is a ripe scholar, an indefatigable worker, and a man of great force of character and pleasant address. He is a liberal Churchman, but somewhat strict as a constructionist of Church law, of which he is a recognized authority. He is a forceful, eloquent and logical preacher.[2]

John Hazen White was born in 1849 in Cincinnati, Ohio, of New England parents. He graduated in 1872 from Kenyon

The Rev. Mr. White began his work as St. John's third rector on Quinquagesima Sunday, the Sunday preceding Ash Wednesday, in 1889. On March 4 the ladies of the parish gave a reception for Mr. White and his wife in the stone building. He inherited an annual budget that was in the black by nearly a thousand dollars, despite the parish indebtedness to the estate of Norman Kittson. The congregation was growing to such an extent that the church building, newly enlarged less than three years earlier, already needed another expansion, but merely as a temporary expedient.

This second enlargement of the church was a much simpler process than the first. In May 1889 the east side of the building was widened at an expense of $636.32, which covered carpentry, the tinting of the walls, the building permit, and new pews and carpet. The expansion increased the seating capacity by about a hundred sittings. Then in November, only six months later, the west side was also expanded to allow for about a hundred more sittings, at a cost of $590.18.

Although the rector and vestry were still dealing with the St. Paul Trust Company over the matter of mortgages, real estate, and indebtedness after Norman Kittson's death, progress was being made within the routines of parish life. The Altar Guild was formally organized on October 3, 1889, with Mrs. J. E. Schadle as president. Among his many accomplishments was Mr. White's reorganization of the music program.

A Miss Hyde had been acting as organist, and she was followed by Charles Tarbox, who was paid $5 per Sunday to play the organ and conduct a quartet of paid adult singers. In May 1889 the vestry voted to reintroduce a vested choir similar to that inaugurated by the Rev. Kittson at the first Christmas in 1881. This new vested choir debuted on Easter 1890.

The rector invited Fletcher H. Wheeler, the organist and choirmaster of Calvary Church in Chicago, to assume a similar post at St. John's, to which he agreed, provided the parish furnish an assistant organist and two good singers—a tenor and a bass—as a nucleus for a good choir. Wheeler began his work in November 1889 at an annual salary of $1,000. With its newly vested choir, the church now needed a suitable organ; the old organ was worn out and useless. It was decided that a suitable reed organ would suffice until the parish had a new building. In May 1890 Wheeler obtained a Mason and Hamlin reed organ from Chicago for $350.

In September 1890, however, Mr. Wheeler notified the vestry that he intended to resign his position as choirmaster and organist, to take effect November 1. Without a large organ he was getting out of practice, and his salary was insufficient. Wheeler's action perturbed the vestry, because he had hinted at no dissatisfaction with the current arrangements.

At the same time, parishioner D. C. Shepard had sent word to the rector that, having heard that there was difficulty in connection with the choir owing to the want of a large organ, he would give $1,000 toward the procuring of a suitable instrument. He believed that other gentlemen in the parish would give enough to make up the difference.

The vestry did not want to lose Wheeler, nor did the rector. They offered, and he apparently accepted, their offer to retain him as both organist and choirmaster for one year from November 1 at a salary of $1,500 and paying the fees for two singers for the choir. Moreover, the vestry authorized the rector to raise funds for the purchase of a new pipe organ, with the instrument and any needed alterations in the building not to exceed $3,000. By January 1891, about $2,700 had been secured in pledges. After considering several bids, the vestry raised the limit of expenses on the organ to $3,500, and authorized Wheeler to purchase an organ from Farrand and Votey Organ Company, of Detroit, which had begun building pipe organs in 1888, in addition to reed organs.[3] By October 1, 1891, the first pipe organ had been installed at St. John's.

In February 1890, the vestry gave the rector a leave of absence to recover from the effects of the grippe (influenza), the leave to last up to one month, if necessary. That same month, because of parish indebtedness, the vestry decided to increase the pew rents by not less than twenty-five percent. Nevertheless, in his annual report the parish treasurer reported a balanced budget of $8,519.85 for the year ending on April 7, 1890.

Concerning a site for a new church, vestryman Emerson W. Peet reported that a Mr. J. N. Rogers had offered to sell his property on the corner of Laurel and Farrington Avenues, but the vestry considered his selling price of $40,000 too high. Three months later, on July 18, the vestry passed a resolution stating that "it is the sense of this vestry that the present site of the parish buildings is not the proper one for the permanent buildings of the parish." The lot now owned by the parish was insufficient in size and the location undesirable for permanent buildings.

On November 26, 1890, the St. Luke's Guild was organized at St. John's to furnish material aid to St. Luke's Hospital in St. Paul. The hospital dates to 1858, but was incorporated in 1873 for the purpose of furnishing a home for orphans and a hospital. The originators of the corporation were Henry H. Sibley (the first governor of Minnesota, in 1858), R. R. Nelson, J. W. Bass, A. H. Cathcart, Amherst H. Wilder, and William Dawson. The home for orphans was not realized, but Bishop Henry Whipple officiated at the opening of the hospital in 1874. The women of St. Luke's Guild made sheets and pillow cases, they hemmed napkins, and they made surgeon's gowns, the materials for which were either donated by the women or paid for from the guild treasury.

THE FIRST "MEMBER" of St. Luke's Hospital was Sister Annette Relf, who trained as a deaconess in 1873-74 at the Deaconess Training School in Philadelphia. In 1875, at Gethsemane Church in Minneapolis, Bishop Whipple consecrated her as Minnesota's first Episcopal deaconess. A nurse herself, Sister Annette was committed to serving Minnesota's youngest and most vulnerable citizens, wearing the long black habit of a nun. She formed a women's religious order in the diocese, and the women lived together and worked as nurses in the hospitals and assisted with parish work in local churches, though never at St. John's.[4] From 1877 to 1882 Sister Annette was involved in the formation of what was to become St. Barnabas Hospital in Minneapolis. She also founded the Sheltering Arms Orphanage, in 1883 (now the Sheltering Arms Foundation), and the Episcopal Home for the aged and infirm, in 1894.[5] The latter, now known as the Episcopal Church Home, and part of Episcopal Homes of Minnesota, struggled through its early existence but was aided on one occasion by a $100 check from James J. Hill.

Sister Annette Relf was the great-aunt of St. John's parishioners Richard Howard Relf, Howard Clark Relf, and Judith Howard Relf.[6] In *The St. John's Evangelist* in March 1907, Herbert Kemper Relf and Judith Howard Relf are named as members of the Little Helpers. Relf family members were baptized and confirmed at St. John's and buried thence.

In February 1891 the Standing Committee of the diocese

St. Luke's Hospital, Smith and Sherman, St. Paul, ca. 1910.

Private room at St. Luke's Hospital, St. Paul, ca. 1895.

Sister Annette Relf.

informed St. John's vestry of its intent to establish a new parish, the Church of the Messiah, to be located between St. John's and the Manitoba Railroad tracks, asking permission to do so, this territory being part of St. John's parish. The vestry gave its consent to the erection of the parish on land west of Western Avenue and north of the center line of Iglehart Street and its continuations.

The minutes of the Annual Meeting on March 30, 1891, show that St. John's was in good shape, as a result of "good work on the part of the rector and his aides. Harmony and good feeling seem to prevail and promise well for the future of the parish." Again the treasurer was able to report a balanced budget of $9,286.01 for the fiscal year now ending. The vestry appointed a committee to find a suitable site for a new building, to be chaired by vestryman John W. White (not to be confused with the rector, John H. White).

At the vestry's next meeting, on May 19, Mr. White's committee reported that the lot on the southwest corner of Mackubin and Portland could probably be purchased for $25,000. A lot on the southeast corner of Laurel and Arundel would cost $1.50 per front foot. And a lot on the southeast corner of Arundel and Holly could likely be had for $18,000. Several other properties were also considered, including the southeast corner of Summit Avenue and Lawton, and the northwest corner of Ashland and Western. The prevailing opinion favored the southwest corner of Portland and Mackubin, but the matter was left for further consideration, with the rector and George Dellinger, Theodore Schurmeier, and Emerson Peet added to the committee.

Mr. White also told the vestry that the trustees of Seabury Divinity School in Faribault had called him to the wardenship of that institution. If he were to accept the position, it would require all of his time. He asked the vestry to consider their wishes in the matter, helping him to determine his course of action. The importance of White's call to Seabury, founded in 1858, lay partially in the fact that the school was the only Episcopal divinity school west of the Mississippi.

VESTRYMAN RICHARDS GORDON submitted his letter of resignation from that body on May 23, 1891, as he did not think he would be able to attend to his obligations. The vestry took no action, but hoped to induce him to withdraw his resignation. In 1901, Gordon returned to the vestry, serving as junior warden for another ten years until his death in 1911.

Originally from Ireland, Richards Gordon founded the Gordon Hat Company, later the Gordon-Ferguson Company, a world-renowned furrier that made the flight suits worn by aviator Charles Lindbergh and by Admiral Richard E. Byrd on his first expedition to Antarctica. Gordon lived at 245 Summit Avenue and later at 378. The vestry wrote that Gordon "fulfilled with care all duties allotted to him. Especially was he identified with the beauty of the Church's worship. He loved a beautiful service and sought to establish a well-trained choir which should adequately render the worshipper's praise to God." He was memorialized by the Richards Gordon Elementary School, built in 1911 at 1619 Dayton Avenue in St. Paul.[7]

As a measure of the increasing health, vitality, and fiscal stability of the parish, the treasurer's report in June 1891 for the previous fourteen months showed that St. John's outreach had blossomed during White's rectorship. Numerous disbursements went to "poor and charitable work:" St. Paul Bethel, city missions, diocesan missions, domestic missions, foreign missions, Aged and Infirm Clergy, Seabury Mission, Sheltering Arms Orphanage, St. Luke's Hospital, the bishop's special needs, and the Home of the Friendless. In response to an appeal from the rector, a member of the parish, John Wann,[8] deposited $1,000 with the St. Paul Trust Company as a perpetual fund for the benefit of Aged and Infirm Clergy.

At some undetermined time, a little company of German people wanting to worship together "in the true Church of the living God and having no house to meet in," St. John's offered them its building, including use of the organ, fuel, light, and the services of the janitor. Over time the small congregation was able to construct its own place of worship, to be known as the German Chapel of Saint Bonifacius. In a letter of gratitude to St. John's, dated June 22, 1891, Pastor Johannes Salinger and two other men wrote to the rector and vestry, saying that "next to God we consider you our benefactors, for which we shall ever remember you in our prayers."[9]

AFTER ONLY TWO YEARS AT ST. JOHN'S, the rector John White wrote to the vestry on June 25, 1891:

> My election to Seabury Divinity School has brought to me the most difficult and trying decision of my life. Emanating from within my own Diocese, urged upon me by both my Bishops as a matter of grave necessity and supported with practical unanimity by the clergy of the entire Diocese and my best advisers outside the Diocese, I have been able to find no ground upon which to base a declination except the happiness and pleasure I find in my present relations.

The vestry replied with a resolution, writing that they were "sincerely loath to yield to the demand to give up their beloved Pastor to the service of the Church elsewhere. The relations between yourself and them have been so pleasant it is not an easy matter to consent to their discontinuance." But the vestry acknowledged the importance and urgency of his call to Seabury.[10]

On July 9, 1891, St. John's vestry appointed a committee to meet with their friend and confidant, Bishop Mahlon Gilbert, to ascertain if he had any names to suggest for the open rectorship. Bishop Gilbert recommended the Rev. Howard S. Clapp, who had been working in the diocese for the past year. The bishop urged the vestry to consult with the Rev. Mr. White, the outgoing rector, "as he knew all about Mr. Clapp." Mr. Clapp was familiar to the parish, as he had supplied for Mr. White in 1890 while the latter was recovering from an illness.

The Rev. Mr. White attended the vestry meeting on July 25, and admitted "that it was a delicate matter to deal with, standing as he did with a deep interest in the welfare of the parish, and at the same time having a great affection for Mr. Clapp who was one of his dearest friends." White went on to say that the parish was in a position where the election of a rector was liable to be accompanied with difficulties. It needed one of the best men in the ministry, a man of wisdom and sound judgment and able to go among the people of wealth and station as well as among the lowly. He said he would rather see Howard S. Clapp elected to succeed him than any other man.

Mr. Clapp had his faults and had made mistakes, White said, but he believed the faults had been corrected and would not again appear, and the mistakes had been rectified and ought not to militate against his usefulness in the ministry. He was of a jovial disposition and loved to tell stories but never any that were unseemly. (The vestry minutes do not disclose the nature of Mr. Clapp's faults and mistakes!)

Mr. White asked the vestry to take definite action upon Rev. Mr. Clapp's name "to enable the Bishop to determine what course to pursue in the matter of presenting Mr. Clapp's

Seabury Divinity Hall under construction in Faribault, ca. 1873.

Richards Gordon, 1854.

Theodore Schurmeier, 1900.

name to another Parish." Complicating the matter, a member of the vestry added the name of Rev. Chauncey C. Williams, rector of historic St. Paul's Church in Augusta, Georgia, to that of Clapp for consideration. A motion that the Rev. Howard S. Clapp be called to the rectorship failed, and the vestry wrote to the Rev. Mr. Williams, inquiring if he would allow his name to be presented as a candidate for the rectorship.

Mr. Williams responded by telegram that he was "not sufficiently informed about Parish and local conditions to authorize nomination. Unwilling therefore to risk compromising you or myself by even seeming to encourage election." The vestry went ahead and extended him a call to the rectorship anyway.

Roughly a month later, the Rev. Chauncey Williams arrived in St. Paul and officiated at a Sunday service at St. John's on September 20, "the church being well filled." The next day he was entertained at an elegant lunch in the rooms of the Minnesota Club, along with Governor William R. Merriam, Amherst H. Wilder, Mr. D. C. Shepard, and some

twenty-five other gentlemen, all prominent residents of St. Anthony Hill.

At their meeting that evening, the vestry agreed that if Williams would accept the call, they would offer him a salary of $5,000 per year, "and also pledge our best efforts to secure the erection of a parish church and rectory within three years." Williams was asked to give an immediate reply but pleaded the necessity of informing his parish in Augusta and "comparative ignorance of the existing conditions in St. John's parish." Mr. Williams wrote later to the vestry, declining the rectorship of St. John's. The vestry asked him to reconsider his decision, but to no avail. In the end, the vestry's best efforts on behalf of two qualified candidates—the Rev. Howard Clapp and the Rev. Chauncey Williams—had failed.

Bishop Gilbert then suggested the name of the Rev. Y. Peyton Morgan, Dean of Trinity Cathedral in Cleveland, Ohio, for the post, being "a desirable person for rector," according to information from various sources.

The Rev. Mr. Morgan came to St. Paul, and on Sunday, December 20, he delivered the sermon at both the morning and evening services, presided at Holy Communion at the early service, and even officiated at a funeral. Members of the vestry entertained Mr. Morgan at the Summit Avenue home of Emerson W. Peet. Two days later, the vestry called Mr. Morgan to the fourth rectorship at St. John's and he accepted. The vestry set his salary at $4,000, less than they had offered the Rev. Mr. Williams.

Meanwhile, at Seabury, the Rev. Mr. White showed himself "possessed of splendid executive abilities."[11] From Seabury[12] he was elected fourth bishop of the Diocese of Indiana in 1895, and later the first bishop of the Episcopal Diocese of Northern Indiana. Bishop White and his wife Mary Louise were buried in the crypt of historic St. James Memorial Chapel on the grounds of Howe Military School in Howe, Indiana, thus establishing a precedent. The first four bishops of the Episcopal Diocese of Northern Indiana are buried there with three of their wives.

Left: The Emerson W. Peet residence at 271 Summit Avenue, ca. 1888.

Below: Theodore Schurmeier's residence at 529 Goodrich Avenue in fashionable Crocus Hill. Designed by St. Paul architect Clarence H. Johnston, who would also design the present Church of St. John the Evangelist, the Schurmeier house was one of the first in St. Paul to have electric lighting throughout. Watercolor by E. Eldon Deane, ca. 1890.

DESIGN·FOR·THE·PRO
POSED·CHVRCH·OF
SAINT·IOHN·THE·EV·
ANGELIST·SAINT·PAVL·DIOCESE·OF·MINNE
SOTA·CRAM·WENTWORTH·AND·GOODHVE
ARCHITECTS·53·STATE·STREET·BOSTON

Svggestion for
Colovr·Decoration.

View looking toward
Morning·Chapel.

RAC· July 91

Rendering by Boston architect Ralph Adams Cram for proposed Church of St. John the Evangelist.

chapter four

THE REV. Y. PEYTON MORGAN 1892-1895
Building the Guild House

YELVERTON PEYTON MORGAN (1853-1899) graduated in 1875 from Dickinson College in Carlisle, Pennsylvania.[1] He was ordained priest in the Diocese of Long Island in 1882 and served St. Ann's parish in Brooklyn as an assistant priest. From 1883 to 1891 he was rector of Trinity Church in Cleveland. In 1890, the parish was offered to the bishop as a cathedral and Morgan was instituted as dean. (We have not been able to locate an image of him.)

In St. Paul, Mr. Morgan began his rectorship at St. John's on February 7, 1892, and took up residence at 427 Portland Avenue. One of his first moves was to hire rising musician Emil Oberhoffer as choirmaster and organist until Easter, with a salary of $1,000 per annum. Born near Munich to a musical family, his father being a well-known composer and regional conductor, Oberhoffer trained in Germany and Paris before emigrating to New York in 1885. He was conductor of the Apollo Club of Minneapolis and founded the Minneapolis Symphony Orchestra (now the Minnesota Orchestra), conducting its first performance in 1903. Hired at St. John's on an interim basis, Oberhoffer remained at the parish until 1895.

Organist and choirmaster Emil Oberhoffer.

THE QUESTION OF a new or enlarged church remained vexing. On May 2 the gentlemen on the church site committee reported that they were considering two sites for purchase. The first included two lots on the southwest corner of Summit Avenue and Summit Court—110 feet on the avenue by 190 feet on the court, and the other on the southwest corner of Portland and Mackubin. The committee unqualifiedly recommended the two lots on Summit, valued at $38,000, judging the second site less desirable. The vestry authorized the committee to purchase the two lots on Summit Avenue "belonging to Messrs. Borup and Rogers" at a price not to exceed $36,600. Meeting a week later at the home of Emerson Peet,[2] the vestry decided to raise the money for the first payment on the Summit Avenue tract of land. Although the vestry minutes were at first silent on the subject, it is clear from the immediate events that controversy was afoot among the members. Albert M. Eddy resigned his positions as vestryman and clerk at the meeting and was replaced by Cortlandt M. Taylor, who himself resigned in June, to be followed by Major Robert B. C. Bement. Senior warden G. W. Dellinger also resigned his position in June.

At a special parish meeting on May 16, 1892, a Ways and Means Committee consisting of seventeen members was formed, with Emerson Peet as chairman, to seek subscriptions from the congregation. The men later reported that reasonable progress had been made, "but as there was no

St. John's choir at Easter 1894. Organist and choirmaster Emil Oberhoffer is surrounded by his ten young choristers.

definite plan agreed upon as to the amount of money to be raised, or the building to be erected, and as the work of obtaining subscriptions was interrupted by the advent of the warm weather and absence from the city of many members of the committees, as well as a number of persons upon whom it was desirable to call, and for other causes, the efforts of the committees were temporarily suspended.[3]

Perhaps frustrated by the slow pace of fundraising, and eager to see St. John's situated on Summit Avenue, parishioner Charles W. Bunn purchased a portion of the lot on Summit Avenue, subject to two mortgages, for the benefit of himself and "certain others who advanced the money," with the un-

derstanding that the church would eventually repay them the money they expended plus interest.

Word of the deal appeared in the church press: "The vestry of St. John's parish, St. Paul have secured a location for their new church on Summit avenue, at the corner of Summit court. They are to pay $33,000 for it, $14,100 of which has been paid."[4]

Then on September 15, the Rev. Peyton Morgan informed the vestry by letter that he had received a unanimous call as rector of Christ Church, Houston, Texas, which he described as the largest parish in the Southwest.[5] Noting that he would visit the parish in October, Morgan wrote: "The call has come unsought and unexpected and is of so great importance that it demands careful consideration." Certainly Mr. Morgan's willingness to consider another call after a rectorship of only seven months merely begged the question of the festering turmoil.

But on the very next day, the rector offered the vestry a resolution stating that, whereas the wardens and vestry

> did of their own free will and accord select and secure for the Parish the lot on [the] Cor[ner] of Summit Ave. and Summit Court for the purpose of erecting thereon a Church and Parish buildings, and Whereas, the Committee of Ways and Means duly appointed has been successful in securing one third of the amount proposed to raise, notwithstanding rumor of discontent and opposition [that] has been circulated through the parish and City,—Be it therefore Resolved: That we Wardens and Vestry of St. John's Parish approve and reaffirm our own action, and hereby express the confident conviction that the amount of $100,000 will be subscribed by April 1st, 1893 and that the work of construction will then be commenced.

The vestry deferred action on both the resolution and the letter. At another meeting three days later vestryman Peet moved that they be adopted. But there was no second to his motion. Instead, action was deferred until the Ways and Means Committee could report on its success with the names given it for personal solicitation.

There were, suspiciously, no further vestry meetings in October, November, December, or January, but the vestry nevertheless devised a plan for raising a definite amount to pay for the lot and erect a church building with a guild house, with specified times and methods of payment. A letter describing these details was sent to each family in the parish on December 27, 1892. (We are not privy to this letter of solicitation.)

Sometime in 1892—though the facts appear nowhere in the parish records—someone from St. John's contacted the office of Ralph Adams Cram, the prolific architect of colle-

giate and ecclesiastical buildings, based in Boston, to provide at least a watercolor rendering of the interior of a new Gothic Revival church for the parish, evidently intended for Summit Avenue. It bears the same elegance and detail of the best of Cram's ecclesiastical work. But the effort at fundraising was faltering.

On January 21, 1893, committee chairman Emerson W. Peet sent an impassioned nine-point letter to the members of his committee asking that "an active, earnest and continuous canvass" be made to secure the necessary subscriptions. He implored that "each member of the committee should devote at least one hour every day, commencing Tuesday, Jan'y 24th, to the work of soliciting subscriptions, and continuing until every person on his list has been induced to subscribe, or has positively refused."

When the vestry met again on February 4, 1893, the men voted to renew for two years the lease of the church's present property on Ashland, doing so through an agent of the trustee of the Kittson estate.

Owing to the lacunae in the vestry records, it is difficult to reconstruct some of the negotiations and diplomacy that went on in the interim period, but fundraising continued for a new church and by February 1893 subscriptions for the project were at $38,600, including a conditional subscription of $10,000 from Mr. D. C. Shepard. A building committee of five was appointed to secure plans and specifications, namely, Robert B. C. Bement, chairman; with Emerson W. Peet, John H. Ames, George C. Squires, and Richards Gordon.

The building committee reported to the vestry in March 1893 that it had engaged St. Paul architect Cass Gilbert to provide preliminary plans at a cost not to exceed $500. (Two years hence Gilbert would be chosen to design the Minnesota State Capitol, springing him to national attention and fame.) The committee made no mention of the earlier architectural rendering from Cram.

In April 1893 the Ways and Means Committee reported:

DAVID CHAUNCEY SHEPARD had the distinction, in May 1858, of turning the first shovelful of sod for a railroad in the new State of Minnesota. Born on a farm near Geneseo in New York, he worked his way west to St. Paul as a civil engineer for several railroad companies. "In this capacity, I learned what it cost to construct railroads, and how to economically employ labor and material." In 1871 he was named general manager of the Northwestern Construction Company, which was organized to construct the Northern Pacific across Minnesota. In succeeding years, in partnership with others, his firms every year received large contracts from nearly every railroad organization in Minnesota and adjoining states and built thousands of miles of railroad.

In 1884, Shepard began the monumental work of his life—the building of the Great Northern Railway. Shepard and his associate partners—Messrs. Shepard, Winston & Company—set construction speed records when they laid 643 miles of continuous track from Minot, North Dakota, that reached Helena, Montana, on November 18. The average work force on the grading was 3,300 teams and about 8,000 men.

Shepard married Frances Aurelia Parsons in Geneseo, New York, in 1850.

Described by a contemporary as "plain, frank, and unassuming [and] an entertaining, intelligent talker," he was notably philanthropic and always generous to St. John's.

After retiring from active work in 1894, D. C. Shepard wrote in a paper, "My generation has seen wonders in all lines of invention and in their application to the comfort, happiness, and well-being of mankind. . . . I doubt if anyone coming after me can ever witness in his generation, the application of so many and such wonderful discoveries for the quick transmission of matter, power, intelligence, and sounds, as I have had the good fortune and happiness to witness and enjoy in mine."

While a careful canvass of a large proportion of the members of the parish has been made . . . The work has not progressed as rapidly, nor been as successful as we hoped, mainly because of the absence from the city of men from whom the committee confidently expected to secure subscriptions for large amounts.

At its meeting on June 15, the vestry adopted a contract dated June 1 stating that the parish debt to Charles W. Bunn in the amount of $16,819.38 plus interest, which he had paid toward the purchase price of the land on Summit Avenue, would be paid to him by St. John's on or before June 1, 1894. When the suggestion of furnishing Mr. Morgan with a rectory came up at the same meeting, the vestry decided with regret that the present income of the parish and the struggles of the building campaign made it inexpedient also to raise the amount of money necessary to pay for the rental of a rectory.

THE REV. MR. MORGAN HAD NOT accepted the earlier call to Houston, and in early November he received the "honor and a grave responsibility" of a call from Christ Church Cathedral in New Orleans, which he described as "easily classed among the most important parishes in the Country." There he would be "relieved of all anxiety and labor regarding the building of a Church" and all the troubles of debts and subscriptions. The compensation would include "a large and beautiful Rectory, combining the comforts of the South and conveniences of the North," placed at his disposal free of rent, with the care of the grounds provided for by the parish.

An urgent parish meeting was called for November 14, whose purpose was to induce Mr. Morgan to decline the call to New Orleans, "which could not but result to a calamity to this Parish." The minutes of the meeting record "the great work which had already been accomplished in the brief administration of the present Rector," and confessed "the highest gratification at the results accomplished in the short period of Mr. Morgan's rectorship, the deepest confidence in their continuance under his leadership, and a most earnest petition that he would remain with us."

As a further expression of their confidence in Morgan, they promised to lift the debts of the parish to the Episcopal Fund and the Farrand and Votey Organ Company, which existed before the present rectorship; to erect a temporary guild house at the corner of Summit Avenue and Summit Court to cost $1,500; and to provide a rectory or additional remuneration. Subscriptions toward the debt were made from the floor by parishioners. General Merritt proposed to be one of ten who should each pledge $100 for the purpose of increasing the rector's compensation by $1,000 for the ensuing year. Such subscriptions were immediately pledged by Messrs. Robert B. C. Bement, Theodore Schurmeier, Alvin W. Krech, Joseph McKee, John A. Humbird, and Mr. J. E. Schadle, with Thomas Irvine proposing to personally guarantee the balance. The liberal offer of Mr. Irvine was declined so that parishioners absent from the meeting might subscribe to the fund.

A week later, on November 22, the vestry again earnestly requested the rector to withdraw his resignation and expressed "their sincere appreciation of the work he has accomplished and their belief that through his future administration of the Parish all the results hoped for will be realized." They renewed their belief that within a reasonable time funds would be raised to complete the payments on the Summit Avenue lots and to erect thereon "suitable buildings" for the parish.

Cheered by their confident expectations concerning the Summit Avenue lot, Mr. Morgan responded the next day that he acquiesced to the wishes of the vestry and would remain at St. John's on the condition that the "suitable buildings" include a church, a guild house, and a rectory.

On December 5, a meeting of the women of the parish was called to devise ways and means for the erection of a suitable guild house. Mrs. George C. Squires was elected chairman and the women pledged their best efforts to secure $100 each by June 1, 1894. The organization was to be known as St. John's Guild.

There were no vestry meetings in January or February, but at their meeting on March 16, 1894, the Ways and Means Committee reported that since their last accounting, at the annual meeting on Easter Monday 1893, "but little progress has been made in securing subscriptions." The committee begged "to express their regret that circumstances seem to have rendered it impossible to make greater progress in the matter at hand." In plain words, the country was weathering the worst economic depression in the United States to date. Railroad overbuilding and shaky railroad financing had fueled the Panic of 1893 that caused six hundred banks and fifteen thousand businesses to fail.

Notwithstanding the financial distress of the parish, the vestry on March 26 formed a committee of five, plus the rector, to present a plan for proceeding with the construction of a new church building "at a future meeting of the Vestry." At a special parish meeting on June 5, 1894, Emerson Peet reported that "now this Parish had before it a tangible plan for the immediate construction of a Church and guild house and that action should be taken, or the idea given up and the subscribers to the fund notified to that effect." Architect Cass Gilbert presented to the congregation sketches of the proposed building drawn

CHARLES W. BUNN was born in 1855 in Trempeleau County, Wisconsin, where his parents had moved from New York. His father, Romanzo Bunn, was a prominent jurist in the Northwest and a U.S. district judge. Charles Bunn studied law at the University of Wisconsin and moved to St. Paul to practice law in 1885. A strong man, physically and morally, he eventually became general counsel for the Northern Pacific Railway, for which he litigated many cases in state and federal courts. His wife was the former Mary Anderson, the daughter of La Crosse businessman Mons Anderson; they had four children. A leading parishioner at St. John's, Bunn paid personally to secure a site for a new church, but plans for a grand new structure at this time came to naught, largely as a consequence of the devastating financial depression of 1893.

to scale, together with estimates of the cost of the construction, indicating that the plan now proposed contemplated building as much of the permanent church as the money subscribed would permit, that the part to be built immediately would seat about 625 people, and that the proposed plan would necessitate the least possible temporary work, but would be practically all availed of when the entire church was completed.

Resolutions were offered by Mr. S. L. Moore, as follows: that the vestry's action in making a contract for the purchase of the lots on Summit Avenue be ratified and approved; that all subscriptions be collected for that purpose as rapidly as possible; that the vestry take title to the lots as soon as they have collected a sufficient sum of money; and that the vestry proceed to the construction of the church edifice on the general plans present at this meeting. The resolutions were adopted unanimously.

But on October 22 the Ways and Means Committee reported that it was "unable to raise sufficient money to take contract to the lots and erect buildings thereon." Four days later, committee chairman Emerson Peet wrote privately to Mr. Morgan that he considered it vital for the interests of the parish

that the enterprise should not be given up at this time. It would be a certain loss of the total amount of the subscriptions that have been renewed and should the present owners of the lots be compelled to take the same back, they can hardly be expected to make any contribution to the erection of a new church until they have been reimbursed for the amount invested in the lots, which, from present indications, may be many years hence.

In Peet's estimation the real problem lay with the Ways and Means Committee itself, which had betrayed a lack of interest and a seeming indifference to the whole project. Many of the members failed to attend meetings, he wrote, and "the manifest unwillingness of many members . . . to cooperate in the enterprise, is sufficient proof to my mind" that they "do not desire to carry on the enterprise and there are quite a number of the Committee who have never done any active work in securing subscriptions." Mr. Peet's letter was read to the vestry on November 5, which immediately discharged the Ways and Means Committee and ordered the clerk to notify Charles W. Bunn, trustee of the Summit Avenue lots, that the Vestry was unable to come to any decision regarding the contract.

Mr. Morgan wrote to Bunn on November 6 and the latter replied on November 8, writing:

I think the vestry is making a mistake and acting so as (without intending it) to be very unfair toward the [seven investors] who have their money in the Summit Avenue Lots. If they cannot pay for them, they ought at least to tell us so—to cancel their contract and claim and place us in position where we can act as owners. . . . Their course prevents our selling elsewhere and keeps such a hold on the lots, without carrying the burden, that we may have to foreclose by suit the rights of the church. This I am sure no one wishes. It seems clear to me that the vestry ought to surrender their contract and quit claim to us, if they cannot pay at least the accruing interest.

Mr. Bunn met with the owners of the Summit Avenue lots in early 1895 and reported that they wished to deed the corner sixty feet to the church subject to the present mortgage thereon of $15,000 plus interest which the church would assume. The church would also convey to the investors the remaining fifty feet subject to the existing mortgage of $7,500 with interest. Bunn asked to be advised promptly whether this proposition was acceptable or not, as foreclosure loomed on at least one of the mortgages unless the interest was paid. The church was in default under its contract with him for the purchase of the lots dated June 1, 1893, and he warned that if the proposition was not accepted he would terminate the contract and request that the church surrender the same and quit claim the property back to him.

At the vestry meeting on January 21, 1895, it was moved to accept Mr. Bunn's proposal. But of the seven men present, John Ames and C. A. Clark voted No, and the five others—Victor Watkins, Emerson Peet, George Squires, Thomas Irvine, and Robert B. C. Bement—all declined to vote. The motion lost, meaning that St. John's would not be relocating to Summit Avenue. The proper officers of the parish were directed to execute and deliver a quit claim deed to Charles W. Bunn for all the rights under the contract of June 1, 1893. A handsome apartment building now occupies this much-discussed Summit Avenue site, two doors west of the legendary University Club, immortalized, for one, by neighbor Scott Fitzgerald.

Mr. Morgan now proposed at a parish meeting on February 24, 1895, that a lot on the northeast corner of Portland and

ARCHITECT CASS GILBERT, ca. 1907, was born in Zanesville, Ohio, in 1859, and moved west with his family to St. Paul when he was nine. St. Paul was also growing up, and at seventeen young Gilbert secured a job in a small architectural firm in the city. When wanderlust soon got the best of him, he traveled to Europe to see and sketch and paint its architectural treasures—enough to inspire him for a lifetime. Back in St. Paul in the 1880s, he formed Gilbert and Taylor with fellow young architect James Knox Taylor. Between 1885 and 1892 the firm designed more than fifty churches, homes, and commercial buildings, including the Endicott Building in downtown St. Paul. His guild house for St. John the Evangelist was also used for services and later incorporated into the present church building.

Kent, with a frontage of 75 feet and a depth of 158 feet, be purchased for the sum of $8,200—leading the way to St. John's present location. The rector, wardens, and vestry were authorized to take title to the property as soon as sufficient funds were subscribed. Subsequent parish meetings took place on March 9, March 15, March 22, and March 29 to report progress on subscriptions. At the latter meeting it was baptisms in the course of the year, five adult baptisms, twelve confirmations, three marriages, and seven burials. In the Sunday School there were 150 scholars—as the children and youth were called for many years—with twenty teachers. The parish had ten organizations, including St. Luke's Guild, the Woman's Auxiliary, the Brotherhood of St. Andrew, the Parish Aid Society, the Altar Guild, and St. John's Guild.

On September 6, 1895, the rector presented to the vestry two resignations: his own and that of Professor Emil Oberhoffer as organist and choirmaster. Both men had been at St. John's about three and a half years. On the same day and hour that the wardens and vestry accepted Mr. Morgan's resignation, their counterparts at Christ Church in Dayton, Ohio, extended a call to him to become rector of their parish, to take effect on October 1, 1895.

Mr. Morgan afterwards read a statement to the members of the parish, explaining that the reason for his resignation was to "relieve the Wardens and Vestry of the burden of their obligations to him." The congregation begged him to remain and—in a startling display of unreality—decided that the rector's salary should be $5,000 instead of $4,000. Morgan, however, as we would expect, said he was unable to accept the offer because he was already under contract with the parish in Ohio. In the years to come, he said, when he should read of the growth and prosperity of the parish "it would be his pride and pleasure to remember that he had had something to do with its work in earlier days."

St. John's wasn't giving up. Bishop Mahlon Gilbert was prevailed upon to prepare a petition asking that Christ Church release Mr. Morgan "for the best welfare of their parish and the Church in Minnesota." But in a telegram dated September 23, the matter was confirmed: "Vestry of Christ Church have declined to release Mr. Morgan."

Thus Mr. Y. Peyton Morgan became rector at Christ Church in Dayton, remaining there until 1899.[7] His health failed him such that he was unable to assume the duties of a new call to the cathedral in Cincinnati. He died in October of that year at his home in Dayton.[8]

The Guild House, including a chapel, was completed in 1895.

reported that $8,500 had been pledged. A total of 181 votes were received on the subject, all being in favor of the purchase, and the lot at Portland and Kent was purchased for St. John's next building. The address was originally 555 Portland Avenue but was eventually changed to 60 Kent Street (which was named in 1855 by Charles Mackubin in honor of Kent County in Maryland.)[6]

THE GUILD HOUSE, incorporating the church, was built according to plans by Cass Gilbert. The vestry awarded the construction contract to Mr. F. J. Romer. A total of $21,800 was spent on the overall effort, including the price of the lot, interest and taxes, building contract, plumbing and heating, pews, architect, and the moving of the organ. The guild house would be used temporarily as a chapel until the church could be completed. Bishop Mahlon Gilbert presided at the opening of the guild house on November 17, 1895.

The vestry had been so preoccupied through virtually all of Mr. Morgan's tenure with the matters of real estate and buildings that little else appears to have been happening in the parish. But according to the parochial report for the year ending May 31, 1895, there were 250 families and 1,000 individuals in the parish. There had been seventeen infant

Acting upon a recommendation from Bishop Gilbert, and after a first candidate had turned down its call, the vestry then called the Rev. Dudley Ward Rhodes of the Church of Our Saviour, an affluent parish in Mount Auburn, Ohio, a neighborhood of Cincinnati, where he had been for twenty years. Vestryman John H. Ames visited Dr. Rhodes in Ohio and was satisfied with his preaching.

On January 9, 1896, the Rev. Dudley Rhodes wrote to the vestry that he wished to accept the call, but begged

> to lay before the Vestry my entire mind. Mr. Morgan was called at a salary of $4,000 and Mr. Ames tells me that there was no difficulty in paying that amount. . . . Should my fortune carry me to St. John's, my lot will be cast in with yours for better or worse and no one will be more desirous that we shall live within our income than I. . . . Should that salary be offered me, and at the end of the year, on Easter 1897, the accounts show that it is too much to be met out of the regular income, I will cheerfully consent that the amount shall be fixed from that time at $3,500.

The vestry urged the Rev. Dudley Rhodes to come to St. John's at the earliest possible moment. He began his duties as the parish's fifth rector at a salary of $4,000 on March 1, 1896. An informal reception for Rev. and Mrs. Rhodes was held in the guild house on February 29, "in accordance with the wishes of the Bishop, and appropriate to the Lenten Season." Rhodes and his wife Jennie lived at 533 Portland Avenue.

The chapel in the Guild House, where St. John's held its services until a new church was constructed.

Parishioner Channing Seabury broke ground for the new (third and present) Minnesota State Capitol on May 6, 1896. Born in Massachusetts in 1842, Seabury reportedly moved to St. Paul to escape the "family disease" of tuberculosis. A partner with Amherst Wilder in a wholesale clothing business, Seabury headed the Capitol Commission, which hired architect Cass Gilbert to design the five-million-dollar Capitol building. Gilbert's design won out over those of forty other applicants and secured for him a propitious future. A Gordon Hat sign can be seen in the middle background.

chapter five

THE REV. DUDLEY WARD RHODES 1896-1900
The Death of a Bishop

TO GIVE A PICTURE OF THE TIMES, during the ensuing rectorship of Dr. Rhodes, the U.S. Supreme Court would decree that racial segregation was approved under the "separate but equal" doctrine. When gold was discovered near Dawson, Canada, the ensuing Klondike Gold Rush caused a boom in travel and gold fever. The first modern Olympic Games were held in Athens, Greece. Jesse W. Reno invented the escalator, and Boston built the first underground public transportation system in North America. The battleship *Maine* exploded and sank in Havana harbor, Cuba; the United States annexed the independent republic of Hawaii; and the peace treaty ending the Spanish-American War was signed in Paris. The islands of Guam, the Philippines, and Puerto Rico were annexed by the United States. Austrian neurologist and founder of psychoanalysis Sigmund Freud wrote *The Interpretation of Dreams*.

Rev. Dudley Ward Rhodes.

he studied at the Philadelphia Divinity School, graduating in 1874, and was ordained deacon in that year. He was an associate priest at St. Paul's Church in Cincinnati from 1874 to 1876, being ordained priest there in 1874. He was subsequently rector of the Church of Our Saviour, which had just organized with twenty-nine members and without any church building or property. He would build a handsome stone church and rectory worth $60,000, with three hundred communicants.

His wife was the former Laura Wiggins, whom he married in 1875, and with whom he had two sons. Laura died in 1883, and in 1885 he married Jennie Allen Handy. Mr. Rhodes and Jennie had one child, daughter Helen Marietta Rhodes, born in 1886, who died in 1894. Mr. Rhodes was a member of the Ohio Historical Society and a member and chaplain of the Society of Colonial Wars in the State of Ohio. He received the Doctor of Divinity degree from Marietta College in 1892.

The Rev. Dr. Dudley Ward Rhodes was born in 1849 in Marietta, Ohio.[1] At the close of his junior year at Marietta College, he spent a year in Europe studying with a tutor. On his return he entered the first senior class at Cornell University, where he won the President's Prizes in English History and Modern History and was the valedictorian of his class, graduating in 1869. After two years studying law,

Dr. Rhodes was a voluminous writer and popular lecturer. In 1879 he published his book *Creed and Greed*[2] and in 1880 he published two more works: *Essays on Marriage and Divorce*[3] and *Dangers and Duties: Talks to Men and Women*.[4] He was also one of several authors of *History of Cincinnati and Hamilton County, Ohio*.[5]

IN CREED AND GREED Rhodes wrote that "we have a city [Cincinnati] as badly sewered, as badly lighted, as badly cleaned, and as badly governed as any city on the continent,"[6] giving cause to one reviewer to brand him "a reformist clergyman."[7] And inasmuch as he "called attention to the poverty, misery, and filth of the rapidly growing tenement districts" another reviewer declared him "unmistakably a precursor of the Social Gospel movement."[8]

Creed and Greed called into question "one of the fundamental assumptions of civic folk mercantilism—the belief in the inevitable harmony of interests in the local society, the assurance that the prospering of one segment of the community would ineluctably benefit everyone else in the city."[9] Indeed reviewer Samuel Haber noted that the relationship between Protestant Christianity in America and the expanding capitalist economy had always been an ambiguous one. "While ministers of most denominations extolled honest industry and accepted wealth as its reward, they also held that wealth could be debasing, even corrupting."[10]

When Dr. Rhodes came to St. John's, the whole country remained under the blight of financial depression. Even many of the rich were poor, and the prospects were dark. But when he entered St. John's for the first time on a weekday in Lent, he wrote, and saw hundreds of faces looking up at his, he took heart. He had never seen such Lenten congregations before and they never failed in the five Lents that he shared with St. John's. He encountered a united and cheerful people who undertook the work that it was possible to do under the stressful conditions of the business world.[11]

Because the parish had a new guild house and church when Dr. Rhodes arrived in March 1896, its building needs were mostly solved for the moment, though the vestry had to deal with the lingering debt. There were also some problems with the pipe organ that lasted for several years, and some financial difficulties, but otherwise the parish during the rectorship of Dr. Rhodes simply went about its daily routines the way churches always do.

Dr. Rhodes had clergy assistance in the services of the Rev. Lewis Gouverneur Morris who married Ruth Myers, the daughter of parishioner Walter F. Myers and sister of Paul N. Myers, who was on the vestry.[12] Morris later became rector at St. John's, Los Angeles. The Rev. Edwin Johnson succeeded Mr. Morris as assistant to Dr. Rhodes and served as superintendent of the Sunday School.

A very large representation from the parish attended the Annual Meeting on April 20, 1896, when receipts for the past year were reported as $11,698.39, with disbursements at 11,601.38, leaving the parish in the black by $97.01. Not bad for a depression. Bishop Mahlon Gilbert came to the meeting and gave "a most cheering and congratulatory address to the Parish and to Dr. Rhodes our Rector, and Stated that this was the largest Parish Meeting he ever attended."

The new guild house saw its first "entertainment"—as such events were called—when the Parish Aid Society held its Christmas Sale to raise money for the carpet fund. The women decorated the Guild Room with framed pictures of three former rectors and Bishop Gilbert, furnished curtains for the windows, painted the floor, and paid half the expense of a sewing machine to be used by the different parish societies—aside from individual donations of dishes, a table, and other useful furnishings.

The St. Luke's Guild had made eighty-five pieces of linen, provided a new screen in the chancel, and joined with the guilds of St. Paul's Church and Christ Church in procuring a new altar for the chapel in St. Luke's Hospital. The Altar Guild made forty-six cottas and ten cassocks for the choir.[13]

The Junior Auxiliary oversaw the Ministering Children's League, organized in February 1893; the boys department of the Brotherhood of St. Andrew, organized in 1894; and the Little Gleaners, organized in February 1895. The Children's League made books and washcloths for the hospital, gave clothing to poor people, and spent one happy hour making Easter eggs for the orphan asylum. Several years later the Little Gleaners gave an alms basin, still in use today, a credence table, and the large brass vases now in the Fireside Room.

SOMETIMES ORDINARY EVENTS prove more significant than they first appear. In 1896, in an otherwise unspectacular moment, the young boy W. Putnam Griswold entered the choir at St. John's, where his choral training prepared him for a career in music. By 1913 he was a player in the St. Paul Symphony Orchestra.

In the parochial report for the year ending March 31, 1896, the rector reported 250 families in the parish, with 1,000 individuals, but only 303 communicants. There were 160 pupils in the school, with twenty-five teachers and officers. The guild house, whose church was said to seat 362 people, was valued at $14,500 while the lots were valued at $8,500, for a total valuation of $23,000. There was no parish endowment.[14]

The resignation of James Blaikie as organist and choirmaster was announced at the vestry meeting in August 1896, and parishioner Alexander A. McKechnie agreed to serve as acting organist and choirmaster. In October the vestry accepted a bid to place an open-work panel for the front of the organ, facing the chancel.

In April 1897 the death of Brevet Major George Q. White, a resident of 86 Western Avenue and a long-time parishioner and worker for the church, both in the parish and the diocese, was reported at the Annual Meeting, with sympathy expressed to his daughters.[15] He was a charter member and recorder of the Minnesota Commandery (founded 1885) of the Military Order of the Loyal Legion of the United States.[16]

The ladies of the Parish Aid Society were reported, at the same meeting, to have held an entertainment for the choir, assisted the Woman's Auxiliary in preparing missionary boxes, distributed 521 garments, of which 241 were sent to the German congregation, 139 to Sheltering Arms, 55 to the Deaconess Home, and the balance elsewhere. They also held a China Social to furnish dishes for the guild house, and in November 1897, a "Silver Tea" that realized

sufficient funds to purchase three dozen forks and three dozen spoons.

In 1897 the St. Margaret's Guild was established as St. John's social service organization, and lasted for many productive decades, helping those in need, regardless of race or color.[17] It assumed responsibility for families recommended to its care by the organized charities of the city. Its members aimed to effect improvement in material and social welfare by visitation and by contributions in whatever form was needed for the comfort of the families, supplying them with food, fuel, clothing, and even money for rent in special cases. The Guild also sent dinners to families in need at Thanksgiving and Christmas time.

Nor did St. Margaret's Guild shun the city streets. Early in 1901, the guild established an industrial service house at 96 Dale Street to be used as its headquarters and workrooms, where the women set up a work exchange, with educational features for poor women. Washing and fine laundering were done on the premises, with the women soliciting laundry, especially the laundry from the bachelors of the city. A crèche (a British term for "day care nursery") was established for the smaller children of the washwomen.[18] Young boys—sons of the washwomen—called for the soiled clothes on Mondays, the washing was done on Tuesdays, and the ironing and mending on Wednesdays, with the cleaned clothes being returned either on Wednesday night or Thursday.

Such an enterprise as the St. Margaret's Guild required constant donations of money and goods. Contributions of money came from Mr. Sedgwick, Mrs. John A. Humbird, Mrs. John Pillsbury, and Mrs. Benjamin I. Stanton, while donations of clothing, furniture, and provisions came from William A. Frost, Mr. Theodore Griggs, and Mesdames E. J. Mairs, Augusta Sibley Pope, and A. B. Sibley.

THE U.S. ECONOMY WAS BEGINNING to recover by the late 1890s, but the lingering cloud of depression was felt at St. John's. At the vestry meeting in March 1898, the treasurer reported that Dr. Rhodes had made a donation to the parish in the amount of $1,000 to be applied toward the payment of diocesan obligations and other liabilities of the

Grace Memorial Episcopal Church in Wabasha, Minnesota, designed by Cass Gilbert and modeled after his plan for St. Clement's in St. Paul. This new Grace Memorial Church building was endowed in 1899 by Thomas Irvine in memory of his wife, Emily Hills Irvine, and her parents, the Rev. and Mrs. Horace Hills. The Rev. Mr. Hills had been rector of Grace Episcopal Church in the 1870s.

parish. The vestry expressed its gratitude to him for his liberal offer, but proposed "to hold the same in abeyance, while they make some effort themselves to raise the funds required to carry the Parish through." In April every regular attendee of the church received subscription cards and envelopes. The church building was mortgaged to the St. Paul Title Insurance and Trust Company for the sum of $6,000 due December 2, 1900, at six percent per annum. At the request of Dr. Rhodes, his salary for the year beginning April 1, 1898, was reduced to $3,500.

At the vestry meeting on May 6, 1899, the gentlemen expressed to Thomas Irvine their "heartfelt sympathy in this his hour of bereavement" upon the death of "his wife and his dearest companion [Emily Hills Irvine] which he has suffered and the loss which the Parish has sustained of an

earnest, faithful and devoted Servant of God, who having finished her labors is numbered with the Saints in Glory. We thank God for her good example."

In the year of his wife's death, Mr. Irvine, who was in the lumber business, endowed the present building for Grace Memorial Episcopal Church in Wabasha, Minnesota, as a memorial to his wife and her parents, the Rev. and Mrs. Horace Hills. Cass Gilbert designed the church, which is modeled after his plan for St. Clement's in St. Paul. The parishioners first gathered in 1859, making it one of the oldest congregations in the Diocese of Minnesota. The Rev. Mr. Hills was rector of Grace Episcopal Church from 1872 until 1877. Thomas and Emily Irvine had a son named Horace Hills Irvine, who grew to prominence in St. Paul, as we shall see.

By October 1899 the treasurer was able to report that parish finances were in "exceptionally good shape," and that pew rents were being paid, but that returns from pledge cards were a little slow.

After only four years in the position, and leaving the church in sound financial standing, the Rev. Dr. Rhodes submitted his letter of resignation to junior warden John H. Ames on February 26, 1900, writing:

My health has been bad for many months and I have been hoping for its improvement through the winter, but I am compelled to believe that I cannot be well except by getting rid of all care and nervous strain for some time. The great need of the Parish is a Church building, even a frame one if no better can be had.

If a sum of $30,000 could be secured, such a Church [could] be built. Every dollar of debt [being] paid, an opportunity to work and grow [may] be seized upon now in prosperous times. I have not the strength to undertake the raising of this sum and a new man will bring and create enthusiasm. You will communicate this resignation to the vestry and say to its members, what they already know, that no relations could be pleasanter than mine have been with all connected with the parish and that I am very unhappy and depressed over this necessity of separation. I hope to go on through Lent and leave you on Easter.

THE VESTRY ACCEPTED THE RECTOR'S resignation with regret. On March 12, Dr. Rhodes submitted the names of three clergymen "from which to make selection as his successor," namely, the Rev. Mr. Thurston of Winona, the Rev. Mr. Slattery of Faribault, and the Rev. Charles S. Scadding of Illinois.

Ten days earlier, on March 2, friend and confidant of St. John's Coadjutor Bishop Mahlon Norris Gilbert died of pneumonia. A private service was conducted in the bishop's residence by the Rev. C. D. Andrews, assisted by the Rev. Dr. Rhodes. His funeral took place at Christ Church, where the multitude of mourners was said to number five thousand. Bishop Gilbert was buried at Oakland Cemetery. As a token of the great affection that the vestry and people of St. John's had for their bishop, a fine, carved wooden episcopal chair with screen, sedilia, and rector's stall was commissioned and installed to his memory in the northwest corner of the chancel.

St. John's search committee for a new rector, consisting of a few vestry members, reported having secured letters recommending "Clergymen located in affluent parts of the Country from Bishops and prominent Clergymen." The committee then contacted and visited these men. At its meeting on April 26, 1900, however, the vestry resolved to call none of them, but instead called the Rev. Theodore Sedgwick, founding rector of St. John's Church in Williamstown, Massachusetts, which he had served from 1894 to 1900. His salary was to be set at $3,000[19]—$1,000 short of Dr. Rhodes' starting salary in 1896, and $2,000 short of the Rev. Mr. Morgan's ending salary in 1895.

On May 29, 1900, after visiting St. Paul, Mr. Sedgwick wrote to senior warden Victor M. Watkins that he would accept the vestry's call only if it would first relieve the parish of its $6,000 indebtedness.[20] Inasmuch as the congregation was scattered during the summer, the vestry

Vestryman Victor M. Watkins was the confidential secretary of Amherst H. Wilder and later president of the Wilder Foundation created in St. Paul by trusts established by the wills of Wilder, his wife, Fanny, and their daughter, Cornelia Day Wilder. Watkins had also served on the boards of directors at the Merchants National Bank, the St. Paul Fire and Marine Insurance Company, the St. Paul Foundry Company, and the Superior Water, Light and Power Company.

Victor Watkins and his family lived at 525 Holly Avenue, ca. 1885.

WILLIAM A. FROST owned the eponymous pharmacy in the turn-of-the-century building known as the Dacotah, at the corner of Selby and Western in St. Paul, where men and women of society went for "drugs, chemicals, and medicines, medicinal wines and liquors, and fancy toilet articles of great variety." F. Scott Fitzgerald resorted to the pharmacy for his tobacco and caffeine. Today the storied building houses the popular restaurant W. A. Frost, founded in 1975 by John Rupp, who grew up in St. John's, and has also renewed and developed the University and Athletic Clubs in St. Paul.

A private service for Bishop Mahlon Gilbert was conducted in the bishop's residence at 18 Summit Court in St. Paul by the Rev. C. D. Andrews, assisted by St. John's rector, the Rev. Dudley Rhodes. This house was later purchased by parishioners David and Perrin Lilly.

pledged its best efforts to eliminate the church's debt by the end of the year. Sedgwick accepted the vestry's call and agreed to begin his work on the first of September.[21] And by the time of their meeting on December 10, the vestry was able to report that they had indeed secured the $6,000 needed to liquidate the debt, fulfilling the agreement between the vestry and Mr. Sedgwick precedent to his call. Mr. Sedgwick resided at 563 Ashland Avenue and later moved to 533 Portland Avenue.

AFTER A TWO-YEAR INTERIM following his departure from St. John's, The Rev. Dr. Rhodes returned as rector to the Church of Our Saviour, Cincinnati, serving from 1902 to 1909. Dr. Rhodes died at his Cincinnati home of a carcinoma in 1925.[22] A *New York Times* article stated that Rhodes was "formerly rector of St. Paul's Episcopal Cathedral, Cincinnati, for decades attended by "elegant and fashionable Cincinnatians."[23]

This Celtic cross marks the burial site of Bishop Mahlon N. Gilbert in Oakland Cemetery in St. Paul.

"NUNC DIMITTIS"

MAHLON NORRIS GILBERT was born in Laurens, Otsego County, New York, in 1848. He studied three years at Hobart College in Geneva, New York, but left school at the beginning of his senior year with respiratory trouble. In 1875 he graduated from the Seabury Divinity School in Faribault, Minnesota, and afterwards went west, where he had pastorates for six years in Deer Lodge and Helena, Montana. Called to Christ Church in St. Paul in 1881, he remained in this city for the rest of his life.

Bishop Gilbert's funeral took place at Christ Church on March 6, 1900. The choir sang a favorite standard, "My Faith looks up to Thee," and at the close of the service, "For all the Saints who from their Labours Rest." The *Nunc Dimittis* was chanted as the cortege left the church, and then from the organ arose the solemn strains of Handel's "Dead March" from *Saul.*

An overflow multitude of thousands of mourners turned out to pay their respects at the funeral of Bishop Mahlon N. Gilbert at Christ Church in downtown St. Paul on March 6, 1900.

This 1910 postcard celebrates the new St. John the Evangelist Episcopal Church at Portland and Kent in St. Paul.

chapter six

THE REV. THEODORE SEDGWICK 1900-1911

"I Had to Eat Another Waffle."

BORN ON AUGUST 2, 1863, in Stockbridge, Massachusetts, Theodore Sedgwick graduated from Harvard College in 1886, and from Berkeley Divinity School, in Middletown, Connecticut, in 1890. Following his ordination at St. Paul's Church in Stockbridge in 1890 he served at St. George's Church in New York City from 1890 to 1894 before founding St. John's in Williamstown. Mr. Sedgwick was single when he moved to St. Paul, but in May 1903 he married parishioner Mary Aspinwall Bend. The couple had four children, three of whom were born during their time in St. Paul, namely, Theodore, Edith Ludlow, and Harold Bend. Son Charles was born in 1912, after the Sedgwicks moved to New York City.

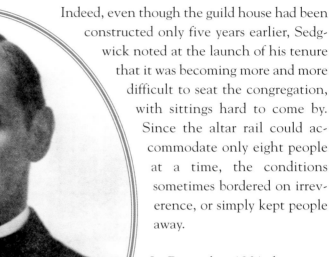

The Rev. Theodore Sedgwick.

The Rev. Theodore Sedgwick began St. John's sixth rectorship at the best of times. The parish had never been in better financial condition, there were no outstanding debts, and all diocesan obligations had been paid. Out of a total of 412 sittings, 342 had been rented by the 220 families in the parish, leaving only seventy seats vacant. The valuation of the parish land and building was approximately $27,000. And by Easter of 1901 the parish showed a balanced budget of $15,413.78. There was still no rectory, nor an endowment, but some $2,000 was already in the building fund for a permanent church.

Indeed, even though the guild house had been constructed only five years earlier, Sedgwick noted at the launch of his tenure that it was becoming more and more difficult to seat the congregation, with sittings hard to come by. Since the altar rail could accommodate only eight people at a time, the conditions sometimes bordered on irreverence, or simply kept people away.

In December 1901 the vestry explored the possibility of purchasing the lot at the rear of the guild house, in order to expand the present building, but considered the owner's asking price of $5,000 unacceptable. A month later they decided to investigate the possibility of using the present property for enlarging the church. In February 1902 the vestry voted to hire Minnesota architect Clarence Johnston to design the contemplated extension of the guild house to extend to Portland Avenue and to accommodate eight hundred sittings.

A close friend and colleague of Cass Gilbert, who had moved to New York City, Clarence Johnston was becoming Minnesota's most prolific architect. As Minnesota State Architect for thirty years, he designed virtually all of the buildings on thirty-five state-owned sites and campuses, including the Stillwater State Prison and the Gillette State Hospital for Crippled Children (the only remaining building of which now houses

Minnesota architect Clarence H. Johnston, 1919.

The children of the parish contributed to the cost of the cornerstone, which was laid on November 9, 1902.

the Minnesota Humanities Commission), which brought him national acclaim and set the standard for buildings of their type. The most sought-after residential architect for two generations of St. Paul's moneyed class, he designed forty-two residences on Summit Avenue alone, the best preserved Victorian boulevard in America. During a career that spanned fifty-four years, 1882-1936, Johnston mastered an enormous range of design types, ultimately coming to regard historical styles as reflections of programming needs and physical context rather than expressions of personal taste—either his own or the client's. One of the hallmarks of his work was its deep sense of humanism, indicated both by his emphasis on long-term functional and structural viability and by his installation of ornamental programs specifically suited to the building's uses.

To start the building fund, Mr. Sedgwick enlisted the interest of the children of the Church School in the new church by placing on display a picture of a large cornerstone. Each week as the children contributed their pennies and dollars they covered the stone with small pieces of paper. A grandfather was persuaded by Sedgwick to double the amount that the children gave. So by the time they had completely covered the cornerstone they had the sum of three thousand dollars.[1] By Easter of 1902 the parish had raised $6,300 toward a project that was estimated to cost between $40,000 and $45,000. The vestry decided to wait until they had $30,000 pledged or in hand. By September of that year they already had subscriptions of $25,275, demonstrating broad parish support for the building project.

Construction began. Work on the new foundation progressed so satisfactorily that the contractor expected to have the floor joists in place and the rough floor laid in time to provide a suitable platform for the ceremony of laying the cornerstone, to take place on November 9, 1902. In the *Centennial History of the Parish of Saint John the Evangelist*, by Robert Orr Baker, we learn, "After the reading of a psalm, a copper box containing a Bible, a hymnal, the records of the church, copies of the addresses of the day, the St. Paul daily papers and a program of the day's activities was placed in the cavity in the center of the stone."

Early in 1903, fearful of the ballooning cost of the project, the vestry decided to make a number of changes to help keep the

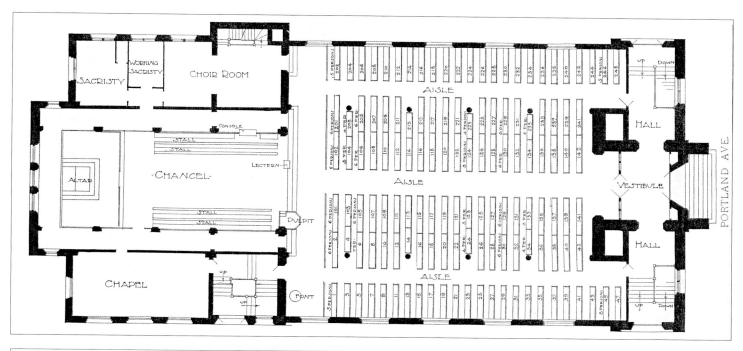

PRICE OF SITTINGS

Pew No.	Single Sitting	Pew No.	Single Sitting	Pew No.	Single Sitting	Pew No.	Single Sitting	Pew No.	Single Sitting	Pew No.	Single Sitting
1	$5.00	24	$25.00	102	$25.00	125	$25.00	206	$6.00	229	$20.00
2	25.00	25	15.00	103	25.00	126	25.00	207	25.00	230	9.00
3	5.00	26	25.00	104	25.00	127	25.00	208	7.00	231	20.00
4	25.00	27	12.00	105	25.00	128	25.00	209	25.00	232	6.00
5	6.00	28	25.00	106	25.00	129	20.00	210	8.00	233	20.00
6	25.00	29	9.00	107	25.00	130	20.00	211	25.00	234	5.00
7	7.00	30	20.00	108	25.00	131	20.00	212	9.00	235	10.00
8	25.00	31	6.00	109	25.00	132	20.00	213	25.00	236	5.00
9	8.00	32	20.00	110	25.00	133	20.00	214	11.00	237	10.00
10	25.00	33	5.00	111	25.00	134	20.00	215	25.00	238	5.00
11	9.00	34	20.00	112	25.00	135	10.00	216	13.00	239	10.00
12	25.00	35	5.00	113	25.00	136	10.00	217	25.00	240	5.00
13	11.00	36	10.00	114	25.00	137	10.00	218	15.00	241	10.00
14	25.00	37	5.00	115	25.00	138	10.00	219	25.00	242	5.00
15	13.00	38	10.00	116	25.00	139	10.00	220	15.00	244	5.00
16	25.00	39	5.00	117	25.00	140	10.00	221	25.00	246	5.00
17	15.00	40	10.00	118	25.00	141	10.00	222	15.00	248	5.00
18	25.00	41	5.00	119	25.00	142	10.00	223	25.00		
19	15.00	42	10.00	120	25.00	201	25.00	224	15.00		
20	25.00	43	5.00	121	25.00	202	5.00	225	25.00		
21	15.00	45	5.00	122	25.00	203	25.00	226	15.00		
22	25.00	47	5.00	123	25.00	204	5.00	227	25.00		
23	15.00	101	25.00	124	25.00	205	25.00	228	12.00		

The floor plan for the new St. John the Evangelist Church as designed by Clarence Johnston, and the "Price of Sittings," ca. 1903.

cost down. Hard brick or sidewalk tile was to be used for the coal room floor and the boiler room, instead of concrete. Slater's felt was to be used for the roof, instead of Cabot's quilt.[2] All the heavy felt paper between the under and upper flooring was to be left out, except in the basement. All floors were to be laid with birch, leaving out the tile in the entrance vestibule. The boiler room ceiling was to be covered with metal lath and only one coat of plaster. But most conspicuously of all, the tower was to be finished only as far as the deck level.

The cost for the general contract, thus altered, was set at $32,690, but the cost of the foundation, glass, plumbing, wiring, gas fixtures, pews, heating, and the architect's fees would bring the total cost to $50,286.60, well above the high-end estimate. In the parochial report for May 1903, Sedgwick reported to the bishop that the cost would come in at $55,000. Sedgewick also sent a photograph of the unfinished tower to the members of the congregation with the comment, "This looks like a turtle." Bowing to popular demand, the

THE LAST SERVICE in the guild house was held on Sunday, June 14, 1903. The first service in St. John's grand new building on the corner of Kent and Portland, encompassing the guild house, was celebrated on October 18, 1903. With the completion of the church and undercroft, the parish land and building were now valued at $86,900, with a declared seating capacity of 712.

vestry added the completion of the tower to the contract, for another $5,500. In the end, the vestry borrowed $20,000.

During construction, it was necessary to gut the interior of Cass Gilbert's nave and chancel, with new chancel arches and columns being added by Johnston, while the new nave was extended south from the Gilbert church, all the way to Portland Avenue. Arrangements were made for St. John's parishioners to worship at Christ Church in downtown St. Paul in the summer and early fall of 1903.

The year before, in late October or early November of 1902, the widow and daughter of Amherst H. Wilder had proposed a marble baptismal font be placed in the church in his memory (see p. 2). Fanny Spencer Wilder and daughter Cornelia Wilder Appleby provided the design for a life-sized angel holding a shell to be executed in Florence, Italy, by the Romanelli Brothers. Fra Romanelli were six generations of renowned Florentine artists and sculptors.[3] By the time the font had arrived, around the beginning of 1904, the two women had also died, adding a sacred melancholy to the font.

Amherst Holcomb Wilder was one of St. Paul's pioneer businessmen, coming to the city in 1859 from his home in Lewis, New York.[4] Over time he accumulated a fortune in the development of the Northwest. A versatile entrepreneur, Wilder's interests included trading, freight and stage coach transportation, railroading, lumbering, banking, insurance, real estate, and merchandising. Wilder married Fanny Spencer, born in Utica, New York, in 1861. Their daughter Cornelia Day (called Day) was born in 1868. As Cornelia approached her sixteenth birthday,

Fanny took her daughter abroad for four years where they toured the continent and Day studied languages and music with tutors. They returned home to "A Baronial Castle," as a St. Paul newspaper described it, that Amherst had built in their absence on the brow of Summit Hill, at the foot of Selby, next door to James and Mary Hill. Designed by Clarence Johnston, the Wilder family home dominated the site now occupied by the Chancery Offices for the Catholic Archdiocese of St. Paul and Minneapolis.[5]

Amherst Wilder had served on the vestry at St. Paul's Episcopal Church when the family lived in St. Paul's then fashionable "lowertown." At St. John the Evangelist, his personal secretary, Victor M. Watkins, was a vestryman. On November 6, 1894, we learn from St. John's parish records, Amherst Wilder was baptized at his home by St. John's former rector, the Rev. Y. P. Morgan. He died several days later at age sixty-six and was buried from St. John's, in Oakland Cemetery, on November 15, 1894. Amherst Wilder provided in his will for a trust to fund the Amherst H. Wilder Charity.

A few years after Wilder's death, Cornelia Day Wilder married Dr. T. E. W. Villiers Appleby, a physician whom she met while serving as a volunteer clerk at the St. Paul Free Dispensary. In 1898 he was elected to St. John's vestry. Dr. Appleby signed a prenuptial contract renouncing any claim to the Wilder family fortune. Four years later Cornelia died at the age of thirty-five from complications following surgery. Her mother died at the age of sixty-five on April 5, 1903, three months after her daughter's death. Both Fanny Spencer Wilder and Cornelia Wilder Appleby left their fortunes to establish separate Wilder charities in memory of their husband and father, respectively.

One of the most popular Wilder programs, suggested by Mrs. Wilder in her will, was the Wilder Baths and Pool, which opened in 1914. Designed to meet the needs of the many St. Paul residents without adequate bathing facilities, it boasted eighty-five shower baths and a 35' by 70' swimming pool. The baths were operated for sixty years.

The Wilder Dispensary created much attention when it opened its doors in July 1924. The dispensary's free medical and dental care to persons without financial resources was a

Amherst Wilder built this "baronial" residence for his family in 1887.

Pioneer St. Paul entrepreneur Amherst H. Wilder (1828-1894).

Fanny Spencer Wilder (1837-1903).

The Wilders' only child, Cornelia Day Wilder (1868-1903).

much needed addition to the Saint Paul community. Physicians and residents from Miller Hospital staffed the dispensary free of charge. The *St. Paul Pioneer Press* heralded the dispensary as "one of the most modern and best equipped in the world." For thirty-five years, tens of thousands of individuals received treatment at the Wilder Dispensary from some of the best doctors in St. Paul. It remained a viable program until 1960 when it was taken over by a hospital association.

At St. John's, friends of Mrs. Wilder who wished to have her name linked with that of her husband, placed in her memory an ornamental oak screen and wall paneling, a window of English stained glass, and a kneeling desk around the marble angel baptismal font that Fanny and her daughter Cornelia had earlier provided in memory of Amherst H. Wilder. The gift included a prayer book and hymnal as well as a brass ewer. At the same time, carved oak screens were being placed in the next two arches in the chancel, following the design of the work within the sanctuary, but the new screens were open to allow access to the communion rail from the ambulatories.

In November of 1904, the vestry approved a plan to arrange what had been the west transept of the original guild house into use for a chapel, providing a platform, an altar, and suitable seating. In those years it was known as the Chapel of the Beloved Disciple, a name that is little used today. The chapel was remodeled several times in the ensuing years.

In his Easter letter of 1904, Sedgwick wrote in eloquent, well-chosen words, with elevated sentiment, a kind of mission statement. The purpose of St. John's, he wrote,

> is to conduct services of worship in our spacious church which shall be dignified, reverent, full of beauty and spiritual feeling, and which shall appeal to the religious instinct of all. We desire nothing sensational, but we want to draw men, women and children to the worship of Almighty God by helping them to feel the beauty of holiness and the strength of things that are spiritual. We want to do this by the divine service which we render, and in which we ask the people to take part.

The newly completed interior of St. John the Evangelist Episcopal Church where congregants gathered for their first service on October 18, 1903. Note the original, lower ceiling; the three lancet windows behind the altar; and the original light fixtures.

Four months into his rectorship, Sedgwick made what was arguably his most important staff appointment when he hired as organist and choirmaster the Canadian-born George H. Fairclough from Kalamazoo, Michigan, who had studied at the Königliche Hochschule in Berlin in the 1890s. Fairclough took charge on January 1, 1901, and in time he erected a musical establishment that achieved wide acclaim across the region. At a salary of $1,000 per year, he came to conduct a large choir of men and boys; organize a new girls choir for the Sunday School, and a new women's choir; run a monthly series of major choral concerts; host summer choir camps for the choristers; present organ recitals during Lent; and purchase not one, but two new pipe organs for the parish.[6]

By Easter of 1902 Fairclough's choir consisted of thirty boys, fifteen men, and a paid solo quartet of men and women, and by 1903 there were over forty boys, including the probationers, and eighteen men (without a paid quartet). But the seating capacity in the chancel was fifty, so that not all the singers could be accommodated. By 1904 there were nearly sixty boys and twenty-three men to fill the more ample choir stalls of the then expanded church, making it one of the largest boychoirs in the country. The Misses Lucy Lord Chapman and Elizabeth Hensel took zealous charge of the vestments.

PARISHIONER ALEXANDER A. McKECHNIE instituted the popular musical services in 1901 that took place on the first Sunday evening of every month (except during the summer), when the choir presented major choral works, often with guest soloists. The first three were under his direction, and George Fairclough continued the programs to great acclaim. It is said that when the soprano Miss Gordon was a featured soloist on the program, "people were turned away in large numbers."

The choir's repertoire for these early services included West's "Seed Time and Harvest," Gaul's "Holy City," Maunder's "Penitence, Pardon and Peace," Stainer's "Crucifixion," and almost the entire first part of Handel's "Messiah." Favorite works in their own day, the first four of these pieces are nevertheless dated, and only the Stainer and the Handel are sung with any frequency today. In later

The reredos above the altar, a wooden depiction of the Last Supper, was carved in quartered oak in Switzerland by Anton Lang.[7] It mimics the original executed in fresco by Leonardo da Vinci in Milan. Both the altar and reredos were given by Fanny Spencer Wilder in memory of her daughter Cornelia Day Wilder Appleby.

years the choir added portions of Mendelssohn's "Elijah" and about half of Haydn's "Creation" to their repertoire.

Fairclough rehearsed the choir boys for an hour and a half on Monday and Thursday afternoons, for two hours on Friday evenings (with the men for much of that time), and on Saturday mornings for an hour and a quarter. This routine took up an enormous amount of the boys' free time, but it was time well-spent; boys in those years were not distracted by school sports, TV, computers, iPhones, Facebook, and Twitter. The parish so loved the boychoir that an occasional couple would entertain the boys in their home, as did Mr. and Mrs. G. D. Taylor one evening, and the rector on another. Mrs. Benjamin Irving (Minnie) Stanton gave a dinner for the boys at the Town and Country Club.

George Herbert Fairclough.

The first choir camp took place in the summer of 1901, beginning a long-time institution fondly remembered by generations of choir boys, including some later boys, Hank Snyder and Fred Myers among them, who are still active members of the congregation. The boys went to Green Lake near Chisago City in the early years, staying for nearly two weeks. They took the 9:10 train from St. Paul's Union Depot, reaching Chisago City at 10:35. A cook went along with them, and at first they refused oatmeal without cream, but the second day they thought it good with only brown sugar. In later years the camp moved to other lakes and other shores in the same general area.[8]

Mr. Fairclough had a number of assistants over the years. Among them were organist Alexander McKechnie, who also tuned and maintained the organ, and Margaret Myers who played for the Lenten services which were sung on Ash Wednesday morning, on daily afternoons during Lent, and on Maundy Thursday evening by the women's choir, which Fairclough established in 1906.

FOR THE FIRST FEW YEARS of his tenure, Sedgwick had no priest to assist him in serving the large congregation and in addition to his duties as rector he took on the

Choir boys delighted in choir camp each summer beginning in 1901, when they took the train to Green Lake near Chisago City. This 1904 photo of the boys and their counselors includes the camp mascot, center stage in the first row!

superintendence of the Sunday School. He did not want to call a priest for less than a $1,000 salary. For the church services he was assisted by lay reader Gen. William Bradford Bend, who held services and delivered addresses at St. Luke's Hospital, the Lilydale mission, and a number of other churches in the area.

The Rev. George W. Smith assisted Sedgwick from July 1904 until July 1905, taking over as superintendent of the Sunday School. Smith later went to St. John's, Randolph, and then to St. Luke's in St. Albans, both in the Diocese of Vermont. Upon his departure, Sedgwick was authorized by the vestry to hire another assistant, but he declined to do so. The vestry noted in August 1906 that he had worked arduously on his own for the past year, again serving as Sunday School superintendent, and offered him a two-month vacation. By September, with no luck finding a suitable priest assistant, Sedgwick proposed to hire "a lady assistant to look after the parish work and to visit the people, under his direction, and also the help of a stenographer to take care of his correspondence." And this he did.

Among Sedgwick's major accomplishments during his eleven-year tenure at St. John's was the increasing strength and vitality of the Sunday School, over which he served for several years as superintendent. By Easter 1901, there were 248 scholars in the school (180 for an average weekly attendance), with twenty-six teachers. He believed that the present and future strength of the parish lay in the school, being "the strongest missionary institution we have, and upon it depends the growth of our work." By 1903 there were three hundred enrolled scholars. It is almost impossible to imagine how so many students could be accommodated in the space allotted to them in the undercroft of the church. The school had a library and the students were expected to check out books to read at home.

Like many Sunday Schools of its era, the school at St. John's was modeled after the adult congregation. The scholars had their own service in the undercroft with an organ, led by a girls choir directed by Mrs. Jehiel W. Chamberlin.[9] They made regular monetary contributions to missions and out-

reach. One year the students sent funds to the Washington Memorial Chapel at Valley Forge, whose mission field covered fifteen square miles.

Over and over, Sedgwick urged parents to make certain that their children attended the Sunday School classes, and that they arrived on time, alleviating the discouragement that teachers feel when they know that a child is allowed to come or not, as he or she pleased. One small girl, when asked if she had a good reason for being late, said, "No, only I had to eat another waffle, they were so good."

The Sunday School had high expectations of the scholars, and their rigorous studies involved homework and report cards. In 1907, they were asked to write short essays on the life of one of the apostles. The next year, the fourth grade studied the history of the English Church from 33 A.D. to 1908 A.D.

For many years the Sunday School season ended with a picnic. One year the primary and main schools chartered the steamer *Minnesota*, with her barge, and followed the river, leaving the foot of Jackson Street at ten a.m., reaching Minnehaha Falls in time for lunch and returning to the landing by five in the afternoon. In 1910 the picnic was held at the Wildwood Amusement Park in Mahtomedi. Built in the late nineteenth century by the Twin Cities Rapid Transit Company at the end of their streetcar line, the park was situated at the south shore of White Bear Lake, opposite the summer "cottages" of St. Paul's merchants, bankers, and capitalists.

On April 17, 1902, the parish sustained the death of Junior Warden Emerson W. Peet who had been a member of the vestry for thirteen years and served many times as a delegate to Diocesan Council. At the time of his death he was the treasurer and a trustee of the diocese, a trustee of St. Mary's Hall for girls in Faribault, treasurer of the Church Foundation fund, and a member of the Standing Committee of the diocese.[10] Mr. Peet was also president of the St. Paul Chamber of Commerce and an actuary of the National Life Insurance Company. His father, the Rev. Stephen Peet, was chief among the founders of Beloit College in Wisconsin.

Charles E. Flandrau, ca. 1895.

In 1894, Mr. Peet founded the Informal Club, which originally met at his home at 271 Summit Avenue. Among its initial members were St. John's rector, the Rev. Y. Peyton Morgan; and men with connections to St. John's: Major Robert B. C. Bement,[11] Joseph G. Pyle, and George C. Squires. Architect Cass Gilbert was also a member, as were Bishop Mahlon Gilbert and James J. Hill. St. John's later rector, the Rev. Julius Schaad; and assistant priest, the Rev. Fred Budlong, were subsequently members, as were parishioners C. M. Griggs, C. W. Gordon, Frank B. Kellogg, Edward H. Morphy, and James H. Skinner, along with Roman Catholic Archbishop John Ireland. The club had a limit of sixty members and met fortnightly. The Informal Club is still in existence. Parishioner Malcolm McDonald is the chief convener.

In December 1904 the vestry acknowledged with gratitude the gift of the elaborately carved oak pulpit placed in the church by Mrs. Emerson W. Peet in memory of her husband.

In the 1890s, Informal Club member Charles E. Flandrau was an affluent St. Paul attorney with the firm Flandrau, Squires and Cutcheon. In that capacity he was a colleague of George C. Squires, who was an active member of St. John's. Mr. Flandrau later served as a judge and was the editor of *Encyclopedia of Biography of Minnesota*.[12] In August 1909 his son William Blair Flandrau, who owned a coffee plantation in Mexico, married writer Grace Hodgson in a ceremony at St. John's.

Grace Hodgson and Blair Flandrau lived in the 1888 townhouse at 548 Portland Avenue,[13] directly across from the Portland entrance to St. John's. Grace Flandrau was the author of novels, short stories, and journalistic pieces, and was

well regarded from the 1920s into the 1940s for her writings about the high society of Summit Avenue.[14] She achieved critical acclaim for several of her works, especially for her novel *Being Respectable*, which F. Scott Fitzgerald thought was "better than Babbitt" and Edith Wharton liked "better than any American novel in years."[15] She produced several pamphlets on early Minnesota history for the Great Northern Railway. Many of her short stories were published in such magazines as *Scribner's Magazine*, *The New Yorker*, *The Saturday Evening Post*, and *Harper's Magazine*. Few women writers in Minnesota have published more or attained greater international fame than Flandrau. She died in 1971, leaving an estate valued at ten million dollars.

General William Bradford Bend, a lay reader, diligent worker and valued vestryman, was a prominent member of St. John's. Both secretary and treasurer of the St. Paul Harvester Works, he was the original owner of the house at 239 Summit Avenue. He and his wife had been members of Christ Church, in downtown St. Paul, but after Mr. Sedgwick married their daughter, Mary Aspinwall Bend, in 1903, they became involved at St. John's and were active parishioners. General Bend died in 1905.

In January of 1904, a Men's Club was organized that met in what was called the Men's Club Room, where the vestry occasionally met. An early request by the club to place a billiard table there was politely ignored by the vestry, but in 1905 Sedgwick expressed his full support, believing that it would keep the younger men "from straying into other resorts."

For a number of years, Sedgwick hosted an annual Men's Smoker during February in the Guild Hall, where the men could "smoke comfortably, be entertained delightfully, eat lightly, and enjoy withal a kindly fellowship." In February 1907 the hall was attractively arranged, with lamps on small tables, and with easy chairs, rugs and palms set round about. The windows were latticed, and in the corners of the room hung large Japanese umbrellas and lanterns. For the smoker in 1908, which drew about 250 men, Minnesota Governor John A. Johnson attended as the guest of honor. The next year, sadly, St. John's hosted a memorial service in October

Author Grace Flandrau (above) and her husband, Blair Flandrau, were married at St. John's and lived at 548 Portland Avenue.

1909 for the popular Democratic governor who died in office after surgery at age 48. The men and boys choir sang for the service. Johnson had sought the 1908 Democratic presidential nomination in 1908, but lost to William Jennings Bryan.

In December 1904 the vestry heard rumors that Mr. Sedgwick had received a call from St. Paul's Church in Englewood, New Jersey. In a letter to him, dated December 6, they declared their hope that he would remain at St. John's, expressing their

> full and unreserved appreciation and approval of the administration of his office and the honor, fidelity and devotion which he has brought to the service of the Parish.

> It is largely to his energy and zeal (which have never faltered) that we owe the new church building. A gratifying increase in the number of its members has crowned his work here.

But in a remarkably candid reply, Sedgwick wrote that

Popular Minnesota governor John Albert Johnson was the first native Minnesotan to be elected to that office, in 1905, and served in the new State Capitol completed that year.

I have felt that the work has been on lines which received the assent of the Vestry in a negative way. As long as it was successful they had nothing against it. What I have felt I have lacked is not *words* of commendation, but an active participation in the life and spiritual development of the parish by the Vestry.

The Vestry are the officers of the parish. They are regarded by the parish and community as leaders in its active effort to enter into its fullest usefulness. But I have not felt that the Vestry recognized any responsibility beyond the attendance on Divine service once on Sunday. There is much spiritual and parish life that their presence and interest would stimulate. To be specific,—

The monthly Evening Musical service, when the Choir would be encouraged by their approval. For the Vestry must remember only two men in the Choir are paid. We are under obligation to the rest.

The special services from time to time arranged at hours to suit the business men.

The monthly preparation service for the Communion.

The occasional entertainments which foster a feeling of fellowship in the Church.

A hospitality shown in the Church to strangers, and to members of the parish.

I have asked members of my Vestry to help me in the work, they have declined. No one man's work can be successful. The rector I believe has a right to expect support in the active work from the officers of the Church.

The Vestry guard very rightly their prerogative of expending the monies of the parish, but has the vestry no responsibility in raising the funds beyond expecting the rector by his preaching, and his energy to fill the pews?

It was a great disappointment when the Church was built that so heavy a debt was laid upon it. It is a heavy burden for us to bear and it hampers any larger activities.

It is for such reasons as I have stated that I questioned whether the Vestry was in sympathy with my work as their rector.

Nevertheless, Sedgwick declined the position in New Jersey, to the certain relief of the vestry.

Mr. Sedgwick was the founder and editor of the parish newsletter, known originally as *The St. John's Evangelist*, with the first issue dated December 1, 1906.[16] It was a weekly in those years and arrived in people's homes every Saturday with an order of worship for the next day's eleven o'clock service. It also contained news of the parish, reports on coming and past meetings of the various parish organizations, news of the diocese and the broader church (including events in the Church of England), learned articles about topics of theological interest (at least to Sedgwick), and news of current events from the broader world. He notified the parish, for example, when the tunnels under the East River in New York were completed (April 1908); when Orville Wright's aeroplane was wrecked and the pilot himself seriously injured (Sept. 1908); and when Halley's Comet passed the earth's orbit (May 1910). When he reported that a major earthquake had devastated the city of San Francisco in 1906, the parish was inclined to send a (very small) contribution for the city's relief.

Among the several organizations available to St. John's women, the Woman's Auxiliary, a missionary organization, regularly sent boxes of clothing and household items to missionaries and their wives and families. In 1902 they sent boxes valued at $423.40 to the widow of a missionary in Cordova, Minnesota, and another to a priest in Brookings, South Dakota. In 1908 they sent a box to Sheltering Arms, containing fifty cans of fruit and vegetables, three dozen packages of breakfast food, a dozen boxes of crackers, several cans of cocoa, and jellies, puddings, and prunes. There were ten boys' Russian blouse suits, nine gingham aprons, eight outing night-gowns, two flannel skirts, two dozen pairs of stockings, three bedspreads, three dozen handkerchiefs, four table cloths, two dozen napkins, and some roller-towels, tea towels, and table bibs. There was also a box of clothing slightly worn, "which will gladden many a heart."

A Junior Auxiliary existed as early as 1893, but the rector's wife, Mary Bend Sedgwick, reorganized the group in February 1904, with an enrollment of seventeen children. It was reorganized still again in 1908 under the efficient direction of Miss Mary Baldy. Intended for children over age nine, the Junior Auxiliary prepared Christmas and Easter boxes for the missions, which included such items as candy bags, scrap books, bead chains, dressing dolls, and Indian baskets. In 1908 the gifts were sent to the Japanese missions. In other years the boxes went to China, the Philippines, the Red Lake Indian Mission in Minnesota, South Carolina, Hawaii, and elsewhere. The Junior Auxiliary met in the Guild Room over the chapel (later known as the Green Room and used today by the parish youth).

The purpose of the Babies' Branch (also called the Little Helpers) of the Woman's Auxiliary was to foster an awareness of mission even among "the little ones." At the request of the Rt. Rev. Samuel Cook Edsall, Bishop of the Diocese of Minnesota, the organization was established in the diocese at the beginning of Lent in 1902. Mrs. Sedgwick was appointed the first Diocesan Secretary of the organization. All baptized children under the age of eight were considered members, the object being "to make every child realize that, by virtue of his baptism, he is a member of the great missionary society, the church, and must do his part in advancing God's kingdom." In 1908, toddlers Louis W. Hill Jr., and his siblings Maud, Jerome, and Cortlandt—all children of Maud Van Cortlandt Taylor Hill and Louis W. Hill Sr., and grandchildren of the "Empire Builder" James J. Hill—were members of the Babies' Branch, as were the two young children of the Sedgwicks: Theodore Jr. and Edith Ludlow Sedgwick.

In July 1907, Rev. Sedgwick named as his assistant the Rev. Frederick G. Budlong, who resided at 434 Laurel Avenue. Budlong remained in the post until April 1909, when he became rector of Christ Church in downtown St. Paul. He later served a parish in Winnetka, Illinois, and in 1915 was called to the rectorship of St. Peter's Church, Chicago, a parish of more than twenty-two hundred communicants, reputed to be among the ten largest parishes in the Episcopal Church at the time.

Maud Van Cortlandt Taylor Hill.

Louis W. Hill Sr.

Maud Van Cortlandt Hill (Maudie); Louis W. Hill Jr.; James J. Hill II (Jerome), possibly in St. Paul, Minnesota, ca. 1907.

PARISHIONER STANFORD NEWEL died in April 1907, bequeathing to St. John's one-sixth of the proceeds to be raised from the sale of his limestone homestead at 251 Dayton Avenue, but the original estimate of $12,000—to be applied to the building fund—seems to have been whittled down to a mere $2,500 by the courts. The Honorable Stanford Newel, identified with the early life and growth of the city, was an attorney and a member of St. Paul's first park board. He was also a delegate to the National Republican Conventions in 1884 and 1892, and served as U.S. Minister to the Netherlands and Luxembourg. In May 1899, the American Commission to the Peace Conference of The Hague, on which he served, met for the first time at the Newels' home. The Minnesota Club in St. Paul was founded principally by Mr. Newel and he was several times its president.[17]

In July 1909 Sedgwick brought on as his assistant the Rev. Robert C. Ten Broeck who remained until August 1, 1910, whereupon he hired the Rev. Deacons John A. Furrer and John F. Plummer,[18] both of whom were later ordained priests

and remained until around the time Sedgwick himself resigned, in the spring of 1911.

In April 1910 the Rev. Ten Broeck was riding his bicycle on Lincoln Avenue, and as he turned onto Oakland Avenue he was hit by an automobile and thrown from his bike with considerable force. Ten Broeck sustained a deep gash over his left temple, with bruises to his left shoulder. He was unconscious for some time and remembered nothing of the incident. An ambulance took him to St. Luke's Hospital, where he was given seven stitches. In later years, the Rev. Ten Broeck became chaplain and instructor in Greek and Latin at St. Alban's School, Knoxville, Illinois.

Parishioner Elizabeth Yardley, who played the organ for the Sunday School and was its secretary, and was also secretary of the rector's Bible Class and second vice-president of the Altar Guild, entered the Church Training School of Philadelphia in 1907, where she trained as a deaconess. The school educated gifted women to assist the clergy in the parishes and to work in hospitals and other institutions that served the poor.[19] Yardley afterwards worked under the Rt. Rev. James B. Funsten, the bishop of the Diocese of Idaho, and served in a small town where the church had no clergyman. In 1909 Marion N. Chapman, a teacher in St. John's Sunday School, also went to the deaconess school for her two-year training.

Lay Reader Fred D. Evanson[20] declared his intent for the ministry and became a candidate for holy orders in June 1908. He had been singing in the choir for some time, was confirmed the previous winter, and began his studies in the fall. He was the first postulant from St. John's in eight years. In the fall of 1910 parishioner John L. Langhorne, the superintendent of the Sunday School at Lilydale, entered Seabury Divinity School in Faribault to prepare for ordained ministry.

In addition to his work within the parish, Sedgwick was active in the wider church in the diocese. In 1907 he was elected a member of the executive committee of the diocesan assembly of the Brotherhood of St. Andrew. He also participated in a Church Congress in New Orleans where he presented a paper on "The Attitude of Our Church to

Protestant Christianity." In 1908 he was elected to the executive committee of the Sunday School Association. He also served several terms on the General Board of Missions, attending meetings in New York City, and he also played a prominent role in the community beyond the church. He once spoke at a noon-day meeting with popular British evangelist Rodney "Gypsy" Smith at St. Paul's Metropolitan Opera House on East Sixth Street, when the preacher was in town in April 1909.

The parish observed its twenty-fifth anniversary on the weekend of December 7-9, 1906, and hoped to mark the celebration in a permanent way by making a reduction in the debt, which now stood at $10,600. With the money raised at the service, a payment of $1,250 was made against the mortgage indebtedness. After the mortgage on the property was paid off on December 24, 1907, Mr. Sedgwick made arrangements for Bishop Edsall to consecrate the building on January 1, 1908.

George Fairclough penned a hymn for this auspicious occasion titled "Forward Be Our Watchword." Printed on card stock, the hymn was reproduced in the diocesan periodical and was made available for sale to the public. Multiple copies of the hymn are still filed in St. John's choir library.

THE MORTALITY RATE among infants, children, and youth at St. John's was fairly high in those years, as it was everywhere before the days of advanced medicine. It was especially bad in 1907, when six parish children died. Mr. and Mrs. Hiram M. Pearce lost their fifteen-year-old daughter Katherine, long a member of the Sunday School, and gave a pair of alms basins in her memory. Six-year-old Marie Caldwell died in July. Two choir boys also died: Stuart Brightman who was memorialized through gifts from fellow choristers and Sunday School children, and the eleven-year-old Homer Ritchie Rothschild, who was memorialized by one of the hand-carved hymn boards in the church. Harold Knox Edwards Jr., the infant son of Harold Knox Edwards and Mary Gallagher Edwards, was buried in Oakland Cemetery. There was also the death of an infant boy in the Berg family, members of the Lilydale mission.

Choirmaster George Fairclough composed "Forward Be Our Watchword" for St. John's twenty-fifth anniversary in 1906.

In 1908, things were no better for young men in their twenties. Twenty-four-year-old Forrest S. Daniels, the eldest son of Mr. and Mrs. John W. Daniels, died at Saranac, New York. Twenty-one-year-old Edmund Barry Dibble, the youngest son of Mr.

and Mrs. Charles A. Dibble and a college sophomore in Amherst, Massachusetts, was suddenly stricken and died despite emergency surgery. And George Ross McMichael, at twenty-four years "a man of high principles, who brought his standard of living into his business, his sport, and his home," died in April after a brief illness. In 1909 three young people died in September alone, in the course of one week: eight-year-old Robert Cargill Farnham, sixteen-year-old Stuart Mason Kerr, and ten-year-old Bessie May Clark.

The Rev. Sedgwick routinely sought prominent churchmen to take the pulpit in his absence. In the 1906-1907 season, for example, no fewer than five bishops preached at St. John's. The Rt. Rev. Samuel C. Edsall, Bishop of Minnesota; the Rt. Rev. John H. White, Bishop of Indiana and former rector of St. John's; the Rt. Rev. Sheldon M. Griswold, Bishop of Salina, Kansas; the Rt. Rev Cameron Mann,

Bishop of North Dakota; and the Rt. Rev. Frank R. Millspaugh, Bishop of Kansas and former rector at St. Paul's, Minneapolis, all addressed St. John's discerning congregation. Millspaugh preached there on a number of occasions over the years.

In April 1907, a senior chapter of the Brotherhood of St. Andrew was formed at St. John's, with William H. Farnham elected as director. Members promised to pray for the extension of God's kingdom, and to act upon their prayer by bringing someone into the hearing of the Gospel or into the activities of the Church. Any baptized man was eligible for membership.

THE ORGAN IN THE GUILD HOUSE proved too small for the much larger space after the expansion of 1902. It was powered by a "water motor," that is, by wind that was pro-

The Rev. Mr. Sedgwick, George Fairclough (at top left), and the choir processing following an obviously elaborate service.

duced by water pressure. The motor needed attention in 1904, and in 1905 it was replaced by an electric equivalent, with a large saving in water rates.

George Fairclough thought a suitable new organ could be purchased for a maximum cost of $10,000, but in 1908 the organ fund had only about $5,000 in hand, and some men on the vestry were opposed to taking on more debt so soon after paying off the mortgage. In the end they decided that as soon as they had $9,000, including what was raised from the sale of the current organ, they would proceed with a new one. In April 1909 the vestry set at $12,000 the limit they would spend on an instrument.

In June 1909 the vestry signed a contract with the Hope-Jones Organ Company of Elmira, New York. Robert Hope-Jones was an innovative British organ builder, becoming famous in England before moving to the United States. One of his greatest works to date was the organ that he built for Worcester Cathedral, "the most perfectly voiced organ in England, and having the most advanced ideas in construction." St. John's organ was among the first large organs constructed by his new American firm, and would be built under the personal supervision of Hope-Jones, the first example of his work in the Twin Cities. The organ would have the Hope-Jones system, boasting all of his patented inventions and giving it as much power and variety of tone as an instrument built by another firm for nearly twice the cost. The console was the most modern available.

Although Fairclough posited in clear terms that the instrument would be a church organ in the fullest sense of the word, the instrument, in fact, had all the trappings of a theater organ. Hope-Jones patented a number of the devices that made the theater organ possible, and other firms adopted or copied many of his innovative and experimental ideas. In October 1909, the organ that had been used in the church since 1891 (beginning in the building on Ashland at Mackubin) was removed from the chambers in the chancel and sent to a Roman Catholic church in Nashua, New Hampshire.

Shortly after the new Hope-Jones organ was installed, it required a new motor because the first one burned out on a Sunday afternoon in March. Other problems ensued in October of 1910, with some of the pipes "ciphering" (sounding by themselves through dust or a malfunction). While the best of organs will occasionally cipher, *The St. John's Evangelist* regretted the fact that the organ had never had the final going over by Mr. Hope-Jones, whose firm was forced into receivership before it completed the instrument.

ST. JOHN'S EARLY PARISHIONERS PROVIDED some handsome memorials. In April 1902, Thomas Irvine gave a silver flagon in memory of his wife Emily. (In our own day, the Thomas Irvine Trust has been a supporter of Episcopal Homes.) In September 1908 designs for a pair of seven-branched gas-lit candelabra, made of elaborately embossed brass and standing eight feet high and nearly five feet wide (said to be patterned after the seven-branched candlesticks in the Temple in Jerusalem), were presented by Mr. and Mrs. James H. Skinner for placement at the foot of the altar steps in memory of her parents, William Augustus Wood and Sarah Elizabeth Wood. These stunning candelabra appear in old photos (see pp. 74 and 143) of the sanctuary but unfortunately were discarded when gas lighting in the church was replaced by electricity.

A silver communion paten, used for the first time on Easter 1909, was given by Mrs. Joseph L. Forepaugh in memory of her daughter Edith. The inscription read: "Peace I leave with you, my peace I give unto you. Edith Forepaugh, 1878-1908." A devoted teacher in the Sunday School, and a member of St. Margaret's Guild, Edith was also memorialized by a copy of Raphael's Madonna, placed on a wall near the place where she taught. The inscription read: "This Memorial is placed here by her many friends. As a teacher in the school, she strengthened the Church, and was much beloved."

Also used on that Easter for the first time were two heavy silver alms basins given by Mr. and Mrs. Hiram M. Pearce in memory of their daughter Katherine. "It is better to give than to receive" is engraved on one side of each basin; and on the other side, "Presented to the Church of St. John the

Evangelist in memory of Katherine Ella Pearce, born April 1, 1892. Entered unto rest April 6, 1907." And on the fifth Sunday after Easter, May 16, 1909, St. John's first memorial window was dedicated, given by his wife in memory of General William Bradford Bend, who for many years until his death in 1905, was a vestryman. The window was made in London by Heaton, Butler, Bayne and Company. Shortly thereafter, the carved wooden screens for the second arches next to the sanctuary were put in place, a gift jointly given by the Sunday School and the Parish Aid Society, thus completing the elaborate gothic screen work in the chancel.

In 1907 the Parish Aid Society hosted a Christmas sale that was organized like a department store. It took place downtown at Smith and Borg during the first week of December, using up the entire first floor and gallery. Churches of all denominations were invited to participate in what proved to be a great cooperative effort. The various departments included toys, millinery, lamp shades, home cooking, table furnishings, baby outfits, carpets, comforters, women's apparel, household goods, men and boys' apparel, paper articles, and a tea room, no less.

The department of paper articles was under the charge of Mrs. Thomas L. Wann. Born Elizabeth Clarkson, she had been a friend of the writer F. Scott Fitzgerald when the latter was a student at Princeton, and the two carried on a lively correspondence.[21] Mr. and Mrs. Wann's daughter, also named Elizabeth, would later marry parishioner Robert Binger.

> **WITH THE WOMEN'S SUFFRAGE** movement gaining ground across the country, the role of women in parish decision-making at St. John's took a leap in 1909 when women, probably for the first time, were entitled to vote at the Annual Meeting in April.

In 1908 a soon-to-be valuable addition to St. John's arrived in the person of Frederick Wigginton, who emigrated with his mother and siblings to St. Paul from England. He wrote to his fiancée Gertrude Livock back home in Ipswich, England, "I am sure we can have a very happy church life there. The church

MAJOR JOHN KELLIHER: The *Yearbook* for 1908 noted the death of parishioner John Kelliher in August, who was a major with the 20th Massachusetts Regiment, losing an arm in the Civil War. Major Kelliher came to St. Paul in 1872 and was a delegate to the Annual Council of the diocese in the year of his death.

seems to have so much life and work in it." "St. John's is more like an English Church than any we have been in since we left, which will soon be two years," he wrote in 1910.[22] After a "very good" sermon by Sedgwick on the need for Christian unity, Wigginton told Gertrude, "The Rector strikes me as being great on Unity, spoke of our unhappy divisions, and the lack of the bond of Peace." Gertrude soon moved to St. Paul and the couple were married at St. John's in 1910.

Mr. Wigginton became an active member of the parish, being named president of the Minnesota Council of Religious Education and captain of St. John's team in the Ramsey County Sunday School Association, not to mention his membership on the vestry, his representation of the parish at the Annual Council of the diocese and at the Church Extension Society, his membership in the choir, and, beginning in September 1929, his service for ten years as superintendent of the Church School, being blessed with a thorough knowledge of church school requirements and a keen business and executive ability. He worked as treasurer of the Emporium, a large department store downtown. Gertrude taught in the Church School for many seasons and was involved in guild work. The Wiggintons' children were also active in the parish, Frederick John eventually going to seminary, and Mary playing the coveted role of herald angel for the Christmas pageant, "The Star of Bethlehem," for which she had to stand on the platform high above the main altar.

With his typical foresight, and ever eager for the growth and prosperity of the community, Mr. Sedgwick called the attention of the parish to the Wells Memorial House that St. Mark's parish in Minneapolis was building in 1908 for philanthropic work. The building was to contain a chapel, a gymnasium, a reading room, a free dispensary, rooms for a kindergarten, day nursery, cooking school, woman's club room, handball court, showers, game rooms, and a large space for a night school. He also noted that Dayton Avenue Presbyterian Church (where St. John's parishioners had held their first services in 1881) had acquired a neighboring property for a men's club house and other purposes.

Sedgwick's point was that though St. John's was in touch with the young life of the community, it needed a building for community outreach. The rector regretted that the boys and young men had to go down below the hill for their exercise and entertainment when they should have been kept nearer home. He later wrote that while he wanted very much to start such a project, there were too many other concerns that had to be completed, and he felt it must be left to a future time. Sedgwick's dream would be realized by his successor, the Rev. Julius Schaad, who erected just such a building for the use of the parish and the wider community.

In *The St. John's Evangelist* of August 20, 1910, Mr. Sedgwick reported that parishioner Alpheus Beede Stickney had delivered an address on the matter of public parks and playgrounds. St. Paul should adopt a plan to provide parks, he said, adding to the health and beauty of the city, and providing playgrounds

attractive to young people. Stickney proposed that a committee of one hundred men and women—landscape gardeners, engineers, architects, physicians, charity workers, social center leaders, preachers, priests, teachers, representatives of labor organizations, mothers and businessmen—be assembled to consider this advancement in the life of the city. Parishioners Paul Doty and Valentine J. Rothschild served on the committee to select this representative group of citizens.

James J. Hill and the former Mary Theresa Mehegan, a Roman Catholic, were married by the Most Rev. John Ireland, Bishop of St. Paul. Together they had ten children, the first of whom, daughter Katherine, died in infancy. Two of their children had later connections with St. John's. The first of these, son Louis Warren Hill, married parishioner Maud Van Cortlandt Taylor. The other was daughter Charlotte Elizabeth Hill, who married George T. Slade, an executive with the Great Northern Railway, who was Roman Catholic. One of their two children was George Norman

Frederick Wigginton and his wife, Gertrude, with their children Mary, Ruth, and Frederick, in a 1929 passport photo.

ALPHEUS B. STICKNEY —he preferred to be called A. B.—settled in St. Paul in 1869 where he entered the growing railroad business. In 1879 he was hired as superintendent of construction for the St. Paul, Minneapolis and Manitoba Railroad, run by James J. Hill, which later became the Great Northern Railway. In 1883 he and William Rainey Marshall (the fifth governor of Minnesota, from 1866-1879) bought all 10,000 shares of stock and the franchise of the Minnesota and Northwestern Railroad Company, which later became the Chicago Great Western Railway, linking St. Paul with Omaha, Kansas City, and Chicago. He also founded the St. Paul Union Stockyards Company. In addition to his railroad work, he was a farmer, a teacher, a lawyer, a business innovator, a civic leader, and a family man. He and his wife, Katherine Wilt-Herzog Hall Stickney, had two sons and five daughters. The family lived in a beautiful house that he built at 288 Summit Avenue, on the bluff, with an expansive view of the river.[23] A long-time personal and professional friend of James J. Hill, the two men disagreed on the matter of government regulation, A. B. favoring it, Hill opposing it.

Slade, who with his wife, the former Elizabeth Carr, had a son named Richard who was raised Roman Catholic and whose wife Mary Ella (Carpenter) Slade was an active leader at St. John's. Ella Slade grew up at St. Paul's-on-the-Hill but moved to St. John's in 1973 and lived on Heather Place. After becoming junior warden in 1996, she served as senior warden during the four-year interim rectorship of the Rev. Michael Tippett (1996-2000).

FOLLOWING A FIVE-MONTH LEAVE of absence in 1910, during which Mr. Sedgwick accepted an invitation from Bishop Nathaniel Thomas of Wyoming to spend the month of July in his diocese. He traveled with two young seminarians doing missionary work around the region, and getting rest and recreation in hunting and fishing, the rector was back in St. Paul for the vestry meeting on December 10. He was also feted at a parish reception, where the congregation expressed their appreciation of his ten years' service among them in no uncertain terms. The parish women presented him with a purse of gold worth $550 and the vestry voted to erect a suitable rectory for him immediately.[24]

One month later, the Rev. Sedgwick tendered his resignation in order to accept a call as rector of Calvary Church, located on Gramercy Park in New York City.[25] The vestry accepted his resignation with regret, remarking that "it is to his untiring fidelity and personal effort that [the] growth and development of the parish are largely due." The Men's Club of St. John's presented Mr. Sedgwick with "a handsome easy chair as a token of their regard." Sedgwick and his wife Mary moved to New York after his last day at St. John's—Easter, April 16, 1911.[26]

Mr. Sedgwick proposed the names of several possible successors, but the search committee met with Bishop Edsall on June 21, 1911, and considered a set of eight candidates, including the Rev. Julius A. Schaad, rector of Grace Church in Kansas City, Missouri. Mr. Schaad won the vote and was offered the seventh rectorship, to begin on September 1, 1911, or thereabouts, at a salary of $4,000, with a $600 housing allowance. Their second choice, should Mr. Schaad decline the invitation, was the Rev. Stanley C. Hughes of Newport, Rhode Island. But Schaad did accept.

MINNESOTA'S STATE CAPITOL

ALTHOUGH OVERSHADOWED as head of the Minnesota State Capitol board of commissioners by Cass Gilbert, the architect he hired, it was Channing Seabury who directed the board's political strategy through six legislative sessions and five different governors; Seabury ran the show. Described as "tough-minded and tenacious," Seabury "rode herd" on finances and deadlines to ensure that the $5 million Minnesota State Capitol was constructed correctly and efficiently.

Top left: This 1910-era postcard celebrates the new Minnesota State Capitol designed by Cass Gilbert. Above Right: The Capitol rotunda with an eight-pointed L'Etoile du Nord motif inlaid on its gleaming marble floor. Above left: Channing Seabury, head of the Minnesota State Capitol board of commissioners, seated, with his fellow commissioners, left to right: Edgar Weaver, John De Laittre, C. H. Graves, George A. Du Toit, H. W. Lamberton, and E. E. Corliss.

Vestrymen: Paul N. Myers, Donald R. Cotton, J. W. Chamberlin, M.D., George C. Whitney, J. D. Denegre.

chapter seven

THE REV. JULIUS AUGUSTUS SCHAAD 1911-1916
A Flourishing Neighborhood Center

DURING THE TENURE of the Rev. Julius Schaad, the *Titanic*—the world's largest passenger liner at the time—struck an iceberg and sank on her maiden voyage. Grand Central Station, the world's largest rail terminal, designed by St. Paul architects Charles Reed and Allen Stem, opened in New York City. The sixteenth amendment to the Constitution authorized the federal treasury to impose an income tax, Babe Ruth made his major league debut, and New York socialite Mary Phelps Jacob patented the brassiere. In 1913 Woodrow Wilson was inaugurated as the 28th president of the United States, the same year Igor Stravinsky's ballet *The Rite of Spring* caused riots in Paris. In 1914 World War I began with the Austro-Hungarian invasion of Serbia, followed by Germany's invasion of Belgium.

The Rev. Julius Augustus Schaad.

following a course at Western Theological Seminary, an Episcopal seminary in Chicago, and was ordained to the priesthood in 1902. His wife was Neenah Marie Wakeman and they had three daughters and two sons, all born before they arrived at St. John's. Mr. Schaad was rector of St. Paul's Church, Lansing, Michigan, from 1902 to 1905, before being appointed archdeacon for the Diocese of Kansas City, a position he held for one year. In 1906 he became rector of Grace Church in Kansas City, Missouri, remaining until 1911, when his departure was the result of an astonishing tale of power over principle.

After his collegiate years, the Rev. Julius Augustus Schaad, born in 1866, in Peoria, Illinois, was engaged in YMCA work in Kentucky and Illinois, from 1893 to 1900, and was president of the West Side Welfare Club, serving the civic and social needs of the people of Kansas City, Missouri. His long and varied experience in social service and institutional work later proved valuable for his work at St. John's. He had originally studied for ordained ministry in the Methodist Church, but quit only a month before his ordination. He subsequently studied theology under tutors,

William Rockhill Nelson was a prominent newspaper mogul in Kansas City who made an imprudent attempt to influence the election of a new bishop for the diocese. Wanting his friend the Rev. Cameron Mann to be elected bishop, Nelson went to the Rev. Schaad, rector at Grace Church, where he was a member, and offered him preferment if he would nominate Mann for the position, or at least second the nomination. Mr. Schaad refused on the grounds that, at age sixty, Mann was too old for the growing young diocese. Incensed at Schaad's recalcitrance, Nelson sold his pew at Grace Church and withdrew his financial and media support of all of the parish's ministries in the Kansas City area. Mr. Schaad was forced to resign.[1]

The Rev. Arthur Wadsworth Farnum.

Promptly after he and his wife arrived at St. John's, the Rev. Julius Schaad bravely made some liturgical changes, asking that the brass eagle lectern standing on the right side of the chancel, adjacent to the center aisle, be moved farther to the right so as not to obstruct the view of the altar. He also asked that a false floor be built in the pulpit, raising the preacher's position about four inches. The vestry consented.

Two months later the new rector recommended a reorganization of the choir; a number of the boys' voices were breaking and it was difficult to find new choristers. He suggested that a temporary mixed choir be formed. Clearly Schaad was not afraid of controversy. By March 1912 a women's choir had been formed at his urging, but the choir of men and boys continued despite his recommendations.

The Rev. Arthur Wadsworth Farnum had become Mr. Schaad's assistant on January 1, 1912. Farnum was a graduate of Seabury Seminary and a grandson of the revered Bishop Benjamin Whipple, the first bishop of the Diocese of Minnesota. Farnum later served churches in Missouri and North Carolina before retiring from St. Mary's in Asheville.

Prior to Mr. Schaad's arrival at St. John's rumors had spread about him. He was reported to be a high-church "ritualist," which was not true. It was also rumored that he locked the church doors in order to compel his parishioners to remain throughout the communion service. Then the newspapers wrote a "sermon" for him and sent it across the country via the Associated Press, quoting him as having said from the pulpit that he would not officiate at weddings unless the women present wore more ample clothing. In 1912 the local papers again spread false information about him, declaring that he was one of the sponsors for an extensive and unusual plan proposed by the YMCA. He had actually refused an appointment on the committee and never attended any of its meetings, and had never seen or assented to the seven-fold proposition that was published in the papers and sent by mail to all the Christian ministers in the city over his name.[2]

We have seen that St. John's first rector, the Rev. Henry Kittson, had high-church predilections when it came to the liturgy. And although it was not true that Mr. Schaad was a ritualist, by 1913 the parish clergy, instead of wearing the low-church cassock, surplice, and tippet for Holy Communion, were vesting in the alb, cincture, stole, and chasuble associated with the increasingly popular high-church approach to the celebration of Holy Communion.

At the rector's first meeting with the vestry, the members proposed that two houses on Holly Avenue be considered as possibilities for a new rectory. But Mr. Schaad, having been at the parish for little more than a week, presented an ambitious building proposal to the vestry, giving them an outline of his view of the special needs of the parish. He strongly advocated building a new parish house, equipping it for the amusement and entertainment of the young people of the parish, and by this means keeping them in continual touch with the church after they had graduated from Sunday School and been confirmed. Such a club house would also express the social consciousness of the church and help to meet the physical, social, and moral needs of "many hundreds of young people of the 'hill' district for which there is nothing whatever now being done." He asserted that such a club house had greater import than the securing of a rectory.

St. John's Girls Choir, 1911. Do you recognize anyone?

His proposal to the vestry was an astonishing feat of bravura and self-confidence, bolstered by his conviction that a vestry and parish that he barely knew would accede to his wishes for a large and expensive new building. It would obviously entail a considerable amount of arm-twisting, promotion, and the winning-over of the reluctant.

In due course, the vestry decided to look into the matter of a rectory at the same time that they agreed to contact a competent architect to advise them of the probable cost of a parish house. They decided upon two lots situated at the southeast corner of Portland Avenue and Dale Street, just one block west of the church. In the meantime the Rev. Julius and Neenah Schaad were living with their family at 658 Lincoln Avenue. They later lived at 661 Lincoln, and later still at 438 Portland Avenue.

In these prosperous pre-war years the parish had 420 families on its rolls, for a total of 1,300 persons, with a building valued at $95,000 and lots valued at another $5,000. In the fiscal year 1911-1912, there were eighteen baptisms, thirty-nine confirmations, seventeen marriages, and nineteen burials, with 262 pupils in the Sunday School, 474 sittings rented in the church, and sixteen active and vibrant parish organizations and agencies.

In a promising coincidence of events, an anonymous "friend of the parish" offered to donate the lots upon which to erect the new parish building, to the value of about $7,000, which could be large enough to serve the dual purpose of parish house and rectory. The new rector was apparently winning the confidence of his parishioners, and the vestry accepted the offer.

The anonymous "friend of the parish" was in fact Caroline G. Stalnaker Humbird, the widow of the late John A.

Caroline Stalnaker Humbird and John Humbird.

Humbird, together with their one son, Thomas J. Humbird, and their five daughters: Mrs. E. T. Koch of Cedar Rapids, Iowa; and Mrs. E. K. Wedelstaedt, Mrs. S. W. Burr, Mrs. C. W. Farnham, and Mrs. Paul N. Myers, all of St. Paul.

In 1882 John Alexander Humbird had organized the White River Lumber Co. in Wisconsin, serving as president, treasurer, and general manager, together with Frederick Weyerhaeuser as one of his associates.[3] Humbird later acquired over 100,000 acres of fine timber land on Vancouver Island in British Columbia and there organized the Victoria Lumber and Manufacturing Company, of which he was president and principal owner. In 1900 Humbird and Weyerhaeuser organized the Clearwater Timber Company; Humbird was president and treasurer. He later became a stockholder and director of the Chicago, St. Paul, Minneapolis and Omaha Railway. The two men reorganized the National German American Bank of St. Paul, where Humbird was a director.

He was also the president of the First National Bank of Sandpoint, Idaho.

At St. John's, a committee was appointed to raise the necessary funds for the erection of both a parish house and a rectory, and to investigate several cities in the East where parish houses were already built. By Easter of 1912, $20,000 had been secured for what was now being called "a parish or church club house—a center for opportunity and influence touching the varied interests of the community." But there had not yet been a canvass to raise an estimated total of $60,000 for the project. Architectural plans for the new structure, by Washington, D.C. architect Frederick H. Brooke, were reviewed as early as the vestry meeting on May 6.

As possibilities for a rectory, the vestry originally considered two houses for sale, one at the northeast corner of Dale Street and Goodrich Avenue, and the other on the southeast corner of Holly Avenue and Kent Street, deciding in January 1913 not to consider the property at Kent and Holly.[4]

At a special meeting on November 29, 1912, the vestry heartily endorsed the proposed plans for the new parish house and pledged to raise the necessary funds. Early in 1913, the Rev. Schaad reported that St. John's neighbor, the House of Hope Presbyterian Church, had recently received $60,000 from one of its members for the erection of a new parish house. But he held that for the purposes of St. John's project it was better that the "Club House" be erected with money secured by popular subscription.

But by February 1913, Schaad saw that parish support for the project was waning. Announcing that bids had been solicited for the plumbing, heating, and electricity, he wrote that such steps were undertaken in good faith by the architect, the building committee, and himself, on the supposition that the repeated official endorsement of parochial organizations and the specific resolutions of the vestry meant what they said. He confessed that he had not seen the cooperation from the parishioners that their words led him to expect. He reminded them that he had stated frankly, in the beginning, that the project would require money and that it was up to the parish

Left: Horace Hills Irvine was active in the lumber business and banking. Right: Mrs. Horace H. (Clotilde McCullough) Irvine with her children: Elizabeth, Thomas, and Clotilde, 1917.

to raise it. He was officially told to proceed, and he did so. But now he wrote: "It is your move." To the parish as a whole, he said, "Please don't delay the game."

In May the vestry decided to proceed with the necessary contracts and agreements for the construction of the club house, but with the following stipulations: the total cost of the structure, including the architect's fees, but excluding furnishings, was not to exceed $90,000; and before any contract could be awarded, $50,000 had to be raised in either cash or pledges (the value of the lot to be included in that amount).

Parishioner Horace H. Irvine was selected as treasurer of the Committee of the Club House, which secured $60,000 (including the value of the lot) in cash and pledges. By July 1913 work had begun and the excavation nearly completed.

In February of 1914 the vestry appointed a board of directors "to have the general supervision over the operation and

The Irvine children: Clotilde Emily Irvine, Elizabeth Hills Irvine, and Thomas Edward Irvine on the front lawn of the Horace H. Irvine residence at 1006 Summit Avenue in St. Paul, ca. 1917.

Paul Jr., Reine, Paul Sr., Zib, and John Myers.

maintenance of the Church Club House and the power to incur obligations in its operation." Appointed to the board were Paul N. Myers, John Townsend, George A. Goodell, Horace H. Irvine, C. W. Gordon, Theodore Schulze, Edward B. Holbert, James H. Skinner, William F. Peet, William D. Mitchell, Jule M. Hannaford Jr., Samuel G. Iverson, Paul Doty, Garrett O. House, and Edgar B. Barton. The Easter offering was posted to the club house building fund, since about $30,000 was still needed.

Board member Jule M. Hannaford Jr. had married Caroline Rose Schurmeier at Christ Church. They lived at 644 Summit Avenue and began attending St. John's because of its proximity. He later became senior warden and treasurer of the parish. His granddaughter, parishioner Caroline Jaffray, recounts that he was active in the Men's Club. William F. Peet, the son of junior warden Emerson W. Peet, was a founding

member of the Town and Country Club, in 1888, and there first introduced the new East Coast game of golf to the club.

Paul N. Myers and his wife, Reine Humbird Myers, lived with their children, Paul Noxon Jr., John Humbird, and Elizabeth at 7 Heather Place, a Tudor Revival house in the style of a Cotswold cottage, on the bluff overlooking the Mississippi River Valley. The house is now on the National Register of Historic Places. Mr. Myers also served as the secretary and treasurer of the Sunday School, was junior warden from 1915 to 1922, senior warden from 1922 to 1929, served as a delegate to Diocesan Council, and was a member of Mr. Sedgwick's Standing Committee. In 1915, Mr. Myers and Michael W. Waldorf created the Waldorf Paper Products Company, merging three separate cooperating companies to produce folding cartons and recycled paperboard.

Club House board member William D. Mitchell began practicing law in 1896 and became a member of the firm How, Butler and Mitchell, with Jared How and Pierce Butler. This firm was the forerunner of Doherty Rumble & Butler, a prominent legal firm in St. Paul. Garret von Oblenis House was a civil engineer and from 1904, secretary, general manager, and director of the Northern Heating and Electric Company in St. Paul.

OPENING CEREMONIES of the Church Club House took place from May 26 to 29, 1915. At the parish dinner, there was an ovation when Mr. Schaad stood to speak. He thanked the people for their help, reminisced about how the building came to be, and spoke of its many purposes. But as a parishioner later wrote, it was the rector who deserved the thanks. He dreamed the dream and brought about its fulfillment. And as the benefits grew and multiplied over the years, the youth and the parents of ensuing years would rise up to bless him for his vision and faith.

The Club House consisted of a dormitory of twenty-one rooms for single men, several parish committee and guild rooms, offices, a dining room and kitchen, an auditorium seating nearly six hundred people, a gymnasium, a swimming pool, bowling lanes, and a billiard room—but not a

St. John's new Church Club House at 614 Portland Avenue, ca. 1915.

rectory. There would be salaries to be paid for ten employees, including a director, office staff, gymnasium staff, janitors, porters, two women for the dormitory, and one attendant.

One of the more public features of the Club House was its equipment for showing movies. Among the first movies shown in the auditorium were *Williamson Submarine Expedition*, *The Man of the Hour*, and the six-reel, $100,000 flick *Samson*. The entrance fee for the movies was ten cents.

In June 1915 the vestry applied for a loan of $23,000 to be secured by a mortgage on the Club House, to provide for the payment of labor and material used in its construction.

The Club House offered various levels of membership to people living in the neighborhood, bringing in just over $5,000 in 1915, when there was a total of 683 members. Rental fees for the auditorium brought in $1,277, the dormitory earned $2,653, and the rental of lockers realized $583. Despite these impressive numbers, the club house ran a deficit of about $3,300 that year, when the payroll had grown to at least fourteen employees. Some effort was made to increase the attendance of Club House men at St. John's Sunday services and at parish social events.

It pleased Mr. Schaad when the St. Paul Academy, located across Dale Street from the Club House, was the first to use the new auditorium for its graduating exercises, on June 4.[5] Its founding institution—the Barnard School—had rented the parish's gray limestone building on Mackubin Street from 1887 to 1889.

To open its activities for the 1915 season, the club held a dinner in October with Minnesota Governor Winfield S. Hammond as its guest of honor, and Pierce Butler the toastmaster. Hammond, a Democrat, represented Minnesota in the U.S. House of Representatives from 1907 to 1915, and was governor of Minnesota from only January to December in 1915, the second Minnesota governor to die in office. Butler was an associate justice of the U.S. Supreme Court from 1923 until his death in 1939, the first justice from Minnesota.

GIVEN ITS PROSPEROUS NEIGHBORHOOD on the hill, and its largely well-to-do membership, St. John's has hosted countless society weddings. One of them, called "the most important social event of Easter week" by a local newspaper,[6] took place at St. John's on April 10, 1912, between Anna Rice Dawson, daughter of Mr. and Mrs. William Dawson Jr. of 720 Goodrich Avenue, and George C. Power (b. 1889),[7] the son of Mr. and Mrs. George C. Power (b. 1858) of 541 Summit Avenue. The paper noted that the wedding united two of St. Paul's oldest families. Indeed the grandfather of Anna Rice Dawson was William Dawson (b. 1825), a native of Ireland, who was the mayor of St. Paul from 1878 to 1881. Mr. Schaad officiated at the wedding and George Fairclough was the organist, assisted by a harpist and the full vested choir of men and boys.

The long St. Paul lineage of present parishioner George C. Power III, on both sides of his family, has distinguished itself through its involvement in community affairs, in railroading, in government, and in the world of finance. Mr. Power is a member of St. John's Adult Choir and the Handbell Choir. His wife Diane, a librarian, is the president of the Altar Guild. In his capacity as a relief worker in the efforts of the American Red Cross, George assisted with the emergency following Hurricane Katrina in New Orleans in 2005. His great-grandfather, also George C. Power, was the first vice-president of the Wilder Charity, in 1910, and helped build Wilder's endowment.

In 1946, George's father, George C. Power Jr. (b. 1914), who attended St. Clement's, joined George A. Mairs Jr. as an investment counselor, and in 1953 became a founding partner in the firm known as Mairs and Power Investment Counsel. A member of St. Clement's parish, he also served on boards for several community organizations as well as the Diocese of Minnesota until his death in 1995.

MR. SCHAAD WROTE PROUDLY in 1912 that at St. John's there was a marked absence of a certain frostiness all too common elsewhere, which deters people from active involvement with a parish church. "We are free from chronic 'kickers' and the chip-on-the-shoulder type of Christian, and we are so because no conditions exist in which these unhealthy types of

Anna Rice Dawson and George C. Power were married at St. John's on April 10, 1912. The bride's father, former St. Paul mayor William Dawson Jr., is to her left. To the right of the groom is matron of honor Mary Dawson Rossum. The other participants in this wedding party, named in various news articles but not necessarily in order in this photograph, are ushers Charles E. Power, William Dawson III, Vincent Dawson, Edgar Russell, Phelps Ingersoll, and Frederick Power; the bridesmaids include Evelyn Konantz, Bessie Robinson, Louise Stubblefield, and Elizabeth Drew. The flower girl in the front row is Gertrude Smith.

Christianity can thrive. All these facts prove that St. John's parish can be a mighty spiritual force in its neighborhood."

The Rev. Schaad also undertook to revive St. Andrew's Brotherhood because its role was to aid the rector in the specifically religious work of the parish. And he oversaw the reorganization of the Junior Brotherhood of St. Andrew.

A man of his time, Mr. Schaad sought to apply proper business methods and sagacity in parochial administration, in the hope of producing greater efficiency. He believed that the modern, scientific method then being adopted by the leading commercial houses had two underlying principles: conservation and concentration of energy, time, and resources. Experts were employed to study and direct the movements of the workers so that the least effort and expense would produce the largest and best results. Schaad be-

lieved the church would benefit by the same practical attention. In the interest of transparency and efficiency, the vestry examined a parish census and revised the parish records accordingly, removing from the rolls the names of people who were members in name only.

Not known for his diplomacy, in an article in *The St. John's Evangelist* for November 22, 1913, Mr. Schaad quoted from a recent sermon he had preached stating that "the crumbs which fall from the rich man's table are not an adequate expression of Christian philanthropy." He declared that charity balls and rummage sales were present-day "crumbs," popularly called "charity." He also called attention to the meager net profits which usually remain for charity "after the florist, the fiddler and the caterer have been paid out of the gross receipts."

Although Mr. Schaad did not know it—a charity ball was

Early advertisement for Maud Borup candies.

MISS MAUD BORUP began making hand-made, hand-dipped chocolates for her family and friends in her home kitchen in St. Paul in 1907. Soon she had a counter at Holm & Olson Florist and was in business for herself. Years passed and new generations carried on her tradition of quality confections inspired by sweet childhood favorites. More than one hundred years since Maud made her first chocolates, Maud Borup, Inc. now sells to specialty stores and Target and Walmart.

At St. John the Evangelist, Miss Maud Borup served on the Rev. Schaad's Standing Committee, which in 1912 reported that parishioners would appreciate having only one appeal for money per year in lieu of many and also recommended the use of the duplex envelope system for weekly giving.

pending in the city. Only after preaching his sermon did he see the account of the ball in a local newspaper. He then wrote: "Well, what is there to say? Only this: That in dealing with a general proposition I inadvertently ran into a special, local situation. If in doing so I offended some of my friends and loyal parishioners I am very sorry." But the damage was done.

The rector then took on another shibboleth when, in *The St. John's Evangelist* of February 7, 1914, he asked rhetorically, "When is drinking to excess not drunkenness?" Answering his own question, he wrote, "The determining factor seems to be the question as to whether a man is taken to jail in a patrol wagon or escorted home in a limousine." Mr. Schaad seemed bent on antagonizing his congregation.

At the same time, however, the rector was dedicated to their spiritual health. In a discussion of the real presence of Christ in the Eucharist, sometimes considered a matter of opinion among Anglicans, Schaad wrote that although we do not know just how Christ is present in the sacrament (contrary to Roman Catholics who believe in transubstantiation), we are bound to believe that he is truly there. "It is a real presence, and not a mere imaginary presence." He quoted this couplet attributed to Queen Elizabeth I:

> Christ was the Word who spake it,
> Christ took the bread and brake it,
> And what his word doth make it,
> That I believe and take it.

The year 1914 saw the death of former junior warden Theodore Leopold Schurmeier. Born in 1852 in St. Louis, the son of a German immigrant, wagon and carriage manufacturer Caspar Schurmeier, Theodore was educated at Baldwin University of Ohio, and worked in James J. Hill's railroad office from 1870, when he was eighteen, until 1875. Afterward he entered the First National Bank as bookkeeper, then teller, and eventually director.

A man of many interests and endeavors, Theodore Schurmeier was a principal in the firm of Lindekes, Warner & Schurmeier, one of the Northwest's largest manufacturers and distributors of wholesale and retail dry goods, known for their fine furs. As president of the Minnesota State Immigration Association, he worked with James J. Hill to encourage the formation of immigration societies and land settlement along Hill's railroads. Schurmeier served as a member of the Board of Regents at the University of Minnesota from 1901 to 1904. He was also a director of the St. Paul Trust Company, and a trustee of St. Luke's Hospital. His wife was Caroline Gotzian Schurmeier.

THE CLUB HOUSE WAS FLOURISHING. During the month of October 1915 its membership increased from 503 to 605, proving its usefulness in St. John's neighborhood. All the dormitory rooms were rented, with applications in advance. During the construction of the Club House, the management had been told repeatedly that women would not take an interest in the athletic department, so the original plan for space assigned to the women was considerably reduced. But, to everyone's surprise, both women and girls took such a great interest in the athletic facilities that the locker and dressing rooms had to be rearranged.

For a number of years the visitation of the diocesan bishop to St. John's fell on Palm Sunday, and it was on that day that confirmations took place. From today's liturgical perspective, a visitation for confirmation on Palm Sunday would not even be considered by a bishop, because of its importance in the run of Holy Week. In 1915 the bishop confirmed thirty-six people of the parish.

Mr. Albert M. Eddy was the last surviving lay incorporator of the parish when he died in June 1915. He had been associated with the Episcopal church in St. Paul beginning in 1870. After many years of valuable service at Christ Church in downtown St. Paul, where he was for a time junior warden, Eddy became interested in the newly planted St. John's and was for many years clerk of the vestry. During nearly the entire period that he was connected with St. John's he was associated in some capacity with the Sunday School, acting at times as assistant superintendent to Mr. Sedgwick, and he had been Sunday School treasurer since 1907. Mr. Eddy was also active in the work of the Church Extension Society, serving as treasurer for many years.

THE STANCE TAKEN by the Rev. Julius Schaad on a matter of national church action proved his undoing at St. John's. When the General Board of Missions of the national church, of which Mr. Schaad was a member, decided to send delegates to a Pan-Protestant Congress in Panama, many Episcopalians opposed the action, including Schaad, but had no thought of doing anything further about it until the next General Convention. But at once, wrote Mr. Schaad, "there came from certain noteworthy quarters in the east the most violent and abusive attacks upon all who opposed the Board's action." Mr. Schaad submitted that "no part of the Church has a right to elect to send delegates to represent the whole Church. This is precisely what the Board of Missions has, without specific authorization, attempted to do." Schaad continued:

Last week the clergy of the Twin Cities, responding to an open call, met and issued an open letter to the House of Bishops, deploring the action of the Board for the following (non-partisan) reasons: 1) the church has been compromised in relation to Protestants and Roman Catholics alike; 2) the Board's action represented a usurpation of the authority of General Convention; 3) it suggests that the Board is independent of control by the church; 4) it suggests that the Board of Missions exists for purposes other than the strict administration of the church's missionary work; and 5) the Board's action has created division in the church's own household of faith and destroyed the spirit of unity.

Mr. Schaad noted that five-sixths of the rectors of independent parishes in Minneapolis and St. Paul (including all of them in St. Paul) signed this letter. Many priests in charge of dependent parishes did so as well. "And so it is both fair and safe to conclude that time will still further prove that, however well-intentioned this visionary group of (chiefly eastern) men may have been, they were in error when they attempted to commit our Church to this Congress."

Some parishioners took grave exception to the rector's position on the subject. Two weeks later Mr. Schaad preached his last sermon at St. John's without realizing it, using the text of St. Paul from II Timothy: 4:6, 7, 14: "I am now ready to be offered, and the time of my departure is at hand. I have fought a good fight, I have finished my course, I have kept my faith." He later wrote that when the vestry subsequently "told me that there was some friction among a few people in the parish over certain of my parochial policies and my expressed views upon the Panama Congress, I felt that the work might suffer from it. And so I resigned." The Rev. Julius A. Schaad submitted his resignation on January 25, effective one week later.

The vestry immediately accepted Mr. Schaad's resignation but continued his salary and housing allowance until September 1 "in order that [he] might suffer no financial hardship while waiting for another field of usefulness."[8]

But there were differences of opinion in the parish regarding the issues that led to his resignation, and Mr. Schaad recounted that he "heard by letter, telephone, or personal call from between two and three hundred families in the parish" who expressed their "personal regard, appreciation, and regret at the termination of parochial relations." Official letters came from nearly every adult organization in the parish, according to Schaad, and the directors of the Club House elected him an honorary life member. A letter sent to him from about seventy parishioners, "representing the strongest and best influences for good in the civic, commercial, and social life of St. Paul," contained "a gift of such magnitude that I am quite overcome by its generosity. It will now be possible for me to go away for a period of rest in Florida or California as soon as I finish certain official business here."

Julius Schaad went on to serve Trinity Church in Bay City, Michigan, from 1918 to 1922.[9] During his rectorship there he proposed the construction of a new parish house, mainly to relieve the crowding in the Sunday School. There was no action on his proposal during his tenure, but in 1923, after he had left the parish, the new Sunday School and parish house were erected, eventually costing the congregation over $80,000. He was lured from Trinity to become general missionary of the National Council.[10]

In 1924, while he was working at the Episcopal Church Mission House in New York City, Mr. Schaad was engaged to give a preaching mission at historic St. Paul's Church[11] in

Augusta, Georgia, established by the Church of England in 1750, where the Rev. George Whitney was rector. Mr. Schaad was in Whitney's home on March 1, when the latter suddenly took ill and died in Schaad's arms. The parish had such a favorable opinion of the Rev. Schaad that they asked him to proceed with the mission as planned and to return as rector, succeeding Mr. Whitney, which he did.

In 1928 *The New York Times* reported[12] that Mr. Schaad, living in Georgia, had delivered a controversial sermon at the Church of the Ascension on Fifth Avenue in New York City, in which he pronounced "a plea to Christians to look upon Christ as one arisen and ruling, rather than one lowly, despised and rejected by the world." He could kneel to the former, he said, but not to the latter.

Julius Schaad was a published author. In 1925 the national Episcopal Church made evangelism its first priority and organized the "Bishops' Crusade" to emphasize the importance of the Christian gospel and to call Episcopalians to renewed fervor. Nearly three hundred bishops, priests, and laity assumed roles of leadership. More than three million copies of printed materials were sent out, notable among them Julius Schaad's book *Evangelism in the Church: An Appeal to Christians*.[13] In it he stressed the quiet, personal work of people in the regular program of the church rather than preaching at mass meetings. Schaad also wrote and published the booklet *Only A Mask: A Comparison of the Teachings of the Christ and of the Christian Science*.[14]

Three members of St. John's vestry constituted a search committee to find a successor to Mr. Schaad that included junior warden Paul N. Myers, vestrymen James D. Denegre, and Samuel G. Iverson. A mere two weeks later, the name of the Rev. Edward M. Cross, of Sheridan, Wyoming, was placed in nomination. Vestryman Louis W. Hill Sr. also nominated a Rev. Crestler[15] of Havre, Montana. The search committee heard the two nominees preach and were in correspondence with other prospects. On April 26, the vestry nominated the Rev. Edward Cross as its new rector, offering him a salary of $4,000, plus a housing allowance of $600 in lieu of a rectory. Mr. Cross accepted the call, but the vestry gave him instead a salary of $5,000, to begin his work on the first of September.

Initial Club House staff: Prof. Carl Rothfus, Physical Director; Marie Rothfus, Women's Physical Director; A. H. Fellows, Managing Director; Harold Helliwell, Assistant Physical Director; Gertrude Weir, Executive Secretary, 1915.

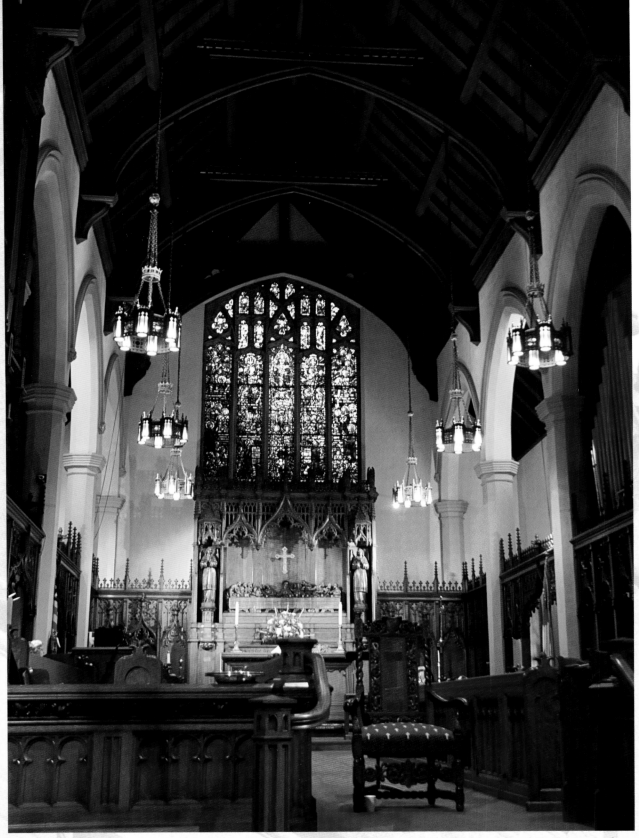

The roof was raised and peaked in the sanctuary to accommodate the World War I memorial *Te Deum* window. Designed by famed stained glass artist Charles J. Connick, the window was dedicated by Bishop McElwain at the Thanksgiving Day service on November 25, 1920.

chapter eight

THE REV. EDWARD MAKIN CROSS 1916-1924
A Real Bath in a Porcelain Tub

THE REV. EDWARD CROSS began his tenure at St. John's around the time Albert Einstein proposed his general theory of relativity. In 1917 the first regular air mail service began with one round trip per day between Washington, D.C. and New York; the United States declared war on Germany and joined the allies in World War I; and the construction of the Panama Canal reached completion. A series of revolutions, collectively called the Russian Revolution, destroyed the Russian autocracy and led to the creation of the Soviet Union. Harlow Shapley discovered that the sun is part of the Milky Way. The worldwide influenza epidemic struck in 1918, killing 645 people that year in St. Paul alone, and nearly fifty million worldwide. In 1919 the Treaty of Versailles was one of the peace treaties that brought an end to the First World War. The League of Nations was founded; it was the first permanent international organization whose principal mission was to maintain world peace. The eighteenth amendment prohibited alcohol, and the nineteenth amendment gave women the right to vote. James Joyce published *Ulysses*, and T. S. Eliot *The Wasteland*, while Eugene O'Neill's first full-length play, *Beyond the Horizon*, marked the beginning of modern American drama and won a Pulitzer Prize. In the winter of 1924-1925 a smallpox epidemic killed nearly four hundred people in the Twin Cities.

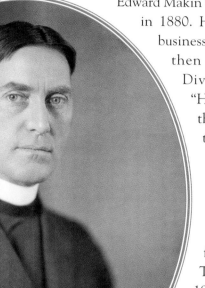

The Rev. Edward Makin Cross.

Edward Makin Cross was born in Philadelphia in 1880. He worked in the mercantile business with his father for six years, then entered the Philadelphia Divinity School, graduating as "Honor Man" in 1907. During three years of his seminary training, Cross had charge of the rehabilitated Epiphany Church in West Philadelphia. After ordination he became a general missionary in the Black Hills of South Dakota, from 1907 to 1910 serving St. Thomas Mission in Sturgis.[1] In 1910 he went to St. Peter's Church[2] in Sheridan, Wyoming, where he remained until his move to St. Paul in 1916.

The *St. Paul Dispatch* reported that in Sheridan Mr. Cross met with a mission of eight people and over time built up a flourishing congregation of more than three hundred members, making it the largest parish in Wyoming, and oversaw there the construction of a church edifice costing $35,000.[3] Described by *Time* magazine as "tall, slender and grey-eyed,"[4] Mr. Cross was active in Boy Scout work and successfully conducted summer camps for the boys and girls of his parish. The magazine reported that "his work in the West has been declared without a parallel in the domestic mission field by a prominent Episcopalian." St. John's vestry called him "a progressive, earnest [and] successful young leader." Like several of his predecessors at St. John's, the Rev. Mr. Cross was a published writer.

The rector's wife, Angela Ware Cross.

St. John's rectory at 581 Portland Avenue (photographed 2014).

While in Sheridan he wrote the book *The Use of Religion: Suggestions for Applying Christianity*.[5]

In July 1916, St. John's vestry purchased the five-bedroom home of vestryman Dr. Jehiel W. Chamberlin and his wife at 581 Portland Avenue,[6] to serve as a rectory for the Rev. and Mrs. Cross. After thirty-five years of existence St. John's finally had a rectory. In 1914 Edward Cross married Angela Ware, who was his junior by thirteen years. She was a reputed beauty, but impish, funny, bright, and creative.

It was love at first sight for Edward, when he saw her performing as Puck in *A Midsummer Night's Dream*, at All Saints' School in Sioux Falls, South Dakota. He leaned over to his friend, commenting, "You might think me a cad, but I'm in love with that girl. And I'll wait for her."[7]

And he did. He visited Angela and her family in Deadwood, near Sturgis, and all the while the Wares thought he was interested in Angela's older sister Jo. He finally popped the question when Angela was about to leave for Vassar College. "But Edward," she is reported to have said, "how can I learn about all there is to know in the world?" To which he replied, "Don't worry, I'll teach you all you need to know."[8]

In August of 1916, before he officially undertook St. John's eighth rectorship, Mr. Cross named the Rev. Edward H. Eckel Jr. as curate, to begin in November. The son of a clergyman, Eckel had won a Rhodes Scholarship and spent three years at the University of Oxford, England. He then attended General Theological Seminary in New York City and subsequently served two mission stations in western Missouri.

Mr. Eckel's first task was to reorganize the Sunday School, where he incorporated a new system of lessons so that each child could learn what it means to be a Christian at his or her particular age. In the new curriculum, called the Christian Nurture Series, five particular interests were woven through all the courses: Christian knowledge (informational material), memory work, church loyalty, devotional life, and

Christian service. As Mr. Cross wrote, "The old fashioned habit of trying to furnish youthful minds with adult conceptions of religion and ethics must now go the way of all outworn systems and every effort must be made to base each lesson upon a normal and natural point of contact with the members of the Church School as divided and graded according to their age and development." It was hoped that this system would help maintain St. John's place at the head of all the Sunday Schools in the diocese.

In the process Mr. Cross declared that the institution would henceforth be called the Church School. The change in name reflected the fact that "the corporate life of the Church, her worship, her creeds, her ordered succession of festival and fast, her ideals of missionary activity and service, properly interpreted to the mind of the child, are the most potent forces we know to develop Christian character." At the same time, the Church School began using *The Mission Hymnal*, finding it more satisfactory than the old *Sunday School Hymnal*. An effort was also made to establish a young people's orchestra—of even two or three instrumentalists—to supplement the piano accompaniments.

For a number of years the member churches of the Church Extension Society in St. Paul had worshiped together annually at a missionary rally at St. John's on Stir-Up Sunday, when the collect for the Sunday before Advent read:

Stir up, we beseech thee, O Lord, the wills of thy faithful people; that they, plenteously bringing forth the fruit of good works, may by thee be plenteously rewarded; through Jesus Christ our Lord. Amen[9]

At the service in November 1917 the church was said to have been filled to capacity with representatives from a dozen different churches of the city who sang missionary hymns and heard a stirring address. A reported 210 singers in the choir sang the "Hallelujah Chorus" under the direction of George Fairclough. One wonders how the chancel could have accommodated so many people.

Out of concern for the comfort and beauty of the chancel,

Mr. Cross observed that the choir stalls had straight backs and flat seats, and unlike the pews in the nave, they had no cushions. He urged that the situation be rectified as soon as possible, noting that $2,000 would probably suffice to complete the furnishings. The Parish Aid Society offered to undertake at least part of the work.

During Mr. Cross's tenure St. John's leadership from time to time took aggressive public positions regarding civic affairs. In December 1916 the vestry signed a petition for the reading of the Bible in the public schools and sent it to the state legislature. Beginning in August 1918, Mr. Cross strenuously urged his congregation to vote "Yes" on the prohibition amendment. Four years later he urged them to attend a mass meeting regarding law enforcement and prohibition at the St. Paul Auditorium. And in 1919 he appealed for their "Yes" votes on a charter amendment for the funding of equipment, maintenance, and salaries in St. Paul's public schools.

Thanks to the Church Club, the parish now had space options. The primary department of the Church School, for instance, moved its classes from the undercroft to the auditorium of the Church Club down the street, affording more space and improved ventilation, while the two clergy moved their offices from the Church Club back to the parish house on Kent Street where they could do their work in quiet.

Like Theodore Sedgwick before him, Mr. Cross addressed the need for improved congregational singing and reminded his flock that the choir is not singing to the people, but for and with the people to God. Congregational singing, he wrote, is the vehicle of our sacrifices of prayer and praise and thanksgiving, and is an integral part of our common worship.

DESPITE PRESIDENT WOODROW WILSON'S long attempt to maintain neutrality in World War I, the United States entered the hostilities on April 6, 1917, declaring war on Germany. It became the burden of Mr. Cross to steer St. John's through the anguish of those years, during which four men associated with the parish laid down their lives in the service of freedom: George C. Squires, Alan Nichols, Cyrus Thurston "Budd" Dorr, and Marshall Peabody. Scores more were willing to do so, including J. B. Lawrence, Thomas D. Lane, Robert Benepe, Louis M. Benepe, Nathiel Lufkin, Robert Schaad, and Guy L. Hill,[10] who were among the first to enlist. By August 1918 a total of 146 members and friends of St. John's had enlisted in the military. Several service flags were hung in the church, each full of stars representing loved ones who had gone to war, including the rector's younger brother.

Upon the declaration of war—in the war to end all war—parishioners and friends of St. John's promptly met in the auditorium of the Church Club to organize groups of women into a Red Cross unit. The plan was to meet on Mondays and Wednesdays to prepare surgical dressings and on Tuesdays and Thursdays to make garments. Classes in first-aid and dietetics were to be offered on Fridays, and a first-aid class for men met on Monday evenings. An impressive 155 memberships were paid to the Red Cross that evening, and by June there were 283. Another auxiliary to the Red Cross was formed at St. Barnabas Mission in Lilydale, in February 1918.

The fruitfulness of St. John's auxiliary becomes evident upon noting the quantities of items made in the course of a single week in that same February:

single compresses	1,600
4 x 4 wipes	2,625
2 x 2¼ wipes	1,400
8 x12 absorbent pads	245
split irrigation pads	70
12 x 24 absorbent pads	122
heel rings	65
triangular bandages	160
scultetus	50
T bandages	8
12 x 18 paper back pads	30
Total items	6,375

Mrs. Jehiel W. Chamberlin was the instructor for preparing surgical dressings for the French Red Cross and Mrs. Louis W. Hill Sr. was in charge of the groups sewing garments. Sewing machines were on loan from the Parish Aid Society and from several parish women.

By 1917 a Girl Scout troop had been formed, known as the Oak Troop, composed mostly of girls from St. John's. It was the first troop of Girl Scouts to be organized in St. Paul and numbered twenty-five girls. The scouts sold $4,500 worth of Liberty Bonds that year to help finance the war effort.

Edward Cross was a great supporter of the American cause at war. In *The St. John's Evangelist* he wrote eloquently:

Unquestionably it may be said of the present war that it is fraught with greater significance and promise with respect to the attainment of an abiding peace such as Christian consciences may approve than any conflict in history. There is a larger consciousness of the ideal and a more widely extended sacrifice for it than ever before. Men are beginning to see the end. They comprehend that without motion life will become stagnant. They know that price in blood must be paid for every advancing step. They are unwilling to purchase a superficial placidity at the cost of mental slavery and moral obloquy.

Late in 1917, Lieutenant Alexander Porterfield, a St. John's boy, who had been with the British Expeditionary Force in Flanders since early in the war, was awarded the military cross for bravery in action; he expected to receive the insignia at the hands of the king. Ironically the Worcestershire Regiment, to which Porterfield belonged, was one of the oldest regiments in the English army and was in fact the first regiment to fire a shot against the American troops in the Revolutionary War.

The congregation was understandably eager for reports from the front. One of the men on the Service Roll, who had been doing service in the trenches in France, enumerated in one of his letters home five things that he hoped to do when he could get to Paris on leave:

to take a real bath in a porcelain tub
to sleep in a bed with real sheets
to eat a real meal that doesn't come out of a tin can
to see a real opera
and to talk with a real lady[11]

The Church Club was the venue for frequent entertainments and dances for some fifty to sixty soldiers stationed locally, as at Fort Snelling, the Overland School, and the Aviation School. Parishioners would provide cakes, the music, and even the cigars. One evening the young people of the African-American Pilgrim Baptist Church gave "a most delightful entertainment" for the benefit of the Soldiers' and Sailors' Club.

Even with the numerous war activities at the church, the daily run of things at St. John's continued unabated. There were roughly six hundred households in the parish, with some 926 communicants. Nearly forty boys and about twenty men were among the ranks of the choir, while the Girls Choir had thirty-six members and the Women's Choir twenty. The Parish Aid Society, the Altar Guild, the St. Margaret's Guild, and the Woman's Auxiliary were flourishing. The Sanctuary Chapter (altar servers) and the Junior Auxiliary were doing well, and the Little Helpers had an impressive ninety-eight young children. As a sure sign that the clergy had not cut back on evangelism, Mr. Eckel had the unique experience in September 1917 of preaching to a street crowd from the mission wagon of the Union Gospel Mission, just off the Bridge Square of Minneapolis.

Edward and Angela Cross had two daughters while they were in St. Paul, Patricia and Angela. The Cross family were able to do much of their rail travel free of charge due to Edward's position as a clergyman plus their relationship with the James J. Hill family. Edward and Angela enjoyed a close personal friendship with vestryman Paul N. Myers and his wife Reine. In fact Paul was a mentor of Edward's. "When Paul committed suicide during the Depression, Edward traveled from Spokane to take the service in the Myers' home, as services for people who committed suicide were not then allowed in the church."[12]

F. Scott and Zelda Fitzgerald. Zelda was pregnant with the Fitzgeralds' only child, daughter Frances Scott (Scottie) Fitzgerald, born in October 1921.

While the Crosses were at St. John's, St. Paul's own F. Scott Fitzgerald and his wife Zelda were living in St. Paul, near St. John's. Married at St. Patrick's Cathedral in New York in 1920, they had moved to St. Paul for the birth of their daughter Scottie in 1921, before moving on to Paris. The Rev. Edward Cross took a broad approach to sermon topics, and once planned to give a sermon on one of Fitzgerald's books. Apparently Fitzgerald got wind of the upcoming sermon and came to church to hear it. Indeed at the evening service on March 26, 1922, to a congregation of about six hundred people, Mr. Cross did speak on Fitzgerald's new book *The Beautiful and Damned*, a portrait of the eastern elite during the jazz age. *The St. John's Evangelist* later reported:

The characters in the book are anything but admirable. They represent the results of the philosophy of nothingness. They are the type—not uncommon today—that makes a god out of the soul-debilitating idleness that often accompanies inherited wealth. The result is a vacuous ennui degrading to the moral, mental, and physical life.

The address was part of a series of services on Sunday evenings begun in 1922 during which Mr. Cross reviewed recently published books. Bolstered by an ample musical offering as well, the services were enormously popular. His sermon on January 29, when he reviewed George Bernard Shaw's book *Back to Methuselah* (1921), was itself reviewed in *The Pioneer Press* the next morning. The services continued through 1923 and became "community" events, attracting many people unaffiliated with St. John's.

According to the Crosses' daughter Patricia, "St. Paul people at the time thought that Angela was woven into some of Fitzgerald's stories." Zelda is said to have met Angela at a gathering in White Bear Lake. Zelda, then perhaps twenty-one or younger, asked Angela how old she was. When told "twenty-six," Zelda exclaimed, "I hope I never get that old!"[13]

An experiment at Christmastime proved so successful when the Manger Service and the Feast of Lights were combined for a Festival Service that many of those present pronounced it the most beautiful and successful children's service in the history of St. John's. The children brought their gifts around the manger, placed prominently in the chancel. The gifts were later distributed among the people of Lilydale and St. Philip's Negro Mission.

Early in 1918, the curate Mr. Eckel, who had now been at St. John's for over a year, accepted a call to the rectorship of St. Paul's-on-the-Hill and was followed at St. John's by the Rev. Christoph Keller, a graduate of the Philadelphia Divinity School and formerly rector of Trinity Church, Bay City, Michigan, where the Rev. Julius Schaad had also served as rector. A longtime friend of the rector, Keller came to St. John's with the understanding that his stay would be temporary. His exceptional qualities endeared him to the

parish, but toward the end of September he left for the Army School for Chaplains in Louisville. Mr. Cross expected to do without an assistant until the end of the war, when younger men in the ministry would become more available. Eckel had also served as editor of *The St. John's Evangelist* and was succeeded in this post by parishioner Joseph Gilpin Pyle, editor, author, librarian, researcher and former associate editor of the *Pioneer Press*, who developed a national reputation as author of *The Life of James J. Hill* (1916).[14]

In January of 1918 a chapter of Christian Stoics, a secret order for boys of high school age, was established at St. John's to teach Christian morals through a system of symbolic ritual. Membership was restricted to those who by their interest in the church proved themselves worthy of becoming "true Stoics," Christian Stoicism being considered a "fine brotherly art." At their fifth anniversary, in 1923, Mr. Cross traced the beginnings of the Stoics back through former parishes where he had been rector. There were six degrees in the lodge, each of which was attained by proper initiation. At the inaugural meeting, nine boys were initiated into the mysteries of the first degree. The chief officer was called Worthy Master, and other officers included a Scribe, a Chancellor, a Guard, a Guide, and a Master of Ceremonies. Later assistant rectors were inducted into the order, among the boys.

Parishioner Ella Haupt Chapman, the wife of Frederick L. Chapman, died on February 28, 1918, in her seventieth year. She had been a member of St. John's practically from the day it was founded. She was president of the Parish Aid Society for many years and "inspired the whole-hearted support of a body of women that sought to emulate her in single-hearted and self-sacrificing service." At her funeral, one of her former Sunday School boys, Mr. Park Learned, sang the solo "Rock of Ages" and the boys of the choir, by request, sang two of her favorite hymns: "Hark! Hark My Soul," and "The Strife Is O'er." In 1919 the Parish Aid Society supplied, in her memory, the resurrection window in the right aisle,[15] at the front, the same year the women supplied the money to adopt a French orphan.

The parish was struck by tragedy on July 2, 1918, when parishioner Helen Nichols Learned, who assisted in the

The Parish Aid Society on the occasion of the twentieth anniversary of Mrs. Ella Haupt Chapman's presidency, ca. 1910.

Church School, drowned at Lake Phalen after her canoe overturned. Her body was not found for several weeks. The Learned family, including her parents and siblings, were active in the parish, including her brother Park, a baritone in the choir.

Just before the war ended, St. John's embarked upon the Forward Movement Campaign to revive parish life and to take an account of the financial situation, with an organization of captains and lieutenants assigned to motivate the congregants in a dozen zones. A man and a woman were appointed to each zone, with as many as eleven lieutenants in each, in an effort to increase contributions to the parish.

Set to begin on October 27, the rector wanted the church full to overflowing for the first of a series of meetings designed to unite and educate the scattered forces. Of more than a thousand people who were approached, fewer than one percent

voiced any objections. In January 1919 a preliminary report indicated that there were 275 new subscribers and a net gain in parish income of roughly $9,100. Edward Cross remarked that this success marked the beginning of a new era at St. John's, with a "determination to do things in a broad and generous fashion and a disposition to take a more prominent and constructive part in all the affairs and enterprises of the church within the state and beyond."

The November 16, 1918, issue of *The St. John's Evangelist* declared victory in the war with Germany. Mr. Cross wrote:

We have spoken brave words, we Americans. They were spoken out of an indignation lashed to a white heat by barbarous cruelty and terrible injustice. We have spoken at our best, and fought at our best; and the best have fought and spoken. Our best foot forward, we have inspired a new confidence in the world.

In 1918 the war claimed the lives of four men whose gold stars appeared on St. John's service flags. Geo. C. Squires was killed by friendly fire during flight in Scotland on May 18; Alan Nichols was killed accidentally during flight in Italy on August 17; Cyrus Thurston "Budd" Dorr was killed by friendly fire in Nashville on December 2; and Marshall Peabody died on October 8 during battle in the Argonne Forest. In January 1923 Peabody was posthumously awarded the Distinguished Service Cross for extraordinary heroism. In charge of the machine gun forces attached to the "Lost Battalion," and though desperately wounded, he left protective shelter and was killed while trying to reach his outlying machine guns in order to direct their fire.

At the service on Thanksgiving Day, called a Special Service of Thanksgiving for Victory, Mr. Cross proposed that a *Te Deum* window be designed for the northern end of the chancel, above the altar, "as a memorial to those on St. John's Service Roll who have given their lives in the war and as an act of gratitude to those who were prepared to do so had they been called on, and finally as an evidence of our gratitude to God for victory." The window would replace the three existing lancet windows and require that the ceiling of the cancel, still flat according to the designs of architect Clarence Johnston, be raised and peaked to allow for the impressive new stained glass. The rector noted that

> Some considerable expense will be attached to the project, and yet this is something with respect to which we hardly dare stop to consider the question of cost. . . . There is a general demand that this window may be as good as money can buy, because it is to tell the story of the spirit of these recent years, and the victory that has come not only to us who will have the privilege of seeing the window from service to service, but as well to our children and their children for generations yet to be. So it must be the kind of window that will live through the centuries, and always tell its story, and tell it well.[16]

With due regard for the architectural problems involved in the plan, the vestry sought the advice of the leading interior church architects in America, including Clarence Johnston, but decided on Ralph Adams Cram who in 1911 had re-

Ralph Adams Cram rendering of interior of proposed Church of St. John the Evangelist.

ceived the commission for the Cathedral of St. John the Divine in New York City. The architect's initial drawings showed the window, the new chancel ceiling, a rood screen,[17] choir stalls, and other lesser improvements. The vestry estimated the cost of these improvements at about $17,000 and decided to proceed at once with a campaign to raise the necessary funds.

A SCAFFOLD WAS ERECTED in the chancel in August 1919, and the early services were moved to the chapel while the later services took place downstairs in the Church School rooms. By September the chancel arch had been raised about eight feet, the ceiling had been torn out, and the roof was being made ready for the mill work that would complete the new arching. By the end of the month the choir took its place in the chancel for the first time, where room was found for a piano and the choir despite the scaffolding. A partition was also built to separate the nave from the chancel, and a tight flooring was constructed on the scaffold in order to keep as much of the dirt as possible off the floor.

Although the preparations for the window were completed in the fall of 1919, it was not until a year later that the stained glass itself, designed by Charles J. Connick of Boston, was ready for installation. Mr. Cross had hoped that the installation would be completed in time for the Thanksgiving Day service. A succession of strikes in the Connick shop had put the plan at risk, but the window was, nevertheless, ready in time. Charles Connick told Mr. Cross that he considered the work his masterpiece, which led the rector to declare with certainty that "we shall have a window second to none in the country." The window was dedicated by Bishop McElwain at the Thanksgiving Day service on November 25, 1920, attended by many grateful parishioners who nevertheless had painful recollections of the war. A recent appraisal placed the value of the *Te Deum* window at one million dollars.

Being lost and then found, as the hymn *Amazing Grace* reminds us, is a familiar image of salvation. The same image—of losing and finding—is also used of personal articles, though of a distinctly lesser value than one's soul. *The St. John's Evangelist* did its best to turn things lost into things found, and was probably successful most of the time. In 1917 the newsletter announced that a parishioner had left a black feather boa in the ambulatory behind the altar, of all places. We trust that owner and boa were eventually reunited. But another tale is told about a lost earring and Mrs. Louis W. Hill Sr. It was winter, and Mrs. Hill had just emerged from the church, only to discover that her pearl earring had fallen into a snow bank. Obliging

ushers came to her rescue, but without success. Mrs. Hill consoled them, telling them not to worry: "they're only paste," she said. "The real ones are in the vault."

In March 1919 the Rev. Bernard N. Lovgren assumed the responsibilities of curate in the parish. A native of Minnesota, the young priest was educated at Cambridge Theological School in Cambridge, Massachusetts, then was ordained deacon in 1917 and priest in 1918.

The Episcopal Church announced in May 1919 that it would be launching a great forward-looking movement to be known as the Nation-Wide Campaign, a three-year spiritual, educational, and financial effort that would begin in 1920 to strengthen and consolidate its work in its present fields and undertake new tasks in hitherto uncultivated fields. The church hoped to enlist 1,600 new workers and raise some $50,000,000, the larger share of which would be spent at home, with the balance for work in the foreign missions. At home, the effort would involve work among immigrants, the training of lay and clerical recruits to carry out increased work, building up and strengthening churches materially, and "finding a real substitute for the saloon," as Mr. Cross put it. The funds would also assist the needs of the provinces, dioceses, and missionary districts. The amount to be raised was based on a weekly per capita contribution nationwide of thirty-three cents per week, but by November 1919 that figure had already been surpassed. Some dioceses were averaging from forty to fifty cents per capita per week. St. John's budgeted $13,425 for each year of the three-year campaign.

In May 1919 Mr. Cross expressed his belief that the pews at St. John's should be free and asked the vestry to consider making them so. He noted that the practice of renting pews was wholly out of keeping with a democratic atmosphere and with the progressive attitude of the parish toward other matters, and that it greatly lessened the opportunity to serve more people. He estimated that only seven percent of Episcopal parishes in the country still used the rental system. The vestry unanimously agreed that the pews should be free and suggested that the rector present the matter at the next Annual Meeting. But the parish did not return to free pews until 1932.

The *Te Deum* window above the altar is a memorial to those on St. John's Service Roll who gave their lives in the war and those who were prepared to do so, and finally, as "evidence of our gratitude to God for victory." The *Te Deum* window replaced the three existing lancet windows and required the raising of the chancel ceiling.

A decade earlier, in 1908 St. Margaret's Guild had established a fund to provide dental work for the needy. Since then, free dental clinics were opened for children and a morning clinic for adults. But because those for adults were open only on weekday mornings, there were no Saturday afternoon or Sunday clinics, forcing some adults to take time off from work. So in 1919 the guild re-established its special fund for dentistry, seeking donations from parishioners.

A Refugee Auxiliary had been established in July 1918 to do work for the Red Cross during the war, and by January 1919 the women had finished 866 surgical supplies. They subsequently began making clothing for French orphans, some 326 garments by May 15. Since then, realizing the pressing need for warm clothing for children locally, the group began making garments for the poor of St. Paul, distributing many of them through the West End Community Center.

Two new stained glass windows in the left aisle were consecrated by Edward Cross on September 28, 1919. Manufactured by the English firm of Heaton, Butler and Bayne, as were the earlier windows on that side, one was given in memory of Cecelia Watkins, wife of senior warden Victor M. Watkins. The other was given in memory of Gertrude Lamborn Peet, the wife of William F. Peet, and their daughter Martha who knew life here "for so brief a space."

The next month, the Rev. Edward Cross received a letter from the vestry of St. Mark's Cathedral in Seattle, Washington, calling him to the position of dean. The parish intended to build a new cathedral and had in excess of $230,000 in cash and pledges to begin the work. They offered him a salary of $6,500, plus a rectory and the prospect of a personal secretary. Cross declined the position, writing in reply that St. John's currently had a program that

would be seriously harmed by my withdrawal; and that so fine is the spirit of cooperation and self sacrifice among our people, that it is impossible for me, certainly at this time, to approach the suggestion of any other field of endeavor with an open mind.[18]

Stained glass windows memorializing Gertrude Lamborn Peet (top), and Cecelia Watkins (bottom).

Mr. Cross had a passion for church pageantry and he promoted the production of mystery plays during Sunday services. A play entitled *The Builders of the City of God* was presented at a morning service in December 1919 by some of the older members of the Church School, with appropriate music by the choir. The play depicted the aims and purposes of the Nation-Wide Campaign, with the various characters representing the resources and needs of the church. The Girls Choir presented a cantata titled *Santa Claus and the Fairy Godmother* at the Church Club only a month later. And for the children's Christmas Eve festivals in 1922 and 1923 a pageant was presented entitled *In the Fullness of Time*, which Cross himself had written.

On January 18, Mr. Cross called a meeting for the purpose of establishing an organization for parish youth fifteen years or older, to induce them to become more closely connected with the church and its work, where their particular problems could be addressed and topics of interest discussed by guest speakers. Twenty-five people attended that first meeting of what came to be known as the Young People's Association, and forty attended in February, when a series of presentations was organized for Sundays through the remainder of the school year.

By 1920 St. John's had developed a strong connection with the Church Home, the diocesan institution for the elderly. In terms of financial contributions alone, the parish stood "at the very top," and in time a number of its members would also serve on the home's board. St. John's parishioners also served on the board of Sheltering Arms Orphanage.

The Church Club continued to be the venue for a wide range of meetings and other gatherings, both by the parish and by outside groups who used the auditorium and its athletic facilities. The annual parish meetings took place there, along with other parish meetings and entertainments of various sorts, but so also did the baccalaureates of Summit School and Mrs. Backus' School for girls.[19] The parish men had their fall and pre-Lenten dinners there, entertained by the Parish Aid Society, and attracted as many as two hundred men. A get-together for fathers and sons became an annual event for young members of the Church Club; in March 1920 about 120 of them sat down for supper with their fathers and older brothers, where the menu consisted largely of beans, bread, and butter. Four hundred fifty meals were served there every week.

Among the outside groups to rent space in the Church Club, in the early 1920s, was Miss Goddard's School for kindergartners and first and second graders. One of St. John's most revered parishioners, the late C. Robert Binger (1918–2012), was in the kindergarten class in 1924; a photo was taken of the children standing on the steps of the Church Club. He played his first piano recital in the auditorium there. Bob grew up at nearby St. Clement's Church, but transferred to St. John's at the time of his marriage with Betty Wann.

As practical evidence of his affection for the parish, the Rev. Cross noted that within the previous ten days he had received calls to two important and strategic parishes of the church, one on the Pacific coast and the other on the Atlantic, but that he had a non-receptive frame of mind for work elsewhere. He felt that St. John's was a great and important parish and that the larger church would become more and more impressed with this fact as the days went on.

A year later, despite his ongoing appreciation for the loyalty of the vestry, both to the parish and to himself, and in spite of the growth of the membership from 835 to approximately 1,250, Mr. Cross described what he called "a critical situation" continuing in the parish for its lack of compactness, that there was no large body of parishioners to guarantee a return of interest on the investment of effort. He noted by explanation that members of the congregation were in the habit of leaving the church before the end of the communion service, that fewer than a half of those that should attend the early communion service actually do so, and he deplored the attitude of some of the children in the Church School, that it reflected a lack of interest, earnestness, and application at home.

Mr. Cross claimed that the parish was twenty-five to thirty-three percent behind other churches of like situation and that the apparent neglect gave him great concern. He thought it possible to increase attendance if he were able to make more parish calls, and believed the problem could be ameliorated by a meeting of the entire congregation, saying that if the members would overcome their Anglo-Saxon reticence to talk to other people about religion, it would have a positive effect upon attendance. The vestry named pairs of members to visit Christ Church, St. Clement's, and House of Hope in St. Paul, and St. Mark's and St. Paul's in Minneapolis, and to report on their findings at a meeting of the congregation on November 4.

ABUSES HAD GRADUALLY crept into the young people's dances hosted at the Church Club, and in 1921 the following Notice to Organizations and Individuals Using the Auditorium of the Church Club for Dancing was issued:

1. All extreme forms of dancing, such as the "shimmy," face to face, cheek to cheek, and other manifestly objectionable or vulgar postures, are positively prohibited on the floor of this club.
2. Immodest dressing such as short skirts with "Scotch stockings" will likewise not be permitted.
3. Smoking by girls or women will not be countenanced anywhere in the building.
4. Men or boys will not be permitted to smoke in the auditorium.
5. Chaperones must be furnished for all "minor" dances.

One of the oldest members of the parish, Kate Ward Rice, the wife of Arthur G. Rice, died early in October. She had

Miss Goddard's School at St. John's Church Club on Portland Avenue, 1924. Later parishioner Robert (Bob) Binger is in the front row, second from right. He played his first piano recital there in the auditorium.

ST. JOHN'S faithful sexton, John Newlander, who had served the parish since June 1886, was seized with an attack of the grippe early in November 1917 and was confined at home for several days. Forgetting perhaps that Newlander had fallen sick seven years earlier, during Sedgwick's tenure, bringing the parish to a standstill, *The St. John's Evangelist* called Newlander's absence in 1917 almost unprecedented. In any case, his illnesses were a stark reminder to the congregation of the dependency that the parish has on its sextons. Turning the heat up at 3 o'clock on Sunday mornings, shoveling and mowing, and keeping the place clean and in good repair late into the evenings during the week, Newlander also had the job of ringing before all services the tubular chimes that hung in the staircase leading down to the Church School rooms. When Newlander retired in 1920, after thirty-four years of service, the vestry voted to pay him $40 per month for the remainder of his life.

connections with the parish under the first rector, the Rev. Henry Kittson, when the church was on Ashland Avenue and had continued to take an active part in parish activities, served as vice-president of the Altar Guild, and was among a small group of people that frequently attended the evening service as well as one in the morning.

As we have seen, Edward Cross launched a number of parish campaigns, and in November 1921 he initiated another: The Bigger and Better St. John's Movement. At an organizational meeting, attended by captains and lieu-

tenants of the parish zones, it was shown that in proportion to its size, strength, and importance, St. John's was not getting the attendance it should. Mr. Cross said there was a danger of self-satisfied complacency taking the place of forward moving missionary zeal and that for the healthful expansion of the parish a more vigorous spiritual interest must be registered. After only a week he noted in the parish newsletter that the five-year movement was already bearing fruit. Including the choir, close to five hundred people attended the 11 o'clock service. In December an All-St. John's Soiree took place at the Club House as the grand opening event of the movement, attracting some seven hundred people.

St. John's frequently had guest speakers on Sunday mornings, many of them itinerant bishops, but not all of them Episcopal clergy. In August 1920, for example, the Rev. Krikor Behesnilian, an Armenian by birth, had come from Tarsus, where he was engaged for several years as a Christian instructor, pastor, and evangelist. During the Turkish massacre of 1909 Behesnilian was under sentence of death and remained for some time a prisoner in a Turkish dungeon. During the war he rendered valuable service to the Allied cause at the War Office of the Intelligence Department in London, because of his knowledge of the Turkish language and customs.

On December 3, 1922, an Armenian noblewoman, Lady Anne Azgapetian, the wife of a general who served with the czar's army in the Caucasus during the war, spoke at St. John's on behalf of relief in the Near East. A war nurse, she had compelling tales to tell of the turbulent regions overseas where American charity in the past three years had saved hundreds of thousands of lives and given approximately $60,000,000 for salvaging the remnants of persecuted, scattered races.

On August 19, 1920, staunch and loyal parishioner Edward Kopper was called to God. Born in Scotland in 1845, Kopper came to St. Paul in 1872 and entered the employ of the Northern Pacific Railroad. He originally became involved with St. Paul's parish downtown where he served for many years as a vestryman, but in January 1897 he and his wife transferred to St. John's. Three years later he was elected secretary of the vestry, and in 1910 he added the position of parish treasurer,

Left: Edward Kopper held many volunteer positions in the church. Right: McNeil V. Seymour, when he was a student at Hamilton College, Clinton, New York.

both of which positions he held until 1919. For the previous twenty years Kopper's name appeared on all important parish committees. And in each one of those years he was a delegate to the diocesan convention. Unassuming and conscientious, Kopper was highly esteemed among his fellow parishioners.

Longtime parishioner McNeil V. Seymour, an attorney and one-time resident of Summit Avenue, died in April 1921. A contributor to the campaign that purchased the property on Kent Street, Seymour also served as usher for Sunday services, and for many years—from 1898 to 1911—was an active member of the vestry, often supplying them with legal counsel. *The St. John's Evangelist* wrote of him that his life "was not spectacular, but it was good. There was a moral soundness about it that contributed in manifold ways to the health and well-being of the city of St. Paul."

In June 1921 the parish lost Dr. Jehiel W. Chamberlin, the son of parishioners Harold S. and Ina Chamberlin. Dr. Chamberlin and his wife Jane were active members of the parish, he serving on the vestry and as delegate to Diocesan Council and vice-president of the Men's Club, and she teaching in the Church School, serving with the Parish Aid Soci-

ety, directing the Girls Choir, singing alto solos as needed, and working for the Red Cross Auxiliary during the war. In January 1923 the fifth window on the right aisle was consecrated to his memory, the gift of his wife and their son Harold.

Longtime vestryman and senior warden Victor M. Watkins was a resident of St. Paul for over forty years. He took a devoted and unflagging interest in religious and civic affairs, especially where these touched the unfortunate and the needy of the city. He was the first president of the Amherst H. Wilder Charity, from 1905 until his death, and was financial secretary and close advisor to Mr. Wilder. The Victor M. Watkins Fund was created by the estate of Anne Watkins Wilder,[20] in memory of her father. The Watkins Fund primarily benefits females over the age of twelve who are in need of services to achieve self-sufficiency. In 1898 Victor Watkins was treasurer of the Breck Mission and Farm School, when Amherst Wilder was president. He also served on the Standing Committee of the diocese and was regularly a delegate to Diocesan Convention. He died in September 1921.

The Rev. Lovgren, who had been serving as assistant to the rector, left St. John's in September 1921 for a position in Norman, Oklahoma. Mr. Cross said of him, that "no man, whether rector or assistant, has ever come into the parish and been more generally and immediately liked than he." After serving as a navy chaplain, Lovgren became a canon at Grace Cathedral in San Francisco and in 1946 he was named its dean.

The rector expected to be without an assistant for an indefinite period, because of the shortage of priests, but in the same month he hired as his assistant a layman named Philip Mercer, an Englishman by birth, an American by adoption, and a Congregationalist by choice. He soon became an Episcopalian and seriously considered holy orders, but nearly a year later, unprepared to make the final steps into Episcopal ministry, he accepted a call from the Congregational Church in Two Rivers, Wisconsin.

THE DOOMED HOPE-JONES ORGAN that was installed in 1910, despite its modern devices and construction, had challenges early on but developed enough problems

A larger-than-life figure at St. John's, active on many fronts, Rufus Harris was elected president of a new men's organization formed in 1923.

over time that by the end of 1921—only eleven years later—it had become apparent to the most casual observer that something had to be done. Surely it was a major embarrassment for organist George Fairclough, who had recommended Robert Hope-Jones as the builder for the instrument.

In any event, by January 1922 an unsolicited gift of $250 had been contributed to the organ fund by someone interested in seeing the proper sort of instrument in the church. Adequate funds were soon in hand, as donors had offered to purchase an instrument for a memorial to Kate Ward Rice. Her husband Arthur G. Rice and their daughter Katherine and son Arthur Ward gave generously of their resources, and

the vestry wrote in their letter of appreciation that "It will bring rest and peace to the weary, and hope to the fallen, and inspire all for greater good who hear its magic voice." The four-manual organ, built by the Ernest M. Skinner Company of Boston, probably the country's most prominent organ builder of the time, was installed between November 1922 and January 1923, and was consecrated on January 28 by the Rt. Rev. Arthur McElwain, Bishop of Minnesota.

St. John's chapel had long needed a serious renovation, and by June 1922 it had been so entirely refreshed that it was difficult to realize it was the same place as before. The dossal, an exquisite piece of fabric behind the altar, was the gift of Mrs. Louis W. Hill Sr. The altar candlesticks were given by Ellen and Easton Senkler in memory of their grandmother Frances Isabella Senkler. And the seven-branch candlesticks at the side of the altar were the gift of the late Victor M. Watkins. The Altar Guild was responsible for the decorated walls, the blue hangings for the windows, the handsome electric light fixtures, and the carpeting.

From at least 1920 Mr. Cross had been driving an automobile that was owned by the parish, a Hudson Super-six. But in October 1922 some members of the congregation replaced it with a brand new Hudson Town Coach. Not knowing who they were, he offered a "General Thanksgiving" in *The St. John's Evangelist.*

Late in 1922 three more memorial windows were manufactured by Charles J. Connick for the right aisle. The window adjacent to the existing first window, and representing the agony in the garden, was the gift of Mrs. John B. Johnston in memory of her husband. The third window, depicting the healing Christ, was given in memory of Edward and Ellen N. Kopper by their daughters. And the fourth window, depicting the nativity, was the gift of Mrs. Vincent O'Brien in memory of her father and mother, Arthur Jay Gillette and Ellen Moore Gillette.

Although the Bigger and Better St. John's Movement was barely a year old, and still underway, another movement, this one for women alone, was launched in December 1922. Called the Women's Church Service League, its purpose was to galvanize the women's organizations under the leadership of an umbrella organization whose officers were drawn from the several existing groups. In this manner a program would be determined each year and every circle of the Service League would work toward that program. The first program was to be devoted to parish interests; a program in the spring would be turned toward outreach. There were seven hundred women in the parish, but only two hundred of them were actively involved in the women's organizations.

The reorganized guilds soon numbered twelve. The Woman's Auxiliary and the Parish Aid Society were banded together under the name of St. John's Guild. Then there were the Altar Guild, the Choir Guild, St. Margaret's Guild, the Emergency Guild, the Rector's Guild, the Church School Teachers' Association, the Social Service Circle, the Women's Choir, the Girls Choir, and the Zone Organization. Each guild assumed its particular task, with the Rector's Guild planning to market a cook book comprising two hundred choice recipes, whose sale would provide a constant source of revenue for the Rector's Discretionary Fund. The book was printed in November 1923.[21]

A new men's organization was also established, and nearly one hundred men gathered at the Church Club in January 1923 for the initial meeting. Rufus E. Harris was elected president; Kenneth G. Brill, vice-president; and Harry S. Given, secretary, with Arthur H. Savage, William R. Langford, Louis M. Benepe Jr., Almon H. Greenman, Joseph G. Pyle, Milton Brown, and Valentine J. Rothschild serving on the executive committee.

At the Annual Parish Meeting on January 15, 1923, the membership voted to encumber the land on which the Church Club stood, with a mortgage from Merchants Trust and Savings Bank. The club had consistently run a deficit; in 1919 it was estimated that the parish would have to underwrite as much as $2,500 annually. The mortgage was for $12,000.

In 1923 the fifth and last of the windows on the left side aisle, manufactured by Heaton, Butler and Bayne, in London—the same firm that had produced the other four windows on that side—was given by Anne Watkins Wilder in memory of her father, Victor M. Watkins. New lighting fixtures were also installed in the nave in March, designed by Ralph Adams Cram, the consulting architect to whom

A high-church Episcopalian and a leading proponent of the Gothic Revival style, Ralph Adams Cram was a prolific architect of ecclesiastical and collegiate edifices. Best-known perhaps for his work from 1907 to 1929 as supervising architect at Princeton University, the school awarded him a Doctor of Letters degree, and on December 13, 1926, he made the cover of *Time* magazine. Together with architect Richard Upjohn and artist John LaFarge, Adams is honored with a feast day—December 16—on the calendar of the Episcopal Church in this country.

everything was referred that involved the beautification of the church. The fixtures, costing $2,900, were made of solid bronze and glass that perfectly harmonized with the interior architecture, and were the gift of the Parish Aid Society.

Despite the fact that the parish was flourishing under Cross's rectorship, and that recent years had seen balanced budgets ($60,682.60 in the year ended December 1922), the budget for

The Rt. Rev. Edward M. Cross, front row, center, the new bishop of the Missionary District of Spokane, 1924. In Spokane, Bishop Cross oversaw the design and construction of the new Cathedral of St. John the Evangelist, named for our St. Paul parish.

1923 required an increase of nearly $6,500 over that of 1922. The rector called the attention of the vestry in November 1923 to the fact that more than $10,000 would be needed to balance the budget in 1924, with each dollar spent as follows:

60¢   Salaries, choir, operating, repairs, church club, etc.
23¢   For the general work of the church at home and abroad
12¢   For missionary work throughout the diocese
5¢   For Bishop, Archdeacon, Executive Secretary, etc.

After Cross had served eight years as rector, *The St. John's Evangelist* of December 1, 1923, announced that the House of Bishops had called the Rev. Edward M. Cross to become the third bishop of the Missionary District of Spokane, comprising the eastern part of the state of Washington. As his consecration was set for the latter part of February, he thought it wise to go immediately to Spokane to spend some three weeks acquainting himself with the district, conducting its Annual Convocation and putting in motion such work as required immediate attention. But he planned to return to St. John's for the last two weeks of Lent and Easter day, bringing his rectorship to a close on May 1. He also asked the vestry to acquiesce in his desire to have the service of consecration at St. John's.

St. John's vestry boldly resisted the decision of the House of Bishops. In an undated resolution[22] to that august body, the gentlemen declared themselves

> confident that the House of Bishops had not been advised of the situation and conditions prevailing in the up-building of the work of this Parish and we feel positive that had they known our peculiar problems and needs they would have hesitated to call to another field a man so splendidly fitted to carry on and complete his work here.

The resolution noted that St. John's had been an unusual parish since its foundation, in that it had been maintained and supported in large part by men who were not churchmen. Never before, they wrote, did the parish have the cooperation and help from such men that it had enjoyed under the leadership of Mr. Cross. They believed that the parish would, in a few years, become "such a cohesive, established unit in the Church that it will be able to carry on and develop under other leadership."

A search committee was nevertheless established by the vestry at its meeting on December 18, and the outgoing bishop of Spokane, the Rt. Rev. Herman Page, sent a letter to the vestry suggesting names of clergymen who might be considered as candidates to succeed Mr. Cross.

Early in his bishopric in Washington, Bishop Cross oversaw the design and construction of the new Cathedral of St. John the Evangelist in Spokane, named after his parish in St. Paul. The new cathedral supplanted the worn frame structure of All Saints Cathedral, which had been swallowed up by neighboring factories and shops, and deemed unworthy to be the cathedral

of any diocese. An imposing gothic structure with French influence, the prominent new cathedral stands high on a hill overlooking downtown and is a familiar landmark in the city. The bell tower that crowns the crossing, known as the Bishop Cross Tower, contains a carillon of forty-nine bells.[23] And like the stained glass that Mr. Cross had installed in the right aisle of his parish in St. Paul, much of the glass in the cathedral was manufactured by Charles J. Connick of Boston. Members of St. John's parish in St. Paul had the opportunity to contribute to the construction of the new cathedral.

Paul and Reine Myers and the Rev. Frederick Butler, Bishop Cross's successor in St. Paul, were among a number of St. Paul people who attended the dedication of the new cathedral in Spokane. Mr. Myers delivered a speech at the celebratory dinner at the Davenport Hotel, attended by about four hundred guests, and Bishop Cross called the cathedral "the daughter of St. John the Evangelist, St. Paul."

Bishop Cross continued to be in demand by other jurisdictions of the church. In 1929 he was extended the invitation to become bishop coadjutor in Philadelphia for the Diocese of Pennsylvania, but according to *Time* magazine on March 11 of that year, he declined, preferring to remain in Spokane.

In April 1924, even before Mr. Cross had departed from the parish, St. John's vestry voted to call the Rev. Richard Townsend Henshaw of Christ's Church in Rye, New York, as the next rector, at a salary of $6,000, but the call was unsuccessful. Senior warden Paul N. Myers and junior warden James D. Denegre subsequently traveled "many thousands of miles at a great expenditure of time and, needless to say, at their own expense," to investigate other candidates for the position. But it was not until their meeting on October 31 that the vestry extended a call to the Rev. Frederick D. Butler, rector of St. Paul's Church in Alton, Illinois, where he had served as rector since 1917. Butler agreed to begin work as St. John's ninth rector, at the beginning of January 1925, at a salary of $6,000, with the use of the rectory at 581 Portland Avenue where he and his wife Marie E. Butler and their son Frederick Jr. were to live, together with daughter Elizabeth Louise, born in 1929.

ST. BARNABAS MISSION

IN 1897 ST. JOHN'S established a mission at Lily-dale, a hamlet on the south side of the Mississippi River, about a mile west of the Omaha Railroad bridge and three miles east of Mendota. The small congregation met in the public schoolhouse that was nearly opposite the viaduct on the upper road leading to Mendota. The clergy and lay people from St. John's who exercised leadership would travel there by boat during the warm months, but trudged across the frozen river during the winter.

At first the mission languished, but in November of 1901, the parish chapter of the Junior Brotherhood of St. Andrew revived the small congregation, where by 1902 there were nevertheless some seventy children in the Sunday School. St. John's parishioner Charles Learned was superintendent of the school, which was held every Sunday afternoon. A church service took place on the second Sunday of each month, with the Rev. Mr. Sedgwick giving his full support to the project.

By 1907 the mission congregation had nearly $700 in a fund for constructing their own building, which they hoped to accomplish that year, but they needed around $1,300 so as not to burden the congregation with too great a loan. A plot of land was purchased in Lilydale on which to build a chapel, and a start made toward gathering the necessary funds, but there was not enough money yet to justify breaking ground. To raise additional funds, the congregation presented the play "The Mysterious Aunt Selin" on November 19 and 20, 1908, followed by dancing and supper. But the benefit was "a great disappointment" in that the people of the parish did not support it. In the meantime the mission congregation continued to use the schoolhouse, which was unfit for either Sunday School or worship.

In May 1910, the Lilydale Building Committee decided to begin the work of building a chapel at once. With a cement foundation of 24 by 40 feet, the interior would be so arranged that, when used for entertainments or other secular purposes, the chancel could be separated from the main room by a rolling screen, and a hundred chairs would be used instead of pews, for easier use by the Sunday School. An appeal was put out for a bell and a cornerstone. St. John's gave two windows that were taken from our church when the memorial windows were installed (the Lilydale windows having the same dimensions as those in St. John's side aisles). St. John's baptismal font that was used before the Wilder memorial angel was given also went to Lilydale.

The cornerstone, with the words "St. Barnabas Mission, Lilydale, 1910," was laid on June 5; it contained a copy of *St. John's Yearbook 1910*, a newspaper, some coins, a list of the names of the committee in charge of the building, and a list of the members of the mission and its Sunday School.

By August of 1910, the chapel was nearly completed, although there was still a need for another seventy-five chairs, a furnace (even a second-hand one), an altar and altar rail with a cushion, and a few other things. The first service took place in the new chapel on October 2, 1910, with faithful organist Evelyn Rumble at the new piano case organ.

Because of its location on the other side of the river, and the absence of a convenient bridge, services at Lilydale were subject to the river's condition. On Good Friday evening in 1917, the service had to be postponed because of the high waters. (Meanwhile, the services at St. John's went on as usual; the combined attendance at all five services on Easter day were said to have exceeded 2,000.)

Work on the chapel was suspended in the fall of 1918, but commenced again in June 1919, with the chapel now completely equipped with the windows taken from St. John's. Services had been curtailed, but at a recent meeting, interested parties decided to hold gatherings twice a month, with regular weekly services to resume in the early fall.

LITTLE BY LITTLE the St. Barnabas Mission began to disappear from the vestry minutes and *The St. John's Evangelist*, and by the spring of 1925 the mission had ceased to exist. In April 1931 the vestry received an offer of $200 for the Lilydale property, which it declined on account of "the use to which the property was to be put by the purchaser."

By May 1934, the St. Barnabas Chapel in Lilydale was seldom used, the neighborhood having changed and church families having moved away, and it suffered from neglect. It would take a great deal of money to restore it to any future use, so the vestry decided to sell the property. The chapel was razed in 1935 and in July 1936 the vestry accepted an offer from Mr. and Mrs. Alexander Manson of $50 cash for the two lots, on which they planned to build a residence. By September 1938 the vestry had received a total of $212.68 from the sale, an amount they sent to the Rt. Rev. Stephen E. Keeler, Bishop of Minnesota, with the expressed wish that it be used as a startup fund for the purchase of a suitable property, preferably in the Highland Park District, where church expansion seemed likely. In 1940, Bishop Keeler was eager to begin the establishment of a new parish in that area, to be called St. Alban's, between Snelling and Fairview Avenues.

Miss Sarah E. Baldy
President, Altar Guild

Mrs. Morton Barrows
President, Choir Guild

Mrs. Sylvester M. Cary
President, Woman's Auxiliary

Mrs. H. W. Fagley
President, Refugee Auxiliary

Mrs. N. S. Poole
President, Parish Aid

Mrs. William H. Merrick
President, St. John's Guild

Miss Dorothy M. Punderson
President, Young People's Association

Mrs. Elma J. Harris
Rector's Secretary

St. John's parishioner and U.S. Secretary of State Frank Billings Kellogg is seated at the table to the left of President Calvin Coolidge in the East Room of the White House, where he is signing the Kellogg-Briand Pact in the presence of members of the president's cabinet, senators, and congressmen in 1928.

chapter nine

THE REV. FREDERICK DUNTON BUTLER 1925-1933
A Secretary of State

DURING FREDERICK BUTLER'S tenure as rector at St. John's, the state of Tennessee passed a law forbidding the teaching of evolution in public schools, setting the stage for the Scopes Monkey Trial. In 1927 Minnesota aviator Charles Lindbergh made the first solo nonstop transatlantic flight in his plane *The Spirit of St. Louis.* In 1929 the stock market crash precipitated the Great Depression. The year 1931 was the warmest in St. Paul's recorded history. In 1932, another Minnesotan, St. Paul Episcopalian Amelia Earhart, was the first woman to fly solo, nonstop, across the Atlantic. In 1933 Franklin Delano Roosevelt was inaugurated as the 32nd president of the United States.

The Rev. Frederick
Dunton Butler.

Because he was an alumnus of Nashotah House Theological Seminary, which trains seminarians in Anglo-Catholic liturgical practice, Butler brought a more catholic consciousness to his work in the parish (as had St. John's first and seventh rectors, the Rev. Henry Kittson and the Rev. Julius Schaad). Mr. Butler appears never to have made liturgical innovations, by introducing incense, for example, but in his writings in *The St. John's Evangelist* he betrayed his leanings by his choice of words and by his teachings. He referred to "our Holy Mother, the Church" and to the "blessed sacrament," and occasionally provided definitions for words not ordinarily found in a low-church lexicon, such as private *absolution, biretta,* and *consecration.* Several times he addressed the Young People's Association on "Ceremonial—The Reason Why." He reminded the congregation of the holy days of obligation (such as the

Frederick Dunton Butler was born in Brooklyn, New York, in 1884. After high school he spent three years in the business world in New York City. In 1903 he entered the Nashotah House Theological Seminary in Nashotah, Wisconsin, graduating with the B.D. in 1908, the same year he was ordained priest. His first rectorship was at St. Matthias Church in Waukesha, Wisconsin, and in 1914 he became rector of Grace Church in Freeport, Illinois. During his time at St. Paul's in Alton, Illinois, Mr. Butler served as archdeacon for the Diocese of Springfield, diocesan representative on the Council of the Province of the Midwest, and deputy to the General Conventions in 1919 and 1922.

Ascension and the Annunciation of the Blessed Virgin Mary), of rogation days and ember days, and he corrected them on the proper use of the word *Reverend*—not to address him as Rev. Butler. Reverend, he said, is correctly used only when it is followed by Doctor, Father, Mister, or the Christian name of the clergyman. He also attended the Annual Meetings of the Catholic Congress, which he once described as "one of the most outstanding events in the Episcopal Church" in the United States of America. At any rate, he was probably careful not to offend too much against the low-church taste of St. John's.

Butler's attention to liturgical matters was prompted in no small measure by the national church's ongoing revision of the *Book of Common Prayer*. The process took some fifteen years and is said to have represented the most radical revision in American prayer books until that of 1979. Butler introduced these extensive changes to the congregation as soon as they became available, both in Morning Prayer and Holy Communion, and he purchased the new book "at once." It was used for the first time on December 1, 1929, becoming the third prayer book to be used at St. John's, after the original American book of 1789 and its first revision, in 1892.

The new Rector's Guild for women was founded very early in Butler's rectorship to raise discretionary funds for the rector to use for charitable purposes. Mrs. Paul J. Kalman was the first president and she was succeeded in turn by Mesdames Springer Brooks, Horace H. Irvine, Harold O. Washburn, and William

Mrs. Paul J. Kalman, left, was the first president of the new Rector's Guild, tasked with raising discretionary funds for the rector. Mrs. Horace (Clotilde) Irvine, right, later presided over this group.

J. Hamm. In later years the guild developed a reputation for snobbishness, with membership highly coveted and exclusive.

The women's husbands were St. Paul businessmen. Mrs. Hamm's husband, William J. Hamm, for instance, had inherited Hamm's brewery in St. Paul in 1903 from his father, German immigrant Theodore Hamm. During Prohibition the company produced soft drinks and food products, and expanded rapidly through acquisitions after the repeal of Prohibition in 1933.

In his first year on the job, Mr. Butler successfully befriended his parishioners. So much so, in fact, that between services on Christmas day in 1925, a man rang the doorbell at the rectory and presented the Rev. Mr. Butler with an envelope containing a Christmas card wishing him and his family a Merry Christmas from "some of your many friends in the parish." On looking outside, he saw a beautiful Master Six Buick Sedan, fully equipped, and was told it was for the Butlers.

For a number of years the furnishings in the chancel had remained incomplete, with the choir stalls, a few parclose screens, and the chancel rails still wanting. The vestry originally intended to have the rest of the work done by the American Seating Company, which had produced the earlier oak work in the chancel, but decided instead to engage the Stillwater Manufacturing Company. The total cost of the stalls, screens, and rails would come to $5,945.

Mrs. Henry E. (Lucy May) Wedelstaedt and her son, Mr. A. H. Wedelstaedt, gave $2,000 toward the cost of the choir stalls, in memory of her husband and his father, Henry E. Wedelstaedt. The furnishings were installed in 1927, whereupon Mr. Butler pronounced that St. John's had "one of the most beautiful chancels anywhere in the American Church."

A prominent St. John's couple to die in 1925 were Crawford Livingston[1] and his wife, Mary Steele (Potts) Livingston. Residents of Summit Avenue, they lived at 432, the second oldest surviving house on the street, known today as the Burbank-Livingston-Griggs house. "An elegant gentleman impeccably dressed with a neat, waxed mustache," Livingston was born of

Scottish aristocracy in 1847. Among his ancestors were signers of the Declaration of Independence and the Constitution, a soldier against the British in the Revolutionary War, a U.S. Supreme Court justice, and the country's first secretary of state.

Before moving to St. Paul, Crawford Livingston lived much of his life in New York (at the Waldorf-Astoria Hotel), where he was associated with the stock brokerage firm White, Livingston and Kendrick. Moving to Winona, Minnesota, in 1870, he was employed by the Winona and St. Peter Railroad. Around 1886 he bought the St. Paul Gas Light Company and served as its

vice-president. He was a director of the Merchant's National Bank, the Title and Insurance Company of Minnesota, the Edison Electric Company (in New York), the Inter-State Investment Company, the Livingston Land Company, and a trustee of The Minnesota Mutual Life Insurance Company. About 1880 he established C. Livingston and Company, and served as secretary of the St. Paul Board of Trade. Livingston built several branch lines of the Northern Pacific, and in 1917 became director of that railway, a position he held until his death. The Livingstons' daughter, Mary, married Theodore Wright Griggs, and the couple subsequently lived at 432 Summit Avenue.

THE BURBANK-LIVINGSTON-GRIGGS HOUSE at 432 Summit Avenue was designed by Chicago architect Otis L. Wheelock and built in 1862-65 for James C. Burbank, a prominent figure in early transportation in St. Paul—stagecoaches and riverboats. Interestingly enough, following the deaths of the Burbanks, the mansion was owned briefly in the mid-1880s by George R. Finch (see pp. 30-31). Crawford Livingston acquired the property in 1887.

MARY LIVINGSTON GRIGGS, a socialite and philanthropist, filled the family home with art treasures and antiques from around the world. Her daughter, Mary Griggs Burke, amassed the largest comprehensive col-

lection of Japanese art outside Japan. Upon Mary Burke's death in 2012, her Japanese collection was divided between the Metropolitan Museum of Art in New York and the Minneapolis Institute of Arts.

PARISHIONER THEODORE WRIGHT GRIGGS had a wholesale grocery business in the firm of Griggs, Cooper and Company, where he served as vice-president, president, and chairman of the board. He was also a first lieutenant in the 15th Minnesota National Guard during the Spanish-American War, in 1898. Confirmed at St. John's, he and Mary Steele Livingston were married there in 1916. He was buried from St. John's in 1934.

PARISHIONER CORDENIO A. SEVERANCE and his wife, Mary Frances (Harriman) Severance, died during Mr. Butler's first year in 1925. Admitted to the bar in 1882, Cordenio entered into partnership in 1887 with U.S. Senator Cushman Kellogg Davis and Cushman's cousin, Frank B. Kellogg, a fellow parishioner at St. John's.

Davis had been governor of Minnesota in 1874-75. Frank Kellogg would rise to U.S. Secretary of State. The firm of Davis, Kellogg, and Severance is today known as Briggs and Morgan. Mr. Severance, a Republican, was president of the American Bar Association in 1921-22. He was also a member of St. John's Men's Club, though he often attended House of Hope Presbyterian Church. Mary Frances Severance was involved with St. John's Altar Guild and the Women's Board of the Church Club. Mary Frances endowed Severence Hall at Carleton College and also Severance Hall at Wellesley, her alma mater. Present-day parishioner Jay Severance, a member of St. John's choir, is a distant relative of Cordenio Severance.

The Severances' country estate in Cottage Grove, known as *Cedarhurst*, was designed by Cass Gilbert and is on the National Register of Historic Places. Cordenio was a friend and longtime client of Gilbert, who also designed the interior of the Severance home on Summit Avenue. Given Frank Kellogg's connections with Washington, the Severances offered *Cedarhurst* as a meeting place for high government officials, who included presidents Theodore Roosevelt, William Taft, Warren G. Harding, and Calvin Coolidge.

The Severances' summer residence outside St. Paul called *Cedarhurst* had been a modest, mid-1850s farmhouse that the couple first enlarged in 1886. Between 1911 and 1917, they transformed the property into a twenty-six-room Neoclassical Revival-style mansion with twin columned porticoes and a one-hundred-foot veranda.

During the course of his rectorship Mr. Butler enunciated three goals that he considered of paramount importance to St. John's future. First of all, the church needed an adequate endowment to meet the future spiritual needs of its changing neighborhood, which was becoming one of transient people of limited means living in apartments and boarding houses—with "very many of our people" moving miles away from the parish. "I warn you, dear friends, that the handwriting is on the wall and that St. John's cannot possibly operate in the future unless our parishioners make provision in their wills now for her future welfare." Two parishioners had lately done so and by January 1932 the fund had $9,300. Butler cautioned that by 1945 the parish would need between $75,000 and $100,000 in its endowment. Secondly, the congregation needed a Parish House in which the Church School could be adequately accommodated. Thirdly, the antiquated practice of renting pews needed to be abolished.

Five months into his rectorship, giving serious consideration to Mr. Butler's second goal, the need for a Parish House, a Church Club Committee was formed, consisting of Royal A. Moore, chairman, with members E. H. Davidson, Rufus Harris, and Julian S. Gilman. The committee investigated the present club on Portland Avenue, assessed its financial state, considered its needs, and made recommendations for the future. Erected at a cost of approximately $100,000, including land and equipment, the building, now free of indebtedness, was appraised at $135,000. The club director for the past seven years, Art Zache, managed a staff of eight persons: a women's swimming instructor, a pianist for physical training classes, an instructor for the business women's classes, an engineer, a porter, a matron, a boys' life guard, and a locker boy.

The second floor was originally intended for the numerous women's guilds, but by stress of circumstances and the endeavor to reduce deficits by placing upon a rental basis "every possible bit of space," these organizations had been relegated to three small, poorly ventilated closet-less rooms. But the greatest criticism of the Club House was that it was in no way adapted for the use of the Church School. So long as the school was forced to use this building, the results would be unsatisfactory. And the fact that the upper school,

Royal A. Moore, left, and Julian S. Gilman, right, were members of the Church Club Committee, which concluded that "If a new building is needed, let us rise up and build it."

which met in the basement of the church, was equally handicapped made the problem even more acute.

In 1924 the Church Club had an excess of expenses over receipts in the amount of $7,445.35 and was almost constantly $2,500 in arrears in its current payments. The committee thought it could and should be operated at closer to one hundred percent of its capacity than it was at the time. Moreover, only 18 of the present 228 members of the club had any real connection with the parish, which offered nothing for the spiritual welfare of the twenty-three young men currently living in the dormitory. Finally, the stage in the auditorium was so high as to make observation difficult from the main floor.

The committee concluded that the Club House did not fulfill ideally the needs of the parish, i.e., (1) it was not contiguous to the church building; (2) it had inadequate provision for the care of the Church School; (3) its use for secular purposes sometimes excluded its use by the parish; and 4) it was costly to operate. In their judgment only a new building could solve problems (1) and (2). Problem (3) could and would be remedied, with parish needs given primary consideration. As for (4), the parish probably could not erect a distinctive parish house for a reasonable cost, even assuming that the church was willing to forego its community work.

Despite this list of concerns, the Church Club had lent prestige to the parish because of the lavish interest it showed in the community. Indeed, throughout the diocese the congregation was known to be generous and civic-minded. But given the changes taking place in the neighborhood, the committee thought it possible that there would be a growing need for the dormitory type of club in that part of the city, suggesting that another wing of dormitories be built over the swimming pool. The first floor could be reconstructed to include a chapel with nearby classrooms for the Church School. The second and third floors would be devoted to dormitory space, with rentals sufficient to carry the cost of the additional investment and provide for the slightly increased overhead. Thus the parish would get more Church School space without any additional cash investment. In summary the committee wrote:

> We have not yet realized to the full the potentialities of the Church Club. If by going forward we may realize them more completely, let us advance. If a new building is needed, let us rise up and build it. But if the real need in this instance is a new vision of usefulness, let us have that too.

Further discussion of the Church Club took place at the vestry meeting on January 31, 1929, when three courses of action were considered: (1) to purchase a site and build a new Parish House, requiring a very large investment; (2) to move the Church Club to a site nearer the church, with the cost estimated at $50,000; or (3) to make alterations and repairs to the Church Club and use the entire building as a Parish House.

Butler strongly advocated for the third plan and submitted an estimate for the alterations and repairs amounting to $14,800. The vestry approved the rector's plan and in March 1929 authorized the expenditure of no more than $22,500 on the project, exclusive of furniture. The congregation was asked for one third of an estimated total budget of $30,000, namely, $10,000. By May 1929 the alterations to the

Church Club were in process and by July the work was nearly completed, thus accomplishing Butler's second goal for the parish.

In the spring of 1928, there had been several instances when strangers and parishioners without sittings had been made uncomfortable by the attitude of parishioners who held rented pews. There was a consensus of the vestry that the day of free sittings was not far off. Indeed St. John's was said to be one of only two or three Episcopal churches in the state still with rented pews. The pew rental system was finally abolished on January 1, 1932, accomplishing Butler's third goal.

A remarkable eight parishioners advanced to the diaconate or priesthood during Butler's rectorship, namely, Alexander R. McKechnie, Guy Louis Hill, Howard Frederick Dunn, Joseph G. Moore, Elliott D. Marston,[2] Crawford W. Brown,[3] Robert H. Kluckhohn, and Paul C. Weed Jr.

Like all of his predecessors, Mr. Butler missed no opportunity to urge his congregation to better attendance at worship. In November 1926, after a particularly dismal turnout, he had these harsh words for his flock:

> St. John's IS your parish, isn't it? Yet, very frankly, one sometimes wonders if many of you, who claim to be St. John's people are really churchmen and churchwomen at heart. . . . Last Sunday, our choir was present, as it will be each Sunday afternoon, from now on BUT the congregation was pitifully small. Was the cause the bad weather or just indifference?

MANY OF ST. JOHN'S PARISHIONERS vacationed in White Bear Lake during the summer, making attendance at St. John's difficult, so *The St. John's Evangelist* for many years posted the times of services at St. John's in the Wilderness in White Bear Lake, in the hope that parishioners would maintain their spiritual observances while on holiday.

The Christmas Bazaar sponsored by the Parish Aid Society in 1926 was deemed a financial success, and with a portion of the proceeds the women made the first payment on elegant new chandeliers for the nave, designed by architect Ralph Adams Cram.

At Christmastime 1928, St. John's Business and Professional Women's Guild, an organization for self-supporting women, hosted a Christmas party and dinner at the Church Club for twenty-five boys and girls who were wards of the Ramsey County Child Welfare Association. There was a Christmas tree, the rector told a Christmas story, and a girls' sextet sang familiar carols. The children were brought to the club in taxis and met in the reception room by Santa himself, "rosy and bewhiskered," who presented a gift for every child and adult, and for each child a box of candy, making the big room "ring with merriment."

In September 1926 Mr. Butler was appointed by Bishop McElwain to serve as chairman of the Diocesan Commission for the Bishops' Crusade, a national effort of the Episcopal Church launched in January 1927, to make evangelism its top priority and to arouse in the hearts of Episcopalians a true sense of their responsibilities as Christians. Parishioner Ernest H. Davidson was a member of the National Commission on Evangelism and played a prominent role in the effort.

Mr. Butler worked tirelessly for the Crusade and was instrumental in its success, both in the Twin Cities and throughout the diocese. By December 1927 his labors in the diocese and the parish were so consuming that his health suffered under the strain and a severe nervous breakdown was said to have been averted only by the relinquishing of his parish work during the winter of 1927-1928. Several parishioners provided funds for a four- or five-week stay in the South, but Butler ended up needing three months away. For two months he was under a strict medical regimen, first at the hospital and then at home. He spent a third month recuperating with his wife in the South.

Beginning in the fall of 1927 the Rt. Rev. Frederic L. Deane, the Lord Bishop of Aberdeen, Scotland, toured the United States in the interests of a proposed Seabury Memorial in the Cathedral Church of Aberdeen. In 1783 the Rev. Samuel Seabury had been elected Bishop of Connecticut and the first

bishop in the American colonies. But as there were no Anglican bishops in the colonies to consecrate him, and because as an American citizen he could not take an oath of allegiance to King George III of England, he went to Aberdeen, whose bishops did not recognize the king's authority, and there he was consecrated the first American Episcopal bishop.[4] Deane's visit to St. John's on January 15, 1928, where he was attended by Bishop McElwain and the clergy of

Crawford Brown was one of eight parishioners who advanced to the diaconate or priesthood in these years.

Parishioner Elliott Dar Marston became the first rector of St. Stephen's Episcopal Church in Edina, Minnesota.

Choir mother Elizabeth Hensel.

the diocese, with the combined choirs of the parish, was his last appearance in the United States before returning to Aberdeen. Parishioners had the opportunity to contribute to the memorial.

In 1928 parishioners Frederick and Gertrude Wigginton took their three children to meet their relatives in England and France (see p. 77). When they visited Canterbury Cathedral, sixteen-year-old daughter Mary took a rock from the reconstruction site at the cathedral. Gertrude Wigginton allowed Mary to take the piece of consecrated material back home only if she made it into a bedside altar. Today at St. John's, the mounted rock with its black cross sits in a niche on the east side of the columbarium, which will be discussed later.

In the spring of 1928, Mr. Butler told the vestry about a growing problem with the choir: there was no discipline and no training, and the choirboys were often late or absent from the rehearsals. After much deliberation, the vestry informed George Fairclough that if he would secure a competent assistant and return the choir to efficiency, they would be satisfied. Within the next few weeks Fairclough had made arrangements with Art Zache to assist with the choir in the capacity of disciplinarian.

A number of women over the years devoted their time to the work of choir mother, assisting the boys, and later the girls as well, with vesting and line-up, helping to make their choir experience a satisfying one. Lucy Lord Chapman had earlier served in the position for twelve years. In September 1928 the vestry marked the twenty-fifth anniversary of Miss Elizabeth Hensel as choir mother, honoring her with a gift

of $50. Miss Hensel served for many more years and also taught in the Sunday School.

Butler, however, foresaw the day when women would assume responsibilities hitherto reserved for men. He wrote,

> There is a time coming and coming fast—we predict it—when women's work in the Church will not be confined to making aprons and embroidery, cooking parish suppers, teaching Sunday School, or even packing missionary boxes. Women will be on the vestries, conducting lay evangelistic missions, linking up the Church more and more with social service work—branching out into many lines of activity that now are closed to them.

Mrs. Louis W. Hill consented in December 1928 to serve as chairman of a committee of women who would raise money in the parish toward the completion of St. Luke's Hospital in Tokyo. Butler wrote in *The St. John's Evangelist*, "We know of no object toward which the General Church is working which will mean more to international good will than the completion of this great hospital in Tokyo."

St. John's lost some of its early and loyal parishioners during these years. James D. Denegre died in January 1927. A native of New Orleans, Denegre was a clerk in Hiler Hosmer Horton's law office in St. Paul before becoming the lead partner in the law firm of Denegre, McDermott, Stearns and Weeks. A Republican member of the Minnesota State Senate from 1911 until 1926, he and his wife, Marion Simpson Denegre, lived at 623 Summit Avenue, and later at the nearby Commodore Hotel at 79 Western Avenue.

Senator Denegre was a prominent Mason, a member of the Ancient Landmark Lodge No. 5 of St. Paul, and Summit Chapter No. 45. He was a Knight Templar in Paladin Commandery No. 21, and a Potentate of Osman Temple, a member of the Red Cross of Constantine, and a 33rd Degree Scottish Rite Mason. A member and Council Commander of the order of Woodmen of the World, he was also a member of the Minnesota Boat Club in St. Paul and a leader in the National Amateur Rowing Association.

A MOST RENOWNED parishioner, Frank Billings Kellogg, a U.S. Senator (1917-1923), then ambassador to the Court of St. James, was U.S. Secretary of State from 1925 to 1929. Of the eighty treaties that he signed while in office, none was as important as the Kellogg-Briand Pact. Sponsored by France and the U.S., and named for its co-authors: Kellogg and French foreign minister Aristide Briand, the 1928 pact renounced the use of

war as an instrument of national policy except in self-defense and called for the peaceful settlement of disputes. Because it contained no provisions for sanctions, and provided no alternatives to war, it had little immediate effect. Similar ideas, however, were later incorporated into the United Nations charter and other treaties. Kellogg was awarded the Nobel peace prize in 1929.

Born in Potsdam, New York, Kellogg came with his family to Minnesota in 1865. From 1889 until his death on December 21, 1937, Kellogg and his wife Clara had a home in St. Paul. Kellogg himself never

Clara May (Cook) Kellogg.

attended college, but in 1937 he established at Carleton College in Northfield, Minnesota, the Frank B. Kellogg Foundation for Education in International Affairs with a $500,000 endowment. Kellogg's life story is well worth a read. Frank B. Kellogg was a Minnesota farm boy, largely self-taught, who rose to international prominence.

New U.S. Secretary of State Frank Kellogg with President Calvin Coolidge at the Summer White House in Swampscott, Massachusetts, July 13, 1925.

The Kellogg residence at 633 Fairmount Avenue in St. Paul is on the National Register of Historic Places.

Marion Simpson Denegre and Senator James D. Denegre.

A member of St. John's for over thirty years, Denegre served on the parish Standing Committee, was a delegate to Diocesan Council, a vestryman, and a regular communicant at the early service on Sunday. He was junior warden for the last five years of his life and also started an endowment fund at the church.

Parishioner Obed Pardon Lanpher died in September 1928. From 1876 to 1915, he was president of Lanpher, Skinner and Company, a wholesaler in hats and furs in St. Paul. Lanpher served on the vestry for many years, for three years was junior warden, and was a delegate to Diocesan Council.

Parishioner Valentine J. Rothschild died in November 1930. His firm of Rothschild and Thurston specialized in real estate and mortgage loans, and Rothschild was for many years identified with St. Paul's civic and social life. He and his family lived at 756 Fairmount Avenue, which is on the National Register of Historic Places.

Alexander A. McKechnie died in August 1931. Active at St. John's for at least thirty-one years, his name first appeared in the vestry minutes when those gentlemen

ATTORNEY CHARLES WELLS FARNHAM died in April 1931. A recognized authority on insurance law, Farnham was a member and president of the Ramsey County Bar Association, and a member of the Minnesota State Bar and American Bar Associations.

Born in 1867 in Buffalo, New York, young Farnham came to St. Paul with his parents when he was five. He earned a law degree at the University of Minnesota and began practicing law in 1895. In 1900 he married Kate Humbird with whom he had five children.

Farnham's later years were devoted mainly to books and travel. He possessed a large library of carefully selected books, many of them signed by their authors. His many personal friends included President Theodore Roosevelt and the poet James Whitcomb Riley, and he spent many of the poet's birthdays at his home on Lockerbie Street in Indianapolis.

thanked him for conducting the choir for ten months in 1900. He had previously served as choirmaster at Christ Church. For a time he maintained and tuned St. John's organ, and for many years was a lay reader, a delegate to the Church Extension Society, and to Diocesan Council. A member of the parish Standing Committee, he also took part in Church School activities. He and his family lived at 572 and then 676 Summit Avenue.

In October 1932, the parish lost Jane Whipple Scandrett, the daughter of the Rt. Rev. Henry Benjamin Whipple, the first bishop of Minnesota. "A lady of the old school, a faithful Christian, a devout Churchwoman, a devoted mother and a loyal friend," Mrs. Scandrett was buried from the Cathedral of

Our Merciful Saviour in Faribault. The Rt. Rev. Frank A. McElwain, Bishop of Minnesota, conducted the service. The chancel was banked by flowers from church dignitaries and railroad executives. She and her late husband, Henry Alexander Scandrett, lived at 9 Crocus Place and had four children. Their son Benjamin Wright Scandrett was junior warden at St. John's from 1929 to 1939. Active in the legal profession, he later became the executive vice-president of the Northern Pacific Railway. Benjamin and his wife, the former Bertha D. Reid, had two daughters, Cornelia (Mrs. Jack Elsinger Hanstein) and Betty (Mrs. Cole Oehler), both of whom grew up at St. John's. Jack Hanstein served on the vestry for many years and was the superintendent of the Church School. Betty Oehler was president of the Woman's Auxiliary.

Betty and Cole Oehler with their six children, left to right: Susan, Cole (son), Peter, Betty, Debbie, Cole, Ben, and Judy, on the occasion of daughter Debbie's graduation from Summit School, 1958. Betty Oehler was the great-granddaughter of Bishop Henry Whipple; the Oehler sons and daughters, who grew up at St. John's, are Whipple's great-great-grandchildren.

> **FROM THE COOKBOOK "Reliable Recipes"**
> Compiled by the Rector's Guild of St. John's Church, 1932.
>
> **ICE BOX COOKIES**
>
> | | |
> |---|---|
> | 1 cup white sugar | 1 teaspoon soda |
> | 1 cup shortening | 1 teaspoon vanilla |
> | 2 eggs | teaspoon cinnamon |
> | 1 teaspoon cream tartar | 3 1/2 cups flour |
> | ¼ teaspoon salt | 1 cup nutmeats |
>
> Makes heavy dough. Knead in nuts and shape into 2 rolls and let stand in ice box over night. Slice thin and bake.
>
> Contributors were the Misses Cecelia Kalman and Maud Hill Sr., and Mesdames Kenneth Bayliss, Springer Brooks, E. C. Brown, Worrell Clarkson, D. S. Culver, B. G. Griggs, M. W. Griggs, Jule M. Hannaford Jr., George Hardenbergh, E. B. Holbert, J. L. Hyde, H. H. Irvine, Harrison Johnston, Thurston Johnston, W. F. Peet, John Peyton, Cecil Read, J. M. Scanlon, G. B. Schurmeier, M. S. Stringer, James Thompson, R. P. Warner, A. H. Warren Jr., Norbert Winter, and E. C. Williams.

An outstanding parishioner of St. John's in these years was Thomas L. Daniels, the son of John W. and Amelia Leonard Daniels, who lived with his wife Frances and their children at 271 Summit Avenue. Formerly an attaché in the U.S. diplomatic corps, he served in Brussels, Rio de Janeiro, and Rome. In 1929 he began working with Archer Daniels Midland Company, where he became president and board chairman. He was also a director of Northwestern National Bank and Trust Company, Minnesota and Ontario Paper Company, Northwest Bancorporation, the Great Northern Railway, and chairman of the board of trustees of the Minneapolis Institute of Arts. The family lived for a time at 7 Heather Place.

THE STOCK MARKET CRASH on October 24, 1929, was the most devastating of such crashes in the history of the United States. Businesses failed and many families were reduced to poverty. The most tragic result of the Depression for St. John's was the death by suicide, on December 3, 1929, of Senior Warden Paul Noxon Myers, described by Mr. Butler as a man of noble life, unimpeachable character, and splendid churchmanship. Butler wrote that it would have been an unbearable calamity but for the faith of the church and wished "that he had not been permitted to bear so many burdens alone." Myers was junior warden from 1915 to 1922 and senior warden from 1922 until his death.

No direct mention was made of the trouble on Wall Street anywhere in the vestry minutes or *The St. John's Evangelist*. It took little time, however, for the effects of the Depression to be felt among parishioners. Many members found it difficult to honor their pledges, and some had to eliminate or reduce their pledges in succeeding years.

In the early 1930s *The St. John's Evangelist* published several "job wanted" notices: a bookkeeper was looking for an accounting position, a woman from the parish needing to augment her much depleted income was looking to take elderly persons or convalescents into her home, and a driver was looking for a chauffeur's position, indicating just how tough the times had become even for people of means. But the wealthiest still had their gardeners, their maids, and their chauffeurs.

Despite the economic slump, a number of memorials were given during the early years of the Depression. Reine Myers provided a new altar for the Chapel of the Beloved Disciple in honor of her mother Caroline G. (Mrs. John A.) Humbird that was installed in May 1931. Her gift facilitated the complete redecoration of the interior of the chapel, featuring a new reredos, a credence table, and an altar. The altar was designed by celebrated St. Paul architect Magnus Jemne, best known for his Art Deco Moderne Women's City Club Building, which was built on the corner of St. Peter Street and Kellogg Blvd. in St Paul in 1931.

The Lawrence King family presented a private communion set together with a new carved oak lectern for the chancel as a memorial for Jane Cotton Edge (formerly Mrs. Samuel D.

Flagg, president of the Woman's Auxiliary).[5] Their gift included a Bible bound in two volumes, containing the old and new testaments, to be used at the lectern. Elmar L. Van Dresar offered a clerestory window on the west side, a memorial for his wife.

William Huntington Fobes was not a member of St. John's—in fact he was a member of the nearby Virginia Street Swedenborgian Church—but he was deeply interested in the parish and frequently attended services. A resident of Crocus Hill, he was treasurer of the North Western Fuel Company. His son, William Huntington Fobes Jr., president of Fobes and Brown Coal and Oil Company, married Elizabeth Irvine.

Mr. Butler enjoyed the distinction of being named to two posts in the national church by the Presiding Bishop, the Most Rev. James DeWolf Perry. In December 1931 he was appointed to serve on the National Commission on Evangelism, and in November 1932 he was appointed Secretary for the Province of the Northwest for the Jerusalem and East Mission, which included the work of the Anglican Church in Palestine.

On March 20, 1933, after a tenure of just over eight years, the Rev. Frederick D. Butler submitted his letter of resignation following a call from Grace Church in Madison, Wisconsin. The vestry accepted his resignation with keen regret, writing that "he has always been able to see clearly what was the right thing to do and has had the courage to act on his convictions." Two weeks prior to his departure from the parish at the end of May, his alma mater, Nashotah Theological Seminary, bestowed upon him the degree Doctor of Divinity.

Elizabeth Irvine Fobes was the daughter of Mr. and Mrs. Horace Irvine and grew up in the present Minnesota Governor's Residence at 1006 Summit Avenue. (See p. 85.) When she died at age forty in 1949, her husband and parents placed an electronic carillon in St. John's bell tower in her memory.

There was an unusually long vacancy after the departure of Dr. Butler, and the Rt. Rev. Frank A. McElwain, Bishop of Minnesota, accepted the vestry's request that he take charge of the parish until a new rector be called. The Rev. Frank C. Greene assisted him as curate on a monthly basis. In June Bishop McElwain was elected Professor of Pastoral Theology at Seabury-Western Theological Seminary in Evanston, a position he accepted with the proviso that he retain his title and jurisdiction as Bishop of Minnesota.

The search for a rector garnered some sixty applications and nominations. The vestry extended a call to the Rev. Conrad H. Gesner of Pierre, South Dakota, at a yearly salary of $4,200. He would also have the use of the rectory (with janitorial services). Gesner accepted the call as tenth rector and came to St. John's on December 3, 1933, the first Sunday in Advent. He promptly declared his desire to hire an assistant, a graduate of a theological seminary, someone who was unmarried and still in deacon's orders, and who would live in the apartment in the Club House.

CHOIR CAMP

NO SINGLE FEATURE OF LIFE at St. John's affected the lives of more young boys and girls as deeply or as memorably as the annual summer camps for choristers. Young children from the neighborhood and from beyond, many of them not otherwise having a family connection with the parish, and numbers of them from relatively poor families, were attracted to the choirs because the parish provided them with streetcar fare and promised them some ten days or so at the summer camp.

Several camp sites were used by the choirboys over the years, including a peninsula on Green Lake, Russell Beach on Chisago Lake, and later another site on the same lake. In 1917 a site on Chisago Lake was purchased for Camp Sedgwick, named in honor of the former rector. Some summers saw as many as fifty boys in attendance. In 1921 a group of former choirboys and men formed an organization to develop the site, which then had only eighteen sleep tents, a dining tent, and a kitchen tent. All they really needed was an adequate road to the camp, and a permanent shelter for an assembly room, dining room, kitchen, and store room. In 1927 they estimated that a minimum of $2,000 would be needed for the purpose and the building was erected that summer. In 1931 the low water level at Lake Chisago—because of a drought— forced the boys to Camp Lawton on Deer Lake, Wisconsin, owned by St. Paul's Church in Minneapolis, some sixty-six miles from St. Paul and eight miles from St. Croix Falls.

The following description of life at Camp Lawton, with its seventy acres, was published in *The St. John's Evangelist* on July 14, 1934, written by a visitor to the camp identified only as R. R. I.

The boys are up almost with the sun. Out on the field by six o'clock, they are given a period of setting up exercises in order to start the day off right. Then breakfast follows; and we are more than fortunate in having an experienced chef at the Camp to prepare this and the other meals of the day. A scale in the "mess" hall that bears signs of much usage, bears witness to the pride with which the boys 'weigh out' as they leave the table, and watch the extra weight being put on.

Following breakfast the boys put their tents in order and make up their beds; for there is no better place for a boy to learn neatness and orderliness than in a camp where he is encouraged through competition with his buddies in the tent to make his bed a little better than any of the others in order to come out first in the daily inspection.

The morning period is devoted to instruction in swimming, in first aid, in all the little tricks of camp life and woodcraft. The schedule is strenuous, but immediately following dinner there is a rest period provided, followed later in the afternoon by the supervised play period and another swim period. Supper is at six in the evening, and immediately afterwards comes the nightly ceremony of lowering

the flag. Finally 'taps'—the lights are put out, and another glorious day is ended. . . .

An unusually fine recreation building, surmounting a small hill overlooking Deer Lake, is well supplied with good books, ping-pong tables, and other equipment to take care of the boys in the evenings. The fireplace was the site of campfires not held at the beach because of inclement weather.

Parishioner Hank Snyder joined the choir when he was eight years old, in 1938, on the recommendation of a friend. He didn't realize at the time how poor his family was, but it was the camp that drew him to the church and the choir. Camp lasted long enough to get homesick, he recalls, but long enough to get over it. He was eventually a paid tenor in the choir.

The St. Cecilia Girls Choir at first went to Camp Ojiketa, on Green Lake, Chisago City, in 1936, the property of the St. Paul Council of Camp Fire Girls, and later to Christ Church Camp outside Hudson,

The girls choir camp, 1959.

Wisconsin, which wasn't as much fun as the rougher Camp Lawton, which had only canvas tents, latrines, and cold water from pumps. The Christ Church Camp had wooden buildings with sophisticated electric lights. Art Zache was in charge of the ten-day camps for girls.

Parishioner and Adult Choir librarian Dorothy Ek remembers attending girls choir camp under C. Wesley Andersen in 1954. Two or three women did the cooking and the food was good, though the girls had prunes every other morning. After breakfast they had clean-up duty (in the kitchen, at the beach, or the latrines). Beds had to be made and the laundry hung neatly from the clothes line. There were wooden orange crates next to their beds to hold personal items. The campers were required to pass boating tests before being allowed in the rowboats. In the evenings they sang songs around the campfire and told ghost stories. Dorothy remembers that the Rev. Lloyd Gillmett, who occasionally visited the camp, told the best ghost stories.

Parishioners William Gardner White and John (Jack) Hannaford. White was one of two crewmen in a torpedo bomber piloted by George H. W. Bush that was hit by enemy flack during a raid on Chichi-jima in the Japanese archipelago in September 1944. The plane went into a dive. Bush dropped the plane's four 500-pound bombs and flew out to sea. After ordering his crewmen to bail out, he jumped himself shortly afterwards. White and the other crewman were never seen again. Bush was rescued by an American submarine. In 1988 George Herbert Walker Bush won the national election to become the forty-first president of the United States.

chapter ten

THE REV. CONRAD HERBERT GESNER 1933-1945

Depression and War

The Rev. Conrad Herbert Gesner.

PROHIBITION WAS REPEALED on December 5, 1933, two days after the Rev. Conrad Gesner began his tenure as rector. During his ensuing eleven years at St. John's, President Roosevelt inaugurated his New Deal, the Works Progress Administration (WPA) was established, and also the Federal Bureau of Investigation under J. Edgar Hoover. George Gershwin combined black folk idioms and Broadway musical techniques in his "American folk opera" *Porgy and Bess*, and Rodgers and Hammerstein's *Oklahoma!* changed American musical theater forever by combining entertainment with serious subject matter.

World War II erupted on September 1, 1939, when Germany invaded Poland. Six million European Jews were put to death during the Holocaust. Japan attacked Pearl Harbor on December 7, 1941, and the United States declared war on Japan. The United States dropped atomic bombs on Hiroshima and Nagasaki in September 1945 to bring the war to a close. The United Nations was established the following month.

Born in 1901 in Detroit Lakes, Minnesota, Conrad Herbert Gesner was the son of the Rev. Anthon Temple Gesner, who taught at Seabury Divinity School in Faribault. The young Gesner graduated from Trinity College in Hartford, and from General Theological Seminary in New York City. He was ordained to the priesthood in 1927, the same year he married Elizabeth Merrell. He was first named canon missionary at Calvary Cathedral in Sioux Falls, South Dakota, serving from 1927 to 1929, then was rector of Trinity Church, Pierre, from 1929 to 1933.

Although Gesner was not a man of big ideas, he had a remarkable missionary zeal. He did not conceive of any major building projects, apart from the installation of the *Benedicite* window over the main entrance to the church, nor did he imagine large-scale initiatives to raise funds or to mobilize the congregation in some way, apart from the Forward in Service campaign. Indeed, he wrote that "The very high regard which I have for the work done by my predecessors makes me more than confident that no changes in the enterprises or organizations of the parish are needed." He is remembered as a sweet-natured man who was conscientious and unselfish in his duties as rector.

Since from at least 1901, the women of St. Margaret's Guild had acted as the social service arm of the parish, reaching out to the poor and needy of the community without regard for race or color. The women undertook particular cases with passion, helping to provide a simple but decent burial for a young girl of an indigent family, for example, and searching for some-

ST. JOHN'S LOST A VALUED MEMBER when Mrs. Samuel Mairs died in December 1942. The former Mary S. Goodell, Mrs. Mairs was assistant secretary, vice-president, and president of the St. Margaret's Guild, a lieutenant in the parish zone organization, a teacher in the Church School, secretary-treasurer of the Rector's Guild, treasurer of the Woman's Auxiliary, and a member of the board of Sheltering Arms, the orphanage and hospital founded in 1883 by Sister Annette Relf to provide a safe and loving haven for homeless and sick children.

Mrs. Mairs was survived by her husband, Samuel Mairs, and their four children: George, Robert, Thomas, and Mary Ann. Her funeral took place from the family residence at 5 Heather Place.

Mary Mairs's widower, Sam Mairs, was born in Hastings, Minnesota. His mother, Abbie Gardner Mairs, was the daughter of Stephen Gardner, an affluent miller and banker in Hastings, who brought his daughter's husband, Samuel Wycoff Mairs, into his businesses. Stephen Gardner died in 1889 and Samuel W. Mairs two years later, at the young age of thirty-seven. Abbie Mairs moved with her four children—Clara, Sam, Helen, and Agnes—to St. Paul, where the family lived in the Crocus Hill neighborhood and attended St. John's. When he reached nineteen years of age, in 1903, young Sam took a job as a bookkeeper for Archer Daniels Midland Company (ADM), bicycling to work each day. In 1947, having worked his way up through the ranks, Mairs was named chairman of ADM (which today is a global food-processing and commodities-trading firm headquartered in Decatur, Illinois).

one to give a mattress to an elderly couple, he ninety-five and she eighty-six. At one point in 1910 they were supporting some thirty families. They helped with rent and fuel, they located a stove, they gave milk for tubercular children, and in 1918 they supplied nine hundred new and used garments to people who needed them. In 1923 they solicited clothes for five African-American boys, aged between one and four years, who wanted to be baptized on Easter Day but had nothing to wear. For a time, in 1928, they were collaborating with United Charities.

The presidency of St. Margaret's Guild was shouldered over the years by the Misses Nellie Cunningham and Harriet Armstrong, and Mesdames Samuel Mairs,[1] Frederick R. Angell, Joseph Milton, Charles W. Gordon, Jehiel W. Chamberlin, Warren A. Dennis, Frank A. Kempe,[2] Benjamin G. Griggs and Harry S. Keech, among others.

Early in his tenure Gesner made it clear where he himself stood on mission:

> An intense interest in sharing with others a Life which has brought joy to our own lives is generosity of a high order. For that reason I should like to see zeal for the missionary acts of parish, diocese and nation pre-eminent in our activities, no matter what else we may essay to tackle.

He called the Church School a missionary agency that should not be looked on as a step-child, but rather as the heir-apparent. Next to it should be the popularizing of the church services. By "popularizing" he meant "giving to strangers and newcomers to the community an opportunity to know what St. John's has to offer them by way of assistance in developing an abundant life." He wanted more people

GEORGE HARRISON PRINCE and his wife Jessie lived at 965 Summit Ave. Mr. Prince was vice-president of the Merchants National Bank, and vice-president and director of the First National Bank of Cloquet and the First National Bank of Carlton, Minnesota. Mrs. Prince was an active member of the parish, having served as secretary and then vice-president of the Woman's Auxiliary and as treasurer of the St. John's Guild. In 1922 she was elected to the General Executive Committee of the Woman's Auxiliary of the national church. When she died in 1938, she left $2,500 to the Endowment Fund, the same year that an anonymous donor gave another $5,000 to the fund.

PRESENT-DAY CHOIR MEMBER and member of the Music Commission Richard Lyman, a lifelong Episcopalian, was ten-months old in 1934 when his businessman father was killed during the deadly Minneapolis Teamsters strike, leaving four children.

C. ARTHUR LYMAN, forty-four, vice-president of American Ball Company, was an open-shop employer, sworn in for strike duty as a special deputy of the sheriff's office. As the Citizens Alliance retreated down Sixth Street on May 22, during the "Battle of Deputies Run," Arthur Lyman rallied twenty deputies to help the men in the front lines escape. "Give the poor chaps a chance," he called. Within minutes Lyman was trapped in the frenzy of swinging clubs. A small, sickly-looking man in dirty coveralls struck him on the head. Dazed, Lyman was thrown over an automobile and worked over with clubs and fists. His unconscious body dropped to the street by the alley, lying there until an improvised ambulance could pick him up. Lyman lay across the laps of six wounded men as they rode to the hospital."[6] His skull badly fractured, Lyman never regained consciousness. A member of St. Mark's Episcopal Cathedral in Minneapolis, he had planned to attend a national conference of Sunday School superintendents in Indianapolis when the riots intervened.[7]

to be aware of the helpful adjuncts that the parish had in its place of worship: "beauty of building; charm of music; atmosphere of reverence and worship; and a spirit of friendliness toward every fellow-worshipper who comes to her doors." Gesner was not unlike his predecessors in his zeal for mission, but he was the first to articulate it in these terms.

St. John's sent a crop of seven candidates for ordination during Mr. Gesner's rectorship. At the outset of his tenure, the vestry endorsed the candidacy of Arnold M. Ross and a few months later they did the same for Perry M. Gilfillan for the order of deacon. The Rev. Paul C. Weed Jr.,[3] the son of Mr. and Mrs. Paul C. Weed, was ordained deacon in June 1934. In that November the vestry authorized the advance to the priesthood of the Rev. Russell R. Ingersoll, St. John's curate, and later on three more men attended seminary, namely, Ware G. King,[4] Frederick John Wigginton,[5] and George Masuda.

The Depression brought a reduced income to the parish, at

least temporarily. But by the annual meeting in 1934, it appeared the worst was over, as the financial position of the parish was by then materially improved over its condition at the end of 1932. In 1937, as evidence of the rallying financial situation, the vestry raised the curate's salary from $1,200 to $1,500.

JULE M. HANNAFORD SR., was a loyal friend and staunch supporter of St. John's. A native of New Hampshire, he began working at age sixteen for the Vermont Central Railroad as a clerk in the general freight office. From 1872 he was employed by the Northern Pacific Railway in a variety of capacities, including general freight agent, traffic manager, and vice-president; from 1913 to 1920 he was president of the railroad, and later vice-chairman and director. The town of Hannaford, North Dakota, was named after him when it was laid out by the Northern Pacific Railway.

Hannaford's great-granddaughter, present-day parishioner Caroline Jaffray, the fourth generation of her family at St. John's, recounts that her great-grandparents lived in the big grey house at 405 Portland Avenue. By virtue of his girth Hannaford required a triple-sized bathtub. She also recalls that he was a great friend of James. J. Hill. So much so, in fact, that when he happened upon a great idea he would take his carriage four blocks in the middle of the night to chat with Hill at his home on Summit Avenue. Hannaford died in September 1934 at age eighty-three. The burial office was read at the Hannaford home by Bishop Stephen Keeler, assisted by Conrad Gesner.

Jule M. Hannaford Sr. with James J. Hill, 1915.

AT THE ANNUAL MEETING in January 1934, Mr. Gesner addressed the congregation (in terms reminiscent of the Rev. Frederick Butler who had sternly recognized that the character of St. John's congregation was changing):

I feel strongly that St. John's is in a period of transition; one which perhaps began some years ago and which has not yet reached its highest point. But transition it is and the sooner we realize that St. John's has lost certain venerable characteristics and has taken on new but none the less valuable ones, the sooner will be our readiness to take our place in the new scheme of things. St. John's cannot remain in the minds of people solely a fashionable Episcopal Church. It cannot truthfully be looked upon as an institution supported mainly by people of great wealth. The sooner we are ourselves impressed with the dignity of belonging to a parish in which all classes and types of individuals are welcomed and fed, the sooner we shall be awake to the choice opportunity which now confronts St. John's.

Two months later the vestry expressed its concern over the "very startling statistical revelations concerning the percent of the budget given by a very few members of the church," awakening "a degree of apprehension for the day when such large gifts may cease."

Mr. and Mrs. Jule M. Hannaford Jr. Mrs. Hannaford was the former Caroline Rose Schurmeier.

The Endowment Fund, a major concern of the Rev. Frederick Butler, fared rather better during the rectorship of Mr. Gesner. In December 1934, the sum of $2,000 was given by Jule M. Hannaford Jr. and Foster Hannaford in memory of their mother and father. Caroline Weed Fobes donated $5,000 to the fund as a memorial to Albert Randall Moore,[8] for use in parochial work. An additional bequest came from the estate of Emma A. Gray, as well as a contribution from Mrs. Theodosia Cary Langford, so that by March 1937 the fund had doubled in three years. By early 1938 it stood at about $40,000.

Senior warden Jule M. Hannaford Jr. claimed that the fund would have to be increased by about $100,000 within the next decade if the church were to maintain its present standard of service and position in the community. Nonetheless, a gift of $1,500 in November 1941 from the will of a member prompted the vestry to write "there is something seriously wrong somewhere when so many parishioners are failing to adequately remember the church, if they remember it at all.

There is a very real and serious problem here." As if in response, the will of Mrs. Frank B. Kellogg included a bequest to St. John's of $5,000 and in 1943 the estate of Miss Mary Baldy left $1,000 to the fund. Mr. and Mrs. Gus Seeger contributed $2,000 at Christmas 1945, and choir mother Elizabeth Hensel gave $525 in war bonds in thanks for all that Mr. Gesner's rectorship had meant to her.

Mrs. Jule M. Hannaford Jr. was appointed a member of the National Committee on Volunteer Services of the American Red Cross in 1944. Active in several capacities at St. John's, Mrs. Hannaford frequently donated flowers for the altar on Sundays, and after her death flowers were often given in memory of her and her husband.

In 1934 a children's altar was given by Mrs. Frank E. Ward, to be known as the Little Sanctuary and situated at the head of the east aisle. Its architect was Harold C. Whitehouse of Spokane, who designed the Cathedral of St. John the Evangelist in that city, the church of Bishop Edward M. Cross. It was given as a memorial to Mrs. Ward's son, Lawrence, who died at age ten in November 1915 and was intended as a special place for the children and young people of the congregation to worship. Coincidental as it was tragic, an accident took the life of seventeen-year-old Howard Comstock, brother of Dorothy Comstock, around the time the Little Sanctuary was dedicated in November 1934. Howard grew up at St. John's and was a choirboy and acolyte at the time of his death.

Reine Myers (the widow of Paul N. Myers) and her son John Myers gave a new Ford for Mr. Gesner's use in January 1935. Three years later the car was replaced by a new 1938 model Chevrolet. Still later the Chevrolet was succeeded by another Ford. When Mr. Gesner left the parish upon his election as Coadjutor Bishop of South Dakota in 1945, the vestry transferred the Ford to him, relinquishing any equity it might have in it.

In March 1936 the men and boys choir gave the first of several Sunday evening broadcasts from the studio of radio station WTCN,[9] a compliment to Fairclough and his singers. Conrad

Gesner delivered a brief message on the program known as The Church Music Appreciation Hour, under the supervision of Mrs. Paul G. Bremer, the prime mover in the effort to bring good religious music to Twin Cities audiences.

In the late 1930s St. John's developed a cooperative relationship with St. Philip's African-American congregation. St. John's St. Cecilia Choir was met with a warm welcome when it sang for a Sunday service in their church at the corner of Mackubin and Aurora in February 1938. St. Philip's used St. John's Parish House for a style show presented in 1938 by their Vitality Club. The auditorium was also the venue for two recitals in 1939, one by a talented young soprano, Dorothy Martin, a member of St. Philip's choir, and another by baritone Lewis I. Williams. The congregation held occasional chicken dinners in the auditorium, as fundraisers for the parish, and in 1940 the Men's Club presented a style show of women's clothing that attracted 250 people.

The Rev. Russell Ingersoll[10] announced in April 1936 that he had accepted a call to St. Paul's Church in Bellingham, Washington. In September the Rev. Tom Greenwood, an Englishman, was named to succeed him as curate, but he in turn left only a year later, to accept an appointment as curate at the church in Greenhill, Harrow, England. By March 1938 the Rev. Thomas Mathers had become Gesner's new assistant. He remained for two years, leaving for a church in South Dakota in April 1940.

In 1936 a room on the third floor of the Parish House on Portland Avenue was given over to the St. Paul Family Nursing Service for office purposes. The two nurses stationed there made home visits where needed through that section of the city. And a photo in The Saturday Evening Post in its November 7 issue that year[11] showed workers from the Works Progress Administration (WPA)[12] engaged in making tennis nets for playgrounds in the gymnasium of the Club House.

In the same year, Mrs. Maude Grant made a gift to remodel the chapel. Nearly the entire interior was replaced, with pews added to seat thirty-five people, and four wooden trusses and rafters on the ceiling above. Architect Clarence H. Johnston drew the plans.

The children and young adults of the parish were no strangers to tragedy during the Gesner years. On July 9, 1936, Channing Seabury, the twenty-one year-old son of Mrs. John E. Seabury, was killed while piloting his airplane over the Minneapolis airport. A year later Dr. and Mrs. Edward C. Emerson lost their infant daughter, Nancy Lou Emerson, in a drowning accident. In November 1940 St. Paul socialite M. Creighton Churchill died at age thirty-three, having married Clotilde Irvine[13] only a few years earlier at St. John's in 1936, and leaving a small daughter, Olivia Ann. Five-year-old Charles Guerdon Guyer, the son of Mr. and Mrs. Reynolds Guyer, died in December 1944 after an illness of several weeks.

MEMBERS OF THE ORDWAY FAMILY have had close connections with St. John's over the years. Lucius Pond Ordway, the patriarch of the Ordway family, was a president and early investor in Minnesota Mining and Manufacturing (later 3M), which was founded in Two Harbors, Minnesota, in 1902. In 1910 Ordway moved the company to St. Paul. The family lived at 400 Summit Avenue. Ordway was also a partner in the wholesale plumbing company of Crane and Ordway, and was instrumental in the building of the St. Paul Hotel. While Lucius himself was not a member of St. John's, his son Richard (Dick) Ordway married Gladys Watson Ford at St. John's in April 1926. Their three children, Gladys Alexandra, Mary Pond (Pondie), and Robert Ford, were baptized at their summer home on White Bear Lake in December 1936, and later confirmed at St. John's. Pondie Ordway and David Strong Nicholson were married at St. John's in September 1950. Their four sons include Ford Nicholson, whose family are current members.

The Kent Street lobby in the parish house was given in memory of David and Pondie Nicholson, and Dick and Gladys Ordway, by the Nicholson Family Foundation. Pondie's sister, Gladys Alexandra (Alex) Ordway Bjorklund and her son, Edwin McCarthy, and his family are also parishioners of St. John's.

Other members of the Ordway family had St. John's connections as well. In November 1945 Bishop Conrad Gesner baptized Sally Gilman Ordway and John Ordway Irvine at St. John's. Robert Ford Ordway was buried from the church in August 1953, as was Mildred Wurtele Ordway in June 1978. The Ordway Center for the Performing Arts is a gift to St. Paul initiated and supported by the Ordway family.

Ford Nicholson's confirmation class, April 28, 1968. Back row: Jorge L'Acosta, David Griggs, Phil Brown, Ford Nicholson. Middle row: Denis O'Pray (teacher), Dawn LaMotte, Gail Benepe, Suzanne Lilly, Christine Andrews, Karen Johnston, Betty Boody, Perrin Lilly (teacher). Front row: Karen Harri, Leta Glenn, Sara Stryker, Laurel Kartarik.

The Rev. Douglas H. Atwill, for thirteen years the rector of St. Clement's Episcopal Church, was consecrated the sixth bishop of North Dakota at the larger St. John's church on January 21, 1937. Ten bishops and one archbishop attended the impressive service. Atwill assumed his new post, as one writer put it, under clouds of depression, drought, and dust.

May and Clarence Johnston, ca. 1925.

ARCHITECT CLARENCE JOHNSTON was buried from his home at 2 Crocus Hill on New Year's Day, 1937. His wife May had died in 1932. Two of the Johnston children, Helen (Mrs. Roger Kennedy Jr.), and Harrison (Jimmy) Johnston, were members of St. John's. Johnston's practice spanned fifty-four years, and he designed more buildings—in a wide range of styles—than any other figure in Minnesota's history. The most sought-after architect for two generations of St. Paul's upper classes, he designed forty-two residences on Summit Avenue, the best-preserved Victorian boulevard in America. For thirty years he also served as Minnesota State Architect. His utilitarian buildings on thirty-five state-owned sites set new standards for institutional complexes. These campuses included the Stillwater State Prison and Gillette State Hospital for Crippled Children. Johnston's son, Harrison Johnston, was a celebrated golfer who won the Minnesota Amateur title seven years in a row: 1921–27. In 1929 he came home to a ticker-tape parade in downtown St. Paul after winning the U.S. Amateur at Pebble Beach, California. Jimmy Johnston served in both World Wars and is buried at Fort Snelling National Cemetery. He was elected to the Minnesota Golf Hall of Fame in 1988.

The ticker-tape parade on September 18, 1929, that greeted golfer Harrison (Jimmy) Johnston when he returned home to St. Paul after winning the U.S. Amateur title at Pebble Beach, California.

LOUIS W. HILL JR., also called "Louie,"[15] was the eldest son of Louis Sr. and Maud Hill. He attended Yale University, Balliol College at Oxford University, and the American Institute of Banking. Louie Jr. married Dorothy Millett at St. John's in 1929. After their divorce, he married Elsi Fors in 1943, and together they had three children: Louis Fors, Johanna, and Mari.

In 1926 Hill went to work for the Great Northern Railway, of which he later became president. In the same year he entered the employ of the First National Bank of St. Paul, eventually serving as board director and major shareholder. He also worked for the First Trust Saint Paul. From 1948 to 1981 he was a trustee of the Great Northern Iron Ore Properties. From 1937 to 1951 he was District 40 state representative in the Minnesota legislature. In 1950 he founded the North Oaks Company to develop the Hill family's North Oaks farm and was its major stockholder, president, and board chair.

LOUIS W. HILL SR. was insrumental in reviving the St. Paul Winter Carnival in 1916. Pictured above on snowshoes, with one of 108 carnival queens that year, Hill decried: "Men who cannot forget their business and get out and take part in the winter carnival are not the kind of men we want in St. Paul!" Monster slides were constructed on Ramsey Hill and Cedar Street. Hill "took the first spin down the Dayton's Bluff slide, formally opened the Jefferson neighborhood slide, and declared the Harriet Island slide 'the prince of them all.'"[14]

Louis Hill Jr. was also the founder, board director, and president of the Grotto Foundation, whose mission is to benefit society by improving the education and the economic, physical, and social well-being of citizens, with a special focus on families and culturally diverse groups. Hill was also a member of the Jerome Foundation, and board director, president, chair and trustee of the Northwest Area Foundation, also Hill family foundations. A member of the vestry, Louis W. Hill Jr. was buried from St. John's in 1995.

SCOUTING WAS BECOMING POPULAR at St. John's during the 1930s. In 1937 the Cub Pack, founded two years earlier, had sixty-five members with a waiting list. In the same year, Dr. Louis M. Benepe, a dentist, was chairman of the troop committee for Troop 2 of the St. Paul Area Council of the Boy Scouts of America. Art Zache was scoutmaster.

Dr. Louis M. Benepe Jr.

Alfred J. Jennings and Ware King, later a seminarian from St. John's. Boy Scouts operated the Golden Rule department store on Seventh Street in St. Paul for a day in 1933.

The many guilds at St. John's enjoyed a cherished independence from the vestry over the years, sometimes doing work, maintaining their own checking accounts, and raising and spending funds, without the vestry's knowledge or oversight. In 1937, for example, the Chancel Guild surprised Mr. Gesner when he discovered a painter at work upon the former rector's office, which had not been used as such since the Parish House re-opened. The last privileged vestige of guild independence came to an end in 2011 when the Women of St. John's, after years running the Huge Sale, spent the last of their treasury on the re-upholstering and refurbishing of the Fireside Room. Thereafter all funds at St. John's fell under the control of the parish treasurer.

Navy Capt. Henry L. Wyman, who married Margaret Myers at St. John's, had the honor of bringing the body of the Unknown Soldier home from France after the First World War. When Wyman died in July 1937, he left several survivors, including his sister Mrs. Donald H. Myers, the sister-in-law of Margaret Myers Wyman. His funeral was held at the Washington National Cathedral, with burial in Arlington National Cemetery.

National leader and St. John's revered communicant, Frank Billings Kellogg, died in 1937 at the age of eighty-one. His funeral took place at St. John's, and was attended by representatives of state and business, with Mr. Gesner officiating, assisted by Bishop Stephen Keeler, the Rev. Francis L. Palmer, and Gesner's father, the Rev. Anthon Gesner. Kellogg's body lay in state at the Minnesota Capitol rotunda before eventual burial in the Washington National Cathedral, whose construction he had supported and overseen. Kellogg left $100,000 to the cathedral in his will.

In 1937, Mrs. Conrad Gesner began to disappear from the pages of The St. John's Evangelist, her relationship with her husband having deteriorated to the point of separation. The Ramsey County Courthouse has no record of a divorce decree. In any case, the Gesners' three daughters—Joan, Rosalind, and Nancy—were cared for after the departure of their mother by a governess and by grandmother Blanche Louise Gesner on her extended visits from Connecticut. If Mr. Gesner's marital status had been thought problematic in the church hierarchy, his election and consecration to the bishopric, in 1945, would surely have been impossible.

Although the exact year is lost to memory, local lore has it that one Christmas Eve either Louis W. Hill Sr., president and board chairman of the Great Northern Railway, or writer F. Scott Fitzgerald,[16] in a festive mood and well primed, set foot into St. John's during the candlelight service, carrying a trumpet. The culprit was accompanied by a chimney sweep named Snooky Norton. The two made their merry way up the aisle and the trumpeter ascended the steps of the pulpit, sounding forth a note on his raised instrument, likely in the manner of a herald angel. The tale is so remarkable that it must be true, whether it was Hill or Fitzgerald.

Louis W. ("Louie") Hill Sr., a Roman Catholic like his mother, was the second son of James J. Hill and took over his father's Great Northern Railway. Louie's wife, Maud Van Cortlandt Taylor Hill, was an Episcopalian and an active member of St. John's. Their four children—Louis Warren Hill Jr., Maud Van Cortlandt, James Jerome, and Cortlandt Taylor—were raised at St. John's. The family lived at 260 Summit Avenue,[17] the home that James J. Hill built as a wedding gift for his son and daughter-in-law.

THE NEW BENEDICITE WINDOW over the Portland entrance to the church was installed in October 1938 and dedicated in December at Morning Prayer, with the St. Cecilia Choir seated in the gallery, and the men and boys in the chancel. When it came time for the Benedicite to be sung, the clergy went to the foot of the window, whereupon the hymn "Angel voices, ever singing" was sung in a new arrangement by George Fairclough. The window's stone tracery and small sections of glass were the gift of a single donor, with the remainder of the window made possible by eleven other gifts,[18] ranging from $175 to $250, given in memory of Minnie E. Stanton, Lemuel and Florella Grange Dyer, Theodosia P. Cary, Frank Hilliard Barton, Lucy Martin Warner, Nancy Emerson, Henry A. and Lucinda Gilman, and William Fellows Peet.

The curate, the Rev. Thomas Mathers, took over as superintendent of the Church School in September 1938, and married parishioner Henrietta Keech the next year in July 1939. Henrietta had sung in the girls choir and taught in the Church School. The Rev. and Mrs. Mathers left the parish in April 1940 for a parish in South Dakota. In September he was succeeded at St. John's by the Rev. Alexander M. Wood as curate, who lived with his wife and family in the remodeled apartment of the Parish House. Wood remained until Easter Sunday in 1944, when he began a tenure at Ascension Church in Stillwater.

Minnie E. (Mrs. Benjamin Irving) Stanton, for forty-eight years a member of the parish, served in nearly every capacity in which parish women could serve, taking great interest in the Episcopal Church and in its every activity. At the time of her death she was a member of the St. John's Guild. Bishop Stephen Keeler officiated at her funeral on June 11, 1938, assisted by the parish clergy. She left $4,600 to the Endowment Fund.

The Parish House was the scene of religious instruction by outside organizations in 1938 and 1939. In October 1938 the vestry authorized the temporary use of a room for the religious instruction of twenty-five children of Greek parentage, under the auspices of the Greek Orthodox congregation that as yet had no church of its own in St. Paul. In September 1939 the vestry accepted a request by the Ramsey County Sunday School Association to use the auditorium each Thursday from 8:30 a.m. to 3:15 p.m. to provide weekday religious instruction for children from the Irving and Webster schools for twenty-four weeks.

Through the years of the Depression, St. John's Parish House thus served useful purposes in the community. Indeed Edward Lee Sheppard noted in his Second Fifty Years: The Diocese of Minnesota and the Diocese of Duluth from 1907 to 1957 that through the depression years to 1939, "virtually no increase in communicant strength was registered by St. Paul parishes." But as the bustling activity at the Parish House indicates, "St. John the Evangelist maintained its neighborhood program, and remained by far the strongest parish despite the fact that it ceased to grow."[19]

Early in 1940 Mrs. Frank B. Kellogg met with pre-eminent stained glass artist Charles J. Connick and made arrangements

Miss Vivian Grace Gibson, left, was a land patent attorney for the State of Minnesota with a fondness for knee-high lace-up bicycle boots. Miss Carolyn Punderson, right, chaired a Red Cross unit at St. John's; more than a hundred women were enrolled and sewed garments, knit sweaters, and prepared surgical dressings.

for the manufacture of a clerestory window in memory of her brother, Major Paul Burns Cook, to be installed on the west side in June.

On April 28, 1940, there occurred a ceremony of singular significance in St. John's baptistery, where Mr. Gesner baptized three grandchildren of Mr. and Mrs. Horace H. Irvine: Horace Hills II, son of Mr. and Mrs. Thomas E. Irvine; Clotilde "Clover" Irvine, daughter of Mr. and Mrs. William Huntington Fobes Jr.; and Olivia Anne, daughter of Mr. and Mrs. Creighton Churchill.

Parishioner Nathaniel P. Langford died suddenly in April 1940, leaving his wife Theodosia Cary Langford and five offspring. A nephew of western historian, vigilante, businessman and bureaucrat Nathaniel Pitt Langford (*Diary of the Washburn Expedition to the Yellowstone and Firehole Rivers In the Year 1870*), St. John's Langford had been a member of the parish Standing Committee, the vestry, and a delegate to Diocesan Council. His son Nathaniel "Tan" P. Langford Jr. also served on the vestry.

In 1940 several parishioners were elected to positions in the diocese. In May Mrs. Kenneth G. Brill was elected president of the diocesan Woman's Auxiliary, a distinct honor both for her and the parish. The next month, at the 83rd Diocesan Convention, Benjamin G. Griggs was elected to the Bishop's Council and Jule M. Hannaford Jr. was elected a trustee of the diocese and an alternate to General Convention. Conrad Gesner was re-elected to the Standing Committee and named a delegate to General Convention.

Miss Vivian Grace Gibson, a practicing attorney since 1929, and a member of the Business and Professional Woman's Guild at St. John's, sought election to the St. Paul City Council in 1940 and became a land patent attorney for the State of Minnesota in 1943. She was fond of formidable knee-length lace-up bicycle boots, made of black leather and fabric with metal hooks and buckles, and marked on the sole with the manufacturer's label "Heffelfinger" stamped over three intersecting bicycle wheels. After her death in November 1954 a private communion set was given to the parish in her memory by family and friends.

After war broke out in Europe, the auditorium in the Parish House became the site of the church's newly organized Red Cross unit. Some sixty-five women joined the effort to produce garments and surgical dressings for the world war, even before the United States itself became engaged. Mrs. Newell H. Clapp Jr. chaired the unit, and by February 1941 there were 149 women enrolled, making garments, knitting sweaters, and preparing surgical dressings. Mrs. Clapp was succeeded in 1944 by Miss Carolyn Punderson.

Two former choirboys came to St. John's for a Sunday visit in the summer of 1940, both of them having become professional church musicians. William Ripley Dorr was organist and choirmaster of St. Luke's Episcopal Church in Long Beach, California, where he conducted a choir of men and boys that was often heard and seen in Hollywood movies.

PARISHIONER ROBERT BINGER, a gentleman of the old school, came to St. John's from St. Clement's Church because he was fond of Conrad Gesner. The latter married him and his fiancée, Betty Wann, at St. John's on April 6, 1942. After graduating from the forestry schools at the University of Minnesota and Yale University, Mr. Binger worked in the logging industry in Idaho until enlisting in the Navy, some six months into his marriage.

Binger was sent to an aerial photography school in Washington, D.C. and eventually served in the amphibious forces at Pearl Harbor and Okinawa. He produced the map of Iwo Jima for use by the battleships bombing the island, with the enemy defenses clearly marked, and was present below the site of the storied raising of the U.S. flag there in 1945, immortalized in the famous photograph by Joe Rosenthal.

Bob returned to his job in Idaho, where Betty Binger was in her sixth month of pregnancy with their first child. Betty fell on some ice and gave premature birth to a son who was blind and mentally retarded. It was a terrible setback for them, and Betty would be in the hospital for a long time. The couple had three sons: Theodore (deceased), Thomas W., and R. Bruce.

Back in the Twin Cities, Mr. Binger was hired by the Minnesota and Ontario Paper Company and remained for twenty-two years, working much of that time in International Falls. Cherishing the goal of becoming vice-president of operations, he achieved his dream in 1962. After the company was purchased by Boise Cascade, he became an assistant to the president of the company. He was then hired by the Northern Pacific Railroad, serving for thirteen years as vice-president for natural resources. Bob's beloved Betty died in 1984. The Rev. Grayson Clary read her funeral service at St. John's.

Mr. Binger married a second time, his wife's name was Mary, and this marriage ended in divorce. Their children are Robert M. and Erica A. Binger. Bob lived into his nineties. He was an exceedingly generous benefactor to the parish and was buried from St. John's in 2012.

Betty and Bob Binger on their wedding day in 1942.

Wedding guests Forrest and Nancy Clarkson Daniels.

The other visitor was Alfred Greenfield, who entered St. John's choir when he was nine years old in 1911, later becoming alto soloist and assistant organist. For sixteen years, he was organist of Fifth Church of Christ, Scientist, in New York City and also served nearly as long on the faculty of New York University, where he was associate professor of music.

During his rectorship, Mr. Gesner held a number of important positions outside the parish. He was a trustee at St. Mary's Hall in Faribault and at Breck School in St. Paul. From 1935 to 1938 he served as chairman of the Forward Movement in the diocese. In February 1937 he was chaplain of the Minnesota State Senate, and in 1940, chair of the interdenominational State Pastors' Conference that was held at St. Mark's Episcopal Church[20] in Minneapolis. He served on the Bishop's Council and was a deputy to General Convention in 1937 and 1940.

The funeral of Miss Annie Isabelle Carpenter was conducted jointly by Bishop Keeler and Mr. Gesner on September 14, 1941. A pioneer member of the parish, Miss Carpenter was generous in providing altar flowers and contributing to St. Margaret's Guild, and zealous for the missionary work of the church at home and abroad. Her will specified a bequest of $2,000 for the Endowment Fund, which now amounted to nearly $60,000.

A synod of the Province of the Northwest took place at St. John's on October 7-9, 1941, attracting twelve bishops and other lay and clerical delegates from its member dioceses, and demanding all the resources of the parish, its members, and its guilds. Most of the delegates had lodging in hotels, with the Commodore Hotel serving as synod headquarters, but the bishops were entertained in the homes of parishioners. Arrangements included a motor corps, headed by Mrs. Chauncey M. Griggs, to transport delegates to and from their hotels and the train depot. Mrs. Louis W. Hill hosted a luncheon for the bishops at her home, and Mrs. Kenneth G. Brill, chair of the Woman's Auxiliary of the diocese, arranged dinner for everyone at the St. Paul Athletic Club—the gala social event of the gathering. Mrs. Frank Kellogg entertained three hundred guests for tea in her home.

Bishop Stephen E. Keeler of the Diocese of Minnesota was the president of the province and presided at the synod meetings. Bishop Douglas H. Atwill of the Diocese of North Dakota was elected to succeed him, the Rev. Conrad Gesner was elected secretary, and parishioner Benjamin G. Griggs was named lay trustee of Seabury-Western Seminary.

ELEVEN VALIANT MEN from the parish did not return home after their service in the Second World War. *The St. John's Evangelist* reported in January 16, 1943, that Russell Bluhm, of the U.S. Navy, who was confirmed at the church in 1939, had been killed in enemy action while aboard the USS *New Orleans*.

Former choir librarian, Capt. Hollister Boody, was first reported missing in action in North Africa. In September 1943 the parish newsletter reported that his death had occurred during the Sicilian campaign.

On September 10, 1943, Dr. and Mrs. Louis M. Benepe Jr., of Dayton Avenue, received notification that their son Lt. Louis M. Benepe III, a bomber pilot with the Army Air Corps, was reported missing in action while engaged in bombing operations over Europe. His plane was shot down over Germany in August 1943. In October he was located in a prison in Germany, where he spent twenty-one months.

Lt. David Hallam Armstrong, a pilot in the U.S. Army Air Corps, died following an airplane accident in November 1943. He had participated in every youth organization of the parish and held office in many of them. A prayer desk to his memory was placed in the chancel by his family and by members of the Brotherhood of St. Andrew.

In June 1944, parishioner Lt. Kay Todd Jr., a paratrooper with the American forces in Normandy, was killed some days after D-day. The son of Mr. and Mrs. Kay Todd, he was a member of St. John's from boyhood and was active in its youth activities. His widow, Nancy Todd, made

LOUIS M. BENEPE'S courageous "Hell's Angels" combat crew. This photo is dated August 1943.

Benepe was captured on August 31 after completing six credited combat missions.

Seven dispatched (6 credited) missions flown by 1st Lt. Louis M. Benepe:

JULY 4, 1943, TO HEROYA, NORWAY
JULY 17, 1943, TO HANOVER, GERMANY
JULY 25, 1943, TO HAMBURG, GERMANY
AUG 16, 1943, TO PARIS, FRANCE
AUG 17, 1943, TO SCHWEINFURT, GERMANY
AUG 19, 1943, TO GILZE-RIJEN, NETHERLANDS
AUGUST 31,1943, TO AMIENS-GILSEY, FRANCE

(Back L-R) 2Lt Richard A. Sagar, 2Lt Raymond J. Cassidy, 2Lt Aubrey L. Emerson, 1Lt Louis M. Benepe, 1Lt Arni L. Sumarlidason, (Front L-R) T/Sgt George W. Buske, S/Sgt Edward J. Cassidy, T/Sgt Stanley J. Backiel, T/Sgt Francis H. Stender, T/Sgt Bruce R. Clemens, T/Sgt Richard C. Grimm.

arrangements for a new memorial window to be placed in the clerestory in his memory.[21] Lt. Todd's father was an attorney with the firm of Todd and Kerr.

Lt. Robert C. Shepard of the 116th infantry of the 29th Division, which was cited by Gen. Omar Bradley for heroic action while landing in heavily defended sectors of France on D-day, was killed in action in Normandy on July 12, 1944. The son of parishioners Mr. and Mrs. George M. Shepard, Lt. Shepard had been baptized and confirmed at St. John's and was an active communicant. The Shepards also lost a second son, William M. Shepard, during his military service, though no information regarding his death is at hand. His wife gave birth to their daughter Jean Anne Shepard in 1945.

In September 1944 parishioner William Gardner White, was one of two crewmen flying in a plane piloted by George H. W. Bush, a Grumman Avenger that Bush had named *Barbara*, after his wife. White was the gunnery officer on the flight, a last-minute addition to the crew. The torpedo bomber was hit by flack in a raid on Chichi-jima, in the Japanese archipelago, and went into a dive, but "Bush managed to drop its four 500-pound bombs and fly out to sea. He ordered his two crewmen to bail out, and he jumped shortly after that."[22] He never saw White or the other crewman again. Bush was rescued by an American submarine and rejoined his squadron two months later. In 1989 he became the forty-first president of the United States.

On October 2, 1944, word was received that Henry N. Klein Jr., son of Dr. and Mrs. Henry N. Klein, had been killed in maneuvers here in the U.S.[23]

On November 11, 1944, *The St. John's Evangelist* reported that Lt. Robert Machray Ward had died of natural causes at a naval base in the Southwest Pacific, having been in that area but a few weeks. The son of Mrs. Frank E. Ward, Robert was a member of the parish from infancy, and was survived by his wife, Dorothy Simpson Ward,[24] and their four-year-old son Frank.

Parishioner Capt. Edwin Alness Daugherty died December 16, 1944, while in training at Panama City, Florida, where

he had been stationed with the Army Air Forces. Daugherty was baptized at St. John's; his mother, May Alness Daugherty, held several offices in the St. Margaret's Guild.

The date is not available, but 1st Lt. Charles L. Weeks "was shot in the back while walking outside the barracks during an air raid while a POW at Oflag XIII-B, Hammelburg, Germany. Permission had been granted by the German camp commandant to allow prisoners to be outside for the purpose of going to the latrine during air raids. . . . Apparently the orders to allow men outdoors during the alerts were not sent down to all guards, for Lt. Weeks was killed instantly by a shot from close range, while strolling towards the latrine with his hands in his pockets." Without hesitation a chaplain ran outside to attend to him.[25]

Major John H. Myers, eventually a prominent member of St. John's, had enlisted in the military as a private in October 1940 and returned to the country in the fall of 1945 after spending about five years in service overseas, mainly in Australia. He received many honors, including the Silver Star, the Bronze Star, the Purple Heart, and three Presidential citations. Myers was seriously wounded twice in New Guinea and was left for dead on a jungle track, but was rescued by an Australian sergeant. He conducted religious services several times in the absence of a chaplain and would read to his men from a copy of the *Book of Common Prayer* that was given to him by the chief chaplain of the Australian Imperial Force. Returning from overseas, Major Myers was appointed by Bishop Cross of Spokane to take charge of a mission in that city for a time. Returning to St. Paul he was commissioned by Bishop Keeler as a lay reader, authorizing him to read services and give addresses in the diocese.

Not all of St. John's service members were men. Ruth Benepe, the daughter of Mr and Mrs. Louis M. Benepe and the sister of Dr. James L. Benepe, was enlisted in the WAVES (Women Accepted for Volunteer Emergency Service) and returned home after the war.

AFTER FORTY-TWO YEARS of service under five rectors, organist and choirmaster George Fairclough retired in 1943. He had founded the department of organ, piano, and theory

BENJAMIN GLYDE GRIGGS was the son of Chauncey Milton Griggs and the former Mary Chafee Wells. He married Martha Dodgson Baker and together they had five children: Elizabeth Taggart (Clark), Martha Baker (Drewry), Benjamin Glyde Jr., Juliana Stevens (Marty), and Mary Wells (Mack). Griggs was executive vice-president and treasurer of the Food Manufacturing and Distributing Company and later executive vice-president, treasurer, and president of Griggs, Cooper and Company. He was also a member of the St. Paul City Planning Board and the St. Paul Board of Zoning. During World War I, Griggs was awarded the *Croix de Guerre* for his service with the American Field Service with the French army. He was a trustee of the St. Paul Institute, vice-president and director of the St. Paul Association of Commerce, and a member of the special gifts committee of the St. Paul Community Chest. A senior warden at St. John's, he was a member of the Standing Committee of the Diocese and a trustee of Seabury-Western Theological Seminary.

Martha Dodgson Baker Griggs, right, with friends (left to right) Elizabeth Griggs (Nichols), Mrs. Roger Cudworth, Elizabeth Ottis, and Maud Hill in 1924.

at Macalester College and for twenty years was organist and professor of music at the University of Minnesota. His long list of published compositions, including *Communion Service in A-flat* and *Benedicite in G*, were sung in Episcopal churches across the country. He was a Fellow in the American Guild of Organists and founded the Minnesota Chapter of the AGO in 1910 at St. John's. He also served as president of the Minnesota Music Teachers Association. Long considered the dean of organists and choirmasters in Minnesota, Fairclough died at age eighty-five in March 1954 in California.

Fairclough was succeeded in the post by C. Wesley Andersen who had charge of the music department at Roosevelt High School in Minneapolis. The vestry paid him $150 monthly. Andersen had a long and successful tenure at St. John's. He retained his church position when, in April 1957, he was appointed superintendent of music for the Minneapolis Public Schools. His tenure at St. John's came to an end in 1972.

A preaching mission titled "A Good Earthquake" took place from September 28 to October 2, 1943, given by the

Rev. Michael Coleman, from All Hallows by the Tower in London, England. Established in the year 675, All Hallows is the oldest congregation in the City of London, narrowly surviving the Great Fire in 1666 and gutted by German bombers in World War II. It was St. John's first such mission in seventeen years. Mr. Gesner estimated that over 550 people attended each service, partially as the result of a canvass of the entire church membership prior to the mission, sixty parishioners visiting all the member households.[26]

In March 1944 a new stained glass window was placed in the clerestory on the east side, the second window from the chancel arch, by Mrs. Francis J. Ottis in memory of her sister, Clara (Mrs. Frank) Kellogg. It is directly opposite the window given by Mrs. Kellogg in memory of her brother. During August 1944 the memorial window given by Fred Baldy in memory of his sisters, Miss Sarah and Miss Mary Baldy, was placed in the narthex of the church, at the foot of the east aisle.

The rectory at 581 Portland Avenue that housed three of St. John's rectors since 1916 was sold in May 1945 for $6,500 to a Mr. and Mrs. James H. Battersby. The vestry then purchased for a rectory the home belonging to Charles M. Power[27] at 751 Goodrich Avenue.

Early in 1945, after some eleven years as rector of St. John's, the Rev. Conrad Herbert Gesner was elected Bishop Coadjutor of the Missionary District of South Dakota.[28] Parish archivist Frederick Myers wrote: "While the attention of the world was focused on epic events in Europe, St. John's had its own epic event in the spring of 1945. The death of President Roosevelt on April 12, the suicide of Adolf Hitler on April 30, and the imminent end of the war in Europe were not enough to prevent St. John's from hosting the consecration of Mr. Gesner on May 2. Admission was by ticket only.

Over a hundred clergymen were present, among them Indian, Negro, Caucasian, Japanese, and Romanian Orthodox representatives, hailing from Wisconsin, North and South Dakota, and all parts of Minnesota. The presenters were re-

tired Bishop McElwain of Minnesota, and Bishop Atwill of North Dakota. The Rt. Rev. Henry St. George Tucker, the presiding bishop, was chief consecrator, with Bishop Stephen Keeler of Minnesota and Bishop W. Blair Roberts of South Dakota serving as co-consecrators. In all, ten bishops were in attendance, and ten committees from St. John's took care of the arrangements. St. John's beloved Art Zache was assistant master of ceremonies. Reynolds Guyer was chairman of the committee on arrangements. Dr. James L. Benepe organized a first-aid station, complete with a nurse, in the undercroft. The presiding bishop commented afterward, "Never before have I participated in a consecration service where arrangements before, during and after the service were as well planned and carried out."

Bishop Gesner served as Coadjutor Bishop of South Dakota until 1954, whereupon he succeeded diocesan Bishop W. Blair Roberts as sixth bishop of the diocese, with jurisdiction. During his tenure the growth of Native American and non-native American clergy flourished. In 1967 Bishop Gesner was adopted into a Dakota Indian tribe, and given the name: First of the Eagles. Upon his retirement in 1970, he moved to Longmeadow, Massachusetts.

In December 1945, thirty-two members of St. John's choir took part in the St. Paul Municipal Christmas Choral Pageant that was held in the St. Paul Auditorium before a reported audience of 12,500 people. Mrs. Paul G. Bremer directed the production. The singing of the massed choirs was accompanied by forty members of the Minneapolis Symphony Orchestra.

Following Bishop Gesner's departure the parish cobbled together a patchwork of clergy who served the parish as preachers and pastors until the new rector, the Rev. Lloyd Russell Gillmett, began in February 1946. Formerly of St. Paul's in Duluth, Gillmett was already known to many of St. John's parishioners because he had preached there and elsewhere in the area on a number of occasions over the years. Gillmett took up his residence in the new rectory at 751 Goodrich Avenue.

ST. PAUL BUSINESSMAN J. GEORGE SMITH died at the Church Home in St. Paul in February 1945. A devoted worker at St. John's, he served on the vestry and was chairman of many important committees. The gallery of the church and the stairs leading to it were planned and executed when Smith was the chairman of the Property Committee. The lighting fixtures that illuminated the balcony were his gift, as was the chiming system heard each Sunday morning from the tower.[29] He owned the J. George Smith Confectionery on East Sixth St.

Parishioner J. George Smith. His popular J. George Smith Confectionary in downtown St. Paul at 108 East Sixth Street, pictured here about 1910, was a favorite gathering place with small, round marble-topped tables, and counters piled high with colorful candies and fruit from the French Riviera. His specialty was homemade ice cream. "My favorite was peach, with great chunks of fresh fruit all through it," remembered one woman from her girlhood.

Men here, men there, men on the rafters—building St. John's Memorial Parish House in July 1955.

chapter eleven

THE REV. LLOYD RUSSELL GILLMETT 1946-1959

Three Houses Moved

THE SURRENDER OF the Japanese Empire had brought World War II to an end on September 2, 1945. During the thirteen-year rectorship of Rev. Lloyd Gillmett, the American Marshall Plan would begin rebuilding European economies, and the United Nations would create the state of Israel. Winston Churchill gave his *Iron Curtain* speech in 1946, the same year that Benjamin Spock published his book *The Common Sense Book of Baby and Child Care*. The 1940s also saw the development of Abstract Expressionism, the first wholly American art movement to achieve international recognition, in New York, which now overtook Paris as the leader of the western art world.

In 1947, Jackie Robinson broke the color barrier in baseball. In 1950, McCarthyism began accusing innocent Americans of subversion, and North Korea invaded South Korea. In 1951, *I Love Lucy* premiered on CBS, sparking the Golden Age of Television. The United States built the *Nautilus*, the first nuclear submarine, in 1954; and in 1955 the arrest of Rosa Parks incited the bus boycotts in Montgomery, Alabama, that led to the end of segregation on city buses. In 1956, Elvis Presley first appeared on *The Ed Sullivan Show*, and Marilyn Monroe married playwright Arthur Miller. In 1957, the Russians launched *Sputnik*, the first artificial satellite.

The Rev. Lloyd Russell Gillmett.

A native of Minnesota, Mr. Gillmett attended Adelbert College of Western Reserve University in Cleveland, Ohio, where he played varsity football and ran on the track team. Upon graduating *magna cum laude* in 1927, he was elected to Phi Beta Kappa, the honorary scholastic society. He completed his theological training at Episcopal Theological School in Cambridge, Massachusetts; and for two years while in the seminary, he was given charge of the services at Old North Church in Boston, of Paul Revere fame. He afterwards served in Boston parishes until 1935, when he became rector of St. Paul's Church in Duluth, Minnesota, until 1942. A lieutenant commander in the chaplain corps of the U.S. Naval Reserve during World War II, he attended his first vestry meeting at St. John's on February 11, 1946.

The Rev. Lloyd Gillmett is remembered by those who knew him as a great preacher who spoke without notes, a scholarly and conservative man who was serious and dignified, well-organized, an introvert, and something of a loner. He married the former Betty Bowman while in Duluth, but they divorced before he came to St. John's, and he remained unmarried for the duration of his rectorship. Fond of hunting, Gillmett had a black Labrador retriever who accompanied him on his forays into the outdoors.

VESTRYMAN HARRY S. GIVEN served as president of the parish Men's Club. His wife was the former Dorothy Mahoney, an active worker in the St. John's Guild and the sister of Mrs. Arthur (Helen "Holly" Mahoney) Gross.[1] Harry Given and Arthur Gross were the founders of Gross Given Manufacturing Company of St. Paul, established in 1935. The company was founded as a sheet metal manufacturer and later became one of the largest producers of vending machines in the United States, with sales worldwide.

Harry and Dorothy's son, also named Harry, was a first cousin of Virginia "Ginny" Gross Edgerton, the wife of Jack Edgerton, members of the parish and the parents of parishioners Kathy, John III, and Scott. The younger Harry Given was confirmed at St. John's and was the founder and owner of the Prom Ballroom

on University Avenue in St. Paul. For forty-five years the St. Paul landmark hosted dances and featured big bands and rock performances by the likes of Count Basie, Duke Ellington, Jerry Lee Lewis, and Buddy Holly. As the popularity of ballroom dancing waned in the 1960s, the Prom morphed into a banquet and catering facility now called Prom Catering, owned by Harry's sons, Billy and Tommy Given.

Harry Given the younger founded and operated the Prom Ballroom on University Avenue in St. Paul for forty-five years.

The Prom Ballroom in St. Paul, where many of us flocked to dance in decades past.

Barely had he arrived at St. John's when he presided at the burial services for World War I veteran Mitchell Scott Rhodes. A life-long communicant of St. John's, Rhodes began serving his church as a boy chorister around 1901. His sons followed in their father's footsteps as choir boys and as soldiers in the Second World War; son Scott served in France and Germany, and Grant with the army in Alaska.

Among those serving on Gillmett's first vestry was investment attorney Kenneth H. Bayliss, who represented Minneapolis Trust Company investment securities, operated Kenneth H. Bayliss and Company, Schuneman and Bayliss Company investment securities, and Kenneth H. Bayliss, investment counsel. A director of the YMCA, he was also a teacher in St. John's Church School. His wife, the former Stella Gould Hill, served on the board of the Woman's Auxiliary.

At the vestry meeting in March 1946, Mr. Gillmett proposed a plan for reconditioning the basement of the church for use by the Church School that met the whole-hearted approval of the Committee on Religious Education. The Parish House had become ill-suited for the large number of children in the school. Indeed, at its next meeting, in April 1946, the vestry decided to sell the Parish House and authorized vestryman McNeil S. Stringer to obtain the best offer possible. The vestry suggested a price of $50,000. In early 1947, the Minnesota Public Health Service offered $49,500 cash and presented a contract for sale and a check for $500. Deal done.

It was a matter of opinion as to how well the Parish/Club House had served St. John's since 1914. (It was referred to both as "Parish House" and "Club House.") Over the years the building and its activities had been a drain on parish finances, and the Club House had lost its identity with St. John's. Surely the greatest value of the building was that for about three decades it served as a bustling community center for the wider neighborhood, meeting the recreational needs of children and adults; running summer camps for boys and girls; hosting civic, academic, and religious organizations and clubs of various types, without regard for anyone's cultural or religious identity; providing lodging for single men; and in

the process establishing St. John's as a place that cared deeply for the welfare of the world beyond its own walls. Indeed, as a form of outreach the old Club House had been immensely successful, a diocesan model, if not a national model, for parish engagement in the community. The former Club House on Portland now houses condominiums. The transom window at the entrance still reads "Club House."

It is worth noting that in all of 1947, with so much activity surrounding the closing and sale of the Club House, only $100 had been contributed to the Endowment Fund, which by March 1948 totaled $87,861.93. In April that year, Mrs. Paul (Reine) Myers gave $40,000 to establish a trust fund in memory of her husband, and added another $10,000 to the fund in January 1949, for a total of $50,000. This Myers trust fund has grown to more than a million dollars and is administered by U. S. Bank for the benefit of St. John's.

In the ensuing years, all the parish activities that had been housed at the Parish House were moved back to the guild house and the undercroft of the church. Space was tight; Church School classes sometimes met in the church, and all community activities were terminated, at least temporarily.

In September 1946, the vestry turned its attention to raising funds for a World War II memorial window, to be placed in the vestibule at the head of the west aisle. Some parishioners, however, thought such a memorial window—small as it was, and in the vestibule—would be an inadequate memorial and favored the building of a new Parish House to serve as a memorial instead. While the matter of a new Parish House was being considered, the memorial window and a bronze plaque listing the names of those who fought and eleven who died in the war was installed after Easter in 1949.

St. John's was also in need of a parking lot, and in April 1951, the vestry purchased the lot on the northwest corner of Summit Avenue and Kent Street. The lot extended north only as far as the alley, not all the way to Portland Avenue. It had been forfeited to the state for taxes and was purchased through the Ramsey County Land Commissioner for only $2,560. It cost roughly $1,500 to prepare and pave the parking lot, which was ready for use in the fall.

The matter of a new Memorial Parish House now emerged forefront. A comprehensive New Parish House Committee, comprising three subcommittees, was organized in February 1952 and met with architects Ellerbe and Company[2] to consider the preparation of preliminary drawings of elevations and floor plans. The new parish house would be a major enterprise on the part of many people in the parish.

Reynolds Guyer Sr. was the chairman of the project, which included the Finance Committee (Augustus W. Clapp, chairman; with Benjamin G. Griggs, Bruce B. Harris, William Ward, John Myers, McNeil Stringer, William Gratz, Julian Gilman and James Stevenson); the Promotional Committee (Russell Moffitt, chairman; with George Dow, John Parish and John Brackett); and the Planning Committee (Reception Room: Mrs. John W. Thompson; Kitchen and Dining Facilities: Mrs. Arthur Gross and Mrs. William Plummer; Church School Facilities: Mrs. Jerome [Ella] Buser; Choir Facilities: C. Wesley Andersen, Mrs. Kenneth P. Grant, and Miss Helen Day; Athletic Facilities: Albert Buser and Ray Scott Jr.; Engineering: George Shepard; General Decorating: Mrs. John Farnham and Mrs. Robert Clark; Women's Work Facilities: Mrs. Robert Ahrens; Auditorium Theatre Facilities: Harry Boranian; Offices and Business Facilities: Oliver Humphrey and McNeil Seymour Jr.; and Landscaping: Mrs. John Abbott). Later on others were added to the group, including Mrs. James Benepe, Irvine Kelliher, Mr. and Mrs. Lawrence King, Nathaniel P. Langford, Mrs. Paul N. Myers, Mrs. Paul Pinkerton, Miss Katharine Rice, and John Brands.

Drawings were ready to present to the parish at the Annual Meeting in January 1952. The new parish house would be built on property St. John's had purchased north of the church with proceeds from the sale of the Club House. Parishioner Richard Boranian Jr., and his father, Richard Boranian Sr., offered to move the three houses occupying the property on which the parish house would be built in exchange for the buildings and materials, an offer the vestry

accepted. Parishioners Jerry Woelfel and Becky Garthofner once lived in the added third floor of the duplex that was moved from Kent Street to 500 Holly Avenue.[3]

A year later, at the Annual Meeting in January 1954, Mr. Guyer, reporting from the New Parish House Committee, indicated that sixty percent, or 240 of the 400 parish households had pledged $185,000 toward the project, just over half the amount needed, while the membership voted to spend up to $273,000 on the project. At the same meeting John Myers made a few points in criticism of "our lethargy as a congregation."

THE PLANS FOR THE MEMORIAL PARISH HOUSE, as shown by architect Thomas Farr Ellerbe in January 1954, had three levels. The basement level included an auditorium adequate for basketball, a large and efficient kitchen and serving area, rest rooms, a bridal room, and a reception hall and cloak room. The street level included offices for the rector, curate, financial secretary, educational director, and secretary, along with a parlor, a women's work room, a young people's room, and a kitchenette. The top floor housed the classrooms, lavatories, and an apartment for the sexton.

In a cost-saving measure that some felt had unfortunate consequences for the building's aesthetic, it was decided in March 1954 to use brick rather than cut stone on the exterior. Later provisions included a curate's apartment in addition to the one for the sexton. Even with the cost-cutting measures, the total estimated cost of the building still exceeded the authorized limit of $273,000 by some $19,482. And this assumed that the bids would come within the architects' estimates for a total of $291,482, which included the architects' fee of $16,000. Bids for the job were due toward the end of July. By May the parish had pledges in the amount of $197,181, as well as a promised gift of $35,000 contingent upon raising $215,000.

A parish meeting was called in August 1954 to take final action on the financing and to win the authority to proceed with the Memorial Parish House. The lowest bid for the project came in at $299,005, considerably higher than the authorized limit of $273,000. Pledges to date totaled about $209,250, or $5,750 short of the $215,000 needed to secure the contingent gift of $35,000. But that evening an anonymous donor pledged $35,000, bringing the pledges to about $245,000. Whether that donor was the person who originally pledged the contingent gift of $35,000 remains unknown, but it seems likely. The meeting then authorized the vestry to spend no more than $300,000 on the project and to negotiate the necessary finances.

By the Annual Meeting in January 1955, the footings were down, the stairs in, and the plumbing and electrical work completed. The plan was to have the basic structure ready by April 15, but because of the cold weather, construction stopped in February. The heavy expense of wrapping and heating required for the pouring of concrete was prohibitive, so work resumed toward the end of March. The vestry decided to add more showers to the plan, and arranged to borrow up to $150,000 from the First National Bank.[4] The date of the dedication of the Memorial Parish House was set for January 8, 1956.

Not always preoccupied by weighty issues of property and finances, the vestry did occasionally attend to lighter matters. At a meeting in March 1946, for example, after the war had ended and just a month after Mr. Gillmett became rector, Mc-Neil Stringer told his fellow vestrymen to drag their cutaways out of mothballs, deep freezers, or whatever else they used as repositories for such habiliments. The haberdashery of St. John's ushers henceforth would be formal on the church's two greatest feasts: Christmas and Easter. The men would be arrayed in grey-and-black striped trousers, grey vests, cutaways, spats, and wide silk ascot ties, with white carnations in their buttonholes. They dressed this way for ten years before the vestry decided to dispense with the morning coats and return instead to dark suits.

In March 1946, all of the women's guilds were brought into one large association known as the Woman's Auxiliary Guild, to promote the spiritual, social, and material welfare of the women of the parish and to enlist their participation in the goals of the congregation and the general church. The new

One of the houses being moved to make room for the Parish House.

Construction of the new Memorial Parish House, 1954.

DUSTY PLATT was vice-president of a new youth organization formed by the young people themselves. Membership was open to everyone fifteen years of age and older. In 1950 the other officers of the Young People's Fellowship were Michael Heverly, president; Marlene Chamberlin, secretary; Dick Kennedy, treasurer; and Lois Wilson, deanery representative.

Dusty Platt was the daughter of parishioners Mr. and Mrs. William Platt.

officers were Mrs. Benjamin G. Griggs, president; Mrs. Roger S. Kennedy, first vice-president; Mrs. Frank W. Fuller, second vice-president; Mrs. Harold O. Washburn, third vice-president; Mrs. Worrell Clarkson, corresponding secretary; Mrs. William H. Plummer, recording secretary; Mrs. Henry G. Dyer, assistant recording secretary; Mrs. John Peyton, treasurer; Mrs. George W. Tilden, assistant treasurer; and Mrs. William E. Ward, treasurer for the United Thank Offering.[5] When parishioner Miss Cornelia W. Scandrett died in May 1946, Bishop Stephen Keeler and the Rev. Lloyd Gillmett officiated at her funeral at St. John's. For many years a devoted member of St. John's, Miss Scandrett was a granddaughter of Bishop Henry Benjamin Whipple, the first bishop of Minnesota. She was survived by one sister, Mrs. Jane Burt, and two brothers, Henry A. Scandrett and Benjamin W. Scandrett.

Parishioner Laura Cook Ottis also died in 1946. The sister of the late Mrs. Frank B. Kellogg, Mrs. Ottis was for many years an active member and worker at St. John's. She served on the women's board of the Church Club and on the board of the Woman's Auxiliary. She lived with her husband Francis J. Ottis in the eight-bedroom house at 675 Goodrich Avenue, now on the National Register of Historic Places, and summered in Mahtomedi. Francis Ottis was a civic leader and president of Northern Malleable Iron Company.

A new "Junior Church" was introduced at the beginning of the new Church School year in September 1946. This service for all young people twelve years of age and older took place at 9:30 a.m. in the church and was a significant innovation for St. John's. The rector conducted the service and gave an instruction. The lessons were illustrated by slides. All young people who would be fifteen years of age by the following May were expected to attend Junior Church in preparation for confirmation. The church had its own choir, its own vestry, its own acolytes, and in due time practically every member of the Junior Church would take an active part in the services.

The Rev. Gillmett was assisted by a number of curates in succession. In October 1946, the Rev. F. Douglas Henderson, curate and director of religious education at St. Peter's Cathedral in Charlottetown, Prince Edward Island, Canada, became curate and director of religious education at St. John's, for a stipend of $2,400 plus living quarters in the Parish House. In June 1948 he assumed the position of director of religious education for the diocese, becoming a canon in the process, and in 1952 he was named headmaster of Breck Episcopal School, then located at Como and Herndon in St. Paul.[6]

Mr. Henderson was followed as curate by the Rev. Charles Holcomb, a recent graduate of Bexley Hall of Kenyon College in Gambier, Ohio, and also a graduate of the University of Minnesota, where he majored in drama and minored in radio. During the war he served as an officer in Europe, taking part in the Battle of the Bulge. Holcomb was named director of St. John's Church School. He married a parishioner, Anita June Williamson, just prior to accepting a call as assistant priest at a parish in Tallahassee, Florida, effective February 1954.

THE NEW MEMORIAL PARISH HOUSE!

BISHOP CONRAD GESNER PREACHED at the morning service for the dedication on January 8, 1956. A processional of parishioners wound its way from the church to the new auditorium, as the gymnasium was then called, where Bishop Stephen Keeler dedicated the structure. The dedication of the Memorial Parish House was certainly a festive moment in the life of the parish, the culmination of years of planning and fundraising. *The St. John's Evangelist* reported that parishioners' hearts were filled with gratitude at having achieved their goal.

Following Mr. Holcomb came Winston F. Crum, who served in the U.S. Army during World War II. He was a senior at Seabury-Western Seminary when he was hired by Gillmett, and before that had held a fellowship in mathematics at Carleton College. He started as curate on June 13, 1954, and was ordained to the priesthood in June 1955 at St. John's. After leaving St. John's, Mr. Crum earned a doctorate at Harvard Divinity School and returned to Seabury-Western where he took a position on the teaching faculty.[7] In February 1955, Herbert Brubaker Cully was assigned to St. John's as an assistant to the rector. He came to the Episcopal Church from the Methodist Church and the vestry recommended him to the bishop for admission to the diaconate.

St. John's basketball team had been formed before the war, and for the 1947-1948 season it won the Central YMCA Church League title, with eleven wins and two losses. A trophy testifying to the fact stands proudly in the glass display case in the undercroft, with the following players listed: Robert Andrews, captain; Roger Olsen, Irvine Kelliher, Ray Scott, Robert Johnston, Robert Zierdt, Jack Olsen, Roger Benson, and coach Herb Lee. St. John's placed three players on the all-star team: Bob Andrews, Ray Scott, and Roger Olsen, the latter being the league's high-point man with a total of 131 points.

Team member John Olsen was a member of St. John's choir in the 1920s, worked in sales at both Texaco and Minnesota Mining, and served a stint in the Minnesota National Guard. A Shakespeare and Civil War buff, John believed that, next to the Bard and the King James Bible, the finest book in English was the *Book of Common Prayer*. His daughter Debora was chosen Miss St. Paul in 1971, and Roger Olsen's son Jeffrey served the parish first as junior warden, then as senior warden, from 2004 to 2007.

For several years, the parish held the popular Feast of Lights on the Sunday after Epiphany. This traditional service, representing the manifestation of the Light to the whole world, was one of the most beautiful of the entire year. A silver tea followed the service, during which the Epiphany cake was cut and the recipient of the ring hidden in the cake duly honored. Cole Oehler received the ring in 1948, being named king, and was therefore the host at the tea party in 1949, with the honor of cutting the cake. King Keith Kennedy was the lucky recipient of the ring that year. In 1950 the winners were Queen Lucille Donham and Princess Betty Hanstein.

St. John's Basketball Team brought home the 1946-47 Central YMCA Church League title and a trophy!

The need for a new organ console and for almost six hundred new pipes had the attention of the vestry at this time. By February 1950 the parish had engaged the Moeller Organ Company of Hagerstown, Maryland, for work that was expected to cost $10,800, and a fundraising campaign was begun, with Mr. William H. Oppenheimer as its chairman. The organ and console arrived in October and were installed and ready for use by the end of November 1950.

Famed organist Dr. Alexander McCurdy, the head of the Curtis Institute of Music in Philadelphia and head of the organ department at Westminster Choir College in Princeton, New Jersey, gave an organ and carillon recital at St. John's in January 1951. A second renowned organist performed at St. John's in March that year. Richard Purvis, who had studied with Alexander McCurdy, was organist and master of the choristers at Grace Cathedral in San Francisco as well as organist at the California Palace of the Legion of Honor. Recognized as one of the greatest organ improvisers in the country, Purvis had written more than two hundred compositions. His recital at St. John's was sponsored by the local chapter of the American Guild of Organists.

Piquing the interest of parishioners, and playing on the power of suggestion, Mr. Gillmett wrote in *The St. John's Evangelist* in January 1950, "They wonder why I announced that the number of men present at our services is going to grow steadily. I didn't tell them why, but I know that is the case and you just keep your eyes open and see." Somehow it came to pass, so that by the end of March there were more men in the congregation than women, with the attendance of men increasing every Sunday since February 4.

A membership contest held in the Church School in the fall of 1949 promised an airplane ride for the boys and girls bringing in the largest number of new students. Provided by Mid-Continent Airlines, the ride took place in February 1950 from Wold Chamberlin Field.[8] The plane flew at an altitude of 1,500 feet down Summit Avenue and circled around the church twice, then went out over the Capitol to White Bear Lake, made a lap over Stillwater, and set down above Hastings. The children were elated. A similar

HORACE HILLS IRVINE, whose home at 1006 Summit Avenue would become the Minnesota's Governor's Residence, died in February 1947. A devoted and generous member of St. John's, Irvine was engaged with his father in the lumber business, and became secretary and treasurer of the Thomas Irvine Lumber Company. He eventually became treasurer and president of the Weyerhaeuser Timber Company, vice-president of Allied Building Credits, and a director of the Northern Pacific Railway, First National Bank, First Trust Company, First Bank Stock Corporation, and St. Paul Fire and Marine Insurance Company. He was survived by his wife, the former Clotilde McCullough, and their four children: Thomas E. Irvine, Mrs. Creighton (Clotilde) Churchill (later Mrs. Ted Moles), Mrs. William H. (Elizabeth) Fobes Jr., all of St. Paul, and Mrs. Robert (Olivia) Jenney (later Mrs. Arthur Dodge), of Boston. Olivia and Clotilde gave the Summit Avenue house to the State of Minnesota in 1965. (See p. 85.)

contest took place in 1958 when the pilot was parishioner Robert Farnham.[9]

A number of memorials were given to the church between mid-November 1949 and January 1950, including a handrail for the stairways from the ambulatory given by Donald Myers in memory of his parents. Altar hangings were given by Mrs. Paul N. Myers; $5,000 was given to the Endowment Fund in the estate of Miss Marion Lanpher; a motion picture projector was given in memory of Amy Constance Moon by

Mrs. Thomas B. Jennings and friends; and the sum of $900 was given to the fund in memory of Miss Moon. Amy Moon had been a member at St. John's since 1920, and a charter member of the Business and Professional Women's Guild for which she served as secretary and vice-president. She had also been a librarian at the St. Paul Public Library.

At the Annual Meeting in January 1953, Senior Warden Augustus W. Clapp reported that the parish was in excellent financial shape and the physical plant in excellent condition. The major challenge, he said, was to increase the average Sunday attendance, which had fallen to a mere 200, made up mostly of women, whereas the total membership was 1,074. Mr. Gillmett's prediction needed repeating!

THE ORDINARY AFFAIRS OF THE PARISH had carried on as usual while the new Memorial Parish House was being imagined, designed, and realized. On July 23, 1950, the Sunday service was broadcast over the radio, a practice that would continue. This was an expensive undertaking, and the broadcasts were given as memorials. In the ensuing months broadcasts were sponsored by Mr. and Mrs. Donald H. Myers in memory of his parents, Walter Frederick and Mary Frances Hovey Myers; by Reine Myers in appreciation for all that St. John's meant to her mother, Caroline Humbird, during her later years; by the Wigginton family and Julian S. Gilman, the son of Dr. and Mrs. Gilman, in memory of Frederick Wigginton and Henry and Lucinda Gilman; and by a number of former choirboys, now grown, in memory of the Rev. Theodore Sedgwick, who died in May 1951. Parishioner and long-time choir member Dorothy Ek recalls that the present "No Parking" signs on Kent Street were originally installed to reserve space for the truck from the radio station.

Former senior warden John Webster Thompson died suddenly in March 1951. After Conrad Gesner left St. John's, Thompson[10] frequently read the Sunday service and preached the sermon. The Word of God was precious to him and he frequently talked about, and was concerned about, its application to his own life and to business and society as a whole. He was an able leader who won the esteem and affection of many.

Thomas Grange Dyer was killed in action in Korea on March 16, 1951. Dyer had grown up in the choir and served as an acolyte for a number of years before entering the military. He was survived by his mother, Mrs. Henry G. Dyer, and his sister, Carol.

In September 1951, James Paulson, a recent graduate of Hamline University was hired as superintendent of the Church School and director of young people's activities. At Hamline, Paulson concentrated on courses in teaching, physical education, and psychology.

Yet another new youth organization was also established that month. Called The University of Life, the group was open to high school students, college students, and young people in business. Despite a rainstorm, the first meeting attracted seventy-four youth who heard the Red River Valley Gang and "raised the rafters" in the undercroft with their singing. They also heard popular Twin Cities WCCO radio host and Episcopalian Bob De Haven speak on "Witnessing to Your Faith." By the next month there were ninety-one enrolled members and a choir was formed to sing each Sunday evening at the group's worship service. Mr. and Mrs. William (Mary Guest) Platt entertained the group in October, and Mr. and Mrs. James Moore held an open house for them in November, when a magician was their guest.

A variety of interest groups soon developed in The University of Life. One of them, called "Know Your Community," brought in a deputy officer of the Ramsey County Probation Office to give an address. Another group, "Know Your Bible," heard an address by a professor of philosophy and religion at Hamline University. Those in "Preparation for Marriage" heard the director of the Family Life Program in the Arts College of the University of Minnesota. The group on "Moral Questions and Christianity" heard a professor from the University of Minnesota. A group on "Drama" welcomed a presenter named Windred Grunke.

In September 1954 St. John's high-school youth formed still another new group, this one called Teen-Tivities. They met every Sunday evening in the undercroft. Their first speaker of the season was columnist Paul Light of the *St. Paul Pioneer Press* who spoke on "European Adventures." For their next gathering they had a Teen-Sing with "Liberace" Andersen— C. Wesley, that is—at the piano, and then a square dance. In October they heard a presentation on "Henry VIII and All That."

LLOYD GILLMETT WAS KNOWN for his fine preaching. In 1952 his sermon titled "The Birthday of Our Eternity" was published in the book *Best Sermons*, edited by G. Paul Butler.[11] The volume included sermons by the Very Rev. James A. Pike, then the controversial dean of the Cathedral of St. John the Divine in New York City, and the Most Rev. Fulton J. Sheen, Auxiliary Bishop of the Roman Catholic Archdiocese of New York, known to radio and television audiences.

And in March 1954 *The St. John's Evangelist* reported that the Rev. Gillmett was once again in print. A friend of his had sent him a card congratulating him on his article in *The Witness*. Gillmett knew nothing about it. But on the cover of the magazine was the title "Infallible Fallacies and the Holy Catholic Church." Gillmett discovered the entire sermon he preached at St. John's had been printed in the magazine.

For several months a group of married parishioners called the "Mr. and Mrs. Club" had been meeting on the second and fourth Fridays for fellowship and "whatever might come along." The "whatever" had developed into an hour's discussion on the church's history and allied fields. The "fellowship" took the form of square dancing. In December 1952 the group renamed itself the "Friday Nighters" and declared itself open not only to married couples, but to anyone in the post-college bracket.

At the end of January 1953, St. John's hosted the 22nd annual Minnesota Pastors' Conference, which usually drew about five hundred pastors under the auspices of the Minnesota Council of Churches, along with the cooperation of the Councils in St. Paul and Minneapolis. Principal guest speakers came from out-of-state. The dinner speaker was Senator Elmer L. Andersen of the 42nd district, later the thirtieth governor of Minnesota.

C. WESLEY ANDERSEN succeeded George Fairclough as organist and choirmaster in 1943 and enjoyed many years as such at St. John's, until 1972. Under his direction, the boys of the choir were honored to be chosen to sing for a performance of the Mahler *Third Symphony* with the Minneapolis Symphony Orchestra, in February 1950 at Northrop Auditorium of the University of Minnesota. In 1951 the choir produced a recording on a vinyl disc that would become a collector's item. The popular selections on the disc were the *Hallelujah Chorus* from the *Messiah* of George Frederick Handel; the *Agnus Dei* from the *Communion Service in A-flat* by George Fairclough; and the seven-fold *Amen* by Peter Lutkin. The records were promoted by the Woman's Auxiliary Guild.

DURING HOLY WEEK in 1953, St. John's presented the film *King of Kings*, about the last weeks of the life of Jesus. Produced in 1927 by Cecil B. DeMille, the movie was seen by more than a billion people worldwide, and was once considered the most enduring picture of all time. The sequence about the resurrection was in technicolor. *King of Kings* attracted citywide attention when it was presented at St. John's, and was repeated for Holy Week audiences for a number of years thereafter. Parishioner Alden Drew recalls that William Boyd, who played Hopalong Cassidy in the eponymous TV series in the 1950s, played the role of Simon of Cyrene. "That was of greater interest to us kids than the movie itself. Spotting him was the highlight of the evening."

For many years a quartet of professional singers had replaced the choir of men and boys during the summer months. In 1953 the quartet was joined by a volunteer adult choir to lead the singing of hymns and canticles. The following year, older boys and girls, as well as men and women, were welcomed as volunteers. But during the academic year, the old choir of men and boys was encountering some hard realities in maintaining its ranks. The difficulty in securing the thirty boys necessary for an adequate choir was not due to any specific cause, except the tenor of the times, and many of the boys had drifted away. It became necessary to augment the group with the Girls Choir, who were now singing a heavy load of two services on Sundays and who, by 1955, boasted nearly forty members. Gradually a mixed adult choir emerged to assume the duties of singing regularly on Sundays during the church year, after the slow demise of the choir of men and boys.

Mrs. Selmor S. Benson, an able teacher and leader, was appointed director of the Church School in February, to begin in April. Enrollment in the school had reached 295 by that time, compared to the opening enrollment of 192, representing an increase of 103 in one year. Benson and the Rev. Winston Crum organized a Vacation Bible School that attracted more than eighty children in June 1954.

The first Spring Fling, sponsored jointly by all the Episcopal churches in the St. Paul Deanery for couples from ages 21

Alden Drew, right, with his brother Bram and father, Adrian Drew, ca. 1957 (probably going to St. John's on Sunday morning).

to 101, was held in the spring of 1954, featuring dancing, entertainment, and door prizes. The second such event, attended by about 550 people, took place at Harry Given's Prom Ballroom with the proceeds given to the building fund of St. Philip's Church. In the third year the Fling was held in the main ballroom of the St. Paul Hotel with music by Wes Barlow's Orchestra. Proceeds benefited the building program of St. James Church. The fourth Spring Fling, in May 1957, featured entertainment by the Clergy Bell Ringers, with dancing to Gil Brabec's Orchestra. The Flings were so successful that in 1957 a Fall Ball was planned for the main ballroom in the Lowry Hotel. The proceeds from the ball in 1958 went to the benefit of work among Native Americans in the Twin Cities area.

THE FIRST ANGLICAN CONGRESS to take place in the United States was held at St. Mark's Cathedral in Minneapolis during August 1954. It was also the first representative gathering of the Anglican Communion to take place outside the British Isles. It was a historic event, as it brought to the diocese some of the world's leading religious figures, including the Archbishop of Canterbury, to witness to our

Jule Murat Hannaford Jr.

WINTERTIME DRIVING can be treacherous in Minnesota, and in December 1952, Jule Murat Hannaford Jr. was killed in a highway accident when a heavy bus skidded into his car. In his early years Hannaford was vice-president of Northwest Electric Equipment Company, then secretary and sales manager of Gordon and Ferguson, Inc., manufacturers of furs and heavy clothing. In 1933 he became president and treasurer of Hannaford O'Brien, Inc., insurance brokers. He was also a director of Waldorf Paper Products Company and director and treasurer of Provident Loan Society.

Hannaford had a long and distinguished association with St. John's and the Diocese of Minnesota. From 1943 until his death he served as treasurer of the diocese, and was a member of several diocesan committees. For the province he was chairman of the Presiding Bishop's Committee on Laymen's work. For several successive General Conventions he was a delegate from the diocese, and at the time of his death he was a member of Seabury-Western Seminary's board of trustees and a trustee of the diocese. He served on the board of trustees of the St. Paul Academy from 1927 to 1952 and became its secretary in 1930. He and his wife, the former Caroline Schurmeier, lived at 644 Summit Avenue with their children, Jule Murat III, John Livingston, and Gertrude.

John Hannaford and Gertrude Hannaford Jaffray on the occasion of her sixtieth birthday in 1982.

common faith and to confer on matters of common interest. All of the bishops, and one priest and one lay person from each of the 325 dioceses in the worldwide communion were invited to attend, coming from six continents. Their deliberations focused on "The Call of God and the Mission of the Anglican Communion." The congress began with an impressive opening service in the Minneapolis Municipal Auditorium. The Diocese of Minnesota planned to raise $50,000 to cover the expenses of the Minneapolis gathering, with each parish in the diocese expected to contribute an amount equal to its 1952 diocesan assessment.

Beginning in April 1955, St. John's supported four displaced persons coming to the United States, including transportation to St. Paul and help in finding a job. The parish first sponsored Mr. Bunia, a Ukrainian Pole, who was an Orthodox Christian and a farmer by occupation. Mr. Bunia did not speak English, making it impossible for him to find employment. Parishioner John Myers gave him gardening work while he took English lessons at the International Institute and later employed Bunia at the Waldorf Paper Company, where he was then vice-president.

The parish also sponsored Mrs. Ilse Tetzlaff, 22, a Lutheran who spoke both English and German and had high-school commercial training; her mother, Mrs. Charlotte Vier, 48; and

The parish marked the death of valued member *KENNETH G. BRILL* in February 1954. Brill had served as assistant St. Paul city attorney before becoming a judge of district court in St. Paul. At St. John's he was a delegate to the Church Extension Society and to Diocesan Council, a member of the parish Standing Committee and the Church Club board, a teacher in the Church School, clerk of the vestry, and parish treasurer. He was married to the former Laura Catherine Cooke who was also very active at St. John's. She held the office of president and other offices for the Woman's Auxiliary, she was a member of the Altar Guild, an officer in St. John's Guild, and a delegate to General Convention in Washington, D.C., representing the Woman's Auxiliary of the diocese, of which she also served as president.

Ilse's daughter, Gisela, age 4. The three had lived on a Bavarian farm and came to St. John's from East Germany through the Episcopal Church's Department of Christian Social Relations. Mrs. Tetzlaff went to work for a firm in St. Paul.

Four new guilds for women were formed in April 1955: the Fellowship Guild, the Salisbury Guild, the Canterbury Guild, and the St. Mark's Guild, each with its own purpose and function. Members of the Fellowship Guild, for example, prayed for individuals and special purposes at designated times during the day. The Salisbury Guild was engaged in sewing and knitting.

Elections for the Woman's Auxiliary were held in May 1955. Mrs. John (Elizabeth) Parish[12] was named president; Mrs. Paul Pinkerton, first vice-president; Mrs. John (Elizabeth) Musser, second vice-president; Mrs. William (Mary) Ward, third vice-president; Mrs. Bruce B. (Clare) Harris, corresponding secretary; Mrs. Adrian (Dorothy) Drew, assistant corresponding secretary; Mrs. W. Lyman (Gertrude) Heitmiller, recording secretary; Mrs. Nathaniel P. (Mildred) Langford, assistant recording secretary; Mrs. John (Betty) Myers, treasurer; and Mrs. Thomas Fifield, assistant treasurer.

It was probably the new building that attracted over three hundred people to the Annual Meeting in January 1956, including four bishops: Keeler, Cross, Atwill, and Kellogg, with many diocesan clergy also in attendance. Nathaniel P. Langford Jr. was elected senior warden, and Charles Alden, junior warden. Robert Andrews, Hubert Haas, John B. Hilton, and Dr. Frederick M. Owens Jr. were newly elected to the vestry.

Parishioner Dickran Boranian was running St. John's new recreational activities on a part-time basis, but the vestry realized that a full-time person would be needed to take advantage of all the new opportunities available at St. John's. Gillmett saw the program as a missionary one. In March 1956 James Soltau, a recent graduate of the University of Minnesota, recently star end on the football team and the recipient of three letters in the sport, was hired as St. John's full-time director of recreational and group work. In October Soltau oversaw three Halloween parties for boys and girls that were attended by more than four hundred children. By November the average daily attendance at recreation was close to seventy. Parishioner Frank Weicher helped with the supervision of the program for twelve years. In 1958–59 Soltau was assisted by parishioner Mrs. Frederick Chapman who was in charge of some of the afternoon programs.

Several members of St. John's were newly elected to board positions at St. Luke's Hospital in January 1956. Benjamin Griggs was named president; Augustus W. Clapp Jr., vice-president; George Dean, second vice-president; and William Gratz, treasurer. Another member of the board of trustees, parishioner Garrett O. House was responsible for the renovation of the Nurses' Home. A major undertaking, the project provided a physical therapy department and many rooms for convalescents.

The spring of 1956 saw a Spring Circus Carnival, chaired by William Nesbitt and Mr. and Mrs. James Chilton, in the new Parish House auditorium. There was a spook house, a fish pond, a rifle range, movie, fortune teller, dart games, horse shoe game, cake walk, pistol target, parcel post sale, make-up booth, pop and ice cream, caramel apples, fudge, a coffee and donut shop, guessing games, and door prizes. Wesley Andersen directed a second event in the auditorium, a musical revue that featured St. John's combined choirs and soloists singing hit show tunes from *Carousel*, *South Pacific*, and *Oklahoma*. The choir girls sang "Summertime," the boys sang (and whistled) "I Whistle a Happy Tune," and the men crooned "By the Light of the Silvery Moon." The soloists and organist-choirmaster appeared in "quite unaccustomed roles."

In April 1956, Mrs. Benson resigned her position as director of religious education, effective as soon as the vestry could find her successor. Gillmett had a hunch that she left because of her heavy workload. Rose Lee Baldwin followed her in the job and was given use of the smaller apartment in the new Parish House but was dismissed in May 1957, three months in advance of her contract, for disloyalty to Mr. Gillmett.

The Rev. John Robert Hanson, the assistant minister of Morningside Congregational Church in Minneapolis, joined St. John's staff as Gillmett's assistant in August 1957. He had studied both at Yale Divinity School and at Oxford. In March 1957 the vestry supported his ordination to the diaconate in the Episcopal Church. After Rose Baldwin left in May, Hanson assumed her duties in addition to his own, receiving an appropriate salary increase. We don't know his rate of pay, only that the vestry promised him a further increase of $25 per month upon his ordination to the priesthood.[13]

Two distinctions came to Lloyd Gillmett in June 1956. First, he received an honorary Doctor of Divinity Degree from Seabury-Western Seminary in Evanston. He then participated in a Sherwood-Eddy Seminar that took him to England, France, Germany, Russia, and Finland, and gave him the opportunity to talk with people prominent in the political and economic spheres in these countries. On August 3 he sailed

GARRETT O. HOUSE was president of the board of directors of St. John's Church Club. An engineer for the reconstruction of the Erie Canal in New York State before coming to St. Paul, he was secretary and general manager for Northern Heating and Electric Company, general superintendent of St. Paul City Water Works, superintendent of St. Paul City Railway Company, manager and director of the St. Paul Division of Northern States Power Company, and vice-president and director of the Northern Federal Savings and Loan Association. His wife, Florence Peasley House, was active in many philanthropic, civic, and social enterprises.

home on board the newly constructed *Empress of Britain*, one of the first North Atlantic ocean liners to have air-conditioning. In 1957 he made a similar tour of Rome, Jerusalem, Damascus, Vienna, Athens, and Cairo and afterwards gave a sermon at St. John's about tensions in the Arab world.

Continuing his travels, in September 1958 Dr. Gillmett went to Independence Hall in Philadelphia to participate in the production of television programs for the American Religious Town Hall, which featured inter-faith dialog on timely topics. The show began on radio in 1952 and is still broadcast on more than three hundred television stations. Dr. Gillmett also attended General Convention in Miami that year.

During Lent in 1957, the women of St. John's and St. Clement's parishes on Tuesday afternoons heard presentations on the English Reformation. Dean Henry Hancock of St. Mark's Cathedral in Minneapolis made several presentations. The Very Rev. James A. Pike, Dean of the

Cathedral of St. John the Divine in New York, spoke on "The Meaning of the Reformation Today." Pike later became the outspoken bishop of the Diocese of California, headquartered in San Francisco, where he distinguished himself by his liberal positions on a variety of controversial causes. He ordained a woman to the transitional diaconate before it was allowed, and he questioned a number of central Christian tenets, including the virginity of Mary the mother of Jesus, and the doctrines of hell and the Trinity. Heresy procedures were begun in the House of Bishops, but eventually it was decided that an actual heresy trial was not in the best interest of the church.

THE CHRISTMAS PAGEANT was an elaborate affair enacted by adults on the Sunday afternoon before Christmas. Titled "Star of Bethlehem," the set for the pageant featured the town of Bethlehem, with scenery designed

and executed by Reynolds Guyer. Because parishioner Mary Wigginton Pinkerton, who sang lead roles in productions of the St. Paul Civic Opera,[14] was one of the angels in the pageant, we suppose it actually merited being called a semi-professional presentation. A number of other young women, among them Betty Myers, Dusty Mairs, Elinor Myers Strebel, and Helen Day played the roles of the herald angels, which required that they climb the steps up to the narrow precipice high above the reredos for the singing of "Angels We Have Heard on High." For several years the angels' parts were played by Catherine Ann Napier and her friends Trudy Kelliher and Margaret Sceli. Catherine remembered her experience:

With our long white gowns, our wings and our trumpets, believe me, it was precarious. We performed for several years. In the last year I must have looked down and started

Above: Christmastime at St. John's, decorated in holiday greenery, during the rectorship of the Rev. Lloyd Gillmett. Above right: Christmastime at St. John's, 2011.

to shake, but my friends supported me. One year in the darkened church as the narrator intoned these familiar words, "And suddenly there was with the angel...", the flood lights shone, and a young child called out, "Oh, mommy, look at the angels!"[15]

The Rev. Dr. Lloyd R. Gillmett had served St. John's wisely and faithfully for thirteen years when he advised the vestry

NATHANIEL "TAN" LANGFORD was one of the co-chairmen of the Calling Committee that conducted a search for a new rector. The committee had been in touch with Bishop Edward Cross who recommended that the Rev. Raymond H. Clarke of St. Peter's Church in Sheridan, Wyoming, come to St. Paul to meet the vestry and the Calling Committee. Bishop Cross himself was serving at St. Peter's when he was called to the rectorship of St. John's some forty-three years earlier. The vestry extended a call to Mr. Clarke that was inadvisably announced in The St. John's Evangelist, because it was unsuccessful. At the end of May 1959 the vestry voted unanimously to invite the Rev. William Henry Mead to be St. John's twelfth rector.

Mr. Langford reminded the vestry that the rectory was in poor condition and suggested that steps be taken to purchase a new house for Mr. Mead. At the end of May the vestry decided to sell the rectory for the sum of $15,000, and in July they offered $30,000 for the dwelling at One Heather Place, to serve as the residence for the Mead family. Architect Cass Gilbert had built the three-story English Tudor-style dwelling in 1894 as his own residence.

on December 3, 1958, that he had accepted a call to become dean of St. Paul's Cathedral in Los Angeles, his resignation to take effect on January 31, 1959. Mr. Gillmett delivered his farewell sermon on January 25, 1959. A reception was held in his honor, and parishioners apparently gave him a large purse. He had recently purchased a new automobile, but in The St. John's Evangelist of February 1, he acknowledged that by their generous gifts it had actually been purchased by the parish. "To say 'thank you' is not enough. I will always be grateful."

Shortly after Dr. Gillmett's departure, and before the arrival of a new rector, there was a generous turnout of the choir for the funeral of Elizabeth Hensel in February 1959. Miss Hensel had been an integral part of the choir's life for about fifty-five years, making hers by far the longest tenure of anyone to hold either a paid or volunteer position in the parish. An issue of The Living Church in September 1958 contained a photograph of her and some of the choir boys with the article: "What Is It Like To Be a Choir Mother?" It would be impossible to number the heads she brushed, the cassocks she kept in repair, and the smiles she gave each little choir boy and girl as they started in procession down the aisle on Sunday mornings. Miss Hensel's father and three of her brothers—Kenneth, Elliott, and Dr. Charles N. Hensel[16]—sang in the choir over the years.

Before Dr. Gillmett left the parish, the Woman's Auxiliary closed its books with the group's last formal report, given at the Annual Meeting in January 1959 by Betty Scandrett (Mrs. Cole) Oehler,[17] its last president. Thereafter the organization began its new life as the Women of St. John's.[18] Its first president was Gertrude (Mrs. Lyman W.) Heitmiller, a graduate of Barnard College, where her discipline was medieval history. She also studied at Havana University during the regime of Cuban dictator and military leader Fulgencio Batista, and had participated in a campaign to wipe out illiteracy in Puerto Rico. St. John's Woman's Auxiliary was the last of the standing guilds exclusively for women. In some ways its demise was testimony that parish women had taken their rightful place as equals with the men at the highest levels of church life and leadership.

ARTHUR F. ZACHE 1885-1977

CAN A PILLAR OF THE CHURCH BE ONLY 5'7" TALL?

For more than fifty years, Art Zache, short of stature but big of heart, was a valued presence at St. John's, always on hand and mindful of what needed to be done. He began living in the Club House soon after it was built, probably in 1915. In 1920 he was named Physical Director of the Club, where he scheduled, organized, and supervised the staff and facilities. His annual salary in 1924 was "$2,000 and room."

In 1923 he was appointed Assistant Choirmaster[19] of the men and boys choir. As such, he was responsible for recruiting, attendance, and discipline of the boys, and for directing the two-week choir camp. The Rev. Frederick Butler said Zache had "the rare faculty of being able to get down absolutely to the level of the boys and still always retain their respect."

In 1929 Art was offered a job that would require that he leave the Club House, but he decided to stay at an increased salary of $2,400. The following year, he was named parish Financial Secretary. Art served also as leader of Boy Scout Troop No. 2 for several years.

In March of 1961, church members organized a testimonial dinner to honor Art. The gym was full with well-wishers of all ages from far and near. The grace before dinner was the traditional one from camp, taken from the book of Psalms:

> *Art*: The eyes of all wait upon thee, O Lord.
> *Response*: And thou givest them their meat in due season.

There were many spoken reminiscences, but Art's reply was memorable: "Thank you all, but this is *not* a retirement party!" Art actually did retire in April 1964. His increasing deafness required the use of a hearing aid, and he eventually moved to the Church Home. After having developed heart trouble for which he was hospitalized, Art died in 1977 at age 92. Many of the former choir boys, boy scouts, and others who knew him were present at his funeral. Ironically, the final sentence in his obituary was the melancholy statement: "There are no known survivors."

—Fred Myers

SHIRLEY HAMMERGREN KARTARIK MICHIENZI

OF THE MANY HUNDREDS OF SINGERS who have raised their voices to the glory of God at St. John's, the one universally regarded for her musicality and the clarity of her lyrical voice is soprano Shirley Kartarik Michienzi, who has been associated with the parish for more than seven decades.

The young Shirley Hammergren won a citywide singing contest in 1936, entitling her to a year of private voice lessons with prominent baritone Grant Kelliher from the St. Paul Civic Opera Company, who was also a soloist at St. John's. A year later she started singing for the parish under George Fairclough. Later organist and choirmaster C. Wesley Andersen would have her stand next to the organ console and sing through the carved gothic arches to support the boy choristers. (Women, in those days, could be heard, but not seen.)

Shirley's four years of high school at the elite Oak Hall School for girls, around the corner from the church, on Holly Avenue, was paid for by a well-known journalist with *The St. Paul Dispatch*, who insisted on anonymity, merely because he liked the sound of her voice. For a long time not even Shirley knew the identity of her benefactor. She went on to study voice at Hamline University and later sang solo roles under the batons of Dimitri Mitropoulos and Robert Shaw.

In 1968 Kartarik attended a church music conference in Detroit. While there she met the Rt. Hon. Geoffrey Fisher, retired Archbishop of Canterbury, and asked him if there were any reason that choirs couldn't wear red cassocks instead of black. Hearing his response, she returned to St. John's where the old heavy black cassocks, lined and hard to keep clean, were soon discarded and replaced with red ones. That's how the cassocks at St. John's came to be red.

After the demise of the men and boys choir, Mrs. Kartarik became the director of St. John's new youth choir. In 1970 she made arrangements for the young singers to join with the boychoir from the Cathedral of St. Paul for performances of Arrigo Boito's opera *Mefistofole* with the Minneapolis Symphony. The performances took place

at Northrup Auditorium and at the Mayo Civic Auditorium in Rochester.

Shirley retired from singing in 1992 and in 1997 she married Dr. Leonard J. Michienzi, for thirty-two years the physician for the Minnesota Twins. She quickly learned to love baseball.[20]

Lobster cookout on the Maine coast: Peter Myers, Bill Mead Jr., Kate Mead, The Rev. William (Bill) Mead, and Kathy Mead.

chapter twelve

THE REV. WILLIAM HENRY MEAD 1959-1964
North Star Flight 85

DURING THE RECTORSHIP of the Rev. William Mead, Congress passed and President Dwight D. Eisenhower signed the Civil Rights Act of 1960, the same year that John F. Kennedy was elected president. The civil rights movement spanned the length of Mr. Mead's tenure. In 1961, JFK established the Peace Corps, oversaw the escalation of U.S. involvement in Vietnam, and launched the unsuccessful Bay of Pigs Invasion in an attempt to overthrow the Communist regime of Fidel Castro. The latter led to the Cuban missile crisis, the closest nuclear confrontation ever to involve the United States and the Soviet Union.

In New York, Avery Fisher Hall, the home of the New York Philharmonic, opened at the Lincoln Center for the Performing Arts in 1962. And in 1963: Bob Dylan released his classic "The Freewheelin' Bob Dylan"; Martin Luther King Jr., standing in front of the Lincoln Memorial, delivered his "I Have a Dream" speech during the March on Washington for civil and economic rights for African-Americans; Betty Friedan published *The Feminine Mystique*, widely credited with sparking the women's liberation movement; and President Kennedy was assassinated in Dallas, Texas, on November 22, 1963. In 1964 the Beatles were greeted by three thousand screaming fans upon their first arrival in the United

The Rev. William Henry Mead.

States, at Kennedy Airport in New York City; and President Lyndon Johnson launched the reforms of the Great Society.

William Henry Mead, born in Detroit in 1921, attended the Cranbrook School, a private college prep boarding school in Bloomfield Hills, Michigan; Lake Forest College; and the University of Michigan. After recovering from a bout with tuberculosis, he was uncertain as to a career path until the Rev. Robert L. DeWitt[1] suggested the ministry. Thereupon Mead attended Virginia Theological Seminary in Alexandria, Virginia, and then became rector of historic St. Paul's Church in that city. He served Christ Church Cranbrook in Bloomfield Hills, Michigan, and was on the staff of the Parishfield Community in Brighton, Michigan, a semi-independent agency of the Diocese of Michigan established to create a ministry of lay people who would further the mission of the church in society. Mr. Mead's wife was the former Katherine Baldwin Lloyd, and they had a son, William Lloyd, and a daughter, Katherine Barton. The family moved into the new rectory at One Heather Place on October 1.

The Rev. Mr. Mead attended his first vestry meeting on September 14, but he was not the only new person in attendance. Mrs. W. Lyman (Gertrude) Heitmiller had been invited to attend the meetings in her capacity as the president

The rector's wife, Katherine Baldwin Lloyd Mead.

A pen-and-ink sketch of St. John's by Katherine Mead.

of the Women of St. John's, thus making her the first female parishioner to attend vestry meetings on a regular basis, though without a vote. She was also the only woman

to serve as a parish delegate to Diocesan Convention in 1960. Her successors in the post of president of the Women of St. John's—Mrs. John (Betty) Myers and Mrs. John (Mary Lou) Brackett—attended vestry meetings in their turn, and by 1962 four women were elected delegates to Diocesan Convention, namely, Betty Myers, Mary Lou Brackett, Mrs. C. E. Bayliss (Mary) Griggs, and Mrs. John (Betty) Musser.

The new Holy Apostles Parish on the east side of St. Paul emerged upon the unification of St. James Church and St. Peter's Church. Several members of the fledgling parish, including the Rev. Robert Crosbie, approached St. John's in October 1959 asking for financial assistance in their project to erect a building upon property located on East Minnehaha near the city limits. Their fundraising campaign had already netted the church approximately $51,000, but they needed another $50,000. There is no record at St. John's to suggest that the parish made a contribution to Holy Apostles. Some fifty years later, however, the two parishes embarked upon a fruitful collaboration after a large contingent of St. Paul's flourishing Hmong community joined the congregation at Holy Apostles.

The Rev. Mead instituted a new baptismal practice during his third month at St. John's. Whereas private baptisms had been the norm in virtually all Episcopal churches, being small family affairs, and for the most part observed at times other than Sunday mornings, Mead was far ahead of his time in declaring the sacrament of baptism a public event best celebrated in the presence of the congregation. It was not until twenty years later, with the promulgation of the 1979 *Book of Common Prayer*, that public baptism became normative in the Episcopal Church.

During these years, the congregation was deeply concerned about the evolving neighborhood north of the church. Rondo Avenue at the center of St. Paul's largest African-American community was being cut through by the construction of I-94, displacing thousands into a racially segregated city with discriminatory housing. By the 1960s the Selby-Dale area, within blocks of St. John's, had some of the worst housing and street

Gertrude Heitmiller.

Bob and Jan Andrews.

Mary and Bayliss Griggs.

crime in the city. Guest speakers were invited to address the congregation on topics of relevant interest. In December 1959, for instance, the director of the St. Paul Planning Commission spoke concerning the problems of the Selby-Dale area and its relation to greater St. Paul.

The parish itself suffered several break-ins during the 1960s. In June 1961, Art Zache's office was vandalized while he was on vacation in Florida, leading to the changing of roughly sixty-five locks and the issuance of fewer keys than before. In December someone broke into the Parish House, jimmying the doors; and in March 1963 Mr. Mead reported that there had been an illegal entry into "The Church of the Open Door." As was the case with an earlier burglary attempt, the would-be thieves were thwarted and left empty-handed.

Irvine Kelliher raised for the vestry's consideration, in February 1960, the question of equitable pay and carfare for boys and girls in the choir, an issue that had long needed discussion. Part of the problem had to do with excessive payments of carfare when they were not especially needed. Under a new plan the children and youth would receive 50¢, 70¢, or 90¢ per Sunday, depending on age and experience, with a

reduction in these stipends if a rehearsal were missed.

Although there had recently been difficulty staffing the choir with boys, and inequity in the payment of the boys and girls, by the fall of 1960 the choir of men, women, boys, and girls had eighty-four members on the roster, seriously crowding the choir stalls in the chancel. It was, by far, the largest choir in St. John's history. Nevertheless, by March, Mr. Andersen was still in desperate need of tenors and basses.

Janice Andrews was general chairman for the Rummage Sale in April 1960 when the net profit was $1,439.59. She served in the same capacity for two more years, and in 1963 Mrs. Vernon (Marilyn) Olson assumed the task. St. John's first Rummage Sale was sponsored by St. Margaret's Guild in 1910.

Parishioner Truman P. Gardner, a real estate and insurance agent, was buried from St. John's in February 1960. Gardner worked with the Investment Service Company in St. Paul during the 1920s and then was secretary and general manager of the Gardner Company real estate and insurance. In 1939 he became president of the First National Bank in

THE REV. DAVID BENSON was hired as Mr. Mead's assistant, to start in September 1961, with a car allowance and a residence in addition to his salary. The vestry had decided that since St. John's would always be a "two-man job," a second house was desirable, with the annual residence allowance for the clergyman going instead toward monthly payments on the mortgage. All that was needed was a down payment.

By June a house was found at 937 Lincoln Avenue with four bedrooms and the possibility of a fifth. It was about forty-five years old, but it was in excellent repair and stood in a good neighborhood. The vestry decided to purchase the house, with the top figure not to exceed $27,500. A down payment of $10,000 had to be raised, but the vestry authorized the borrowing of that sum from the endowment fund, if it were necessary. By September the house had been purchased for the new associate rector and his family.

Thirty-three-years-old when he came to St. John's, Mr. Benson did general parish work and was not restricted to any particular ministries, as was usually the case with assistant clergy, who were often assigned to the youth or the church school. Mr. Mead allowed him to preach at least once a month and make frequent calls upon parishioners. Benson considered Mr. Mead a good pastor and an exemplary preacher, and recalls that his superior preached his best sermons on Christmas and Easter, when he could reach many people who never attended church otherwise. As a pastoral man, he said, Mr. Mead was endowed with fine counseling skills, a good bedside manner, and with empathy for people of all walks and conditions of life.

Hastings, Minnesota. He and his wife lived at 301 Summit Avenue. An oak prayer desk to his memory was carved to match the existing prayer desk in the chancel.

Cole Oehler observed at a vestry meeting that the Rev. Robert Hanson, Mr. Mead's assistant, did not like, nor was he trained for, the job of handling the Church School. It was announced in June 1960 that Hanson would resign his position at St. John's, effective on August 31.[2] By the start-up of the Church School in September, Mr. Mead had been unable to find a director of religious education. Mrs. Margaret Hill was subsequently hired as director of Christian education in 1961.

John Parish was chairman of the Stewardship Campaign in the fall of 1960, and in December he reported that the campaign had been a success. With a few pledges still to come in, a total of $83,079.80 had been pledged thus far for 1961.

Mr. Mead observed that it was the first increase in pledges in five years, while many older and more established churches were having a real struggle to make ends meet.

The vestry received the good news in March 1962 that the estate of Adele Lanpher, who died in December 1961, left $5,000 to the parish.[3] But a year later they learned, certainly to their regret and perhaps to their censure, that the bulk of the $300,000 estate of Mrs. John (Mildred) Finehout, the widow of Judge John W. Finehout,[4] had been left to the Humane Society for the care and nurture of animals, thus snubbing St. John's. Parish treasurer James Stevenson commented that there had been some failure on the part of the parish with regard to Mrs. Finehout. She left a more modest $1,000 to the church.

Also in March 1962 the house on the southwest corner of Portland and Kent went on the market, with an asking price of $17,500. The lot was 92 feet by 140 feet, on which an estimated twenty-four cars could be parked. The vestry purchased the property for $18,000 with a down payment of $4,000, the balance to be secured by a mortgage. The vestry voted the next year to demolish the buildings on the lot for a maximum figure of $2,000 and bring it to rough grade and investigated the cost of blacktop. These plans were subsequently put on hold, however, because of strained finances at the church. Indeed, circumstances were such that in December the vestry voted to discontinue choir salaries for the boy and girl choristers, and either to reduce the frequency of *The Evangelist* or eliminate it altogether.

Although the pledges for fiscal year 1964 came to $90,300, representing an increase of $3,400, or 4 percent, over 1963, it was a tight budget that allowed no frills.[5] The budget reflected a cut in what the parish spent on itself and an increase in outside giving, "a good and healthy sign," and was the direct result of vestry action toward that end.

The rectorship of the Rev. William Mead, as we shall see, lasted for only five years, but it saw four major contributions to the life of the parish: (1) the formation of commissions to work in tandem with the vestry, (2) the sponsorship of refugees from Communist Cuba, (3) the exhibition of religious art, and (4) the awakening of the parish to civil rights issues and racial injustice.

THE FIRST ACHIEVEMENT was an important and lasting addition to the infrastructure of the parish, namely, the institution of a commission organization to work in collaboration with the vestry, an organization that continues to this day. The original seven commissions were set up in February 1961: Worship, Christian Education, Christian Social Relations, Fellowship, Finance, Property and Memorials, and a Communications and Promotion Commission. Each commission was chaired and co-chaired by members of the vestry.

The commissions took up their challenges in earnest, one reporting on problems in the Church School and another making suggestions relative to newcomers. Among their concerns were the fact that a number of parishioners were moving into the suburbs,[6] that the choir desperately required more tenors and basses, and that rehearsals were needed to improve congregational singing.

A new guild, called the Coventry Guild, was established in November 1961 for young women. The first officers were Dusty Henry and Mary Thomas as co-chairs, with Judy Diedrich as secretary-treasurer.

Among the problems in the Church School was the evident lack of success of the curriculum then in use. The Seabury Series was the official curriculum of the national church and it had been in use at St. John's for six years, presenting apparently daunting challenges to the teachers. Mr. Mead believed that the teachers were inadequately trained to use the series effectively, and said that next year the teacher training would be on a weekly basis rather than monthly. In his view, though the series was not in itself too sacred to change, it deserved a better chance than it had been accorded. And it was given that chance. Mr. Mead remarked that the greatest single parish improvement in 1962 was in the Church School and that the teachers made the greatest difference in creating the improvement.

THE RECTOR'S POLITICS WERE PRIVATE, so much so, according to the Rev. David Benson, that when John Kennedy ran against Richard Nixon, "Not even Kate knew who I voted for." Indeed, although Mr. Mead was concerned about world issues, in the mind of Benson he avoided politicizing the parish. A perfectionist, Mead was a tough man, not a pushover, and it was during his tenure that St. John's began to shed its reputation for aloofness. Nevertheless, the parish remained a wealthy, white upper-middle class congregation, and though its neighbors to the north were never turned away, they did not feel welcomed.

Both Benson and Mead were committed to civil rights, racial justice, and the relief of the dispossessed. After leaving St. John's, Mr. Benson joined other clergy and lay people in one of the civil rights marches from Selma to Montgomery, Alabama. He called it a transformative experience. And

Mr. Mead is remembered for the time he disguised himself as a homeless man and lived among the homeless, receiving attention in a news article.

Vestryman Frank Wiecher had been serving as director of the neighborhood Recreation Program for some time, and Richard Benepe, the son of Dr. and Mrs. James L. (Gladys) Benepe and a teacher at Wilson High School, was devoting three nights every week to evening sessions for neighbors in the twelve-to-twenty-one age group. Mr. and Mrs. Al Hanner, experts in the field of recreation, came in on four afternoons a week for the boys and girls in the six-to-eleven age bracket. The recreation program for the neighborhood was flourishing. After twelve years as chairman of the program, Frank Wiecher would resign in May 1967.

Neighboring St. Clement's Episcopal Church was operating a full summer program at a storefront that included a food shelf on Selby Avenue with several seminarians on the staff, and they invited St. John's to become a co-sponsor. By the end of 1964, four area churches had signed on to the project, with Nobuo Murakami, Charles Stryker, and John Edgerton Jr. from St. John's serving on the executive committee. For an eight-week summer program in 1965, three seminary students (two men and one woman) became involved, and by the end of the year the storefront was financially secure, with an effective program operating on Wednesday and Thursday afternoons, and on Saturday mornings. So rosy were the prospects that by January 1966 the project was said to have an unlimited future, with an annual budget of $113,770. In February the storefront had moved to a new location, at 649 Selby, but in September 1968 the sponsors terminated the lease.

THE SECOND CONSIDERABLE ACHIEVEMENT in the life of the parish during Mr. Mead's rectorship was the program titled "North Star Flight 85," which emerged in July 1962. The Christian Social Relations Commission, spearheaded by Jerome Buser and Adrian Drew proposed to bring eighty-five Cuban refugees from Communist Cuba to new homes in the diocese. Both Presiding Bishop Arthur Lichtenberger and Bishop Kellogg had committed the

church to this effort, and parishioners Dr. and Mrs. James (Gladys) Benepe[7] were named chairmen for the diocesan program. All of the Cuban men were said to be skilled, semi-skilled, or professional people. The vestry accepted the challenge. St. John's was asked to sponsor one family, to find a house for them, and to secure a job for the head of the family.

At the last minute, the family that was expected by the parish did not come. Instead Mr. and Mrs. Enrique Portell came with six other family members, including Enrique Portell Jr., who had a wife, Maria Louisa, and a son, aged two, named Enrique III. The daughter of the senior Portells, named Concepcion, had a one-and-a-half-year-old daughter named Maria. Then there was five-year-old Santiago, son of another Portell daughter, who would stay with his grandparents until his mother arrived. Enrique Sr. spoke English and could arrange to give Spanish lessons, while Concepcion was working in a garment factory. The Portells were settled in the duplex on the property recently acquired by the parish for a parking lot on the corner of Kent and Portland.

Jerome (Jerry) Buser led the Christian Social Relations Commission, which brought Cuban refugees to the diocese.

The success of this first settlement of Cuban refugees led to another in 1963, when the parish received Mr. and Mrs. Arturo Codina Sr. and their family. For twenty-two years Mr. Codina was head of the physical education department of the high school in Manzanillo, Oriente Province. He was also a skilled physical therapist and masseur. Mrs. Codina was a cateress, specializing in buffet suppers for weddings. Their daughter Joaquina and son-in-law were Mr. and Mrs. Bernardo Utset, who had a three-month-old boy named Bernardo Jr. Sixteen-year-old Arturo Codina Jr. had been in St. Paul for the past year, attending Central High School and living with an aunt and uncle who had arrived the previous July with

The Portell family with Marilyn Olson (in striped dress) and the Rev. Grayson Clary.

the first group of Cuban refugees sponsored by the Diocese of Minnesota. The Codina family lived at 35 N. Grotto Avenue in St. Paul.

In the last months of 1962, members of the vestry shared with *The Evangelist* their dreams for St. John's and the neighborhood. Reynolds W. Guyer Sr. was vice-chairman of the Communications Commission and taught in the Church School. He looked to the task "of strengthening and increasing the image and effectiveness of St. John's within our community," and believed that the parish had "an opportunity to be a far more positive force within the area for delivering the gospel and providing recreational assistance to the immediate neighborhood." Mr. Guyer was the founder of Reynolds Guyer Agency of Design, and was for many years the vice-president of research and development at Hoerner-Waldorf.

Guyer's multi-talented son, Reynolds W. (Reyn) Guyer Jr., inventor, artist, and songwriter, became chairman of the board and chief executive officer of his father's design agency. He also founded Winsor Learning, whose materials and products for educators focus on a multi-sensory approach to teaching, reading, writing, and spelling. Reyn was the voice of the characters, and co-writer of the Curly Lasagna stories and songs. He also developed and licensed the party game Twister (Milton Bradley) named the Game of the Year in 1967, as well as the Nerf Ball (Parker Brothers). Over four million of the foam balls were sold in Nerf's first year. Many of Mr. Guyer's artworks, including sculptures, are found in corporate and private collections.

A former member of St. John's, William M. Ripley, son of parishioner Edna B. Ripley and nephew of parishioner Mrs. James Benepe, was ordained to the priesthood in Hutchinson,

FRANCIS G. OKIE, an earlier parishioner of St. John's, was another inventor. Okie invented waterproof sandpaper in 1921, contributing significantly to improved worker safety and ending the health hazards associated with dry sanding. Waterproof sandpaper played a key role in the growth of the Minnesota Mining and Manufacturing Company. It launched 3M on the road to broad product diversification, opened the door to international expansion, taught the company the importance of patent protection, and provided funds to finance future growth at a critical time in the firm's history.[8] Mr. Okie served on St. John's vestry in the 1920s.

Francis Okie was inducted into the Minnesota Inventors Hall of Fame in 1980.

Kansas, in September 1962. Ripley was a recent graduate of the Episcopal Theological Seminary of the Southwest in Austin, Texas.

In the spring of 1964, parishioner Irvine A. Kelliher was admitted as a postulant for holy orders in the Diocese of Minnesota. He intended to study for the perpetual diaconate, meaning that he would remain in deacon's orders without proceeding to the priesthood, at the same time retaining his secular employment.

THE THIRD SIGNIFICANT accomplishment of the Mead tenure was a major exhibition at the church of religious art that ran from November 25 through December 2, 1962. "The Christmas Exhibition of Religious Art," as it was called, featured medieval and contemporary art treasures, including paintings, sculpture, and vestments. The exhibition was a collaboration between St. John's and the Minneapolis Institute of Arts (MIA), whose director, Carl Weinhardt, generously offered to prepare the show. Parishioner Thomas Daniels was chairman of the board of MIA, and it was he who negotiated the arrangements, though his wife Fannie was general chairman of the effort.

Most of the art objects were on loan from MIA including a fifteenth-century polychromed statue of the Virgin, but objects from private collections were included: an alabaster piece from Mrs. Theodore W. Griggs, art objects loaned by the Daniels family, by Mr. and Mrs. Louis W. Hill, the family of Mrs. Frank E. Ward, Mr. and Mrs. John R. Savage, Eleanor Quantrell, Dr. and Mrs. Vernon Olson, and Mr. and Mrs. H. H. Grace. Parishioner Reynolds W. Guyer Sr. was in charge of publicity and promotion, and Betty Myers was responsible for hospitality. The show was open to the public without charge and was toured by about two thousand people.

The Chapel of the Beloved Disciple had already seen makeovers in 1922, 1931, and 1936. Although the renovation in 1931 was the gift of Mrs. Paul (Reine) Myers, she had the chapel completely renovated again in 1962. Reine and Paul Myers always sat in pew 111, on the left side of the nave in the church. A small ledge on the back of that pew was installed for Reine, who was too short to rest her elbows on the top of the pew and needed a lower support. The discreet shelf continues to mark her customary seat.

After only two years on the job, Margaret Hill resigned her position as director of Christian education in March 1963, effective on July 23, to take up a similar post at St. Mark's Church in San Antonio, at the time the fourth largest parish in the Episcopal Church. Marla Shilton, then director of Christian education at Calvary Episcopal Cathedral in Sioux Falls, was hired to succeed Hill at St. John's in May 1963 and reported on August 1. Shilton attended Union Theological Seminary and the Windham House in New York City, graduating *cum laude* with a master's degree in religious education.

In June 1963, organist and choirmaster C. Wesley Andersen was honored for his twenty years of service to the

Fifteenth-century polychromed wood Madonna, Florence. Minneapolis Institute of Arts.

The John H. Myers family: John, Bruce, Peter, and Betty.

parish at a reception that followed the annual spring choir concert. Parishioners were given the opportunity to contribute to a testimonial purse for Mr. Andersen, which came to a total of $500, with which he purchased an air-conditioner for his automobile.

THE FOURTH MAJOR accomplishment of Mr. Mead's tenure, and perhaps the most important of all, was the awakening of the parish to civil rights issues and racial injustice. The movement challenged clergy, staff, vestry, and laity alike, and it engaged adults at worship no less than the children and youth in the Church School. No one could ignore it. There were meetings with black leaders from the community and exchanges with the black congregation at St. Philip's Church. There were store-front efforts and hands-on campaigns in the neighborhood.[9]

There was plenty of soul-searching by the vestry, as well as the commitment of funds, not to mention the ongoing recreation program for neighborhood children and youth in St. John's gymnasium. The efforts were zealous even if not always successful.

The Christian Social Relations Commission continued its discussion of civil rights in June 1963. Dr. Clarke Chambers pointed out that the subject was a concern of parishioners nationwide, sparked by a recent letter from the presiding bishop. The vestry sent a letter to the membership reminding them of the presiding bishop's plea on Whitsunday, indicating that the vestry would send a minimum gift of $300 to further the work of the Urban League of St. Paul and inviting additional contributions from parishioners. The purpose of the league was "to eliminate racial segregation and discrimination in American life; and to give guidance and help to Negroes so that they may share equally the responsibilities and rewards of citizenship."

The parish continued to undertake projects designed to stir interest in racial equality and civil rights. Reynolds Guyer, for instance, took his ninth-grade Church School class to visit their counterparts at St. Philip's Church. The students had a healthy discussion of race relations, and St. Philip's planned to return the visit. In 1964 Mrs. William (Liz) Perry and Mrs. Robert (Priscilla) Farnham took their fifth-grade girls to visit the Hallie Q. Brown Community Center, a private, nonprofit social service agency serving the Summit-University area that was established in 1929 for the support of African Americans. W. Lyman Heitmiller[10] and Enrique Portell Jr. took their sixth-grade boys on a tour of the neighborhood. And Mrs. Eugene (Joan) Ware Jr., a teacher of the third-grade class, invited the Dale-Selby Action Council to show pictures of its children's activities to the three lower grades.

An opportunity for further parish engagement emerged after *The Evangelist* noted in November 1963 that "sometime within this month an experiment of real importance will begin in our neighborhood." The Planned Parenthood Center of St. Paul was to open a clinic and information center at 671 Selby Avenue, near the corner of St. Albans. It would be an experiment in that its storefront location would make its services readily accessible and visible to all the people of the area. It would be controversial in that it would raise the subjects of birth control and over-population. The newsletter quoted from the report of the 1958 Lambeth Conference, in which the bishops of the Anglican Communion wrote:

> The responsibility for deciding upon the number and frequency of children has been laid by God upon the consciences of parents everywhere; this planning, in such ways as are mutually acceptable to husband and wife in Christian conscience is a right and important factor in Christian family life and should be the result of positive choice before God.

The Evangelist gave its unqualified support to the experiment, believing it to be a real service to the neighbors, and invited women in the parish to volunteer as hostesses in the new clinic.

In November 1963 the commissions of the vestry met with leaders of St. Paul's African-American community to discuss informally the situation in the city with regard to race relations. It was not a conclusive evening, and no decisions were reached on the part of the parish, but the black leaders gave the commissions much to think about, and in several cases challenged well-established points of view.

In September 1963 it was announced that three families from the parish offered to cover the cost of a new sacristy and new offices for the rector and assistant rector, permitting more privacy for counseling purposes and better all-around efficiency and comfort. The rector's study originally occupied the room where the photocopier is today, adjacent to the office administrator. Mr. Mead believed that the rector's study should not be on the main thoroughfare of parish house traffic:

> Many people who come to see us are emotionally upset, or become so, and would like to be able to arrive and leave with some privacy. Our regular desk work, our writing and study, as well as our pastoral counseling, is presently being done in surroundings which remind one of no place quite as much as Grand Central Station.

The new offices were located to the east of the chancel, below the chambers for the organ pipes, and occupy part of what was originally the east transept of the 1895 guild house designed by Cass Gilbert. In April 1964 it was divulged that the donor was in fact Mrs. Paul (Reine) Myers whose "generous loyalty and concern for this parish and its needs have been expressed in many ways through the years and this latest gift is but another example of that concern." Mrs. Myers gave the offices in appreciation for all that St. John's had meant to her.

The diocese had established a Long-Range Planning Commission in 1960 to survey its needs and challenges into the future, and to achieve a clearer understanding of its goals and purposes. Bishop Hamilton Kellogg was its chairman, but in September 1963 the Rev. Mead was appointed to the post. It was an honor for him and for the parish, but it was

ARTIST CLARA GARDNER MAIRS (pronounced "Mars") was buried from St. John's in June 1963. Born in Hastings, Minnesota, the daughter of Samuel and Abigail Gardner Mairs, Clara moved to St. Paul with her mother and three siblings after Samuel died at the young age of thirty-seven in 1891. The Mairs family lived first in a fashionable brick and brownstone rowhouse at 123 Nina Street, then after 1898 at 407 Holly (the present site of the Commodore Hotel).

In 1923 Clara moved to Paris to study with cubist teacher and artist André Lhote and at the Académie Julian. Known for her genre scenes of women and children, Mairs achieved a national reputation through her etchings in the 1920s and 1930s, and was prominent in the upper Midwest for her paintings and prints. She had several one-woman shows and her works are held in the collections of museums across the country. Clara and her partner, artist Clem Haupers, lived at 377 Ramsey Hill.

Clara and her brother Sam Mairs in 1888. Sam would distinguish himself as chairman of Archer Daniels Midland Company.

Clara Mairs, *Ramsey Hill*, etching.

Clara Mairs with portrait of serviceman on her easel.

also a burden, and both he and the parish would be called upon to make certain sacrifices into the future. It was not a full-time job, partly because an executive director had also been hired, but it would nevertheless be a demanding and time-consuming occupation, taking Mead away from some of his parish duties. The vestry offered him their support and understanding and hoped every parishioner would do the same.

A MAJOR GENDER BARRIER was shattered in January 1964 when at the Annual Meeting Ella Buser was elected to a post on the vestry, along with John Edgerton Jr., Charles Richards Gordon, and Nobuo Murakami. For the previous seventy-seven years, membership on the vestry—indeed, on all Episcopal vestries everywhere—was synonymous with prominent men of stature in the community: business or professional men, or men holding positions of public trust. While it would be difficult to specify how the presence of women influenced the deliberations of St. John's vestry, it won decisively for the future a better representation of the mixed complexion of the parish in its leadership.

Early in 1964 the Christian Social Relations Commission obtained authorization from the vestry to use one or two Sundays to promote civil rights. Tables were set up at the coffee hour and equipped with stationery and essential information, so that individuals could write to their representatives in Congress to urge passage of the landmark Civil Rights Act. Over fifty letters supporting the legislation were mailed to U.S. Senate leaders, and on July 2, 1964, the bill outlawed major forms of discrimination against blacks and women, including racial segregation.

At a January 1964 meeting of the Dale-Selby Action Council, a non-partisan campaign was organized to increase voter participation as an effective way of making the needs of the neighborhood heard at city hall. Parishioner Marilyn Olson was appointed chairwoman of the Voter Participation Committee, which included parishioner Robert Farnham. The committee took on voter registration, voter education, and a get-out-the-vote campaign for the city primary and the general election. The campaign opened in the first week of February with over eighty participants, including parish-

ioners Annie Laurie Baker, Jenny Chambers, Nancy Shepard, and Marla Shilton. This group canvassed one-third of the 153 blocks in the area and sent questionnaires regarding specific areas of residents' concern to all candidates for mayor and city council. It also held an open meeting, which all candidates in the general election for mayor and city council were urged to attend.

In February, Presiding Bishop Arthur Lichtenberger sent a letter to congregations around the country announcing a two-pronged effort to deal with racial inequity. The National Council of the Episcopal Church sought to raise $150,000 to work toward racial justice, and the National Council of Churches, to which the Episcopal Church contributes, made an appeal to raise $45,000 to deal with special crises arising from the racial situation. The vestry ordered that the Maundy Thursday offering be sent to the presiding bishop, with not less than $250 to the fund for racial justice.

AFTER A RECTORSHIP of less than five years, the Rev. William H. Mead announced to the parish that he had accepted a call to be dean of Christ Church Cathedral in St. Louis, Missouri, with his resignation effective on May 3, 1964. He wrote in the April issue of The Evangelist, "I cannot remember ever having been happier than I've been at St. John's." The vestry accepted his resignation "with deepest regret" and wrote in a resolution that Mr. Mead had served in "a very superior manner" and that the parish had been "singularly blessed" by his presence. Indeed, he was esteemed for his "compassionate counseling coupled with wisdom and insight for those who sought his help; his forthrightness and honesty in communicating with people; his vision of the church's mission, and his ability to work for its accomplishment."[11]

The vestry asked the associate rector, the Rev. David Benson, to be locum tenens from the time of Mead's departure, serving as acting rector until a new rector was elected. Benson agreed to commit himself to St. John's through July 1964, but would stay beyond that date until such time as a new rector took up residence in the parish, or until he found another position, in which case he would try to give sixty days' notice.

John H. Myers was elected chairman of the Calling Committee and he asked Cole Oehler to serve with him as co-chairman. The other members on the committee were Annie Laurie Baker, Richard Benepe, Ella Buser, Dr. Clarke Chambers, Edward Divett, Dorothy Drew, Mrs. Benjamin Griggs Sr., Dusty Henry, Irvine Kelliher, Blair Klein, John Musser, John Parish, John Pierson, Blake Shepard, Charles Smith III, and James Stevenson Sr.

By mid-March a list of sixty-three names had been pared to eighteen prospective candidates. John Myers had also talked with Bishop Kellogg, who was entitled by canon law to suggest nominees for the rectorship within thirty days. Urging the committee to consider clergy from within the diocese, the bishop suggested three candidates: the Rev. John Hildebrand of St. Paul's, Duluth; the Rev. Wendell McGinnis of Calvary, Rochester; and the Rev. Webster Barnett of St. David's, Minnetonka Village.

At the vestry meeting in May, John Myers named four final candidates who would be invited with their wives to visit St. John's: the Rev. Robert L. Green Jr., of Wilton, Connecticut; the Rev. John Hildebrand of Duluth; the Rev. Jon H. Vruwink of Tulsa, Oklahoma; and the Rev. Sidney Grayson Clary, of Charleston, South Carolina. In June, the vestry voted to call Mr. Clary, who was presently serving St. Philip's parish in Charleston, a church of eleven hundred communicants, where he enjoyed an effective ministry. He and his wife, the former Olive Jean Beazley, of South Orange, New Jersey, who, like her husband, was a graduate of the College of William and Mary, had two sons, Bradley and Richard.

Mr. Mead's last service fell on Confirmation Sunday, May 3, when Bishop Kellogg was present. After the service there was a reception in the gymnasium to honor Mr. Mead, his wife Kate,[12] and their children Kathy and Billy.

It was a season of departures and retirements at St. John's, for at precisely this time Arthur Zache announced his retirement after more than forty years of faithful service. Al Hanner succeeded Zache as director of the choir camps that summer, which took place at the Christ Church Camp at Bass Lake, Wisconsin. Mr. Zache's long ministry had endeared him to young and old alike, from boy and girl choristers to the parish hierarchy.

The Rev. William Mead enjoyed additional ecclesiastical distinctions after becoming dean of the cathedral in St. Louis. The Virginia Theological Seminary awarded him an honorary Doctor of Divinity degree in 1966, and in 1968 he was elected seventh bishop of the Diocese of Delaware. As bishop, Mead served on the national church's Committee on the Integration of Women's Work. He died in office in 1974, at the young age of fifty-three, apparently of a heart attack. John and Betty Myers, John and Betty Musser, and Mary and Bayliss Griggs from St. John's attended his funeral in Wilmington.

In 1966 the Rev. William Henry Mead was elected seventh bishop of the Diocese of Delaware. John Myers served as the attending layman at his consecration.

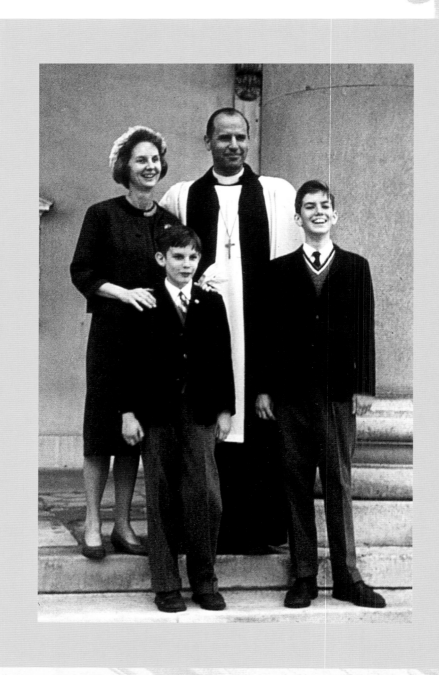

The Rev. S. Grayson Clary, his wife Jean, with their two sons, Richard (left) and Bradley, on the steps of St. Marylebone's Church in London in 1963, the year before they came to St. Paul.

chapter thirteen

THE REV. SIDNEY GRAYSON CLARY 1964-1986
A Priest's Priest

SOCIAL TUMULT throughout the country marked the beginning years of the rectorship of the Rev. Grayson Clary. In 1965, as the Vietnam War was ratcheting up, the Students for a Democratic Society and the Student Nonviolent Coordinating Committee led the first of several anti-war marches in Washington, D.C. Congress passed the Voting Rights Act, Medicare and Medicaid were enacted, and African-American Muslim activist Malcolm X was assassinated in Harlem.

The first Super Bowl was played in 1967, with the Green Bay Packers defeating the Kansas City Chiefs. Race riots in Detroit precipitated the "long hot summer" when similar riots erupted in 159 cities nationwide. The following year both Robert F. Kennedy and Martin Luther King Jr. were assassinated. Neil Armstrong and Buzz Aldrin landed their space module Apollo 11 on the moon in 1969. The same year, Stonewall riots in New York City marked the beginning of the gay rights movement, and the Woodstock Music Festival drew half a million hippies to a farm in the Catskills.

In 1973 the Vietnam War officially came to an end. The next year Richard Nixon resigned the presidency in the wake of the Watergate scandal. Film producer and director George Lucas created *Star Wars* and Indiana Jones, and in

The Rev. Sidney Grayson Clary.

1978 Jerry Falwell founded the Moral Majority, the same year that Apple introduced the first operating system for its computers. In 1980 Beatle John Lennon was assassinated on a sidewalk in New York City and Ronald Reagan was elected to the presidency. In 1981 AIDS was described for the first time in a U.S. medical journal. The winter of 1983-1984 was the snowiest in St. Paul's recorded history (98.4"), and in 1986 the space shuttle *Challenger* broke apart after its launch, killing all seven astronauts.

Born in Virginia in 1921, Sidney Grayson Clary graduated from the College of William and Mary in 1943, receiving the Algernon Sydney Sullivan Award in recognition of his "heart, mind and helpfulness to others." During World War II, he served on the USS *North Carolina* as Lieutenant JG in the Pacific, for a period of thirty-two months. After the war he attended Virginia Theological Seminary and was ordained deacon in 1949, and priest in 1950.

Between 1948 and 1951, Mr. Clary served Episcopal parishes in Newport News, Lawrenceville, Alberta, and Callaville, all in Virginia. In 1951 he went to Calvary Church in Tarboro, North Carolina,[1] a small tobacco-growing town in the eastern part of the state, leaving in 1957. From then until 1964 he served St. Philip's Church in Charleston,

South Carolina, founded in 1680 as the mother church of Anglicanism in the Carolinas and the oldest Anglican congregation south of Virginia. Mr. Clary took a leave of absence in 1962-1963 in order to assume the pastorate at St. Marylebone's Church in central London, England, in an affluent inner-city area in the City of Westminster. While in London he had occasion to preach at St. Paul's Cathedral.

In the 1950s and 1960s Mr. Clary was a prominent civil rights activist in North and South Carolina, so much so, in fact, that the family endured harassing telephone calls and even death threats. People would cross to the other side of the street rather than walk by them. According to their son, parishioner Bradley Clary, his parents used to say, "We had some of our best friends and some of our best enemies in Charleston."[2]

The Rev. S. Grayson Clary assumed his position as thirteenth rector on the first Sunday in September 1964. During the first week of his twenty-two-year tenure, the longest of any priest at St. John's, Mr. Clary's first formal act was to officiate at the funeral of parishioner Reine Humbird Myers, widow of Paul Noxon Myers and mother of John H. Myers, Elizabeth Myers Parish, and Paul Myers Jr., for many years an indefatigable worker well-regarded for her lavish benevolence.

In November 1964, the sixty-first General Convention of the Episcopal Church, meeting in St. Louis, elected the Rev. George Theodore Masuda as Missionary Bishop of North Dakota, with the Rt. Rev. Conrad Gesner serving as co-consecrator. Known for his pastoral care and simplicity, Bishop Masuda was at one time a member of St. John's and a trustee of St. Mary's Hall in Faribault.

Just three blocks north of St. John's, Selby Avenue had been a respectable address and was a prosperous streetcar route until the railway was replaced by buses and automobiles in the early 1950s. It depends on one's perspective as to when St. John's neighborhood began its slow decline. But as early as the late 1920s, as we have seen, new apartment buildings and rentals were replacing single-family dwellings, leading

REINE MYERS was a benefactor of Carleton College (Myers Hall was named after her) and she had connections with the American Hearing Society, the Schubert Club, and the YWCA. Three former rectors participated in her memorial service: the Very Rev. Dr. Lloyd Gillmett from Los Angeles, the Rt. Rev. Conrad Gesner from South Dakota, and the Very Rev. Dr. William Mead from St. Louis. In 1957 the Myers Foundation established the Reine Humbird Myers Fellowships in audiology and speech at Northwestern University. As Mrs. Myers was an excellent violinist, the Reine Humbird Myers chair for principal violist in the Minnesota Orchestra was endowed by her family—John and Betty Myers, John and Zib Parish, and Genevieve and Paul Myers Jr.

Shortly after her death, the vestry learned that Mrs. Myers had bequeathed her property at 880 Goodrich Avenue to the church. The vestry wrote the following resolution in tribute to her:

> Profoundly thankful as we are for this characteristically generous bequest, we wish to express...our gratitude and joy for the many years of Christian fellowship we of St. John's Church shared with Reine Myers. The devoted and loyal friend of bishop, priest, and layman alike, she was a good and faithful steward; her many acts of kindness were carried out in the quiet spirit of service that glorifies God.

For the sum of $40,000 in cash, the vestry sold the Myers property to Wells Farnham, who purchased it for his mother, Kate Humbird Farnham, the sister of Reine.

Confirmation class, May 15, 1966. Back row: Mr. Lyman Heitmiller, Richards Gordon, Mark Harrison, Tom Wood, Richard Clary, Peter Myers, Mrs. Newton B. (Sally) Frost. Middle row: Peter Melges, Deborah Larson, Barbara Boody, Wynne DeCoster, Virginia Stryker, Gregory Brooks. Front row: Ben Griggs, Ted Kohn, George Johnson, John Ware, Chris Brown, and Gordon Brown.

to a transient and unstable environment. By the 1950s St. John's was becoming involved in efforts to save and restore the neighborhood, becoming active in race relations, and it took little time for the parish to endorse the challenge as a moral responsibility. By the late 1960s the neighborhood was in serious decline and in 1968 the city's worst race riots took place at Selby's intersection with Dale. Buildings were boarded up or torn down and businesses closed or fled. When Bishop Kellogg came to St. John's for Confirmation one year, his chauffeur parked the bishop's black limousine on Holly Street. He returned to the car to discover that a brick had been hurled through the window.

In September 1964, in an effort at further engagement with

its neighborhood, the vestry considered the establishment of a neighborhood Study Center at St. John's, to provide an agreeable place for reading and study, along with books and reference materials, and supervision and encouragement. Motivation for learning basic skills and interest in study and school work had been stimulated by similar study centers in other areas, as in Chicago, where they tended to prevent school dropouts and juvenile delinquency.

At nearby Marshall Junior High School a recent report showed that fifty percent of the eighth-grade students were at least one year behind in their reading ability. At the neighborhood Webster School the principal and several teachers supported the Study Center for many of their students. The target date for the start-up of St. John's Reading Program was January 1965, for grades one through six, to be open for five weekday afternoons and Saturday mornings, if feasible. The center would have all necessary books, furniture, equipment, and supplies. There would be an advisory committee, comprising representatives from the Selby-Dale Action Council and Webster School, with two lay persons from St. John's and a member of the staff, but the program would be administered by the rector and vestry, with a chairman selected from the membership of the parish. An initial grant of $8,000 for the center came from the Myers Foundation with an evaluation to be made after a period of two years. The proposal was passed unanimously by the vestry.

The program ran successfully for several years, but by 1968 it was running into a financial bind, and the committee decided to seek funding from other sources. In December parishioners David and Perrin Lilly contributed to the program. Vestryman William Ward, president and treasurer of the Gokey Company, contacted the Hill family for an additional donation. Jerome Hill and Cortlandt Hill both made contributions. In acknowledgement of their gifts, the two men consented to the placing of a medallion in memory of their mother, Maud Taylor Hill, which hangs above the choir stalls in the chancel. It contains her image in relief, taken from a photograph.

Medallion in memory
of Maud Taylor Hill.

In April 1965, Grayson Clary announced that Reynolds Guyer Sr. and Augustus Clapp Jr. would be the co-chairmen for the Advance Fund Campaign at St. John's, a long-range diocesan effort with an overall goal of $1,400,000. The parish exceeded its quota of $98,100, while the diocese exceeded its goal by a substantial sum.

After the death of revered parishioner Reynolds Guyer Sr.,

ten years later, the vestry published a resolution dated June 19, 1975 that read as follows:

> He lived a life dedicated to the Christian faith, served as vestryman and warden, showed forth the Holy Gospel by example, personal evangelism, and stewardship, giving generously of his material possessions, and was a living example to his fellowman in his own robust and unique fashion that one's God-given gifts are for the service of mankind.

The rector of St. Thomas Church, Fifth Avenue in New York City,[3] the Rev. Frederick M. Morris, preached at St. John's in June 1965. He was dean of St. Mark's Cathedral before moving to New York in 1955, and his parents, the Rev. Lewis and Ruth Morris, were married at St. John's. Parishioners Fred Myers, John H. Myers, and Elizabeth Parish were cousins to the Rev. Frederick Morris.

In July 1965, the Rev. David Benson, the assisting priest, announced his resignation from St. John's, to become vicar for the parishes in Sauk Centre and Paynesville, Minnesota. He later took the post of associate rector at St. Peter's Church in Ladue, Missouri, an affluent parish in an inner-ring suburb of St. Louis. A farewell reception for the Benson family took place in August, at which the parish gave them a silver service.[4]

Parishioner John M. Musser, president of the General Timber Company, a subsidiary of the Weyerhaeuser Company, served the larger community in his role as general chairman of the St. Paul United Fund Campaign which, in October 1965, exceeded its goal of $4,028,096, providing hope for a homeless child, comfort for an aged woman, recreation for an adolescent, and counsel for a troubled marriage. He also served in leadership roles with the Boy

Scouts, the St. Paul Urban Coalition, and the Nitrogen Fixing Tree Association, in Hawaii, and was a trustee of the Aspen Institute for Humanistic Studies. In 1984 he was elected to the office of president of the St. Paul Chamber Orchestra Association. Musser died in 1990.

Also serving the broader community at this time was parishioner C. E. Bayliss Griggs who was recently elected president of the St. Paul Council of Arts and Sciences, an organization that attended to the cultural needs of the city—from Theatre St. Paul to the Science Museum.

St. John's was not immune to the turmoil of the Vietnam War, which raged from 1955 to the fall of Saigon in 1975, bringing dissent and riots to the shores of the United States and exacting a huge toll in casualties. Several members and friends of the congregation served in the military during that time, including Kenneth Dean Bellanger, Robert K. Brands, Thomas Brooks, Alden Drew, Richard M. Dunlop, Andrew H. Glenn, John W. Glenn, Charles Gordon, Milton W. Griggs II, Robert L. Harris, Peter A. Liebelt, Glenn Miller, Michael Norton, William Norton, Richard Paul Nuessle, Walter Nuessle, Cole Oehler Jr., Warren E. Olson, Michael M. Parish, Robert S. Parish, Charles T. Platt, James E. Stevenson, Mark J. Tobias, and Doreen L. Wells.

Parishioners Benjamin Griggs and John Myers were appointed to serve on the Minnesota Episcopal Foundation in February 1966. At the same time, upon request from the vestry and Mr. Clary, Bishop Kellogg transferred to St. John's the perpetual deacon, the Rev. Robert Orr Baker, who would assist on the first-Sunday services of Holy Communion, but be available to serve elsewhere on other Sundays of the month. Mr. Baker was assistant corporate secretary of the St. Paul Companies. He had several stints in the military, as a member of the Medical Battalion, Minnesota National Guard, and as chemical, biological and radiological officer for the 47th Infantry Division. In 1970 he was appointed civilian aide to the Secretary of the Army and was awarded the Outstanding Civilian Service Award by the Army in 1974. A president of the board of Riverview Memorial Hospital, he held a like position on the committee on capital improvements for the Metropolitan

Husband and wife Betty and John Musser were prominent in activities at St. John's and in the community. Betty Musser is credited with saving St. Paul's Landmark Center building.

Hospital Planning Council. He was a member of the board of St. Joseph's Hospital and the American Red Cross, and chairman of the Ramsey County Historical Society.

In March 1966 Mr. Clary nominated Joseph Madison Clark to be curate of the parish, to begin in June. A native of Kansas, Mr. Clark graduated from Northwestern University, and in May from Virginia Theological Seminary. He and his wife Sharon had one child and expected another at the end of the summer. Ordained a deacon in June, Mr. Clark was ordained to the priesthood at St. John's in March 1967. After only a year in the position, he left to take a mission of his own. Mr. Clark left parish ministry in the 1970s to do community organizing and engage in political action in Baltimore, and later joined the staff of the Maryland governor.

The vestry voted in May 1966 to commit the parish to an educational program called Project Summer. To be conducted at six area schools and churches for children in grades one through five, the morning program had a maximum enrollment possibility of 320 children from a low income level. The goals of Project Summer were to develop skills and provide cultural enrichment through classes in music, art, and sewing. Six centers would be open in the afternoons and evenings, one each at the school of the Cathedral of St. Paul, St. Peter Claver Church, the Ober Boys Club, Dayton Avenue Presbyterian Church, Park Baptist Church, and St. John's. The total program would have a budget of $38,872, with a majority of that coming from the federal government and the balance coming from local sources, including donations of space, utilities, and janitorial services. There would be fifty-six teachers, of whom thirty-one were Roman Catholic nuns and Christian Brothers,[5] with twenty-five lay persons.

WHEN RACIAL TENSION WAS HIGH in 1969, in the neighborhood north of St. John's, a School of Fine Arts was established at the church in collaboration with the Schubert Club, of which Shirley Kartarik was then president, for the teaching of art and music to the mostly African-American children who lived nearby. Shirley taught singing, the nationally known artist and parishioner Nell Hillsley taught art, and Prentice Harris, an African-American woman

respected in the black community, taught piano. But the children did not like going to the big white church. So the program was moved to the Martin Luther King Center and was named Project Cheer. The program still exists at that location, under that name, with continuing support from the Schubert Club, and the music lessons are still free.

Linda J. Rhodes, a graduate of Macalester College, was hired as director of Christian education beginning in September 1966, but she resigned her post the following spring to accept employment at the St. Paul Fire and Marine Insurance Company. She continued to work in the church school and with the Episcopal Young Churchmen on Sundays.

In June 1968 the vestry extended a call to Avis Haskell to fill the director's position. She was a graduate of St. Margaret's House in Berkeley, California, where she received practical as well as academic training. She had worked with Mexican immigrants and served in the Missionary District of Nevada for four years, where she had charge of two missions.

At the start-up of the Church School the following September, some 160 students were enrolled, a considerably smaller number than in earlier decades. By December the enrollment had risen to 175 (with attendance at only 50 percent), and by January 1969, eight children were coming from the neighborhood, three of whom also sang in the choir. Ms. Haskell retired from her position in 1976, after an eight-year tenure. In 1979 parishioner Dusty Henry agreed to be Christian Education Coordinator until a new assistant be hired, but remained in the post until January 1984.

By the fall of 1966 over 150 children were registered for the recreation program, the reading room, and the craft room. A cooking and sewing class for teenage girls under the direction of Gertrude Hannaford Jaffray was under way with ten girls and three volunteers participating. When the season ended in June 1967, total book circulation for the year was just under one thousand. One girl took out 112 books.

At the diocesan convention in February 1967, several parishioners were elected or appointed to important positions in the diocese. Nathaniel P. Langford[6] and Mr. Clary were appointed to the nominating committee for a new bishop coadjutor, which included twelve laymen and twelve clergy. C. E. Bayliss Griggs was elected to a term on the Standing Committee of the diocese, Mr. Clary was elected a member of the Diocean Council, and John Parish was elected to a term on the University Episcopal Center Board.

MR. AND MRS. JOHN PARISH and Mr. and Mrs. John Myers contributed a total of $25,000 to constitute a Challenge Fund in the spring of 1967 for the reduction of the debt on the Memorial Parish House, which remained at $95,923.26. Mr. and Mrs. Charles Smith III promptly made the first contribution toward matching the fund.

No stranger to the congregation, the Rt. Rev. James A. Pike, Bishop of the Diocese of California, returned to St. John's pulpit in May 1967 at the height of the controversy surrounding him. In 1966, Pike's son had taken his own life in a New York City hotel room, following a period of recreational drug use. Shortly after his son's death, the bishop experienced poltergeist phenomena—books vanished and reappeared, and open safety pins indicated the approximate hour of his son's death. Pike led a public pursuit of various spiritualist and clairvoyant methods of contacting his deceased son. In preparation for his visit to St. John's, two study meetings were held to discuss his books. Some 750 tickets were available at one dollar each for those wanting to hear his lecture, with the overflow crowd listening to him over a loudspeaker in the undercroft. Two years later Bishop Pike and his third wife drove into the Judean desert, where he died.

At their meeting in June 1967 the vestry opted to sell the property at 937 Lincoln Avenue, either to the University Episcopal Center, for use as a rectory, or to another party. The house had served St. John's as a rectory for the assistant priest, the Rev. David Benson, and his family. But the Bensons had vacated the house in 1965. In November the transaction was completed, with a check for $20,293 being applied to the retirement of the debt on the Memorial Parish House. A balance of $46,291 remained on the debt.

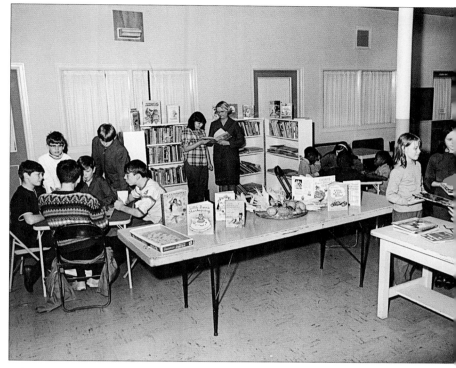

The reading room on the lower level of the church.

The Rev. Grayson Clary giving basketball tips at the Recreation Program.

John and Elizabeth Parish.

Confirmation class from the early 1970s, taught by Avis Haskell, second from left, top row, and Fred Myers, center.

CHRIST EPISCOPAL CHURCH IN DOWNTOWN St. Paul, at Sixth and Pleasant, learned about this time that its property was slated to be surrounded on three sides by the new freeway cutting through the city. Attorney Jack Lightner,[7] representing Christ Church, solicited the assistance of St. John's in order to delay the action of the Minnesota Highway Department by having the mayor and city council hold up the action. As if in direct response to the goals newly established by the Long-Range Planning Committee, St. John's vestry sent a resolution to the mayor and council on behalf of the vestry and the congregation of Christ Church. Under the evolving plans, the area around the church would become noisy, there would be an air-pollution problem due to the physically depressed area in which the church would stand, and access to the property would be inconvenient for cars and virtually impossible for pedestrians. St. John's offered its sister church support, encouragement, assistance, and the use of its facilities. Parishioners John Musser, John Myers, and John Parish served on a special committee formed by Christ Church to study its future and negotiations with the Highway Department. In the end, Christ Church relocated to the suburb of Woodbury, east of St. Paul. Its building downtown was deconsecrated in December 1973 and subsequently demolished.

Thaddeus Ingersoll was named chairman of the Every Member Canvass for 1968. In 1965 the pledges had been approximately $83,000 and in 1966 they were $95,610—a gain of over $12,000. Ingersoll had reason to be hopeful for 1968. Indeed, by December the pledges were coming in better than the parish treasurer, Charles E. Smith III,[8] had anticipated. In fact, he said, it was the first year the parish had been so lush in a long time. And by mid-January the debt was reduced to $38,988.

As we have seen, St. John's had a long association with St. Luke's Hospital, and in the fall of 1967 the hospital's Service League began its twentieth year of operation. Parishioner Augustus Clapp, for a total of eight years the president of the board of trustees, awarded past-president pins of the American Hospital Association to each of the eight past presidents. Parishioner Mrs. Patrick J. Towle had been the

ANNIE LAURIE BAKER, the sister of the Rev. Robert Orr Baker and a prominent social worker, was appointed in May 1967 to serve on the Selby-Dale Action Council, and Benjamin Griggs Jr.[9] was named delegate to the Summit-University Federation, an umbrella organization for the urban renewal of the area between the Cathedral of St. Paul and Lexington Avenue.

Ms. Baker was the director of social services at the University of Minnesota Medical Center and received the 1967 Minnesota Welfare Association District Service Award for "creative contributions and achievements to social welfare." She was also a past president of the organization and had been a board member for fifteen years, having represented "Minnesota social work from the pre-depression era to the present," and having "contributed actively to the social philosophy and policies of our state and even to the national social work philosophy and program." She held a term as national president of the American Hospital Association Social Work Society and worked in the Red Cross during the war, caring for casualties from Pearl Harbor and Guadalcanal. She then became assistant director of the Red Cross hospital program in Great Britain. After the war Ms. Baker supervised the Red Cross program at the Bikini Islands during the atom bomb tests and became director of Red Cross military hospitals throughout the Far East.

The Baker family had originally been members of Dayton Avenue Presbyterian Church.[10] Annie

Annie Laurie Baker and the Rev. Robert Orr Baker.

Laurie and Robert Orr were only two of the nine children, but sister Betty was the first to transfer to St. John's, because the Presbyterians had no programs for youth. She joined the Girls Choir and entered into all the youth activities and later became a singer with the St. Paul Opera Company and still later a professional singer in New York City. Annie Laurie and Robert followed their sister to St. John's; Annie liked swimming at the Church Club House. Robert became president of the Young People's Fellowship at a time when the organization held dances on Friday nights with a WPA orchestra. Another sister, Marguerite, married David Robinson Frost at St. John's. Their son David Robinson Frost III was a boy chorister and became a professional percussionist and composer.[11]

second president of the association. Other members of St. John's were among the founding members, namely, Ella Buser, the first secretary; and Mrs. Louis Hill Jr., the first chairman for the redecoration projects.

At the Diocesan Convention, early in 1968, Mr. Clary was elected a clerical delegate to the Provincial Synod. He was

also appointed by the bishop to serve on the Board of Examining Chaplains, the Ecumenical Commission, the Architecture Commission, the Liturgical Commission, and the Church Building Fund. Parishioner John H. Myers was appointed to the board of directors of The Episcopal Church Foundation, a national organization that had been established by General Convention for the purpose of

MARY GUEST SMITH PLATT was elected president of the Women of St. John's in May 1971. She took advantage of the occasion to note that she was situated right in the middle of five generations at St. John's. Her mother was Mrs. Charles E. (Esther) Smith Jr., whose husband was a public health officer for St. Paul, and her grandmother Eliza was the wife of physician Charles E. Smith Sr. Her daughter was Mrs. John (Dusty) Henry,[12] who raised four children of her own in the parish, making five generations in all. Dusty's cousin, Sarah K. Smith, a singer in the parish choir, enjoys the same heritage (Dusty's mother and Sarah's father were brother and sister). Sarah's daughter Eloise Teisberg is the fifth generation of her family. Two great-great-grandsons baptized at St. John's, making the sixth generation, are Eloise's son, Thomas Giambetti, and Dusty's great-grandson, Braylon Minor.

Though she never graduated from an American school, Mary "Gare" Platt had an interest in creative writing and in languages, fostered in the years she spent as a girl in Paris; Florence; Rome—and Geneva, where she attended the International School, and later at the University of Minnesota. Gare, as she was known, served on the diocesan board of the Episcopal Church Women and gave long years of volunteer service at Children's Hospital, and at Miller and St. Luke's Hospitals. She was for several years a delegate to diocesan convention and had said, "Let's not be complaining eternally about necessary and inevitable changes. Let's get along together and progress." Her husband William T. "Bit" Platt was vice-president in charge of personnel for Midway-Platt Company, which owned Knox Lumber. He also spent many years as general manager of General Refineries, Inc., a division of The Patterson Company.

Top Right: Dr. Charles Eastwick Smith Sr., Dr. Charles Eastwick Smith Jr., and Charles Eastwick Smith III, representing three of five generations of the Smith/Platt family at St. John's. Bottom left: Esther Easton McDavitt Smith. Bottom right: Mary Guest Smith Platt.

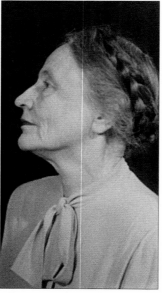

receiving gifts for investment purposes. The income from the foundation was used for theological education and building new church facilities, and for graduate fellowships for those serving in the ministry.

A program for senior citizens had been established at St. Clement's Church, where an average of 150 people were participating in the program and having lunch together on Wednesdays. The so-called Leisure Age Center was co-sponsored with St. Paul's United Church of Christ. An invitation was extended to St. John's and six other churches to join the collaboration. In the end, the program, later known as the United Leisure Age Center, was co-hosted by St. John's, St. Paul's United Church, St. Luke's Roman Catholic Church, and House of Hope Presbyterian Church, each congregation contributing only $20 per month.

The parish newsletter reported in May 1968 that the national church had produced a proposed liturgy of the Holy Communion, looking toward the possibility of incorporating it in a new *Book of Common Prayer*. General Convention had authorized the trial use of the service with the specific request that the reactions of persons to the service be compiled in a report and sent back to the Liturgical Commission for evaluation. A small group at St. John's made a study of the service the previous fall and it was used at Wednesday services after All Saints Day. Mr. Clary announced that beginning with the first Sunday in May, and for the next six months, the parish would be using the proposed liturgy. Those familiar with the service particularly liked its greater flexibility, but the new liturgy created strong differences of opinion within the congregation.

In January 1971 the bishop's office notified parishes of the diocese that they were to use the trial prayer book, known as "The Green Book," both freely and fully during the period 1971 through 1973, but only after study and preparation, and with no deviation from the literary form. Evaluations and recommendations were to be made afterward. By March 1972 St. John's had used the trial services at various times for morning prayer (Rites I and II), both communion services, as well as the baptismal, marriage, and burial offices.

Some favored the new liturgies while others clearly did not. St. John's buildings bore the scars of the turmoil in this era. The bulletin board outside the church, for example, had bullet holes in it, and even the large *Benedicite* window over the Portland Avenue entrance endured the indignity of a bullet hole. Though the harm was reflected in the substantial reductions in baptisms, confirmations, marriages, deaths, and transfers from 1957 to 1968, the parish did not retreat from its commitment to its various neighborhood programs.

In August 1969 an article[13] about St. John's appeared in the Episcopal publication *The Living Church*, written by parishioner Thomas M. Johnson, a World War I correspondent and the author of several books. It was featured in the journal's series on distinguished congregations. In the first paragraph Johnson wrote:

> This is a changing neighborhood. Many of its comfortable homes are being scuffed by the feet of variant and thronging newcomers who suffer from many needs, spiritual and physical. St. John's 800 communicants are striving to meet these needs. Although the congregation includes, according to leading local columnist Gareth Hiebert, "many of the most affluent, well-educated old-line Saint Paul families," yet it "vaunteth not itself."

Mr. Johnson credited the Rev. Grayson Clary with the continuing success of St. John's efforts "to face . . . the social and racial problems besetting American cities and the crucial need for the Church's help in solving them." Among St. John's numerous programs, the article highlighted the Friday-morning sessions for some fifteen persons who had been hospitalized for emotional problems and who now lived in halfway houses in the neighborhood. "They meet at the church for a change of scene, for group therapy, exercise, and some counseling."

The article was right about Mr. Clary. In fact, it may fairly be reckoned of him that his greatest legacy to St. John's was exactly that passion for civil rights and social justice that had first compelled him in South Carolina, along with his support for the practical means to achieve them. He kept St. John's doors open even when they were subject to abuse.

C. WESLEY ANDERSEN loved being a teacher, both in the Minneapolis public schools and at St. John's, and he could relate well to both children and adults. He played everything from his favorite Bach to music from Broadway musicals. He loved the organ at St. John's and truly enjoyed playing it. He expected to retire from the Minneapolis schools in June 1972 and hoped to have more time to devote to the parish. But instead Mr. Clary accepted his resignation and the Music Commission began a search for his successor.

In September 1970, long-time loyal parishioner and youth worker John R. Palarine began his studies at Seabury-Western Seminary in pursuit of holy orders. He was ordained to the diaconate at St. Mark's Cathedral in June 1973 and to the priesthood in 1974. In May 1976 he was finishing a two-year contract as curate at St. Peter's Church in Chicago, where his field was youth ministry and Christian education. He was interested in working part-time at St. John's while at the same time developing an education center in the Twin Cities. The vestry offered the position to Mr. Palarine for a one-year period. He began his work on July 1 and was allowed to develop his Education Resource Center at St. John's.

At its meeting in November, the vestry learned that they had reached zero indebtedness on the parish house. The members promptly sang the doxology and on December 27, which is St. John the Evangelist Day on the liturgical calendar, a facsimile of the mortgage note was burned in the church. Nevertheless, at the same meeting John Musser suggested that the vestry give some thought to St. John's working with, or even merging with, some of the other Episcopal churches in the city. The vestry took the thought seriously enough to refer it to the Long-Range Planning Committee, to be studied in depth. But nothing ever came of it.

Things were indeed looking up in 1971. The parish started the fiscal year with a cash balance of $7,000, 120 children

ROBERT L. KENDALL, assistant professor of organ at St. Olaf College in Northfield who had just resigned from the Cathedral of Our Merciful Saviour, in Faribault, began his work at St. John's in September 1972. In 1974 his recording "Robert Kendall at the Boe Memorial Chapel Organ," at St. Olaf College, became available in local stores. Mr. Kendall announced his intention to terminate his duties, effective June 1, 1976, staying on through the summer if necessary, because of the cost of driving back and forth from his home in Northfield. Instead he renewed his contract at a $500 increase in salary and served until 1983.

were enrolled in the Church School, with an average attendance of 116, there was $300,000 in the endowment fund, and several of the outreach programs were now in their fifteenth year.

After assessing what they already knew about the neighborhood and what they did not know, the Long-Range Planning Committee reported in September 1971 that in order to further their objectives, they would conduct a survey of parish families, inaugurate a series of neighborhood group meetings, and send out a promotional brochure describing the activities and aims of the parish. Dorothy Drew was named chairwoman of the committee in 1975.

The Christian Social Relations Commission conducted its own survey that was analyzed by Annie Laurie Baker. The conclusions drawn by her and parishioner Mary Stites, a former professor in the School of Social Work at the University of Tennessee, were that this was a very transient community; the programs did have value and were appreciated; and that there was a feeling of fear relative to any parish programs that involved leaving the house at night.

It was in 1971 that Grayson Clary introduced the now long-popular Christmas parties, thinking December a good time for fellowship. The first such event was modest in scale and featured ice cream sundaes, topped by a variety of delectable sauces whipped up by several parish men. The parties later involved elaborate progressive dinners, with buses transporting the revelers from various parishioners' homes to the church for dessert. In recent years the festivities begin with delicacies, savory hors d'oeuvres, and merry egg nog in the Fireside Room. Dinner follows in the gymnasium, aptly disguised by holiday decorations and dimmed lighting, and concludes with the singing of Christmas carols, accompanied by pianist Shirley Kartarik. The last carol is always *Silent Night*, with parishioners circling the gym and joining hands. Caroline Jaffray, hearing impaired since birth, has been known to "sing" the carol using American sign language.

In 1972 Dorothy Drew was elected St. John's junior warden, the first woman in the parish and the diocese to hold such a position. It was to her particular credit that she was elected to this post, because fourteen years earlier, coming to St. John's from Missouri in 1949, and with no connections to the established Crocus Hill crowd, she had not initially felt welcomed in the women's guilds. Her achievement, therefore, was all the more notable. Nine other women followed her as junior warden, namely, Mary Gare Platt, Lola Ferguson, Nancy Martin, Shirley Sailors, Mary Probst Halvorson, Ella Slade, Cammie Beattie, Becky Garthofner and Elizabeth Snelson, seven of whom—Ferguson, Probst, Sailors, Slade, Beattie, Garthofner, and Snelson—subsequently served as senior wardens.

Ever since the Rev. David Benson resigned his position as assistant rector, in 1965, the Rev. Grayson Clary had been without an assisting clergyman, and in 1972 the vestry gave some thought to hiring someone for the position. Mr. Clary supported the idea but noted that earlier discussion on the subject had been unproductive, because of the cost. He was now prepared to hire someone, but he wanted a priest with experience, not someone who needed to be trained. The package cost for such an assistant would run about $18,000 for salary, housing, utilities, car allowance, insurance, and pension. But on the basis of the discouraging returns from the congregational survey, it was clear that too few were willing to increase their pledges to enable the hiring of an assistant.

THE SUPREME COURT of the United States issued its decision overturning the abortion laws in the states in January 1973. Mr. Clary emphatically declared in the parish newsletter that "FOR A CHRISTIAN NOTHING HAS CHANGED." Insisting that the Christian is subject not only to the laws of the state, but also to the demands of God, he wrote that the teachings of Christianity clearly require a commitment to the sacredness of life. "The Christian is constantly confronted with difficult decisions, and when we do not have the support of legal guides, the decisions may be even harder." One wonders whether the rector knew that parish women had served at the Planned Parenthood clinic that opened on Selby Avenue in 1963, a year before he came to St. John's.

Parishioner Denis O'Pray, who had served on the vestry and on the Long-Range Planning Committee, was admitted to postulancy for holy orders in 1972. In February 1973 the vestry commended him to the diocesan Standing Committee for admission to holy orders. O'Pray was currently studying at United Theological Seminary in New Brighton, and was ordained to the diaconate in June 1975.

In March 1973 Mr. Clary was re-elected president of Episcopal Community Services (ECS), founded in 1963 by the Diocese of Minnesota to address the health and welfare needs of communities within the diocese, and Marilyn Olson and Mary Stites were re-elected to the board. Olson, who worked at St. Luke's Hospital, had been president of the Women of St. John's. She also operated the religious bookshop at Gethsemane Episcopal Church in downtown Minneapolis.

Alice Borup walking her dog, 1945.

and, at seventy-three years, were the longest running institution within the parish, apart from the Church School, and were an extremely effective ministry among the children and youth. But after years of decline, the Christian Education Commission considered whether to discontinue the camp, given the difficulty of finding a good director for a two-week period and the cost of about $1,300. In 1974 Cindy Brooks was named director for what was now a co-ed camp. In the meantime the commission began urging families and individual children instead to attend the Cass Lake Camp owned by the diocese. In the summer of 1975 the vestry supported each choir child wishing to attend Cass Lake, bringing the choir camps to a peaceful end.

In the 1970s the ordination of women in the Episcopal Church—whether they should be ordained or not—was the *cause célèbre* of the day. A diocesan conference on the subject was held at Breck School in April 1975, to which each parish was expected to send the same number of people as were delegated to the Diocesan Convention. Only four people attended from St. John's, but the parish continued to wrestle with the subject.

In September 1973 parishioner and attorney John Livingston Hannaford advised the vestry that in her will the late Alice Borup had bequeathed her house at 18 Summit Court to the church. This house was formerly the home of Bishop Mahlon Gilbert (see p. 56). The parish took legal possession of the property and parishioners were given the first opportunity to bid on it. It was subsequently purchased by David and Perrin Lilly, for the sum of $38,500. The home remains the Lilly residence to this day.

At the same meeting, it was learned that Mr. and Mrs. Charles E. Smith III had named the church as the owner and beneficiary of their Prudential Insurance policy. The vestry decided to credit the policy to the general endowment fund, with the income going to the rector's discretionary fund. Mrs. William J. (Katherine) O'Brien, a long-time member of the parish, also provided a gift to the parish in her will.

The parish choir camps had begun in the summer of 1901

Ladies had always worn gloves and hats at St. John's, at least into the 1960s. It was the fashionable thing to do. And gloves were the first to go. But in June 1975, when the rector's wife, Jean Clary, a last holdout for hats, first appeared in church without one—so goes the lore—lightning struck the church tower not once but twice, shattering some of the stonework.

Vestryman Charles Adamson reported for the Christian Social Relations Commission, in the same month, that its members had voted to respond affirmatively to a Vietnamese Resettlement Program. Housing for a family had already been offered by a member of the congregation. The need for food, clothing, medical care, and employment had been worked out by other churches, and the experience had not been a long-time financial burden. St. John's had already had the experience of resettling Cuban families. The vestry approved the proposal,[14] but the "family" turned out to be a single man named Nguyen Thuc Ho, age thirty-two, a

Buddhist with a fair knowledge of the English language and a degree in pharmacy, who was met at the airport by Charles Adamson, Lola Ferguson, and Gert Jaffray. His father was killed by the Viet Cong, after which his family moved to Saigon. By mid-December he had assumed a full-time job at the Lyngblomsten Home, a health-care facility for seniors in St. Paul, affiliated with what later became the Evangelical Lutheran Church in America.

In another response to the needs of refugees, St. John's accommodated three young men, refugees from Ethiopia—Gebru, Germai, and Tesfai—who arrived in St. Paul in September 1985. They were a teacher, a plumber, and a welder. Parishioners responded with furniture and household items, and with help finding jobs and providing transportation for them to attend interviews and classes.

SEVERAL WOMEN IN THE PARISH had undertaken needlepointing projects by December 1975 to provide kneeling cushions and chair cushions for the chapel and the high altar. The kneelers in the chapel were completed by September 1976 by Mary "Gare" Platt, Gert Jaffray, Jean Millin, and Lucille Biorn Guyer who produced one cushion each, using designs by Kitty Biorn Parfait, daughter of parishioners Norman and Betty Biorn and niece of Lu Guyer. Virginia Colin Stees, the sister of Dusty Henry, made the original rug that lay in front of the chapel altar. Lucille Guyer made the kneelers and chair cushions for the sanctuary of the main altar soon after the cushions in the chapel were completed.

The financial situation for 1976 was as tight as it had ever been and the vestry was facing a deficit of $20,598. Some parishioners who had already pledged had the potential of pledging more, some eighty-six potential pledging units had not yet pledged anything, and an astonishing fifty percent of those on the rolls did not pledge at all. All three groups were to be contacted in the following weeks in order to present a budget to the Annual Meeting, which had been delayed to February. It surely was a surprise to everyone that somehow they were able to adopt a balanced budget of $129,800, with only $92,959 in total pledges.

The program called Teens Encounter Christ came to use St. John's facilities in February 1977 for the first of many times to come. Open to students in grades nine through twelve, the purpose of the three-day retreat is to introduce youth to the paschal mystery, to a deeper relationship with Christ, and to a richer participation in Christian community.

A NUMBER OF LARGE GIFTS were left to the parish during the Clary years. Frances Daniels left $10,000 in her will, in May 1969, to be added to the endowment fund. In March 1971 the estate of Bertha (Mrs. Byrd) Crowell bequeathed some $17,000 to the church, and the bequest was later enlarged by an additional $3,700. At the same time a cash bequest of $5,000 was left by the estate of McNeil V. Seymour. The late William Gratz bequeathed an eighth of his estate to St. John's upon his death. The sum of $60,000 was received and invested by the middle of September 1975. In June 1977 the parish received a memorial from Thomas Daniels by way of $10,300 in Archer Daniels Midland Stock. In May 1978 the parish received a bequest of $10,000 from the estate of William Nesbitt, the husband of Dorothy Hand Nesbitt. William Clymer bequeathed $40,000 in May 1985, and Ruth Cathcart left a bequest of $10,000 in October 1986.

In his continuing drive to introduce the congregation to the new liturgy, and to attract new people who might appreciate a contemporary approach to worship, Mr. Clary established a Sunday schedule and changed the service times to accommodate three services. The early service would be Holy Communion from the 1928 *Book of Common Prayer*, as usual, but a middle service would use the contemporary services for Morning Prayer in the chapel on most Sundays and Holy Communion on first Sundays. The substance of the later main service would not be affected in any way.

In 1977 Jean and Grayson Clary decided they wanted to relinquish the rectory at One Heather Place and to build some equity in a home of their own. With the sale of the rectory, the Clarys received a housing allowance and the vestry assisted them in the purchase of their new home, a house at 2299 Edgcumbe Road.

Parishioners Betty and John Myers, at right, with the Rt. Rev. John M. Allin, presiding bishop of the Episcopal Church, and Mrs. Allin; and the Most Rev. Donald Coggan, Archbishop of Canterbury (center), September 18, 1976. The distinguished gentlemen were in town for the General Convention of the Episcopal Church (held every three years). The Myers celebrated their visit with a dinner party under a tent in their yard.

As was the case for the Borup house at 18 Summit Court, St. John's parishioners were given early notice about the sale of the rectory. Appraisers set the base price at $95,000 and the committee agreed to an asking price of $110,000. In December 1977 parishioner Allan Klein[15] offered that amount for the house. For the sum of one dollar the vestry also sold the electric stove in the house to Jean Clary "to have and to hold as her personal property in perpetuity."

On the docket for the Diocesan Convention in October 1977 was the election of a bishop coadjutor to succeed Bishop McNairy upon his retirement. Rumors had spread that there were no diocesan clergy among the search committee's nominees, so a group of clergy and lay friends approached Grayson Clary and sought his permission to place his name in nomination. They thought his credentials were good, and at age fifty-five he gave his consent. Some people supported Mr. Clary because they believed he was opposed to the ordination of women, but that was not the case; indeed during the convention he went on record as being in favor of it. The three main nominees were the Very Rev. Robert M. Anderson and the Revs. Richard Grein and John Miller. Mr. Clary was nominated from the floor, but he withdrew his name after the ninth ballot, and the election went to Mr. Anderson. Grayson Clary made it clear to the parish that he had not sought the nomination and that he still liked parish ministry and found it meaningful and satisfying.

The Every Member Canvass Committee for 1978 had a discussion about St. John's still being perceived as "cold." Although the parish had come a long way in friendliness in recent years, the committee suggested that they still had work to do to make people feel at home. To some extent, at least, they apparently succeeded, as 1977 was a year of growth for the parish. Attendance at all services increased by 1,739 persons, the number of communions increased by 764, baptisms by eight, confirmations by five, and transfers-in by nine.

ST. JOHN'S NEIGHBORHOOD has a number of beloved old institutions. The University Club is one of them, along with the former Blair Hotel[16] (now condominiums), as well as W. A. Frost, formerly a drugstore but now a popular dining

The Very Rev. Robert M. Anderson was elected bishop upon the retirement of Bishop McNairy.

spot. Another is the landmark Commodore Hotel at 79 Western Avenue. It had been a destination in St. Paul for decades, and a number of St. John's parishioners lived there over the years, along with such notables as F. Scott Fitzgerald and Sinclair Lewis. An early advertisement reported that the Commodore offered "a high class residential service . . . in the most aristocratic and quiet section of the city." Its website declares that "socialites and flappers, businessmen, writers and artists of all sorts found their way to the Commodore, attracted by the same things then that appeal today . . . marvelous Art Deco decoration and comfortable furnishings, a wonderful location in a glamorous and convenient neighborhood and a relaxed, welcoming style that makes you feel right at home." But on February 8, 1978, a gas leak caused an explosion at the Commodore. St. John's assistant priest, the Rev. John Palarine, or Father John as he was called, was the only clergyman to assist at the conflagration. Designed to be reminiscent of an ocean liner's cocktail lounge, the Art Deco Bar was spared.

At the vestry meeting in October 1978, Father John Palarine submitted his letter of resignation, effective January 1, 1979. He planned to work under the direction of Bishop Anderson as coordinator of Youth Ministries for the diocese. At the same meeting Charles Smith announced his intention to retire as parish treasurer, after a stint of fifteen years in the post.

Grayson Clary was given the honor, in the spring of 1978, of being asked to submit one of his sermons to the "Selected Sermons" section of the Seabury Press Publications. He submitted one titled "Here Is the Man." Those who remember his preaching will also recall that he began every sermon with the following beautiful prayer:

> Heavenly Father, help us to be the master of ourselves
> that we may become the servant of others.
> Take our minds and think through them.
> Take our mouths and speak through them.
> Take our hands and serve through them.
> Take our hearts and set them on fire
> with the love of Christ our Lord. Amen.

For his annual report in 1979, Mr. Clary quoted from the song "Sorry-Grateful" from the musical *Company* (music and lyrics by Stephen Sondheim), in which Harry sings: "Everything's different, nothing's changed; only maybe slightly rearranged." That's how Mr. Clary said he felt about St. John's at the end of the year 1978. There were lots of changes, and yet he felt the basics were the same. Even so, the overall attendance increased from 12,699 to 13,678, and the number of communions increased from 4,681 to 6,391, dramatic figures by any reckoning.

Nevertheless, for fiscal year 1979, the vestry had to face the fact, once again, that a balanced budget would not be possible without drastic cuts in programs. All vestry members present at the January 1979 meeting agreed to increase their 1979 pledge over their 1978 pledge and proposed that other congregants do likewise. The Christian Education Commission reduced its budget by twelve percent, and the music budget was reduced to $6,000 from the requested

Active in the parish from her youth, Judy Diedrich was president of the Women of St. John's in 1979.

$7,300. John Myers agreed to contact persons who did not sign pledge cards for 1979 but had contributed in the past.

Judith Diedrich held the presidency of the Women of St. John's and was involved with the rummage sales, being active in the parish from a very early age. The daughter of Zib and John Parish, she and her husband Richard Diedrich have a home in Sarasota, Florida, and they attend the Church of the Redeemer where St. John's fourteenth rector, the Rev. Richard Lampert, is assistant priest. The Diedrichs visit St. John's during the summer.

Michael Kent Hansen, a parishioner from St. Christopher's Church in St. Paul and a graduate of the College of St. Thomas, attended United Theological Seminary and was ordained a deacon in June 1979. He became Mr. Clary's assistant that July, and was ordained to the priesthood in December. With a background in teaching and consulting, Mr. Hansen was soon asked to serve on the diocesan Liturgical Commission and the Commission on Ecumenical Relations. His wife Donna Knight was director of the Governor's Task Force on Educational Policy. Mr. Hansen resigned his post at St. John's, effective June 1981, to become associate rector at St. Martin's-by-the-Lake in Minnetonka Beach.

Senior Warden Thaddeus Ingersoll, in January 1980, pressed the issue of friendliness at St. John's. As worshippers of God and his son, Jesus Christ, he said, we should accept all Christians as friends. It is so natural to be nice to the people you know, he continued, and to ignore those you do not. St. John's, he pointed out, was making an effort to break down this barrier. For several weeks at the end of the service Mr. Clary extended the peace of the Lord to the congregation, in a now-familiar gesture that was introduced with the new liturgy, whereby Christians memorialize their love for Christ by exchanging his peace with their neighbors. But the gesture was not well received by many in the congregation.

Organist and choirmaster Robert Kendall announced in April 1980 that he would be away for one year, beginning on September 1, to study at Westminster Choir College, in Princeton, New Jersey, and in England. He was replaced by Carl Stout, who, like Mr. Kendall, was on the faculty at St. Olaf College. In March 1983 Mr. Kendall shared with the vestry his intention to take a ten-week vacation that year, paying for his own substitute, but on August 6 he submitted his resignation instead, to be effective on August 31.

In October, Gregory Larsen was the successful candidate to succeed Mr. Kendall. With an undergraduate degree in Music Education from the University of Minnesota, and a masters degree in arts education from the University of Montana, Mr. Larsen pursued a graduate degree program in arts administration at Indiana University.

The vestry agreed to a major Capital Fund Drive in advance of the parish centennial in 1981, and in April 1980 adopted the goal of $200,000. They asked Ralph and Rosemary Klosterman to chair the drive, which exceeded its goal in December. With the funds collected, the vestry would attend to deferred maintenance: repairs and improvements in the parish plant, including work on the roof and the electrical system, insulation, a more energy-efficient heating system, the parking lot and landscaping, the repair of the narthex wall, caulking around the church, exterior painting, electrical work, and an audio system.

DOROTHY AND ADRIAN DREW chaired the Centennial Celebration Committee. The year-long observance began with the Festival of Lights in January to commemorate the organization of the parish; there followed a service commemorating the organization of the congregation with the sermon of 1881 by Woodrow Keljik

Wedding at St. John's, February 29, 1980. Front row: Adrian and Dorothy Drew, bride Mimie Pollard, and groom Alden Drew. Back row: Tish Halloran and Bram Drew.

Dorothy MacDonald and Jean Clary on the occasion of St. John's Centennial Picnic in Irvine Park in 1981.

(March); a service to recognize St. John's by city, county, and state officials who participated in the service (April); a parish picnic with an 1880s theme at Irvine Park, featuring a three-legged race, an egg toss and a spoon race, with the

Former rector Lloyd Gilmett and Bishop Gesner with rector Grayson Clary.

Butch Thompson Trio playing in the gazebo (July); a recognition Sunday for all twenty-five to fifty-year members (September); a homecoming Sunday for choir members, organists, and boy scouts—called Art Zache Sunday— followed by an all-parish luncheon in the gymnasium, to which former rectors and assistant rectors were invited (October); recognition Sunday for fifty-year and more members (November); and a rededication Sunday with Bishop Anderson and former junior and senior wardens participating (December).

St. Paul Mayor George Latimer and City Council President Ronald Maddox, an insurance man, politician, bar owner, and downtown booster, participated at the centennial service on April 29, along with the Honorable Robert J. Sheran, Chief Justice of the Minnesota Supreme Court, the only person to have been appointed to the high court twice by two different governors. The two men addressed the congregation in recognition of the important role that St. John's parishioners had played in the civic and business life of the city and the state.

In appreciation for Dorothy and Adrian Drew's highly

successful leadership of the Centennial celebration, Grayson Clary presented to them a copper skillet, engraved with a suitable inscription, at the Annual Meeting in January 1982. During WWII Adrian had worked for Northwest Airlines in Dayton, Ohio, and his best friend there was William "Bit" Platt. When the Drews had the opportunity to move to Minnesota in 1949, the Platts found a house for them in Crocus Hill and invited them to St. John's even though Adrian and Dorothy were not Episcopalians. As their son Alden remarks, "It stuck." Between 1949 and 1979 Adrian owned a number of materials handling companies, notably Adrian Drew Co., Drew & Co. and Distribution Systems Inc. He and Bit cooked most of the dinners in the new parish kitchen in the late '50s and early '60s. He also designed the lift in the back of the nave as well as the baggage carousels at the airport.

The Christian Social Relations Commission reported in March 1981 that parishioners Patricia Hart and Diane Rankin were looking to secure tutors who would work with Hmong[17] residents four hours every week for one year, teaching them English as a second language. The vestry approved the use of St. John's facilities for this purpose, and Hart subsequently took a tutorial course on Hmong. The tutoring began in September with forty-nine people in attendance. St. John's relationship with the Hmong in St. Paul was just beginning.

The Rev. Robert Orr Baker retired as St. John's perpetual deacon on December 25, 1980, after nearly fifteen years in the position. Having already written *The Muster Roll: A Biography of Fort Ripley Minnesota*,[18] in 1981 Mr. Baker authored a history of the parish titled *A Centennial History of the Parish of Saint John the Evangelist*,[19] to which his sister Annie Laurie Baker, Lucille Guyer and Mary Thomas also made contributions.[20]

PARISHIONERS JOHN AND CAROLINE FITCH made a name for themselves as experts at English brasses and were featured in an article in *The St. Paul Dispatch* in 1978.[21] John was a member of the vestry and retired assistant headmaster at St. Paul Academy. The couple mounted exhibits of their brass rubbings at the College of St. Catherine (November 2-27, 1975) and at the College of Saint Benedict (December 14, 1975-January 10, 1976), for which a commemorative brochure was produced. Titled *Monumental Brass Rubbings*, the booklet gave a brief history of English monumental brass rubbings, from the medieval into the Renaissance eras (1277-1631), and included descriptions of the thirty-five rubbings on exhibit. In September 1981, Caroline made a gift of three large rubbings in memory of her husband, and in 2005 the pieces were framed and hung. One of them, executed by the couple at the Church of the Blessed Virgin Mary, Higham Ferrers, Northamptonshire, England, depicts an ordinary medieval priest named Laurence de Sancto Mouro (dated 1337). The piece was hung on the ambulatory wall on the epistle side of the chancel, in a handsome frame given in memory of Janice E. and Robert Andrews, by their family. Another rubbing hangs in the ambulatory on the gospel side of the chancel, behind the organ console, also given in memory of Janice and Robert Andrews. The third hangs in the staircase outside the chapel, donated to the church and framed in memory of John H. Hannaford, by his family.

In the fall of 1981 the rector announced that Rite II Eucharist in the new prayer book—constituting a major reorganization of the communion service and the use of modern English—would be used on the third Sunday of the months of November, January, February, March, and May, as a second monthly Eucharist, after which the experiment would be evaluated. A year later Bishop Anderson advised the clergy of the diocese that they were not to do too much experimenting with the new *Book of Common Prayer*.

The Clarys' son, Bradley, and his wife, Mary-Louise, were members of St. John's for the duration of Grayson's rectorship—in fact he married them on a blistering hot day in July 1982 and later baptized their sons Benjamin and Samuel—and they continue to be active members of the congregation.

Among Brad's fondest memories of St. John's are his times serving as an acolyte with his father and hanging the greens at Christmastime, making sure that the wreath behind the cross above the altar hung straight, which he has done since early adolescence every year but one since arriving at St.

Mr. Clary baptized his grandson, Benjamin (Ben) G. Clary, December 22, 1985. Pictured in front of St. John's angel baptismal font are, left to right: George R. Hunt, Alyce D. Hunt (holding baby Benjamin), Mary-Louise Clary, Bradley G. Clary, Jean B. Clary, and the Rev. S. Grayson Clary. The Hunts were Mary-Louise's parents, baby Benjamin's maternal grandparents.

John's. He and his father hung the wreath together while his father was rector. On her part, Mary-Louise remembers being on Altar Guild duty one weekend, when she had to change the altar frontal for the next day's service. Finding it too large for the altar, she folded it and tucked it in so that it would fit. Her father-in-law Grayson pulled her aside the next morning to tell her that he had changed it, as she had used the casket pall.

Mary-Louise's parents returned to Minnesota toward the end of their lives and their remains are buried in the columbarium. She and Brad have places in the columbarium as well, as do Brad's parents, Jean and Grayson Clary. Brad and Mary-Louise like to joke that eventually there won't be any dispute about which family to visit on Christmas, "since we will all be together!"

After a survey inquiring about the desire and need for a

One of three large brass rubbings made in England by parishioners John and Caroline Fitch.

St. John's columbarium, behind the main altar, designed and constructed by parishioner Jonathan Frost. The Platt memorial window is seen at the far left.

columbarium was circulated among the congregation, a Columbarium Committee was established, in November 1984, whose members were Adrian Drew, chairman; Lola Ferguson, Rob Beattie, Rosemary Klosterman, and Edward Johnson.[22]

In April 1985 Carol Daniels Toombs of Rye, New York, came to St. John's for a service and asked if the parish had any projects that needed funding. She wanted to do something at St. John's to honor the memory of her adoptive parents, the late Thomas Leonard and Frances Hancock Daniels. Grayson Clary mentioned that plans were in the works for a columbarium, a project that appealed to her, as her parish in Rye had one. Mrs. Toombs gave the funds for the columbarium,[23] which provides a solemn burial place directly behind the main altar, with 252 crypts designed to hold the cremated remains of either one or two people.

Work on the columbarium, designed and constructed by twenty-four-year-old parishioner Jonathan Frost, of Frost Cabinets, Furniture and Design, was completed in the spring of 1986. Mr. Frost hand-picked the oak lumber, so that the facing of each row of niches is cut from a single board, making the grain continuous from top to bottom. When Bishop Gesner saw the columbarium sometime later, he asked "Why didn't I think of that years ago?" The columbarium was dedicated on Pentecost Sunday, May 18, 1986.

A program called Putting It All Together, or P.A.T., was organized by Episcopal Community Services, and began its work in the fall of 1982, to provide counseling and clothing for women looking for employment, and to help them develop interviewing skills. Enjoying ecumenical support, the effort helped teenaged mothers as well as women who were heads of households. Operating out of St. John's undercroft, P.A.T. was established by parishioner Nell Hillsley, who served on the board. The effort lasted for several years at St. John's, but eventually had to move to larger quarters.[24]

THE ACOUSTICAL PROPERTIES of the church have been an acknowledged problem ever since the nave was

ST. JOHN'S LOST ONE of the most prominent members in its long history when John Humbird Myers, industrialist, philanthropist, confidant of bishops, and former senior warden, passed away in June 1984, leaving his wife Betty and sons Bruce and Peter. Apart from his many activities in the parish, he was a co-chairman of the Anglican Congress that met at St. Mark's Cathedral in 1954, and chairman of the St. Paul Urban Coalition. He served on the boards of the National Chamber of Commerce and the St. Paul YMCA. He was decorated with the Silver Star, the Bronze Star, and the Purple Heart for his service during the Second World War.

After attending Carleton College and the Stanford Business School, Mr. Myers became assistant mill superintendent for Capital Flour Mills in Minneapolis and then joined the sales department of the Waldorf Paper Company, founded by his father Paul N. Myers, later becoming vice president for research and then in 1966, president and chief executive officer of Hoerner-Waldorf. In 1997 the company was acquired by the Rock-Tenn Company, which is today one of the largest U.S. manufacturers of 100-percent recycled paperboard.

Mr. Myers was the chairman of the boards of a number of non-profits, including the Minneapolis Symphony Orchestra (now the Minnesota Orchestra), the St. Paul Chamber Orchestra, St. John's University in Collegeville, the St. Paul United Way, the St. Paul Chamber of Commerce, and the Upper Midwest Division of the Metropolitan Opera. He was a trustee of Carleton College and served on the national boards of the National Association of Manufacturers in Washington, D.C. and of the Episcopal Church Foundation in New York.

Members of the St. Paul Chamber Orchestra, in a fitting tribute to one of their greatest supporters, presented a concert—giving their services—to memorialize Mr. Myers at St. John's, in the September after his death, performing under the direction of world-renowned violinist, violist, and conductor Pinchas Zukerman. The chancel was incapable of accommodating all twenty-eight players at a given moment, so they appeared in sextets and octets, with Zukerman performing a solo.

completed in 1903. One organist after another has bemoaned the absence of the reverberation that would make congregational singing more effective and satisfying. As it is, the acoustical "deadness" jeopardizes good congregational singing, a problem bemoaned as well by a string of rectors, because each member of the congregation feels isolated in the singing. Various acousticians have been brought in to imagine remedies to the problem, none of which have much succeeded. So when the old carpeting needed replacement, the Music Commission requested that it not be replaced, hoping that the hard wooden surfaces might make a difference. But in 1983 the Property Commission put it to a congregational vote: whether to replace the carpeting or to leave the floor bare. Two thirds of the parishioners preferred recarpeting. Eventually glass panels were placed behind the arches of the oak parclose screens in an effort to provide a "soundboard" behind the choir, making it easier for the choir singers to hear each other and for the congregation to hear the choir.

In the fall of 1983 the Rev. Mr. Clary became the Rev. Dr. Clary, having been awarded the honorary Doctor of Divinity degree from Seabury-Western Theological Seminary. The school's tribute to him was lavish in enumerating his achievements:

> Parish, community and diocese have benefited from Mr. Clary's faithful, firm and wise leadership. Under his rectorship, the church of St. John the Evangelist continues to provide a vital expression of the Episcopal Church's worship and outreach within a changing neighborhood. In St. Paul his leadership in ecumenical endeavors has been an inspirational model for others, particularly through his service on the governing boards of the Minnesota and St. Paul Area Councils of Churches, the United Hospitals, St. Paul Area Social Services Programs, and Clergy Associations. He has held virtually every major elective or appointive leadership position in the diocese. His wisdom and pastoral skills have been especially important as he served for six years as President of the Standing Committee, and now serves as Vice-President of the Diocesan Council. He has served in leadership positions in the Diocesan Departments of Christian Education, Missions, Finance, and Christian Social Relations; has served as an examining chaplain; and has been a key leader in the work of the Minnesota Episcopal Community Services. He has served the diocese and the national church as a delegate to the Provincial Synod and as Alternate and Deputy to General Convention. The Minnesota Challenge Program has depended upon his capable leadership as the Diocese enters into new and challenging opportunities for the ministry.

To all of this Bishop Robert Anderson added that "Grayson Clary is a Priest's Priest," many of his clerical colleagues in the diocese and elsewhere in the church having found him to be a wise mentor, a priest who listens and responds to their questions and needs. Those attributes, noted Anderson, stem from the long experience of a faithful parish priest and pastor, experience nurtured by prayer and scholarship, experience expressed quietly, with dignity, and in love. Undoubtedly, this accounts for the fact that he was one of the most loved and trusted priests in the Diocese of Minnesota.

THE TOTAL BUDGET for fiscal year 1984 was $241,500, the largest operating budget, to date, in the history of the parish. Under the leadership of James E. ("Jim") Johnson, the parish had the most successful Every Member Canvass in its history. Jim maintains that its success depended on so many people giving out of "guilt." Every member of the parish had been invited to attend an evening event at someone's home—usually coffee and dessert. The first event, at the home of John and Betty Myers, was very successful (drinks and hearty hors d'oeuvres instead) and there Jim Johnson and Rob Beattie addressed the needs of the parish. Other events were less successful, however. Hardly anyone attended the gathering at Judy and Dick Diedrich's home, for instance, and the only person who attended the event at Gert Jaffray's home—thirty ladies who would not go out at night were invited to an afternoon gathering—was someone who had Alzheimer's disease. So Jim's hunch is that the canvass succeeded on the guilt of those who attended none of the social events. But he understood the situation: the parish was still socially stratified in those years, and many of its members did not venture outside their comfort zones.

Several other pillars of St. John's died in 1984, including Charles E. Smith III, for fifteen years treasurer of the parish; Mary Platt, his sister, who was elected to the board of the Minnesota Episcopal Foundation at the 1982 diocesan convention and served as St. John's junior warden, and whose other distinctions within and without the parish were numerous; and vestryman Ross Norton, who was chair of the Property Commission and a delegate to diocesan convention.

Since 1981 Mr. Clary had been without an assistant rector until the **REV. THOMAS HARRIES** was hired in June 1984. Harries had been ordained a deacon the previous December and served at St. Edward's in Duluth. He was coordinator of the youth groups for five parishes and minister-in-charge for the congregations in Cloquet and Proctor, Minnesota. After beginning at St. John's he was invited to serve on the Diocesan Lay Ministry Commission.

Like most of his predecessors on the staff at St. John's, Fr. Harries left his mark in many wonderful ways on the identity and life of the parish. Unlike most of them, however, he once used paint and a paintbrush to make that mark. There is a room above the chapel, now used by the parish youth, which for some inscrutable reason came to be called the Green Room. How long ago, nobody really knows. But Mr. Harries saw to it that the room was painted blue.

At the vestry meeting in April 1986, senior warden Jim Johnson announced that the Rev. Grayson Clary, whose twenty-two years was the longest running tenure of any of St. John's rectors, had submitted a letter resigning his post, effective on All Saints Sunday, November 2. On October 30 a farewell party was held to honor the Clarys at the Town and Country Club in St. Paul, attended by parishioners past and present, community leaders, and diocesan officials, including Bishop Robert Anderson, and many friends of the Clarys. Seeing the faces of so many people who rarely attended church, Mr. Clary stood up and asked the three hundred gathered: "Do you all go to St. John's?" After

twenty-two years of service, someone calculated that Clary had attended 7,486 meetings of various groups. He and Jean were presented with a purse of $22,000, representing a thousand dollars for each year of their ministry, along with the keys to the church's Pontiac.

It is a token of the esteem with which Mr. Clary was held at St. John's that he was named *rector emeritus* in 2004. After all the years that have passed since his departure, he continues to be held in high regard as the epitome of the proper rector. His southern charm was beguiling.

But his legacy is more complex than that. In what is probably a compliment in the minds of some and a criticism in the minds of others, he has been called the last of the old-fashioned rectors. He continued to use the 1928 *Book of Common Prayer* at the early service, for example, long after it had been banned, while he pioneered lay ministry and took conspicuous steps at the later service to introduce the congregation to the new prayer book. He ran a straightforward liturgy, allowing little variation. He refused to move the altar away from the wall, but he was the first to welcome girls among the ranks of acolytes,[25] and he ordered enough copies of *The Hymnal 1982* for the pews as soon as they became available in 1985.

Though reserved and formal, he was gracious—he always remembered to send anniversary cards to the couples he had married—and he took pains to develop parish fellowship. Indeed he and Jean hosted a party every year for the vestry members and he introduced the Christmas dinners that the parish continues to enjoy. He successfully met the challenge of holding the congregation together in the face of changing demographics, increasing community outreach to the neighborhood, and he carefully steered the parish through the turmoil of the '60s and '70s.

He himself said that he probably stayed too long. As a civil rights activist he was too liberal for Charleston, yet by the time he left St. John's he was thought by some to be too conservative. He was an excellent spiritual guide to many people. Upon leaving the parish, Mr. Clary became vicar and then interim rector in Troy, North Carolina. The Rev. Dr. S. Grayson Clary died in St. Paul on December 14, 2013, and is interred in the columbarium at St. John's. Jean Clary died on February 14, 2014.

On June 27, 1986, two months after Mr. Clary announced his resignation, tragedy struck the family of Richard and Nancy Ellsworth. Their son Theodore Ellsworth, a recent high school graduate, was paralyzed after a diving accident in the St. Croix River. He spent eleven months at the Courage Center in Golden Valley, and his attitude was remarkably positive as he underwent daily therapy. He subsequently attended Stout State University in Menomonie, Wisconsin, where he studied for a degree in hotel and restaurant management.

Nancy Ellsworth was a made-in-Canterbury Episcopalian, a "Defender of the Faith," and the daughter of a priest, but she

was quite liberal and felt that the church must change as society changes. Richard served as Church School superintendent. The couple served on the vestry at different times and were both career teachers in the St. Paul public schools, she at Ramsey Jr. High, and he at Central High School.

LOLA FERGUSON AND ROB BEATTIE were appointed co-chairs of the large search committee of over twenty people for a new rector. It was the first such search in the parish to follow new diocesan mandates. Under the guidance of a consultant from the bishop's office, weekly meetings were held and a list of candidates from all parts of the country was reviewed. Five candidates were invited to visit St. John's for a single mass interview on a single weekend in November 1987—a somewhat unorthodox approach—involving a Friday dinner, an early Saturday communion service, and a series of interviews by the committee, to determine who would be the best fit. During the service, when the priest

The Rector Search Committee: Front row: Pat Brynteson, Sarah K. Smith, Nancy Martin, Shirley Sailors, Dusty Mairs, Jim Johnson. Second row: Mary Newbold, Florence Hensel, Susan Barker, Fred Myers, Kate Briggs, Jill Greene Thompson, Nell Hillsley, Mary Thomas, Rob Beattie. Third row: Gertrude Jaffray, Betty Myers, Lucille Guyer, Sally Frost, Lola Ferguson. Men at the back: John Brands, Don Husband, Bob Andrews, Newt Frost.

Dusty Mairs preparing burgers for the Search Committee.

asked to discern something together, not just take part in a beauty pageant!" By the time things were drawing to a close, the clergy couples had a conversation in which all but one of the couples agreed that St. John's was probably not quite ready to call a new rector. While Dr. MacBeth did not precisely recall what the issues were, they had to do with the liturgy and what some people were still calling the "new" prayer book. "But there was obviously some healing to be done and some further discernment needed about the parish's vision."

Dr. MacBeth probably did the parish a service by declining the invitation. Doing so forced the congregation to look very deeply into its divisions. The youngish Rob Beattie, about to become senior warden, thought it wise to select a junior warden who would represent the interests of older parishioners, and Nancy Martin accepted the position. At the annual meeting in January 1988 Mr. Beattie addressed the congregation and enunciated the apparently contradictory qualities desired by the parish in a successful candidate: a dynamic leader and preacher who would at the same time retain the liturgical traditions. Many in the congregation considered the two hopes irreconcilable.

Some parishioners wanted the assistant priest, the Rev. Thomas Harries, a very fine preacher, to be offered the rectorship, but the majority opinion was that he was too young. In any case, Bishop Robert Anderson, in a pledge with Jim Johnson, had permitted the parish to retain Mr. Harries as interim rector on two conditions: that he not be considered for the permanent rectorship, and that the parish discontinue all use of the 1928 prayerbook. The vestry consented. In the meantime Mr. Harries helped steer the congregation toward liturgical renewal.

The search committee was reconstituted, then took up its new challenge and compiled a whole new list of candidates, but with a modified interview process: the candidates would come at separate times.[26] The interviews ran from April to June 1988, after which the committee agreed on the choice of the Rev. Richard B. Lampert, who accepted St. John's call as fourteenth rector and began

announced the sign of peace, the committee realized the extent to which St. John's had resisted the new liturgy. Many would admit that the parish needed a new rector who could successfully effect a transition to the 1979 *Book of Common Prayer*. Most were uncomfortable exchanging a gesture of peace.

In a near-unanimous decision, the committee offered the position to the Rev. Andrew MacBeth, who declined the offer in December 1987, saying that he had already had the experience of transitioning a parish from the 1928 prayer book to that of 1979, and that he did not want to do it again. The diocese would not permit the parish to offer the position to the second-favored candidate, so the committee had no choice but to start the process all over again.

The Rev. Dr. Andrew MacBeth, who was serving as interim rector at Christ Church in Grosse Point Farms, Michigan, in 2011, recalled that the parish was very hospitable to the candidates and their wives. "It really felt like we were being

St. John's choir posed on the front steps of the church in 1965.

work in October 1988. He was then serving as vicar at St. Stephen's bi-lingual, multi-racial mission in South Boston. It was nearly two years since the Rev. Grayson Clary had left the parish.

Meanwhile Tom Harries noted that the tone of the parish discussions about the prayer book had changed. "The vehemence which used to accompany statements about the liturgy at St. John's is gone. In its place I find a healthy passion. People still have strong opinions about worship. . . . But we also respect the thoughts and feelings of those who differ from us."

MUSIC AT ST. JOHN'S has not always been Bach, Beethoven, and Brahms, as became clear during Mr. Harries' interim. In 1987, when the Minnesota Twins were in the

World Series, organist Gregory Larsen improvised a fugue for the postlude based on the Twins' fight song, *We're gonna win, Twins.*

During the summer of 1988, Mr. Larsen resigned his position as organist and choirmaster in order to accept a similar position at St. Stephen the Martyr in Edina. He was succeeded in September by William Stump, an experienced teacher of music in the St. Paul public schools, who was also the organist and choirmaster at Roseville Lutheran Church. With a graduate degree in music education from Michigan State University, and private organ study with the renowned composer and pedagogue Nadia Boulanger, in Fontainebleau, France, he also served for two years as assistant organist at Christ Church Cathedral in Indianapolis, Indiana.

St. John's choir under the direction of William Stump. Front row, left to right: Shirley Kartarik Michienzi, Jill Greene Thompson, Barb McGowan, Gail Lorenz, and Kate Briggs. Middle row, left to right: Sarah K. Smith, Mary Johnson, Maggie Thompson, Susan McCoubrie, Kelly Giese, and Ann Marcachini. Back row, left to right: William (Bill) Stump, Rich Pietz, Dan Bowers, Jim Langler, Mark Heimenz, John Thompson, and Chris Raudenbush.

A farewell dinner for Father Harries was held on September 1, after four years in the parish. As a thank-you offering to the church that had employed him, Mr. Harries gave an aumbry to St. John's upon his departure, a free-standing wooden chest designed by Jonathan Frost in which the consecrated wine and bread are reverently reserved in the sacristy, to be taken to the sick or homebound. After leaving the parish, Father Harries became rector of St. Nicholas Church in Richfield, then went to the Church of the Holy Communion in St. Peter. He also became active with the Minnesota Episcopal Environmental Stewardship Commission and served as a Total Ministry mentor.

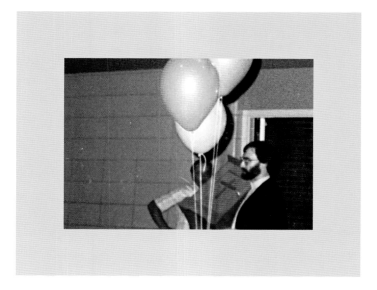

Right: Father Tom Harries with aumbry.

PICTURES FROM THE EIGHTIES!

Baptism of Robert Humbird Farnham, 1986. Left to right: Christopher Farnham (uncle), Thomas Farnham (uncle), Charles W. Farnham (uncle), and Robert Michael Farnham (father) with baby Robert H. Farnham.

Kent Larson and Christine Podas-Larson with their children Linnea, and Molly.

Virginia Brodeen with her children Patty and Lizzie.

Rob and Cammie Beattie with their children Anne, Virginia, and Charles.

Andrea and Jim Bachman with their children Karen, Michael, Niki, and Matthew.

Bob Yaeger and Justin.

Dorothy and Art MacDonald.

Kathy Yaeger and Bree.

Mary Newbold, Jim Johnson, and Dagny Gryttenholm.

Fred Myers and his sister Elinor Strebel.

Jill Greene and Mary Lou Brackett.

Rosemary and Amy Klosterman, and Zola Sailor.

Monica and Ed Cook, Adrian and Alex.

Sarah Smith and Eloise Teisberg.

Susan Barker, Sarah Smith, and Mary Johnson.

Adrian and Dorothy Drew.

Ethelyn Rupp.

Ellie Motter.

Kathy Meyer.

Bernice Jensen.

Jack and Nan Lightner with their sons Drake and William.

At the Plummer cabin, left to right: Margaret Plummer; Rosemary Klosterman, assistant treasurer; the Rev. Thomas Harries, interim rector; Bill Plummer, treasurer; Ed Cook, warden; Monica Cook; John Thompson, chair, finance committee; Elizabeth Thompson.

Winton and Eleanor Hartman.

Lucy and Ted Owens.

Barbara and Crosby Sommers were married at St. John's on June 27, 1980. Their wedding party included, left to right: William Plowman, Richard Figge, Judith Pinkerton (to the right of newlyweds), Edward Sommers, and John Nicene.

MYSTERY DINNERS!

IN THE LATE EIGHTIES, Cammie Beattie and Paige Hagstrom, assisted by their husbands Gary and Robert, organized the first Murder Mystery dinner, which would be continued on occasion several more times, even into the 2000s. In April 1999 parishioners were invited to join the eccentric amateur archaeologist, Lord Arthur E. Fax, and his collection of fascinating accomplices, for an evening of fine food, wine, and murder most foul at Fort Ap Aachih on the banks of the Tigris River (actually the Fireside Room).

Each of the forty-some guests was apprised in advance of the evening's mystery and assigned a character to impersonate; all came dressed accordingly, whether in evening gowns or wielding a samurai sword. During dinner, each course was accompanied by a round of clues. With luck, the mystery would be solved by dessert time. Other dinners featured: "Hu Hung Woo" and "The Great Train Robbery."

Cammie and Rob Beattie.

Ed and Monica Cook.

Kristi Yore and Paige Hagstom.

Dick Yore.

AT THE BEACH!

FUN AND FROLIC was the order of this sunny summer day in 1988, when parish families picnicked at Priscilla and Bob Farnham's residence in St. Mary's Point on the St. Croix River. Mary "Gare" Platt and Henry and Gertrude Jaffray organized this particular summer outing. In subsequent years, parish picnics were often held at other venues, including city parks.

This young man is delighting in running through and smashing a sand rampart.

Who are these little girls who are all now grown up?

Building a dike!

Molly Lampert and Mary-Louise Clary.

Castle builders!

Fun in the Sun! This party includes Cammie Beattie (standing, in white), Paige Hagstrom, and others whom you might recognize!

Caroline Fitch, Carol Stovall, Gert Jaffray, and Nancy Shepard.

Jim Johnson, unidentified, and Susan Barker.

Gabrielle Lawrence and Don Postema wed at St. John's on an ominous day in June, 1998 (see p. 248).

chapter fourteen

THE REV. RICHARD B. LAMPERT 1988-1996
Awakening the Dream

THE EIGHT YEARS of the Rev. Richard Lampert's rectorship saw tremendous positive changes and advances in our world, but also devastating social upheaval. On the plus side, we cheered when African-American Barbara Harris was consecrated suffragan bishop of Massachusetts, becoming the first female bishop in the Anglican Communion. In 1988, Republican candidate George H. W. Bush defeated his Democratic opponent Michael Dukakis to become the 41st president of the United States. That same year a terrorist bomb brought down Pan American flight 103 over Lockerbie, Scotland. In 1989 more than two thousand peaceful demonstrators died after troops opened fire in Tiananmen Square in Beijing. In East Germany, citizens demolished the Berlin Wall, paving the way for the reunification of Germany. Two years later, the Soviet Union dissolved into its several republics. The First Gulf War followed Iraq's invasion of Kuwait, and Osama Bin Laden and other militants founded the terrorist organization al-Qaeda in the late 1980s.

Chief among artistic achievements, August Wilson's play *The Piano Lesson* won the Pulitzer Prize and Steven Spielberg directed the film *Schindler's List.* Travelers and tourists could now ride trains from London to Paris via the Channel Tunnel or "Chunnel" under the English Channel. The world applauded

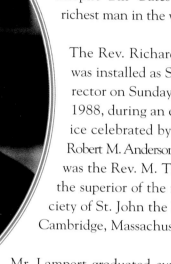

The Rev. Richard B. Lampert.

Nelson Mandela when he became the first president of the new democratic South Africa. Then a massive bomb destroyed the federal building in downtown Oklahoma City. Microsoft founder and philanthropist Bill Gates became the richest man in the world.

The Rev. Richard B. Lampert was installed as St. John's new rector on Sunday, October 16, 1988, during an evening service celebrated by the Rt. Rev. Robert M. Anderson. The preacher was the Rev. M. Thomas Shaw, the superior of the monastic Society of St. John the Evangelist in Cambridge, Massachusetts.[1]

Mr. Lampert graduated *cum laude* from Lawrence College in Appleton, Wisconsin, in 1964, and in 1969 earned a M.S.W. degree from the Boston College School of Social Work. He was awarded the B.D. degree in 1970 from the Episcopal Theological School (now the Episcopal Divinity School) in Cambridge, Massachusetts, and ordained to the priesthood in 1971. While in seminary he ministered at St. Stephen's Episcopal Mission Church in the South End of Boston. His wife, Molly, was a graduate of the Harvard Divinity School. From 1975 to 1977 Mr. Lampert was priest-in-charge at the Church of the Holy Family in Monterrey, Mexico, and then rector of Christ Church parish in Binghamton, New York, until 1981. Dick and Molly moved to Minnesota with their son, Brigham, who attended Mounds Park Academy in St. Paul.

Brigham, Molly, and the Rev. Richard Lampert.

AT HIS FIRST MEETING with the vestry, in September 1988, Mr. Lampert acknowledged that the search committee wished him to maintain St. John's strong traditions, while at the same time moving the parish forward in certain areas, such as liturgy. The general preference was for a blend of the traditional and the modern.

One of the most important goals identified during the search process was the pressing need for parish growth. Many parishioners had expressed concern that the active membership base needed to be expanded in order to sustain parish life. Mr. Lampert noted to the vestry that while church growth was desirable and necessary for the well-being of the parish, resistance to it stemmed from the fear of losing closeness within the parish. In his view the vestry needed to devise a strategy to increase membership and implement it; in 1989 the vestry made parish growth one of its top priorities.

CRAIG LINDEKE was in charge of the planned resettlement of more Ethiopian refugees early in 1988—a young married couple from the northern region of Gondar who were elementary school teachers before political turmoil forced them to leave. Unfortunately the couple was detained in Khartoum, Sudan, and instead the parish received a family of four Cuban refugees on September 30: Julio Buch, his wife, Angela Lopez, and their children, Michael and Yuneisy. With only two days notice that the family was arriving, Craig rented an apartment on the West Side of St. Paul and reserved a motel room for the family's first few days. During the ensuing weeks, Craig and Linda Lindeke, Molly and Dick Lampert, Kate Briggs and Tom Edman, and others, spent days and hours helping in the resettlement process, others donated furniture and household items. The Ethiopian couple eventually arrived on September 12, 1989, when John Edgerton III chaired the Refugee Resettlement Committee.

Tom Edman and Kate Briggs with children Sarah and Robert.

John Edgerton III.

Parishioners and siblings Craig and Barbara Lindeke are descendents of Johanna and Frederick Lindeke who came from Germany to the United States in 1852.[2] Their youngest son, Albert, was one of the founders of St. Paul's prosperous wholesalers Lindekes, Warner and Schurmeier, which became one of the Northwest's largest dry goods and manufacturing companies. Albert and his wife Louise lived with their family at 295 Summit Avenue, across from the Weyerhaeuser home. Their daughter Louise married Rudolph Weyerhaeuser.

Craig and Barbara's grandparents were parishioners Clarence and Alice Rose Lindeke, who struggled during the Depression and moved from house to house in an effort to make their rent payments. The siblings' father, William, and their uncle Clarence sang in St. John's choir as boys, though they couldn't carry a tune. Craig and Barbara are also related to the Hannaford family and are distant cousins of parishioner Caroline Jaffray. Craig has worked in the book department in the Huge Sale at St. John's for many years.

BILL AND SONA PLUMMER lived on Portland Avenue, in the same block as St. John's, and remembered Dick Lampert as a godsend after their son Christopher was injured in the run-up to the first Persian Gulf War. Chris was serving on the USS *St. Louis* in 1988 when it was caught in the flight path of Iraqi planes attacking Iranian targets. Exactly what happened to the crewmen on deck remained for some years a matter of contentious debate. The CIA knew the identities of those on the deck but long refused to acknowledge that their injuries were indeed the result of the Iraqi attacks. Chris himself was never sure what caused his injury, but all signs now point to the likelihood that the men were sprayed with sarin gas, a chemical weapon of mass destruction that causes permanent and completely debilitating neurological damage. The Veterans Administration required evidence that Chris's injuries were caused in the Persian Gulf in 1988, but eventually acknowledged the seriousness of his dementia and deteriorating condition, awarding him back pay and financial support for his family. The Plummer family remains confident that in time the military will declare their son's condition a service disability.

Christopher Plummer, William (Bill) Plummer, and Woodrow Keljik. Woody was a relative of Bill's Armenian wife, Sona.

Sona Plummer.

As if Christopher's tragedy were not enough for the Plummers, on January 12, 1994, his sister and only sibling, Elizabeth Plummer, suffered traumatic head injuries in a car accident and required a great deal of physical and occupational therapy. Again, Dick Lampert was at the family's side. Elizabeth was determined to walk again, and today she is an active member of the parish. In the fall of 2011, Elizabeth hung an art exhibit of her photographs titled "World Visions" in the hallway outside the Fireside Room.[3] She also spoke about her work at a Sunday Adult Forum. Bill's beloved wife—Chris and Elizabeth's mother—Sona, a stalwart of St. John's parish, died following a long illness and was buried from St. John's on May 10, 2014.

When parishioner Winton Hartman, an experienced professional fundraiser, and Jill Greene agreed to chair the Every Member Canvass for fiscal year 1989, it was with the understanding that some $30,000 more than what had been raised in 1988 would need to be pledged. The campaign was an astonishing success! By the close of Pledge Sunday, 154 pledges were in hand, as against 74 pledges by that time the previous year. Indeed, 128 households increased their pledges over 1988, and the church could count on an overall addition of $35,967 for the coming fiscal year.

TED DIVETT had by now been chairman of the hanging-of-the-greens every Christmas for some forty years. Gary Hagstrom, who lived with his wife Paige next door to Ted in Highland Park, began assisting him in his later years, and took full charge after Ted retired in 1988. Ted gave Gary explicit written instructions (where to buy the wreaths and garlands, which today cost around $1,500) and diagrams (where the wreaths and garlands were to be hung in the church). Gary remarks that his new job was not a vestry appointment, nor was he elected by the congregation; he just took over. Parishioner Les Blanc was a loyal assistant for many years, and continued climbing those ladders even into advanced age. Another was Dick Yore, who won the award in the bad-joke category: "I once fell from a forty-foot ladder," he would say. "I was on the bottom rung." The most difficult part of the effort comes long after Christmas is over, however, when the sexton has the dubious fortune of having to vacuum up all the dried and gummy needles from the carpet.

Hillie and Ted Divett.

The Rev. David Gillett had served briefly as parish deacon. Following his departure in December 1988, Mr. Lampert hired Ms. Cricket Cooper to assist him. Ms. Cooper held a bachelor's degree in creative writing from Northwestern University and expected to complete her graduate degree in theology from Seabury-Western Seminary in May 1989. She had done chaplaincy work at Dartmouth-Hitchcock Medical Center in New Hampshire and been a vocational trainer of mentally ill and retarded adults in Vermont. It was Dick Lampert's decision to hire a woman, and parishioners were urged to direct their queries about it to him. Ms. Cooper was ordained to the diaconate on June 14 that same year and to the priesthood in December. She was only with the parish a few years. In the early 1990s she moved to Massachusetts, and afterwards became rector of St. Andrew's Church in New London, New Hampshire.

Gary and Paige Hagstrom with daughters Cydney and Sarah.

IN THE SPRING OF 1989 the Diocese of Minnesota began construction of a House of Prayer on five wooded acres provided by St. John's Abbey in Collegeville, the world's largest Roman Catholic abbey of Benedictine monks. The result of a friendship between Bishop Robert Anderson and Abbot Jerome Theisen, the House of Prayer would be a powerful witness of ecumenical relations and a contemplative ministry for spiritual transformation. St. John's parishioner Nell Hillsley[4] was on the founding board of directors and parishioner Kathy Brown later served on the board until 2011. Over the years, St. John's vestries have made retreats there, the Rev. Michael Tippett held two of his Gifts Course retreats there, and individual parishioners continue to visit the House of Prayer for the development of their contemplative lives.[5]

Nell Hillsley is a nationally known artist who gave away her paintings to raise money for the Nonviolent Peaceforce, an organization whose purpose is to promote, develop, and implement unarmed civilian peacekeeping as a tool for reducing

Kathy Brown with children Cliff, Julia, and Marty.

violence and protecting civilians in situations of violent conflict. In 2007 she dreamed that 125 of her art works might raise $30,000, enough to fund "one courageous peace-keeper." Instead she raised $64,000. "I was never happier in my life than I was after that weekend!" she exclaimed.[6]

St. John's historic organ, constructed in 1922 by famed American organ builder Ernest M. Skinner, and revoiced and enlarged by the Moeller Organ Company in 1950, was in need of major repairs by 1989. Gould and Schultz, Inc., a local pipe organ builder, estimated that the repairs and restoration would cost in the neighborhood of nearly $127,000. The vestry signed a contract for a portion of the work, at a cost of $49,386, for work that would commence in the summer of 1990.

Eager to continue the work of Father Harries toward liturgical renewal, Mr. Lampert mediated discussions about how the new prayer book would be fully implemented. The parish was still using Morning Prayer and Rite I Eucharist more frequently than other Episcopal congregations. At the same time St. John's leadership wanted to be inclusive of the entire congregation, avoiding a scenario by which anyone would feel the need to leave. So the decision was made to include Rite II Eucharist in a twice-monthly rotation with Morning Prayer and Rite I Eucharist, a pattern that so effectively met the spiritual needs of the congregation that eventually it satisfied virtually everyone. In the succeeding years, newcomers to St. John's have simply liked the variety.

There were few significant changes during Mr. Lampert's first couple of years, but part of the agreement with him when he was called was that the main altar would be moved forward, away from the reredos, enabling the priest to stand behind it and face the congregation during the Eucharist. Most Episcopal parishes had made such changes in their own sanctuaries years earlier. The congregation was less concerned about the direction faced by the priest than that the appearance of the church not be changed.

In June 1989 funds were received for a memorial to the McNeil Stringer family and designated for moving the main altar forward, at a cost of roughly $6,600. Some vestry

members received negative phone calls about the plan, but the majority of the vestry approved it, with one dissent and one abstention. Mr. Lampert arranged for parishioner and expert woodworker Jonathan Frost to bring the altar forward. The change was so imperceptible that from any distance it was impossible to see that the altar had been moved.[7] As senior warden Rob Beattie later remarked, "it was a non-event."

A HANDBELL CHOIR was on the mind of parish organist Bill Stump and in September 1989 he brought the idea to the vestry. The vestry embraced the idea, but the motion to spend $4,500 for bells and equipment from the Memorial Fund was defeated as imprudent, the other needs of the parish being considerable. Nine months later, in June 1990, the Women of St. John's provided the funds for Mr. Stump to purchase three octaves of bells. The charter members of the new ensemble were Pat Brynteson, Dorothy Ek, Dusty Mairs, Sona Plummer, and Shirley Sailors.

Left: Behind the altar: the Rev. Barbara Mraz (deacon), the Rev. Jered Weber-Johnson (rector), and the Rev. Keely Franke (assistant rector), 2012. Right: The Handbell Choir in 2012. Front row, left to right: Dusty Mairs, Paige Hagstrom, Sona Plummer, Phyllis Merrill, Dorothy Ek, and Terri Fishel. Middle row, left to right: George Power, Helen Boyer, Kate Graber (director), Becky Garthofner, and Shirley Sailors. Back row, left to right, Helen Michaels, Barbara Lindeke, Johannah Frisby, and Jeannie Holmes.

RICHARD LAMPERT WAS ASKED by Bishop Anderson and assisting Bishop Sanford Hampton in January 1990 to chair the new diocesan effort toward evangelism in the so-called Decade of Evangelism, as designated by the national church. He took on the assignment, saying, "This is an area where I have a track record . . . in which I believe the Episcopal Church needs to move."

In Lent 1990 the congregation had the honor of hearing the renowned American writer Madeleine L'Engle, best known for her young-adult fiction, particularly *A Wrinkle in Time* and its sequels. L'Engle taught at St. Hilda's and St. Hugh's,[8] a private Episcopal school on the Upper West Side in New York City, and became a volunteer librarian at the Cathedral of St. John the Divine, serving for many years also as the cathedral's writer-in-residence. She died in 2007 and is buried in the cathedral.

Parish pillars Bill and Margaret Plummer.

After twelve years of service as parish treasurer, William Plummer Sr. stepped down on June 30, 1990. A reception for Bill and his wife Margaret was held to honor them for their good work in the parish. Mr. Plummer was succeeded in the post by Jack Lightner, who was in turn followed by John Thompson, in 1993.

One of the more ambitious proposals to be undertaken at St. John's in recent years was the accessibility project,[9] which would provide ramps, a lift, and an elevator for people needing assistance. An accessibility report was presented in 1989, reflecting many hours of work, consultation, and study over a period of years, but the proposal languished. In May 1991 Linda Lindeke and Dusty Mairs urged the vestry in a letter that this vital project move forward. The vestry agreed and committed itself to making St. John's property accessible to all persons, regardless of handicaps. The Property commission was charged with obtaining a plan and cost estimate by September 1, 1991.

Two ramps would be needed: one to replace the three steps in the hallway just north of the rector's office, and the other to replace the steps at the door next to the Little Sanctuary. A lift would also be needed at the west entrance to the narthex, from Kent Street. The lower entrance to the lift would open south into the narthex while the upper door would open to the north, into the rear of the church. In September 1992 the vestry approved an agreement with McGuire Courteau Lucke Architects of St. Paul whereby Adrian Drew would design and Charlie Stryker provide the lift and Jonathan Frost would complete the woodwork surrounding it.

A NEW MEMORIAL WINDOW on the west side of the columbarium, overlooking the Kent Street entrance to the parish house, was fabricated by Gaytee Stained Glass in Minneapolis and installed by Jonathan Frost in August 1991—a gift in memory of William Theodore Platt (1908-1973) and Mary Guest Smith Platt (1912-1984) from their children: Mary Dustin, Elizabeth Alexandra, William Theodore Jr., Virginia Colin, and Charles Thomas. Made of clear glass, the memorial was designed by Susan K. Platt, granddaughter of William and Mary Platt, and approved by the Minnesota Heritage Preservation Commission.

A new full-time assistant rector arrived in June 1991 in the person of the Rev. Bradley S. Hauff, formerly deacon-in-charge for four small mission congregations in Yankton, South Dakota. A member of the Oglala Sioux tribe, Mr.

PARISHIONER JOHN 'SOJI AGBAJE, a native of Nigeria, sought and obtained in December 1989 vestry approval for his pursuit of holy orders, and by March 1992 he had been accepted as a postulant. He planned to enter Virginia Seminary in September. With a wife and three children, Mr. Agbaje would need financial assistance, so a scholarship fund was established for his support, into which donations could be made, to help supply the family with $3,000 to $4,000 per year of seminary. Following his ordination to the diaconate, Mr. Agbaje began his ministry at St. Paul's in Brainerd, where he and his family "affected the community mightily."[10] He was ordained a priest there in January 1996, and in 1997 he became assistant rector at St. Edmund's, an inner city church in the heart of Chicago. In 2001 he was awarded the Doctor of Ministry degree by the Lutheran School of Theology in Chicago. The Rev. Dr. John Agbaje is now rector of St. James Church in Portsmouth, Virginia, and adjunct assistant professor at Tidewater Community College.

The Rev. John Agbaje with his wife Bunmi, John Jr., and Esther.

Hauff held the master of education degree from South Dakota State University and a master of divinity from Seabury-Western Seminary. After coming to St. John's, he was ordained to the priesthood on October 23, 1991.

Around June of 1991, Richard Lampert presented a written report assessing his first years as rector.

> I believe that much progress has been made over the past three years. The gap between tradition and vision which Rob [Beattie], Lola [Ferguson] and Jim [Johnson] so correctly identified has narrowed. The main altar was moved. We had a woman priest at St. John's. We have introduced parish retreats and hymnal supplements[11] and children's sermons. We have become more formal and more traditional and more liturgical in some of our Advent and Christmas and Lenten and Easter services. We have also become more inclusive and more informal and more contemporary in our regular 10 am Sunday morning services.

But Mr. Lampert acknowledged that though the gap between vision and tradition, as he defined it, had narrowed, it still existed.

At the vestry meeting in February 1992, Jim Johnson proposed several new programs for St. John's, including at least two that continue today: a men's breakfast series to take place one Saturday every month, and a Bible study in addition to the one that already existed on Sunday mornings. The breakfasts now take place on the second Saturday of every month at the gym kitchen.

In March 1992 the vestry undertook consideration of a Strategic Planning Process with assistance from Cathy Cowling, a diocesan consultant. A committee was formed in July, with members Jim Johnson, Kate Briggs, Carol Ryan, Cammie Beattie, Maggie Thompson, and Lola Ferguson, along with the Revs. Richard Lampert and Bradley Hauff. Three sub-committees were formed to deal with St. John's history, statistics, and demographics. At the annual meeting in 1993 the Strategic Planning Committee proposed the following mission statement:

> The Church of St. John the Evangelist is an Episcopal parish. We are a strong community whose people have chosen to come together to worship and know God. We

strive for spiritual growth across generations through excellence and variety in liturgy, music, education and fellowship. We support these values through a partnership of clergy and lay leadership.

With God's help, we are called to strengthen our spirit and sense of community, to love one another, and to use our gifts to reach out and serve the broader community.

The committee issued three charges to relevant parish commissions. The Outreach Commission was charged with improving the visibility and ownership of the outreach programs; to match volunteers with particular projects, providing information about outreach and its connection to values and faith; and ensuring that outreach be a systematic activity in the life and structure of the parish.

The second charge was addressed to the Christian Education, Adult Education, and Spiritual Growth Commissions, who were to foster spiritual growth among youth and families, use adult education to include new people and diversify adult education on Sunday mornings, and provide workshops on liturgy and music. They were also to hire a full-time director of religious education.

The third charge was not addressed to the Liturgy and Music Task Force, as might be expected, but was retained by the vestry for its own action. Dick Lampert was concerned that whatever process was used, it needed to be clear to the congregation that the parish leadership supported his decisions in the area of liturgy and music.

In any event, the charge was to continue offering a variety of liturgical expressions; increase the level of participation in liturgy and music; and add a spiritual dimension to the work of the choirs; while educating adults, newcomers, and the children's choir about Anglican liturgy, and simplifying the mechanics of worship to make the service more accessible to newcomers.

WILLIAM STUMP submitted his resignation as parish organist in the late spring of 1992, after a tenure of less than

Organist and Choirmaster Larry Blackburn.

four years. By August the parish had hired Larry H. Blackburn as Mr. Stump's successor. Since 1988 Mr. Blackburn had been guest organist at the Mormon Tabernacle in Salt Lake City, where he played numerous recitals, and was also dean of the Santa Barbara Chapter of the American Guild of Organists. Prior to that, he was organist at All Saints-by-the-Sea Episcopal Church in Santa Barbara and half-time lecturer at the University of California in that city. In addition to his work as staff musician at St. John's, Mr. Blackburn served as assistant treasurer.

After assuring the congregation, two years earlier, that the gap between tradition and vision had been narrowed in the liturgical and musical life of the parish, by March 1993 Mr. Lampert had to face the failure of his own innovations. "It was painfully obvious to me this past week," he wrote, "that my strategy of a full-blown contemporary musical service on

The choir during the tenure of Larry Blackburn.

the second Sunday of the month is not working." He had been experimenting with this approach in an effort to attract more people into the parish. "While all of the staff enjoy much of the new music, I must hasten to add that Larry Blackburn [the organist] has simply done what I have asked him to do. I am afraid that to date our contemporary service may have kept more parishioners away from than drawn new people into the church." He confessed to his sadness about this development, but acquiesced to his responsibility as rector to adjust to the realities of the parish.

Thereafter, except on special occasions, a balanced mix of contemporary songs and traditional hymns would be used. At the same time, however, it was Mr. Lampert's sense that the monthly rota of three different liturgies (Rite I and Rite II Eucharist and Morning Prayer) struck a healthy balance and was generally well received. Receiving the vestry's unanimous support for a blended liturgy, Mr. Lampert remarked that ". . . God speaks and people respond in all sorts of liturgical and musical settings and that the Almighty is not confined to any one liturgical setting. Thank God!"

Shirley Sailors.

In the middle 1980s St. John's had become involved in Loaves and Fishes—a program supplying meals for the needy at several Twin Cities locations— under the leadership of Shirley Sailors and Bill Plummer. In 1989, due to a shortage of funds, Loaves and Fishes withdrew from the Neighborhood House location on the west side of St. Paul. The contributing churches, recognizing the continuing need, formed a new organization called Food for Friends. Ms. Sailors continued to chair St. John's effort, with Bill Plummer as chef, until 1991 when Pat Brynteson took over the leadership with Kari Donnelly. People from the community came for a nutritious evening meal five days a week, the numbers ranging from 65 to 150, including many children, who often enjoyed home-baked desserts provided by Annie Laurie Baker and Lola Ferguson.

THE YOUTH OF THE PARISH produced the Broadway rock opera *Jesus Christ Superstar* by Andrew Lloyd Webber, under the direction of organist Larry Blackburn in May 1993. Eloise Teisberg played the part of Jesus; C. J. Hagstrom was Judas Iscariot; Annie Beattie played Mary Magdalene; Jane Raudenbush portrayed the other Mary; Alison Crossley was Caiaphas; Bill Lindeke played King Herod; Sarah Hagstrom was Pontius Pilate; Sarah Reynolds and Glen Lindeke were the high priests; Tim Hayes played the role of Peter; and Ben Thompson, Charlie Beattie, and Alex Cook were the Roman soldiers. Dick Lampert observed that

> The entire performance was filled with energy, terrific music, and a spirit-filled abandon not often seen in this parish.

Paige Hagstrom had served as Christian Education Administrator for a time, until Marjorie Grills became director of the Church School in 1993. Marjorie remained in the post until 1997, when she left to study for a master's degree in elementary education at the College of St. Catherine. She continued, however, to lead Godly Play at St. John's on Sunday mornings.

Loyal parishioner Doris Mills was active during Grayson Clary's tenure and with Ruth Benepe assisted the residents of local halfway houses at their regular Tuesday bingo sessions at St. John's in those years. When Doris died in 1993, she left her house to St. John's. Legal questions complicated the estate and a compromise was eventually reached with her nephew. In August 1994 the vestry resolved to use her legacy toward the salary of the new associate rector. At the same time an anonymous parishioner gave $60,000 to be used for the Building Enhancement Fund, which by February 1994 had grown to $110,000, to be used for the renovation of the Kent Street lobby and the installation of an elevator. In November 1994 the parish also received a generous pledge for $80,000 for the lobby and elevator in memory of Art and Holly Gross from their family.

Holly Gross.

Eloise Teisberg, an acolyte and a life-long member of St. John's, played the role of Jesus in the rock opera *Jesus Christ Superstar* at the church.

But still these improvements remained on the waiting list.

After three years as assistant to the rector, the Rev. Bradley Hauff announced his resignation, to take effect in June 1994, having accomplished what Mr. Lampert considered a superb job with the youth group. A farewell reception for him and his wife Jodi took place on June 19, giving parishioners the opportunity to express gratitude for their ministry. The couple moved to Dallas, Texas, where Mr. Hauff served a parish as assistant priest. In 2011 he was serving as rector at St. Thomas Church in Palm Coast, Florida.

THE REV. MICHAEL TIPPETT[12] was hired as the associate rector on the heels of Mr. Hauff's departure. Mr. Tippett and his wife Krista[13] arrived on August 15 with their infant daughter Alexandra. It was something of a coup that Mr. Lampert was successful in winning them for St. John's, as they had been courted by parishes in the East. A native of Scotland, Mr. Tippett was educated at Oxford University in theology, attended the Royal Military Academy Sandhurst, and for thirteen years was a British Army officer in the Royal Scots Dragoon Guards. He had just graduated from Berkeley Divinity School at Yale, and on June 11 was ordained a deacon in the Diocese of Connecticut. Krista had also just graduated from Yale Divinity School, though she did not intend to pursue ordination. Michael was ordained to the priesthood at St. John's on March 22, 1995.

KRISTA TIPPETT lived in a divided Berlin for most of the 1980s, as a freelance journalist for *The New York Times* and as a freelance correspondent for *Newsweek*, *The International Herald Tribune*, the BBC, and *Die Zeit*, later becoming a special assistant to the U.S. Ambassador to West Germany. Soon after graduating from Yale, she began to imagine radio conversations about the spiritual and intellectual content of faith that could open imaginations

The Rev. Michael Tippett.

Krista Tippett.

and enrich public life. In 1999 she launched her radio program "Speaking of Faith"—about religion, meaning, ethics, and ideas—as an occasional series on Minnesota Public Radio, and it became a monthly program on MPR in 2001. Krista's program began its present weekly run over National Public Radio stations across the United States in 2003 and is now known as "Krista Tippett on Being." Ms.

Tippett has authored two books: *Speaking of Faith: Why Religion Matters—And How to Talk About It*[14] and *Einstein's God: Conversations About Science and the Human Spirit.*[15]

A survey on Parish Life Orientation and Worship conducted at St. John's during the spring of 1994 revealed the surprising statistic that the 30-to-40 age group preferred Rite I Eucharist over Rite II. It was not a surprise, however, that there continued to be heavy support for a variety of services.

In the early 1990s Eleanor Hartman was serving as president of the Women of St. John's and in 1995 she was followed by Margery Jeddeloh. After Ruth Brooks retired as head of the

GERTRUDE JAFFRAY had a contemplative, thoughtful side. After her children were grown she had a little more time for her backyard garden, reading, and travel. She remained vitally interested in what went on at St. John's and never stopped being available to help in any way she could. Jim Johnson, a close friend of hers, referred to her in his address to the congregation the day of the dedication as "a true Christian," meaning that if someone called her in the middle of the night needing help to shovel snow, Gert would respond by saying, "I'm putting my coat on."

She cared deeply about the liturgy of our worship services and was known to offer insights about it and other aspects of our corporate life. She was outspoken in a friendly, sensitive, caring manner, full of humor and love. A loyal, steadfast, and constant source of strength, concern, and action in all aspects of parish life, she went about her duties in an unobtrusive and happy, "can-do" way. If something needed doing, Gert was there. Her many friends testify to her impact on lives, both personally and corporately.

Dick Lampert called Gertrude "one of the great saints of our parish." The Jaffray Garden is a fitting tribute to a remarkable woman.

Gertrude Jaffray was always ready to help in any situation.

Margery Jeddeloh.

Huge Sale, Marge issued a call for a volunteer to take the reins. Finding none, she assumed the post herself and headed up many years of successful sales, retiring after the October sale in 2008. Earlier in life, Marge had been working toward her degree in elementary education, first at Macalester College and then at the University of Minnesota, when she met George Jeddeloh. Together they had five children and many grandchildren.

A NEW GARDEN on either side of the Portland Avenue entrance to the church was dedicated to the memory of Gertrude Hannaford Jaffray on November 19, 1995. Gertrude served on the vestry, was "temporary" chairman of the Altar Guild for eight years, and was a mainstay of the Women of St. John's. Baptized and confirmed at St. John's, she was also a Sunday School teacher and served on the Christian Education Commission. Her commitment to parish outreach was constant—from the Reading Room of the 1960s to the parish food collection program, which her daughter Caroline took up after her. Young Caroline was baptized at St. Mark's Cathedral but confirmed at St. John's. For five years she taught Sunday School and served both on the Junior Altar Guild and on the Altar Guild. Caroline Jaffray worked for the rummage sale for fifteen years, since she was ten, and also served as its chairman.

During the preparation of the Jaffray Garden, a serious leak in the basement of the church required excavation that inflated the cost of the garden nearly four-fold. Gert's brother, parishioner Jack Hannaford, and his three nieces generously augmented the existing funds for the garden. The printed program for the garden's dedication was lavish in its praise for Gertrude's selfless life and her tireless commitment to parish activities.

Shortly after the dedication of the Gertrude Jaffray garden, intrepid parish sexton Steve Kartak installed an artificial owl in the church tower to discourage pigeons from perching there. (There was a similar owl at the Hill mansion.) As Steve put it, "this $12.95 solution sure beats spending upward of $400 to have an exterminator come in." Fred Myers quipped: "Are we ready to have a name-the-owl contest? Watch as you approach the church; if you spot the owl . . . does that make it a spotted owl? Whooooo knows?"

The owl worked for a while, but a year later the pigeons persisted in perching on the top ledges, resulting in messy front steps below. It took Steve three trips to the top,

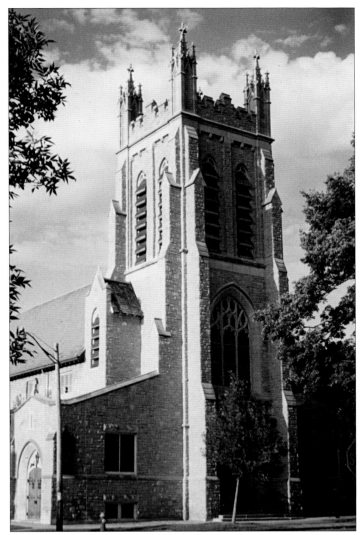

St. John's church tower, inside of which our stalwart sexton Steve Kartak fell some seventy-five feet while placing an artificial owl at its top to discourage roosting pigeons.

climbing through pitch blackness up the seventy-plus feet inside the tower. The first time, the wind dislodged the owl. The second time, the owl needed to have one of its eyes glued into place. This trip ended abruptly and horrifically as Steve fell down to the bottom of the tower where he was unable to move for two hours. Thankfully, he was not injured except for shock and scrapes. On the third trip up, Steve secured a decoy to one of the lower ledges.

MR. LAMPERT ANNOUNCED in a letter to the parish dated December 18, 1995, that he had decided to accept a new position as rector of Grace Church in Union City, New Jersey, on March 1. He described the parish as a mix of working class and poor, with white and black and Hispanic cultures. Mr. Lampert wrote in his letter that over the past year it had become clear to him that in the months to come it would be time to move on. Four factors motivated his decision to leave.

> First, I truly believe that I have about given what I can to St. John's and it is time for a change and new ideas. I have done my very, very best and I do believe that St. John's has progressed over the past seven and a half years. Second, in two months I will turn 55 and the conventional church wisdom is that if you hope to change jobs one last time, now is the time to do so. Third, as many of you know, Molly and I both truly love Hispanic work; in my case I have done it off and on for sixteen years. Fourth, and finally, I feel God calling loud and clear. I did not seek this position; it sought me out. For a period of months I gave God and myself all sorts of reasons why I couldn't do it. In the end God answered all of my doubts and questions and fears and now I am excited and I will follow Him.

Dick's letter was received by the vestry "with dismay and regret," and a discussion ensued at their meeting on December 19 regarding the procedure to be followed in securing an interim rector and a replacement for Mr. Lampert, who planned to leave after Ash Wednesday (February 10). Michael Tippett was asked to consider serving as interim, but he made it clear that the canons prohibited him from

becoming the rector. In January he told the vestry that he accepted their invitation to serve as the interim.

Several parish leaders took the occasion of Mr. Lampert's announcement to address the state of affairs in their reports to the Annual Meeting early in February 1996. In his own report, Mr. Lampert reviewed his rectorship, beginning with the turn of events that preceded his arrival in 1988.

At the January 1988 Parish Annual Meeting, in the midst of a stalled rector search process, Rob Beattie rose and challenged the congregation to become more flexible and open as it moved into the future. As the story goes, the response to the challenge was very mixed indeed, which led Rob to believe that the months ahead would at the very least be "interesting." Nevertheless, the revised Church Deployment Office Position Search Request did list the following challenging parish goals: develop the sense of community, spiritual growth, growth in numbers and participation and diversity, a more active presence in the city.

Mr. Lampert then enumerated the progressive events made during his early years, in an effort to achieve the parish's stated goals, but he noted that in 1991 "the momentum began to slow again and once more the parish's response and support for the changes and challenges was very mixed." St. John's was a traditional parish, after all, and was slower than most to change. Still, he wrote, "the clergy, vestry, and staff persisted and in the summer of 1992 the first-ever parish mission statement was written, and five-year parish goals were adopted."

Outgoing senior warden Jim Johnson offered his own assessment of Dick's tenure in his report to the Annual Meeting in 1996. The ability to build community was one of the qualities St. John's search committee sought in a new rector, and Dick's skills in this regard had impressed the search committee on his visit to St. Paul. Mr. Johnson pointed out that St. John's was now a much younger parish than it was in 1988, thanks to Mr. Lampert—that Dick had deepened the parish commitment to evangelism, and the parish had become a stronger spiritual community, with an expanded concept of outreach into the broader community. The parish had strengthened the Food for Friends program, for example, and begun to build a partnership with its neighborhood through the New Beginnings Center.

Nevertheless, while parish programs had expanded, Mr. Johnson noted, the financial support did not keep pace. Sound financial footing would be a critical step in the next search, he forecast, if the parish was to convince the new rector that St. John's was the parish where his or her ministry would thrive. The budget for 1996 showed expenses exceeding income by approximately $17,000—a situation that must not continue. Mr. Johnson warned that "If we decide to cut programs, we will have difficulty calling the rector we want."

AS ASSOCIATE PRIEST, Michael Tippett also weighed in on the present temper of the parish, acknowledging in his report that "1995 has been a roller-coaster, a year of considerable promise and some disappointments." Michael counted himself pleased with the Gifts Course that he had presented, with various retreats and Bible studies, the healing ministry in embryo, Teens Encounter Christ at St. John's, and the Youth Group's summer venture to Chicago, among other activities that fell under his charge. The disappointments, he admitted, were "hard to catalogue:" there was still no solid connection with the neighborhood and no Vacation Bible School.

The parish feted outgoing rector Dick Lampert and his wife Molly with a social hour and brunch at the University Club after the service on February 11. "All Our Best Wishes" were conveyed to the couple upon the new chapter in their ministry.

In June 2000, while serving as rector of the bi-lingual congregation at Grace Church in Union City, New Jersey, Mr. Lampert was awarded the Doctor of Ministry degree from the Virginia Theological Seminary. He became the first rector at the Church of the Good Shepherd in Venice, Florida, where he served for nearly six years, and since 2006 he has served the Church of the Redeemer in

Sarasota, with 1,600 members the largest parish in the Diocese of Southwest Florida. Serving first as Hispanic missioner, two years later he was named assistant priest. During his tenure there, the Hispanic congregation has doubled in size.

There was no abatement of more mundane matters while the vestry dealt with the departure of its rector and the transition into an interim period. At their meeting in December 1995, for instance, the vestry took up the matter of the aging gutters and authorized a five-year loan of up to $50,000 to replace them. An anonymous gift of $10,000 had been received and was applied to the gutter project.

For the stewardship campaign for 1996, the congregation was given a breakdown showing how their pledges toward the goal of $359,865 would be spent, as follows:

Ministry and Worship: 32%
Administration: 25%
Diocesan Pledge: 20%
Building: 12%
Music: 7%
Youth and Christian Education: 3%
Community Outreach: 1%

Perhaps the most troubling figure was the extremely low percentage of funds—only 1 percent—given to community outreach, which in earlier years had deserved nearly thirty percent of the annual budget.

As the new priest-in-charge, the Rev. Michael Tippett made it clear in a letter to the parish, dated February 22, 1996, that the budget for that year would not admit the possibility of a clergy assistant, and that comparatively little was allotted to educational programs, including spiritual growth—which had been a parish motto for several years. Moreover, the parish would be spending only a paltry amount outside its own borders, other than the pledge to the diocese. He called for a parish meeting on March 3 to examine and confirm "who we aspire to be now and in the future—and then to ensure the checkbook follows faithfully along."

Architect Mark Baumhover with parishioner Dusty Mairs, Building Committee representative.

At the March 3 meeting, Mr. Tippett pointed out that although attendance had risen steadily in the last three years, the number of pledges was down to about one hundred and fifty for the current year, though the amount pledged had remained level. Current membership in the choir, which had fallen to about twelve in 1995, had risen to twenty in the present year. A deficit of $64,000 had been carried over three years. Someone proposed from the floor that the parish mount a capital fund drive to complete the accessibility project, retire the debts from the gutter and sewer renewal, and to separate operating costs from capital expenditure, by bringing the building up to good and economical operating standards, and establishing capital reserves.

AND SO ANOTHER CAPITAL CAMPAIGN was begun, with a long wish list of dreams for the future, from better lighting and a neighborhood children's choir, to a more spiritual place and a more relaxed community, including even the construction of a supported living facility for struggling single-parent families, older people, and widows and widowers looking for easier accommodations. By July the Capital Campaign was in the final stages of conception. Of all the items on the wish list, however, one

piece was indispensable: the Kent Street lobby and elevator—the accessibility project that had been in the works for over three years.

But there were other urgent demands on the budget. For the past several months, Cammie Beattie and others had been trying to determine how to stop the youth program from falling apart. They concluded that a lay person had to be hired for a period of three years and suggested that funds for a youth minister's position be included in the campaign—costing some $90,000 for those three years. They reasoned that because pledge and plate income to date were significantly larger than predicted in the budget, along with growing parish enthusiasm, the congregation could fund this hire from the parish surplus, in anticipation of the campaign.

A Needs Assessment Committee was formed in July 1996 to accompany McGuire Courteau Lucke Architects on a walk-through of the length and breadth of the parish buildings, to make a concrete wish list of jobs that the architect had so far seen only on paper.

In time the campaign was given a name: "Awakening the Dream." Its primary goal would be to remodel the Kent Street entrance and install an elevator and also restrooms to guarantee full accessibility to all.

In an undated brochure titled *Awakening the Dream*, Michael Tippett wrote that "these times are marked by the way our church has been filled: on Sunday by joyful worshippers, during the week by delegates to the Ramsey County Youth Gang Task Force seminar, or two hundred children from the Webster Magnet School, an 'Animal Adventure' or All Saints Party for our children and grandchildren, the Youth Group baking apple pies, the Teens Encounter Christ weekend." In short, he announced:

we are already stepping out vigorously in faith towards our vocation. This leaflet is an invitation to take the challenge, and the fulfillment, another step forward. Here you will find a plan of vision and action which reflects the memories, concerns, and hopes we have been sharing with each other. We have called it Awakening the Dream. Both I and your Vestry believe that it is not only our congregation's dream, but God's dream as well.

The plan included a new entryway and lobby on Kent Street, to be glass-fronted, well-lit, and secure. An elevator in the lobby would give handicap access not just to the basement but also to the Sunday School and youth rooms on the upper floors. To complete this part of the plan, the sum of $280,000 needed to be raised.

BUT OTHER STEPS were necessary to make St. John's space useful for its own expanding needs and for those of the community. The undercroft itself was worn, dark, and difficult, there was an urgent requirement for more office space and for more congenial meeting space, and for bigger, better space for the increasing number of children. These initial steps would cost another $150,000.

The new minister for youth, young adults, and families would be a key point of liaison and administration for outreach to families inside and outside the church walls, including the Portland Avenue Neighborhood Association, the Webster Magnet School, the Selby Avenue Police/ Community Storefront (with whom the parish was a partner in a family and youth project), all of which were flourishing. This position would require $90,000 over three years. Susan Fischer assumed the post in 1996 and in the following year she also took on children's education.

Arguably less glamorous items also required urgent attention: the boiler, the lighting, and acoustics, for example. Some of the church's most precious windows, including the *Te Deum* window over the altar, needed urgent maintenance. These items, together with an accumulated debt of some $64,000 incurred in the maintenance of the building over the last few years, totaled about $160,000.

The total funds needed for Awakening the Dream were therefore $680,000, and by November 1996 the campaign was well under way. By January 1997 it was announced

The new and present glass-fronted, fully accessible entry on Portland Avenue to St. John's lobby and elevator.

that $676,714 was in hand, thus meeting the conservative target of $680,000, with the goal of $950,000 a comfortable possibility. Formal permission was given to start work on the lobby. By March the amount of $739,774 had been reached, and on Pentecost Sunday the parish celebrated the completion of the first stage of the Awakening the Dream campaign and the groundbreaking ceremony for the new lobby.

At their May 1997 meeting the vestry authorized the widening of the hallway outside the Fireside Room, co-opting the space that then accommodated "bleachers" for the gymnasium. They also agreed to offer the parish building—in transition as it was—for a five-week enrichment program called Freedom School, whose purpose was to enrich low-income children's academic skills, match them with mentors, and provide them with nutritious meals as a positive alternative to the streets during the summer months. The nationally acclaimed program was held in forty cities around the country, created by the National Children's Defense Fund. The program met five days a week and was sponsored locally by Project SPIRIT of the St. Paul Area Council of Churches and by the Minnesota Children's Defense Fund. The program occupied all three floors of the building while the construction crew was at work inside and out.

Larry Blackburn announced his resignation as staff musician at the end of the summer in 1997 and a purse was collected for him in gratitude for his years in the position. The parish then hired Roderick Kettlewell, the artistic director of the Bach Society of Minnesota, to be St. John's music director and choir conductor, beginning in September. Mr. Kettlewell held a degree in music history from the University of Southampton in England, and did post-graduate work at the Académie Maurice Ravel in France and at the Guildhall School in London. Concentrating in classical piano studies, he became the first recipient of the masters degree in accompaniment from the Juilliard School in New York City.

Howard Don Small.

A separate organist was needed as an assistant to Mr. Kettlewell. After several interim organists, Howard Don Small assumed the post in August 1998. For many years the distinguished organist and choirmaster of St. Mark's Cathedral in Minneapolis, Mr. Small had retired in 1998 after some twenty-seven years as canon musician, with a remarkable career that garnered national recognition for its excellence and innovation.

George Mairs, Bob Martin, Ella Slade, and Lucy Fellows.

Two months into his tenure at St. John's, Mr. Small established and made the first donation toward a fund to support and perpetuate the evensong program at St. John's. The Winifred Bean Evensong Fund is named after Winifred Bean, an Episcopalian, philanthropist, and lover of church music, who contributed generously to the St. Mark's Music Series when Mr. Small was at the cathedral. He started the Evensong Fund with an annual gift of $1,500.

A year and a half had passed since Richard Lampert's departure from the parish, when senior warden Ella Slade, in September 1997, began preparing the particulars for the committee that would search for a new rector, but the vestry decided that the search should not begin for another year. As Michael Tippett remarked, various events kept pushing back the formation of a search committee, two of which were the capital campaign and the challenge of staff changes, especially in music and Christian education. Mr. Tippett questioned whether it was too soon to initiate a search. In a letter to the vestry, dated October 16, 1997, he wrote of the need "to establish some goals and a timeline, built around what it will take to get us ready for a search, which will carry us forward from here." The vestry decided at its meeting in January 1998 that the search would begin promptly with the appointment of a search committee and the guidance of a diocesan consultant.

At the vestry meeting in December 1997, Mr. Tippett noted the growth in new members and visitors, increased Sunday attendance, and the larger number of children in the Sunday School. He reminded the congregation that five years earlier they sought worship that encompassed the riches of the prayer book and adopted the mixed monthly routine. "We want it all," he wrote, "and with good reason." He was also optimistic that the parish would reach two hundred pledges for 1998, a significant increase over the previous year. There would be only one hundred and seventy pledges, as it turned out, but treasurer Robert Martin[16] reported that it had been a stellar year, with sixty-nine increases in pledge amounts.

THE NEW ELEVATOR had already been installed by February. The Building Committee reported that work in the undercroft would require a great deal of demolition, asbestos abatement, and a lot of mechanical and electrical reworking, to bring the space up to code. The architects' proposal included climate control to improve air circulation, making air-conditioning in the sanctuary a distinct possibility. The plans included new meeting rooms, a meditation area, an enlarged and improved nursery, a library, an archives room, restrooms, a new kitchen, and a large fellowship area.

Much of the money had already been raised, including the $50,000 for a new childcare center, officially the Gesner Nursery, that was provided as a memorial to the Rt. Rev. Conrad Gesner, St. John's former rector, by his daughter Rosalind Gesner Johnson and her husband Lloyd.[17] At their meeting in March 1998 the vestry revised the goal of the Capital Campaign upward from $950,000 to $1,300,000, thus allowing the renovation of the undercroft.

In the same month the treasurer reported that the parish was doing very well financially, with about $6,000 above expenditures as compared to 1997. The situation was favorable enough that a search had begun for a deacon to assist Mr. Tippett, though no deacons were currently available. The search turned to a part-time interim priest for pastoral care, outreach coordination, and preaching, but assistant priests were just as scarce. In October, however, the Rev. Deborah Brown, who had just finished a two-year interim period at St. Christopher's in Roseville, was hired for a twelve-hour per week position in pastoral care. Ms. Brown remained in the post for nearly two years and left St. John's about the same time the Rev. Michael Tippett resigned.[18]

The interim period between rectors had been one of building and preparation, and by April 1998 wardens Ella Slade and Donald Husband were able to report that "we are very well-prepared, with committed, confident, and optimistic membership."

In May 1998 the Search Committee for the permanent rector had been formed, with the search expected to last about one year; Jeff Olsen and Mary Halvorson agreed to serve as co-chairs. In February 1999 an all-parish survey was conducted and a series of focus groups formed so members of the congregation could define St. John's identity and determine its goals for the future.

The survey revealed that the parish sought timeless worship, with ageless traditions made relevant for today. While the congregation preferred a variety of services, they resisted schisms. They also differed in their attitudes to worship: formal versus relaxed, quiet versus active, slow paced versus brisk. The parish was proud of its music program and felt close to God when they sang together, but they wanted a greater variety in the music and an active children's choir. With preaching important to the congregation, the membership wanted sermons to stretch them intellectually and move them emotionally. The real desire for community was thought to be threatened by a troubling lack of involvement in non-worship activities and a reluctance to assume leadership roles. As for lay ministry, "What we do, we do well. But we have not been doing a lot." The parish sought a spiritual leader who would be intentional about spiritual development. They wanted a strong Church School and they wanted their youth to be vital, integrated members.

The revival of the youth program, so recently in dire straits, became evident in 1998 with summer plans to take the youth to the famous ecumenical monastery in Taizé, France, a destination for countless international youth on pilgrimage. St. John's youth raised $750 from parking lot fees on Grand Old Day, falling short of their goal by $800. But the gap was made up by generous donations by parishioners. Four of St. John's youth took the trip.

Mr. Tippett officiated at a unique wedding on June 27, 1998, when Gabrielle Lawrence and Don Postema were married under forbidding circumstances. Happily distracted by the wedding preparations, the couple failed to notice the impending weather and were surprised to learn from guests arriving at the airport that they had encountered, as Gabrielle wrote, "delays, endless circling, high winds and tornado warnings. The sky that night was ominous, filled with huge, roiling, glowering clouds and lit from within with a white lightning. Ferocious straight line winds swept through the city all night long." The next morning Gabrielle awoke to the sounds of a neighbor's chainsaw. Several large trees had fallen around her house and "of course there was no power."

Nor was there electricity at St. John's. "The wonderful church ladies rounded up every candle they could find to light the sanctuary. The string quartet set themselves up in the entrance, where they could see from the light coming in the windows. John Stanley's *Trumpet Tune* sounded odd but valiant on the piano. It was very dim, people could not read the programs or the hymnal very well, and it was very hot." Michael Tippett was calm and reassuring as he led the couple through the ceremony. Then as they turned to the altar for communion, the power was restored and the church was suddenly filled with light. "God has a wonderful sense of timing!" After the final prayers, the organist thundered out the *Toccata* of Charles-Marie Widor, a family favorite, and everyone gathered on the front steps for a photo with Gabrielle and Don, no one looking the worse for wear.

For well over fifteen years parishioner Mary Johnson was the alto section leader of the parish choir, until she retired in the fall of 1998 and found herself sitting out in the nave . . . and enjoying it. Mary studied at MacPhail School of Music and sang with a number of professional choral ensembles, including the Bach Society of Minnesota, the Minnesota Chorale, and the Minnesota Opera. She also sang at the Cathedral of St. Paul during the years of former Vienna Boys Choir director Gerhard Lang.

In September 1998 Lizabeth Renken was hired as the new Christian Education Director. A mother of three with a strong background in theology, pastoral care, and Godly Play, Ms. Renken was a member of St. Clement's parish. At the same time Susan Fischer retired from her position with youth, young adults, and families, to move to a large Methodist church in Eden Prairie. There were currently more kids in the youth program than at any time in the previous five years.

In November Kesha Anderson came on as the new full-time minister for youth, young adults, and families. She had worked in Ecuador at a "cultural survival" school, in El Salvador for the Episcopal Diocese, studying the effects of war trauma on children, and with domestically and academically challenged children and youth in St. Paul. She was also supervisor at Chrysalis, a resource for women in crisis, and worked with her father in Indian ministries in Minnesota and elsewhere. She was leaving a job with the Wilder Foundation Achievement Plus Education Reform Project.

John Oldfield.

The fundraising rummage sale that had been operated for so many years by the Women of St. John's under the mundane name Rummage Sale, in 1998 took on a more grandiloquent name as the "Huge Sale." It continues in good hands, though its original sponsor, the Women of St. John's, no longer exists as such, and raises funds that are put to good use both inside and outside the parish. In recent decades the sale has been chaired by Gert Jaffray, Ruth Brooks, and Marge Jeddeloh, followed by the team of Claire Eckley and Mary Warren for several years. After the Women of St. John's disbanded, the sale has been overseen by the Faith in Action Committee with a subcommittee appointed to take care of details and hands-on work of this parish/community outreach effort.

John Oldfield was hired as assistant treasurer in the summer of 1999 and tutored in the position by his predecessors Larry Blackburn and Marv Cadwell. Mr. Oldfield came to St. John's with a strong background in corporate administration, particularly in book-keeping, accounting, and human resources.

BISHOP JAMES L. JELINEK attended the vestry meeting on September 30, 1999, after receiving the names of semi-finalists for the rector position. Vestry members acknowledged they had a strong, shared sense of being "on the brink of something big," with a general optimism about the future of the parish. The bishop indicated that he found a healthy and broad range of perspectives that seemed to be well-representative of the state of the congregation, with the parish apparently much healthier than it was three and a half years earlier. He thought the parish had an increased capacity for imagination and creativity. He also explained the reasons behind Michael's unusually long tenure as interim, and noted that pangs of concern about what the parish was not doing in the community were good signs of the health and stability of the congregation.

In a letter dated November 23, 1999, senior warden Ella Slade advised the congregation that the twelve members of the search committee, working for more than eighteen months, recommended that the Rev. Frank E. Wilson be named the fifteenth rector of St. John's. The vestry accepted the committee's recommendation. Ella wrote that Frank, currently the rector of St. Luke's in Minneapolis, was "a warm, spiritually mature priest whose enthusiasm for the roles of priest and rector is evident and contagious."

Bishop James L. Jelinek was not only our bishop but also a parishioner at St. John's.

The Rev. Michael Tippett had imaginatively led St. John's through four years of spiritual and numerical growth and healing, in the process raising an enormous amount of money for Awakening the Dream, and completing the first phases of major work on the parish plant. The vestry meeting in December 1999 was his last, and his last Sunday was January 9, 2000. The parish hosted a high tea to honor and bid farewell to Michael and Krista immediately after evensong that afternoon.

And so another cycle of leadership
at St. John's had come to a close.

Teens Encounter Christ (TEC), 2011. St. John's hosts TEC weekends twice a year for high school students. It is a three-day experience of learning about God, making new friends, and growing in faith.

chapter fifteen

THE REV. FRANK E. WILSON 2000-2010

A Voice for Peace

DURING THE TENURE of the Rev. Frank Wilson, it took the U.S. Supreme Court to determine the outcome of the close presidential contest between Republican candidate George W. Bush and Democrat Al Gore in 2000. Bush came out the winner. California Democrat Nancy Pelosi became the first woman to serve as Speaker of the House of Representatives in 2007, and in 2008, Barack Obama became the first African-American elected to the office of president. Health-care reform gave birth to the Tea Party, and social networking revolutionized communication.

In 2001 nineteen Islamic terrorists hijacked four passenger planes, flying two of them into the World Trade Center in New York City, a third into the Pentagon in Arlington, Virginia, and the fourth into a field in Shanksville, Pennsylvania, killing a total of nearly three thousand people. In 2003 the space shuttle *Columbia* disintegrated upon re-entry into the earth's atmosphere, killing all seven astronauts. The United States invaded Iraq and launched Operation Iraqi Freedom. In 2005 Hurricane *Katrina* brought incalculable damage to New Orleans and the Gulf Coast. Massachusetts became the first state to legalize same-sex marriage. United States cyclist Lance Armstrong won his seventh successive victory in the Tour de France, later losing the titles in a doping scandal, and the pilot of a

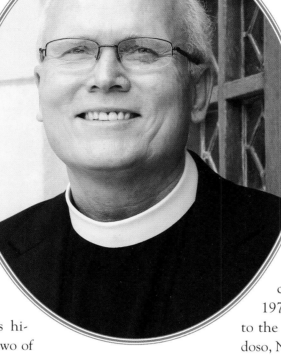

The Rev. Frank E. Wilson.

US Airways flight landed his passenger plane on Manhattan's Hudson River with no loss of life. In 2007 the I-35W bridge in Minneapolis collapsed into the Mississippi River. A global financial crisis followed the stock market crash in September 2008.

The Rev. Frank E. Wilson was born in Big Spring, Texas, where his father had returned following World War II. After attending grade school in Albuquerque, he went to boarding school at the New Mexico Military Institute. He was graduated from the University of New Mexico in 1971 and from the Episcopal Seminary of the Southwest in 1974. Frank and his wife, Alys, moved to the Church of the Holy Mount in Ruidoso, New Mexico, for his first ministry appointment. Before coming to Minnesota in 1993, he served at St. Mark's Cathedral in Shreveport, Louisiana, as sub-dean and canon pastor. At St. Luke's in Minneapolis, he helped to bring that distinguished parish from a low place in its history to a place where it was enthusiastic, welcoming, fiscally sound, growing, and full of young families. Frank and Alys had three grown children, Claire, Katherine, and Mark, and they lived on West Minnehaha Parkway in Minneapolis.[1] At St. John's, Frank inherited a historic parish ready for new directions. He took up the task on March 1, 2000, and was formally installed on Sunday, May 21, at the ten o'clock service.

In one of his earliest messages to his new congregation, in *The Evangelist* of April 2000, the Rev. Frank Wilson introduced one of the prominent themes of his rectorship: friendship with God. He wrote:

> As we journey in faith together it is my prayer that we build on the strength that we have and search for new ways to learn what it is to be friends with God. All we do, our worship, our education, our outreach, our social activities, strengthen our relationship with God and bring us into a closer relationship with each other and those we are called to serve.

There were a number of personnel changes upon Mr. Wilson's assumption of his rectorship. Robert Martin resigned his position as treasurer in May 2000, due to ill health, and Jim Johnson was named to follow him as interim treasurer.[2] Jim assumed his new post upon the vestry's discovery that the church urgently needed tuck-pointing, along with other repairs, to cost an estimated $140,000.

In August of 2002, Wendy Audette Johnson was hired as the new Youth Minister. Ms. Audette had recently been the communications coordinator for a youth-oriented nonprofit, the Minnesota Organization on Adolescent Pregnancy, Prevention and Parenting. Before moving to St. Paul she worked in government in Austin, Texas. She had also been a board member of the City of Lights Program at Gethsemane Church in downtown Minneapolis.

THE REV. KATHRYN JEFFREY accepted Frank's invitation to join the staff as associate rector, beginning in October. With a law degree from Georgetown University and two degrees from Yale Divinity School, Ms. Jeffrey had recently been the interim priest at the Church of the Holy Cross in Huntsville, Alabama.

Mr. Wilson believed that the renovation of the undercroft, which, of all the rector candidates, he saw as an asset rather than a liability, should become a priority in order to open the parish to an invigorated spiritual and community life. It was to be a new day at St. John's.

A small group of parish youth joined a mission trip to Tegucigalpa, Honduras, in July 2000, to work at El Hogar de Amor y Esperanza (The Home of Love and Hope), an Episcopal-funded home and school for boys aged five through eighteen. Then home to about one hundred and sixty boys, the school had been founded twenty years earlier by North Americans and Hondurans. Sarah Edman, Margot Harrington, and Lisa Lindeke were accompanied by Ellen Harrington, Kate Briggs, and youth minister Kesha Anderson, along with the Rev. Mariann Budde,[3] rector of St. John the Baptist in Linden Hills, and several youth from her parish; and the rector and some youth from Trinity Church, Excelsior. As Kate Briggs later wrote in *The Evangelist*,

> We weren't sightseeing or amusing ourselves. Though we worked hard, it was not a business trip. It was not a spiritual retreat, though we were constantly aware of the presence of God. It was not a family visit, although we were treated with extraordinary hospitality and kindness. It was something more than all these—glorious, extraordinary and bewildering.

In October 2000 the interior of the church was being painted when an incident nearly brought catastrophic damage to the structure. The painting contractor had told the parish that ladders would be used for the higher reaches of the walls near the roof peaks. Instead, as Mr. Wilson recalls, "a huge piece of equipment was driven into the nave of the church, and as it approached the first pews in the back, a crack was heard. The beams below gave way." Frank called parishioner Edward Cook who rushed to the church and saw "this monstrous machine, halfway on its way to crashing into the undercroft." The contractor managed to remove the machine from the church but broke some of the stone front steps in the process. In Mr. Cook's estimation, "It was a complete disaster." A structural engineer designed a repair for the broken joists and a masonry contractor repaired the steps. The painting was completed some weeks later with the help of ladders, as originally planned.

Senior warden Brad Clary noted in January 2001 that the vestry had been reorganized, the parish had a record fundraising drive, and there had been many accomplishments and substantial progress. He proposed that the vestry launch a campaign to raise $1,500,000 for the next step in becoming a welcoming community, one million of which would be for the undercroft and tuck-pointing, and a half million for other property needs—including a new tower roof—and the endowment.

ON MONDAY NIGHTS IN THE SPRING, while the vestry held its meetings in the Fireside Room, the Apollo Center,[4] a drop-in program for people with mental illness, used the gymnasium for basketball practice. The Inner City Youth League, which helped at-risk youth seek positive alternatives, also used St. John's gym, for their drill teams and the planning group for their justice program. Alden Drew chaired the committee that worked with the Apollo Center, assisted by Jill Greene. Rush Tully headed the committee working with the Inner City Youth League, assisted by Joe Flores.

Elizabeth Berry succeeded Marcelyn Smale as director of the Children's Choir in February 2001, Lizza, as she was known, was certified to teach K-12 instrumental music and K-8 vocal music. After teaching early childhood music classes, she helped establish the children's music program at St. Clement's in 1994, and directed the elementary grade choir there until the spring of 2003. At St. John's, Lizza directed the Children's Choir and the annual Christmas pageant, and assisted with music in Godly Play. As the founder and director of the Youth Choir and the Evangelist Choir she brought growth and transformation to the music programs for children and youth.

In April 2001, in direct response to the Children's Faces Project, Dick Yore, then a member of St. John's vestry, awakened his colleagues to the urgent need to house people who are temporarily homeless. Dayton Avenue Presbyterian Church, a participant in the Project Home Family Shelter Program, had offered to provide such housing in their facilities during the month of June, and needed a bewildering twenty-eight volunteers from St. John's for one week of that month. But Dick and his wife Kristi Yore presented the proposal to the congregation the next Sunday morning and were met with "volunteers brimming with enthusiasm" who signed up to staff the evening and the overnight shifts at Dayton Avenue. Mr. Yore also persuaded the vestry to establish a parish Commission on Homelessness.

The Youth Choir in 2011. Back row: Johannah Frisby, Emma Grundhauser, Eva Gemlo, and Lizza Berry. Front row: Alex Joyce, Tim Krall, and Lucy Grundhauser.

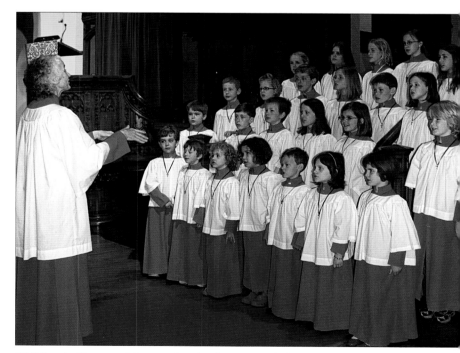

Children's Choir in 2011 under the direction of Elizabeth Berry.

The band of angels, in preparation for the Christmas Pageant in 2010. Right: Helen Baxter and Tessa Johnson.

On the subject of children: Artist and former parishioner *NELL HILLSLEY* spearheaded a Children's Faces Project by engaging artists and school children to paint hundreds of life-sized portraits of children's faces, representing the plight of the homeless in the Twin Cities. The project was displayed at the state capitol, at St. Mark's Cathedral, and elsewhere. At St. John's the portraits were placed on the altar and hung from the columns for an exhibition that lasted several weeks in Lent of 2001, spearheaded by parishioner Esperanza Parrish. As Dick Yore wrote, "The faces 'looked' at us for three Sundays, a reminder of the plight of children, and a plea for social justice . . ."[5]

THE PROJECT HOME FAMILY SHELTER is an outreach program to temporarily homeless parents and children, an effort of the St. Paul Area Council of Churches that provides overnight housing whenever the main Ramsey County shelter in Maplewood has exceeded its capacity of fifty-five beds. At the outset twelve churches and synagogues offered their facilities for twelve months. The need became so great that in 2001 another twelve congregations were enlisted.

In the beginning there was resistance to Project Home on the part of a few parishioners at St. John's who found the concept objectionable, one person even threatening to leave if it went forward. But most parishioners were profoundly touched by meeting their guests at Project Home. So in the fall, when the Council of Churches asked St. John's to host the program in its own facilities during the month of March 2002, the vestry consented unanimously, even though the parish facilities were then undergoing major reconstruction. The homeless families were housed on three floors of the building. "Beds were set up in several Sunday School rooms; the Fireside Room was a place of common rest; and the lower kitchen and a small area off it in the gym added to the space we used that month!" And in time, the one parishioner who at first objected to the concept professed himself proud that St. John's had taken the risk.

In 2011 Gary Hagstrom and John B. Edgerton III succeeded the Yores as coordinators of Project Home, after Dick and Kristi, who cheerfully shepherded the effort from the very beginning, retired to Florida. The son of Jack B. Edgerton Jr. and his wife Ginny, and the husband of Heidi Gesell, Mr. Edgerton is also a teacher in Godly Play and a counter of the Sunday offerings.

The youth took a number of mission trips during Mr. Wilson's tenure. In the summer of 2001 they raised over four thousand dollars for a mission trip to Petersburg, Alaska. Christina Ball, Andrew Aldridge, Miles Cudworth, Jessica Swanson, Alex Diaz, Megan August-Hau, Margaret Jeffery, Sarah Jeffery, Caroline Jeffery, and Brittany Olson all took the trip. They visited Juneau, saw the Mendenhall Glacier, and had the opportunity to ride in a floatplane. In July 2002, thirteen youth and three adults took a mission trip to the White Earth Indian Reservation to spend five days at St. Columba's Church, building a raft and converting a garage into a community center. The youth out-

distanced themselves in 2004 when they raised sixteen thousand dollars for another mission trip to Alaska's Last Frontier, living without running water for four days in a town of thirty people and going sleepless under the twenty-four-hour sun.

In June 2006, the parish youth attended the Episcopal Church's General Convention in Columbus, Ohio, when the Rt. Rev. Katharine Jefferts Schori, Bishop of Nevada, was elected Presiding Bishop of the Episcopal Church of the United States. An airplane pilot and former oceanographer, she was the first woman bishop in the 520-year history of the Anglican Communion.

In August 2001 the vestry unanimously and enthusiastically decided to proceed with the next steps of Awakening the Dream. Jim Johnson, chair of the Building Committee, distributed to the vestry packets of information outlining the proposed work to be done in the undercroft. This new Phase II would involve asbestos abatement, gutting the undercroft (rendering it unusable during the renovation), along with tuck-pointing, and stained glass restoration. The vestry authorized the Building Committee to launch the project that was estimated to cost

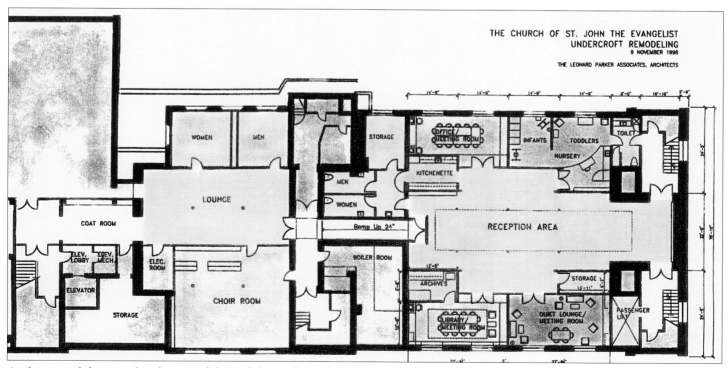

Architectural drawing for the remodeling of the undercroft.

$1,585,879, of which $1,305,879 would be for the undercroft, $200,000 for tuck-pointing, and $80,000 for restoration of the stained glass. After demolition of the undercroft began, the adult choir was forced to move its rehearsals and the music library to the gymnasium.

THERE WERE SURPRISES, AND COST OVER-RUNS, of course. In the very next month, the vestry learned that the church's two largest stained glass windows, the *Te Deum* window above the altar and the *Benedicite* window above the Portland Avenue front entrance, were in urgent need of repairs that would cost $71,000. Another $200,000 had to be factored in for a new retaining wall on the east side of the church in order to remove the soil from the basement windows and reopen them to daylight. The vestry decided that the cost of the retaining wall should come out of the property budget and not be a part of Awakening the Dream. There was still another problem on the south side of the church: all the plantings in the Jaffray Garden had to be temporarily removed to accommodate the waterproofing of the foundation. By July 2002 the vestry estimated that the final cost for Phase II of Awakening the Dream might reach $1,800,000, but no more than that. By November 2002, however, the parish had spent $2,143,834.

The Kent Street entrance prior to the remodeling.

The Jaffray Garden was planted on both sides of the Portland Avenue entrance to the church.

Another surprise could have been catastrophic. Upon the removal of the ceiling in what is now the Music Room, it was discovered that many years earlier the joists there and throughout the undercroft had been notched several inches to accommodate the installation of a gas conduit for the original lighting in the church. As a result, the integrity of the superstructure was severely compromised. As parishioner Ed Cook tells it, "At one point the contractor doing the remodeling job told us that with the slightest provocation the organ [console] could have come tumbling down into the undercroft." Each of the joists had to be structurally augmented. Mr. Cook has more than thirty years of experience as a mechanical engineer, working in the fields of building systems, energy supply and demand side management, and utility infrastructure for institutional, commercial, and industrial facilities. His wife Monica has worked at Miller and United Hospitals.

In April 2002 Frank Wilson wrote in *The Evangelist* that the renovation of the undercroft would not only provide space for St. John's ministries to thrive, but would fulfill the dream that we make a difference in this world by "what we do, what we think, what we pray." It was a gigantic step for St. John's, "and I give thanks that there has been a tremendous commitment not only to this project but to the mission of our parish to be open to the Spirit of God active in our lives." Jim Johnson chaired the Building Committee and Dusty Mairs was project manager, overseeing the daily progress and devoting untold hours to the construction.

Brad Clary tirelessly chaired the fundraising and as senior warden helped St. John's embrace the dream. Ed Cook chaired the Property Committee,[6] served on the Building Committee, and ensured that all was done correctly. Bob Horn chaired the final part of the fundraising.

By June the interior walls were up in the undercroft so that parishioners could see the new nursery, library, office area, the meditation room, the five new bathrooms, the serving kitchen, the archive room, the choir room, and the central space for gathering—worshiping, learning, and celebrating.

Bishop Jelinek came to St. John's for the dedication of the undercroft on September 8, 2002, at the same time celebrating the hundredth anniversary of the laying of the cornerstone for the nave above it. Frank added his sentiments to the observance: "It was a dream. At times it seemed way beyond our reach. At times it seemed like too much money, too much trouble, too much risk. And then the dream began to become reality." After the service, the congregation visited the second annual Ministry Fair, then everyone went out to Kent Street—which had been closed to traffic between Portland and Holly—for a picnic lunch and a block party with games and other activities. Roxie and Pat Markie[7] chaired the celebration, and as head of the Fellowship Committee, Jay Clark[8] organized the picnic and party.

In the fall of 2001, the Rev. Kathryn Jeffrey left St. John's to become interim rector at St. John's in the Wilderness in White Bear Lake, Minnesota. On the heels of Ms. Jeffrey's departure, Frank Wilson introduced to the staff the Rev. Barbara Mraz, a permanent deacon with a wide reputation as a preacher and writer, who had served at St. Luke's and St. James on the Parkway in Minneapolis, and was at the time serving St. John the Baptist in Linden Hills. She was also teaching senior-level social studies and English at Blake School in Minneapolis, where she had been a member of the faculty for twenty-six years. Bishop Jelinek assigned Ms. Mraz to continue working in Linden Hills for two Sundays a month while adding St. John's to her duties on the remaining Sundays, where she would preach once a month and assist with adult education.

Barbara has been a deacon in the diocese for thirty-two years, being ordained by Bishop Anderson[9] in 1982. Her articles have appeared in *The Living Church* and *The Anglican Digest*, and her book *Finding Faith at the Movies*, was published in 2004 by Morehouse Publishing.

Frank Wilson mentored a number of candidates for holy orders during his tenure as rector. The first was Elizabeth "Elsa" Cumming, a member of the vestry, who was recommended for postulancy in October 2001. At the annual meeting in 2004, Mr. Wilson introduced Letha Wilson-Barnard, a member of the

Pastor Frank Wilson embraced Awakening the Dream and was ever at the ready to pitch in wherever there was work to be done.

Interior walls were going up in the undercroft.

Church of the Messiah and a postulant in contextual education at Luther Seminary in St. Paul. Parishioner Patrick Markie was in discernment for the permanent diaconate, and Mary Ramos and Wendy Audette Johnson[10] had completed the discernment process, both being approved to continue their education toward the priesthood. Mary Ramos and Pat Markie were ordained to the diaconate at separate services at St. Mark's Cathedral in June 2006. Elsa Cumming was ordained in October, in New York City, though she was ill with cancer and required surgery.[11] Another parishioner, Cecie Titcomb, was ordained a deacon at the Church of Bethesda-by-the-Sea in Palm Beach, Florida, in November 2004. Keely Franke and Margaret Fell were also mentored by Frank Wilson.

In August 2002, the Library Video Company came to St. John's to produce a video series titled "World Religions for Children," designed for students in grades four through seven to foster tolerance for diversity in religious expression. Besides Christianity, the series included Islam, Judaism, Hinduism, and Buddhism among its subjects. St. John's was selected to be the Christian congregation. Most of the project was filmed at the church—some of it during a Sunday service—but the crew also filmed a few individuals and families in their homes.

In the summer of 2002 a faithful member of the parish gave a beautiful new gilt cross to be placed at the peak of the roof above the *Te Deum* window. It was designed after the cross that hangs over the main altar directly below it. The donor wrote a prayer for the cross that read:

> Let it represent a beacon for the community in which your church resides and for the community of believers within. May it also remind us of Christ's sacrifice for us and of our commitment to share his word. And through the power of the Holy Spirit, help us to lead others to know Jesus Christ, so that they too may share in God's eternal kingdom and while in this life experience the fruits of the Holy Spirit: love, joy, peace, patience, kindness, goodness, faithfulness, gentleness and self-control, each and every day.

In May 2002 Frank Wilson announced a change in the monthly routine for the Sunday services at ten o'clock. The family service would be an adaptation of Rite II Eucharist and would take place on the first Sunday of the month, with the Godly Play children attending the entire service. Frank wrote: "We will be using liturgies designed by members of our parish and other resources to help us in our quest to become better friends with God." Rite I Eucharist would take place on the second Sunday, Rite II on the third and fifth Sundays, and Morning Prayer followed by communion in the chapel on the fourth Sundays. The new routine was introduced in the fall of 2002.

THE ARTARIA STRING QUARTET has been in residence at St. John's since 2002. Formed in Boston in 1986, the quartet was featured on a Peter Jennings World News Tonight broadcast and has given numerous live performances on WGBH Boston and Minnesota Public Radio. The group has also appeared at celebrated venues across the United States, being featured also at the Banff Centre in Canada, Festival de l'Epau in France, and the Tanglewood Music Center in Massachusetts. In 2004 they won the prestigious McKnight Fellowship for performing musicians. The quartet has presented Haydn's "Seven Last Words" at St. John's on Good Friday every year since 2002.

The Artaria Chamber Music School for high school string players was formed in 2002 by Ray Shows and Nancy Oliveros, both members of the Artaria String Quartet, and took up residence in the undercroft at St. John's at the invitation of music director Roderick Kettlewell. The school is one of the nation's premiere chamber music programs for advanced string players through grade twelve. The student quartets are coached by the four members of the Artaria String Quartet, and by 2010–2011 there were twelve quartets in the weekly coaching program, one of which was selected to perform on the nationally broadcast program *From the Top* at the Caramoor Festival in June 2011. Every year the young artists present a series of concerts at Episcopal Homes and they occasionally perform for Sunday services at St. John's.

The Rev. Frank Wilson with five clergy he mentored, left to right: Rev. Mary Ramos, Rev. Barbara Mraz, Rev. Keely Franke, Rev. Frank Wilson, Rev. Patrick Markie, and Rev. Margaret Fell.

The Artaria Chamber Music School in 2011.

In the fall of 2002, the Summit-University Frogtown Community Circle Project, which began in May 1998, found meeting space at St. John's on Monday evenings. This project for restorative justice placed peacemaking and sentencing directly within the community by partnering with the criminal justice system, thus achieving consensus on appropriate sentences. Community circles use traditional rituals and structures to create a respectful space in which all interested community members, the victim (or representative) and the victim's supporters, the offender and the offender's supporters, the judge, prosecutor, defense counsel, police, and court workers share equal roles in the process. The primary goal for such an approach is to restore the victim, the community, and the offender to a state of wholeness, to the greatest extent possible.

St. John's also became involved with the private, non-profit organization World Citizen, headquartered on Ford Parkway in St. Paul. Founded by a group of citizens from the Twin Cities on United Nations Sunday in 1982, its mission is to involve as many people as possible, starting with children, in activities that promote a peaceful, healthful, non-violent world. Among its other activities, World Citizen promotes the establishment of International Peace Sites around the globe. The first dedication of such a site in Minnesota was in May 1988 at the Longfellow International Fine Arts Center, an elementary school in Minneapolis. At the vestry meeting in October 2002, parishioner Roxie Markie proposed that St. John's become a Peace Site and install one of World Citizen's now familiar peace poles in the Jaffray Garden. On May 4, 2003, when the Peace Site was dedicated after the morning service, St. John's became the first Episcopal church in the state of Minnesota to be so designated. The site is rededicated every year on the first Sunday in May.

While parish spirit was high in 2003, the vestry faced a deficit of $40,000. At the annual meeting in January 2004, Brad Clary suggested that the Collect for St. John's serve as a shorthand version of the parish vision statement, then pointed out that in the last two to three years the parish had completed about fifty years of work on the building, raising

an astonishing sum of money in the process, but that the project entailed more work than anticipated and required a bank loan of $750,000 to pay for structural renovation. While the loan was now down to $650,000, thanks to the generosity of a parishioner, the parish was paying $30,000 in interest per year. In 2004 there were 204 pledges for a total of $415,786, representing twenty-four new pledges and a ten percent increase over the previous year.

PARISHIONER DON POSTEMA wrote in *The Evangelist* in March 2003 that St. John's had been working with other churches in the area to form a group that would participate in a Habitat for Humanity Summer Workcamp. The result was the formation of a ten-member coalition of churches to be known as "Faith Builders." The other congregations were Assumption Catholic Church, the Cathedral of St. Paul, Central Presbyterian, House of Hope, St. Clement's, St. Mary's Catholic, St. Paul Reformation Lutheran, St. Peter Claver Catholic, and Virginia Street Swedenborgian Church. St. John's made a financial

St. John's parishioners worked to complete this Habitat for Humanity House at 707 Virginia Street.

commitment to the effort and pledged to provide volunteers for the construction of a home in St. Paul that summer. There were twenty-one volunteers, but room for only fifteen, who worked on the rehabilitation of the house at 707 Virginia Street.

Parishioner and stained glass artist Helen Boyer designed, constructed, and installed art glass panels for three office doors at St. John's to bring the formerly all-wood doors into compliance with Safe Church requirements.[12] The three windows featured the Trinity and were named Creator, Redeemer, and Sustainer. In 2004 she also designed replacement windows for the narthex stairwell. Helen contributed her services, the cost of materials being covered by memorial funds.

Frank Wilson asked parishioner and textile artist Mimie Pollard to create a chasuble for use at the Eucharist on occasions such as Palm Sunday and Pentecost when the liturgical color is red. While contemplating a design, Mimie encountered a magazine article about chasubles that the French painter and colorist Henri Matisse created for the entire liturgical year at the Chapelle du Rosaire in Vence, France, sometimes called the Matisse Chapel. "His red one," as Mimie relates, "was the standout." It featured a gold palm tree and black crosses on the back, which she used as the starting point for her design. Matisse's method was to create paper cutouts of his design and then have others do the sewing. A few years after completing her chasuble for St. John's, Mimie visited a Matisse exhibit at the Metropolitan Museum in New York and saw the very cutout that Matisse had used. And in 2010 she visited the Matisse Chapel and saw the chasuble itself. Frank Wilson later asked Mimie to create a green chasuble and for that design she drew from a wood carving directly above St. John's organ console. She liked its uniqueness and its resemblance to laurel leaves.

THE 74TH GENERAL CONVENTION of the Episcopal Church took place at the Minneapolis Convention Center between July 30 and August 8, 2003, the triennial gathering of deputies, bishops, visitors, and friends from around the world to consider the state of the church and its work in the world. It was at this convention that the Houses of Bishops and Deputies gave sanction to the consecration of the Rt. Rev. V. Gene Robinson as bishop of the Diocese of New Hampshire, the first openly gay, non-celibate priest to be ordained an Anglican bishop. Several of St. John's parishioners volunteered their services to the convention. Dusty Mairs helped to coordinate the diocesan volunteer effort, and organist Howard Don Small[13] conducted the massed choir for the festival Eucharist, with St. John's choir participating. The parish handbell choir joined similar ensembles from around the diocese, and Laura Kochevar coordinated St. John's volunteers. St. John's also made its facilities available to the youth that were attending the convention from across the country.

Like most clergy in the diocese, both Mr. Wilson and Ms. Mraz staunchly supported the rights of gays and lesbians to full membership in the Episcopal Church, including their access to holy orders, and they made their theology clear from the pulpit. At the vestry meeting in December 2006, Frank Wilson commented on the several parishes in Virginia that were leaving the Episcopal Church over these issues and aligning themselves with the Convocation of Anglicans in North America. He declared himself thankful that this was not happening at St. John's.

At the diocesan convention in the fall of 2003, parishioner Malcolm McDonald was elected to serve a three-year term as a trustee of the diocese, and he eventually served as vice-president of the trustees for four out of a total of six years on the board. Mr. McDonald was a banker at First National in St. Paul, and afterward senior vice president with the industrial real estate firm Space Center, Inc., tasked with community relations. He has served and continues to serve on the boards of numerous nonprofit organizations, including more than forty years with the Wilder Foundation, where he was a trustee member of the investment committee. In his "retirement," Mr. McDonald serves the Advisory Council of the Minnesota State Board of Investment and on the board of Home Federal Bank in Rochester. He is especially concerned all pre-schoolers have the advantage

Malcolm and Patricia McDonald were married at St. John's in October 2005.

Joan Potter.

Mark Maronde.

Committee was formed after the hiring of Jim Frazier in September 2004. Joan Potter served as chair, with members Mark Maronde, Malcolm McDonald, Betty Myers, and Rob Beattie.

THE NEW ORGAN console, designed to resemble the original 1922 console by Ernest M. Skinner, was installed and dedicated in November 2005, replacing the one built by the Moeller Organ Company in 1950. It contains various digital devices typical of modern organ consoles, including a recording mechanism that re-plays the organ live. The gothic carved-oak panels from the cabinet of the old console were co-opted for use on the ramp in the undercroft where they now serve as frames for the panes of glass on which the names of donors to the Awakening the Dream campaign are etched for posterity. Phase I of the organ project was complete.

of premium daycare to adequately prepare them for kindergarten and works with various community groups to reach this goal.

For six years it had been no secret in the adult choir that Howard Don Small and Roderick Kettlewell, superb musicians in their own ways, took contrary approaches to the conduct of a choral program, eventually leading to their departures. Don's last Sunday was in May 2004, and Roderick followed him on June 6. Joan Potter led the search for a new musician.

During his tenure as organist, Howard Don Small had called the attention of the Music Commission to the need for modest tonal work on the parish organ, but there was no plan for any major project to restore or enlarge the organ until an Organ

On Sunday, January 8, 2006, to observe the 125th anniversary of the founding of the parish and to launch Phase II of the organ project, the parish came together for evensong, a brief organ recital and dinner, and for an "organ crawl." Participants were invited to "crawl" into the organ chambers to see what the inside of a pipe organ looks like.

In the same month Mark Maronde, chair of the Music Commission and member of the Organ Committee, reported to the vestry that $163,000 had been raised toward the $335,000 that would be required for Phase II. The first notable contribution toward Phase II was given by Phyllis Merrill in memory of her recently deceased husband, Bob Merrill, when she offered the funds needed for a new rank

MIMIE POLLARD'S CHASUBLES

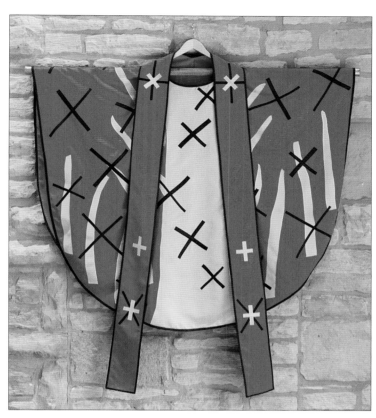

Mimie Pollard, the Rev. Frank Wilson, the Rev. Barbara Mraz.

JAMES E. FRAZIER began his work as organist and director of music in September 2004. Leaving a similar position at Trinity Church in Excelsior, he was previously the director of music for the Roman Catholic Archdiocese of St. Paul and Minneapolis, having earlier served Episcopal churches in Hartford, Connecticut, and Rumson, New Jersey.

Bob and Phyllis Merrill.

The Shepherd Band, for junior high and senior high youth who play musical instruments, is named for the first song they played together, *Rise Up, Shepherd, and Follow*, which is a staple in St. John's Christmas pageant. The band was formed in 2005 by Jim Frazier, and its members in 2011 included Johannah Frisby, Cameron Gemlo, Eva Gemlo, Alex Joyce, Linnea Krall, Charles Olsen, and Eli Weinkauf.

In April 2005 Mr. Frazier took to the vestry a three-phase proposal from the newly formed Organ Committee, with bids from several companies: (1) to replace the ailing organ console; (2) to clean, repair and re-voice the existing pipework and add new ranks of pipes; and (3) to install an antiphonal organ on the balcony rail at the rear of the church as an aid to congregational singing. The Schantz Organ Company, of Orville, Ohio, was engaged for all three phases of the project. Parishioner Robert Binger made two significant contributions to the effort by funding both the new console, which he gave in memory of his wife, Betty Wann Binger, and the new digital carillon for the bell tower, which would be playable from the new console.

by September the goal had been exceeded by $4,000, thanks to major contributions by two donors—eliciting from Frank Wilson one of his characteristic phrases: "How great is that!"

The organ project was going so well that by December an anonymous donor had contributed $80,000 toward Phase III (the antiphonal organ), promising another $40,000 after it was matched by other donations. And by May 2007 the Organ Committee reported that funds had again exceeded the goal, allowing the establishment of a contingency fund for future major repairs on the instrument.

Phases II and III of the organ project were completed in the summer of 2008, allowing for the dedication of the chancel and antiphonal organs on October 5 by Bishop James Jelinek. The success of the organ project was due in overwhelming measure to the generous contributions, large and small, made by so many parishioners, all of them in gracious acknowledgement of the importance of music in the worship life of the congregation.

There were many staff changes in 2004 and 2005. In November 2004 parishioner Ellen Harrington, who had accompanied parish youth on their trip to Honduras, was hired as director of children's ministries and of the Sunday morning curriculum "Godly Play." Ms. Harrington is a cradle Anglican from Canada, coming to St. John's in 1994, and is passionate about helping children develop a relationship to the Mystery as the foundation of their faith.

of pipes in the main division of the organ. In March the vestry authorized the signing of a contract for Phase II once the committee had raised $250,000 in cash and pledges, and

The Handbell Choir during Mr. Wilson's tenure was directed by Jane Riedel, a Ph.D. in musicology whose dissertation dealt with the musical practices of the Anglican Church in the American colonies. She retired from that position in January 2005 but remained a loyal member of the adult choir. Kate Graber was named to succeed her as handbell director. Kate had been a member of the Twin Cities professional handbell ensemble Bells of the Lakes since its inception nine years earlier, and directed the handbell choir at Hennepin Methodist Church in Minneapolis for two years before that.

Shirley Sailors, a founding member of the handbell ensemble, came to St. John's in 1982. She has served as junior and senior warden, and as a lay reader and a member of the Faith in Action Committee. After working at the U.S. Department of Housing and Urban Development since 1971, she retired in 2004. Shirley has since worked as a reading volunteer at Webster School and a tutor at the Rondo Library Homework Center, and she participates in Shinparam, a traditional Korean drumming group, as do parishioners Peggy Olsen and her son Charlie Olsen.

In July 2005 Wendy Audette Johnson retired from her position as youth director in order to spend time with her family. She was succeeded by Jean Hansen, a graduate of the College of St. Catherine, who began on August 1 as the youth and family minister, leaving a position as director of Christian formation at St. James on the Parkway in Minneapolis. She and her husband, Rob Hansen, had two sons at the time, Paul and Luke, and were later joined by daughter Meredith.

A number of parishioners participated in the Home Place dinner on a Sunday in July 2004, preparing and serving a meal to homeless families, about thirty-five guests including two infants and many young children. Gabrielle Lawrence, Tom Lawrence, Don Postema, and Meghan Longley-Postema were among the parish crew, along with Marvin and Sue Cadwell, the Rick Olson family and friends, Gail Markey, Robbin Clamons and friends, Pat Brynteson, and Frank Wilson. Cammie Beattie and Meghan Longley-Postema provided home-baked desserts. Pat Brynteson observed:

My perception was that most of the adults entered the dining area in almost sullen moods. But as we served salads, fruits, pastas with sauces, and they saw brownies to look forward to, our guests relaxed and visited with us. I sat next to a gentleman who had spent the afternoon at The Home Place searching the Internet for job opportunities.

In June 2005 Alden Drew published an article in *The Evangelist* about St. John's endowment, drawing attention to the fact that the parish was among a small minority of Episcopal parishes fortunate enough to have endowments, thanks to the foresight and generosity of parish forebears. At that time St. John's endowment, the result of nearly 125 years of large and small bequests, and valued at approximately $1,750,000, was a portfolio of investments managed by U.S. Bank and overseen by the parish Investment Committee. Mr. Drew noted that income from the fund had almost always been a stable part of the annual budget, though parish dependence on that income for operations was very low compared to many other endowed parishes. He urged parishioners to make provision for the church in their wills, so that outreach programs could be funded in perpetuity. Parishioner Thomas Baxter,[14] recently elected to the vestry as Finance Chair, offered to use his professional expertise to help anyone who needed advice and guidance on the subject.

In October 2004 the Baxter family generously gave new vestments for the parish lay readers. The albs were a gift of thanksgiving from sisters Helen and Maggie, the young daughters of Tom and Aimee—with a little help from their parents.

THE INVESTMENT COMMITTEE began work on what came to be called the Cornerstone Trust and persuaded the vestry to move the existing endowment into it. The work was done primarily by Jim Johnson and Tom Baxter, and by Mary Probst

Mary Probst Morrison.

Morrison who actually drafted the documents. The purpose of the trust was to move the funds away from direct vestry control, as there were countless examples of other parishes' vestries having spent their endowments, including at least two such parishes in the Twin Cities, and nearly a third. Indeed, the committee had heard from potential major donors that they would not leave money directly to St. John's for fear that it would be spent by some future vestry, when it was the wish of the donor to have the money last in perpetuity. The Cornerstone Trust thus safeguards the intent of the donors. The trustees are elected to three-year terms on a staggered basis, their ultimate goal being that the endowment income cover all general operating expenses, with pledges covering all the program costs and payroll. In the opinion of the Finance Committee, a 3.5 percent draw is the prudent aim for the future.

There were promptly two more gifts to the new trust. In September 2009 the parish was remembered in the estate of Olivia Dodge who grew up in what is now the governor's mansion. The funds were designated to the Hand Fund, to be used for the trees and shrubs bordering the parking lot, about which more will be said below. And in the same month a bequest from Betty Garrett, permanently endowed a portion of her annual pledge along with the altar flowers on Christmas.

Rick Rinkoff was among the first trustees of the Cornerstone Trust. After finishing his studies at Carnegie Mellon University in Pittsburgh, Rick entered the investment business. In 1977 he moved to the Twin Cities to work for First Bank (now U.S. Bank) and stayed for nineteen years. In 1996 he joined with two colleagues from the bank to form the new investment company Woodland Partners. Rick is married to Julia Ferguson, a jewelry designer, who is the daughter of the late senior warden Lola Ferguson and parishioner Dr. Daniel Ferguson. The Rinkoffs have two sons, William and Thomas. The family lives in a Prairie-style house at 590 Summit Avenue that was built by Ellerbe and Round in 1913.

Early one morning, perhaps in 2006, as St. John's sexton Steve Kartak was unlocking the building, he encountered a young mother at the Kent Street door about to abandon her infant in a car seat. With some quick thinking on his part, Steve talked with the woman for a while—"that's a pretty fine baby you have there"—and reasoned with her, then offered to drive her and her baby to United Hospital downtown. A physician attended to the baby and the mother was assisted by a social worker. Christ the Son of God, after all, has taught that whoever receives a little child in his name receives Christ himself.

In the fall of 2003 the parish committed itself to Adopt-A-Family, a program of Episcopal Community Services, to provide Christmas gifts and a $50 gift certificate for groceries to each of the adopted families. ECS chose the families and sent the parish a wish list for each member, including the first name, age, gender, and clothing and shoe sizes, with suggestions for three small and three medium-sized gifts for each family member.

Soon after the formation of the Cornerstone Trust, the parish learned that it had become the recipient of a very significant bequest—the largest in its history, to date—from *DOROTHY OFTELIE HAND NESBITT*, giving the Cornerstone Trust its first great impetus.

Dorothy Nesbitt's parents, Ida Barbara and Oscar Oftelie, and Dorothy and her brother, Oscar Jr., were members of St. John's, and Ida was confirmed there in 1907. Ida was involved in the Parish Aid Society, served as general secretary of the St. John's Guild, secretary of the Women's Auxiliary, and assistant treasurer of St. Margaret's Guild, and she taught in the Church School. Oscar had citrus groves in Texas, owned an island off Cuba that grew mahogany, did shipping in South America, and made and lost a series of fortunes, until the stock market crash of 1929, when he lost everything, including his home on Avon Street. Oscar Jr. and Dorothy were confirmed at St. John's in 1921. Dorothy herself also taught kindergarten in the Church School. Oscar Jr. died in 1928 and Mrs. Oftelie died in 1939. Dorothy bought a small house for her father and lived there with him for a while, and inherited a substantial sum of money from a cousin in Texas.

Dorothy was a medical technician and was smart enough to buy 3M stock in the 1940s. She apparently saved her money all her life, in the event times got bad again, and married Robert B. Hand, who was confirmed at St. John's in 1939 and died in 1971. She later married William Nesbitt, a friend from church, but the latter died on their honeymoon.

Jim Johnson occasionally drove Dorothy to church after she got older, and during the Awakening the Dream campaign he wrote to ask if she would be interested in giving $100,000 to name the undercroft. Not fond of the idea, she made a modest gift instead. Jim and George Mairs later met with Dorothy over lunch and talked with her about her plans for her estate. Though she had fine clothes and jewelry, and several fur coats, and though she took two ninety-day cruises around the world, Dorothy lived simply all her life. Becoming infirm and malnourished, she moved to the Episcopal Church Home and promptly regained her health. After she died, Frank Wilson and Jim Johnson went to the probate hearing at the Ramsey County Courthouse and learned that St. John's was the residual beneficiary of Dorothy's estate, which she wanted to benefit youth and young adults. Eventually the parish received slightly over $3 million from the estate, eighty percent of which went into the Cornerstone Trust, and twenty percent into the restoration of the parking lot and most of the re-roofing then underway. With the trust in place, others can now bequeath their estate to St. John's in a way that was not possible previously, because the principal is safe in perpetuity.

St. John's Stained Glass Treasures

WE ARE BLESSED to have in our midst at St. John's some of the most beautiful stained and art glass windows in the Twin Cities metropolitan area. These windows can be appreciated in a number of ways—through an understanding of their history, their biblical references, or their colors and forms. They can be appreciated for the way in which they sometimes make us feel closer to God. They facilitate contemplation and meditation, promote a greater understanding of the biblical stories illustrated, and encourage further exploration of the church's tangible and intangible assets.

The diagram below shows the placement of the art glass windows in the church. The first of these are the Narthex windows, followed by the Nave, the Canticle, and the Clerestory windows. The Chapel and extra windows complete this presentation.

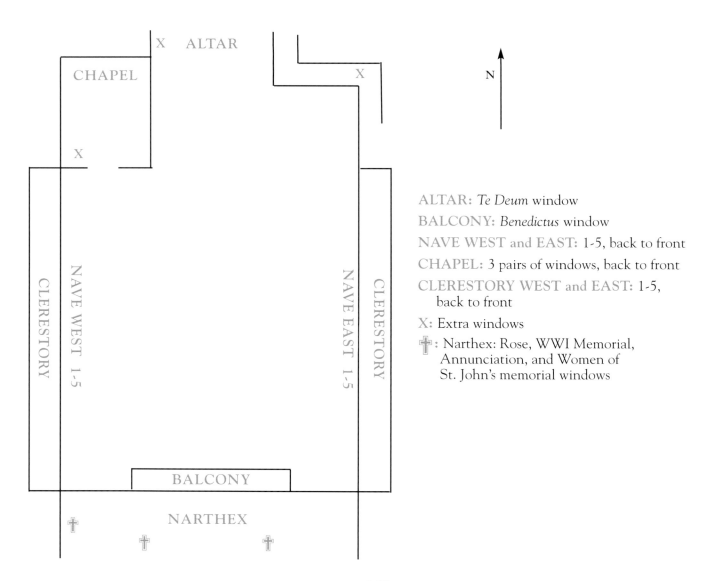

ALTAR: *Te Deum* window

BALCONY: *Benedictus* window

NAVE WEST and EAST: 1-5, back to front

CHAPEL: 3 pairs of windows, back to front

CLERESTORY WEST and EAST: 1-5, back to front

X: Extra windows

✝: Narthex: Rose, WWI Memorial, Annunciation, and Women of St. John's memorial windows

Left: The Annunciation Window, a two-panel Baldy memorial window in the east side of the narthex, was designed by Connick and Associates and installed in 1944. The left window depicts Gabriel, the angel of the Annunciation; the right panel, Mary, mother of Jesus. Right: The World War II Memorial Window in the west side of the narthex was designed by Connick and Associates and installed in 1949. St. Michael, the angel messenger of God, appears in the left panel; in the right panel is the Archangel Raphael, healer of all humanity.

The Women of St. John's Memorial Windows in the east and west stairwells were created by parishioner Helen Boyer and installed in 2005. Vibrant blue and red glass and kiln-fired painted scriptural verses from the Gospel of John provide connections to the Annunciation, WWII memorial, and the Rose windows.

Opposite page: St. John's Rose window dates to the church Cass Gilbert designed in 1903 and was reconstructed in 2004. The five-petaled rose symbolizes the Virgin Mary. A rose window traditionally marks the west entrance to a church.

NAVE WINDOWS

Five sets of stained glass windows in the west wall of the church, designed by the English firm of Heaton, Butler and Bayne, are shaped by three gothic arches with open traceries and illustrate biblical stories with memorial citations. These windows on the west side feature more muted colors than those seen in five similar sets of windows on the east side of the church, which contain jewel tones similar to colors in the clerestory windows.

SCENES DEPICTED IN THE WEST WALL
(from the back of the church to the front):

- Jesus welcoming and nurturing little children: Gertrude and Martha Peet memorial

- Jesus with friends Mary, Martha, and Lazarus: Cecilia Watkins memorial

- Jesus's parable of the Good Samaritan: Victor Watkins memorial

- John the Baptist pointing to a star, the Christ: William Bend memorial

- Jesus being baptized by John the Baptist: Fanny Wilder memorial

SCENES DEPICTED IN THE EAST WALL
(from the back of the church to the front):

- Nativity scene with the Magi and shepherds: Ellen and Arthur Gillette memorial

- The boy Jesus teaching in the temple: Jeheil Chamberlin memorial

- Jesus, the healer, with people in need: Edward and Ellen Kopper memorial

- Jesus in the garden of Gethsemane: John Johnston memorial

- Easter morning with Mary Magdalene and others: Ella Chapman memorial

Jesus's parable of the Good Samaritan: Victor Watkins memorial (top). John the Baptist pointing to a star, the Christ: William Bend memorial (above).

THE CANTICLE WINDOWS

Songs of Praise in Glass

The Canticle windows were designed by the Charles J. Connick studio of Boston. The *Te Deum* window above the main altar (pictured on p. 104) was installed in 1920, and the *Benedicite* window at the rear of the nave in 1938.

The *Te Deum* window features the text of the canticle *We praise the, O God*. It is dedicated to parishioners who fought in WWI and is located above the main altar. Angels, prophets, kings, early priests, disciples, saints, and martyrs surround the figure of the risen Christ in the center lancet. Children, birds, and flowers help to complete the glass panels.

The *Benedicite* window features the text of the canticle *O all ye works of the Lord, bless ye the Lord*. It portrays angels, children, Abraham, Moses, Solomon, David, and St. Luke—along with the sun, moon, clouds, a lamp, lily, and lamb.

The *Benedicite* window (right).

CLERESTORY WINDOWS

Five sets of three-part clerestory windows are located high on both the west and east sides of the church, above the nave windows, near the ceiling of the sanctuary. Installed as memorial windows between 1924 and 1963, these windows illustrate Old and New Testament men and women.

EAST SIDE MAIN CHARACTERS
(from the back of the church to the front):

- Patriarchs—Moses, Jacob, Abraham:
  Elizabeth Hensel memorial (pictured below)

- Kings and prophets—Solomon, David, Samuel:
  Laura Cook Ottis memorial

- Old Testament women—Esther, Ruth, Rebecca:
  Jennie Nelson Butler memorial

- Prophets—Jeremiah, Isaiah, Elisha:
  Clara Cook Kellogg memorial

- Apocalyptic voices—John the Baptist, Daniel,
  Ezekiel: Cortlandt and Mary Taylor memorial

WEST SIDE MAIN CHARACTERS
(from the back of the church to the front):

- St. Mattias, St. Jude, St. Simeon:
  Obed and Emma Lanpher
  and their children memorial

- St. Timothy, St. Paul, St. Titus:
  Lt. Kay Todd Jr. memorial

- St. Mary of Magdala, Mother Mary, Mary of Bethany:
  Luna Van Dresar memorial

- St. James Major, St. Peter, St. Phillip:
  Paul Burns Cook memorial

- St. Andrew, St. Luke, St. John the Apostle:
  Samuel D. Flagg memorial

CHAPEL WINDOWS

There are three pairs of windows in archway insets in the chapel, originally called the Chapel of the Beloved Disciple. The designs for the lancet-shaped windows are drawn from events in the Life of Christ as conveyed by the Gospel of St. John. These windows were designed and fabricated by the Connick studio and dedicated as memorials to Alvin and Isabel Macartney in 1942 and to Maud Macartney Grant in 1956.

Right: The west wall of the chapel with two of its three pairs of stained glass windows.

EXTRA WINDOWS

Additional art glass windows exist in spaces ancillary to the sanctuary. They include:

The Seabury memorial window (1976) is located in the stairwell near the chapel. Two rectangular panels depict the Virgin Mary with Elizabeth and St. Francis of Assisi and his sister, St. Clare.

The Platt memorial window (1991) is located near the columbarium. Designed by a granddaughter of the Platts in collaboration with Gaytee Glass of Minneapolis, it uses clear and textured glass and bevels to connote grace and beauty.

The Trinity windows (2003) are set into the doors to the sacristy and the offices of the clergy. Crafted and donated by Helen Boyer, they depict the Creator, Redeemer, and Sustainer.

The Hospitality windows (2007) with welcome and trinity symbols are located in the Kent Street foyer to greet visitors coming into the church. Crafted by Helen Boyer, they reflect the diverse styles of the Platt memorial window and original Guild House pastel squares adjacent to the foyer.

Right: Artist and parishioner Helen Boyer with the Creator window she crafted.

NOTE: *The publisher thanks parishioner and stained glass artist Helen Boyer for her research materials and considerable explanations from which these six stained glass pages were compiled.*

Mary Dustin Platt (Dusty) Mairs is a fifth-generation parishioner at St. John's.

ST. JOHN'S HAS MANY TREASURES—its beautiful stained glass windows, its vintage pipe organ, its marble sculpture, its splendid hammerbeam ceilings, and its exceptional ornamental woodwork. But among all its finery is the still more prominent treasure of Dusty Mairs.

Mary Dustin Platt Mairs, the fifth generation of her family at St. John's, was baptized, confirmed, and married at the church on Kent Street. She was a member of the choir as a young girl, active in the young people's organization as a teenager, and the "token" youth on the search committee for Grayson Clary. In her adult years she taught in the Church School, co-chaired the Choir Mothers, and was the project manager for the development of the undercroft and a

member of a committee on long-range parish planning. She has held a number of offices in the parish, and before its dissolution, was a member of the board of the Women of St. John's.

A graduate of Summit School, Dusty attended Wells College and the University of Minnesota and taught at the Crocus Hill School formerly on Summit Avenue and now housed at St. John's, where she worked with four-year olds. She has four grown children of her own: Alexandra, Elizabeth, Thomas, and Catherine.

Dusty remembers proudly the time when the Rev. Grayson Clary decided he wanted to host a Christmas party—St. John's first. She took charge of all the arrangements and soon realized that the committee that organized the event, with Adrian Drew and her father the capable chefs, was, in effect, St. John's first Fellowship Commission, and she its first chairman.

Dusty began her ministry at St. John's in the area of Christian education, teaching confirmation. She still occasionally hears from some of the boys in her class. Soon she became professionally engaged as the Christian Education Director, before Paige Hagstrom assumed the post. In the 1980s she left St. John's to work for the Rev. Denis O'Pray as office administrator at St. James in Minneapolis for about nine years, and then took on a similar position with the Rev. Ernie Ashcroft for eleven years at Church of the Messiah.

She was drawn back to St. John's when she was asked to computerize the parish register—the records of baptisms, weddings, and funerals—though she wasn't given a computer (and the job remains unfinished). After a few years she realized that she was actually doing the work of a parish administrator—as a volunteer. And through her work with assistant treasurer John Oldfield, she increasingly realized how much was involved in such a position, with many of its dimensions left undone.

Dusty believes the clergy should be free to do what only the clergy can do, and not have to worry about mundane things—like boilers, shingles, and gutters. The parish administrator can oversee the various commission meetings, make sure the staff is on the right track, ascertain that there are no scheduling difficulties, see to it that the building is well used by the neighbors, and in general ensure the material well-being of the parish in faithfulness to the vestry's goals. Indeed just as the vestry is responsible for the earthly affairs of the parish, so the parish administrator is the vestry's extension into its daily operations. Continued growth at St. John's is inevitable and Dusty's position will become a paid necessity.

It brings Dusty great delight that she is part of something that came from the past and is leading toward the future. She likes the continuity and the tradition that St. John's represents for her. But she also likes progress. As she says, "We've waded through change very carefully. We've kept up with the times and we've changed well, aiming to do it right for our next hundred years."

Outside the parish, Dusty serves on the board of trustees for Episcopal Homes of Minnesota, which deliberated on the disposition of the property on University Avenue that formerly belonged to their long-time neighbor, Porky's, since 1953 the Twin Cities' iconic drive-in restaurant. Porky's served its last burger and root beer float in April 2011. Episcopal Homes bought the property and has expanded its campus on the site.

Dusty holds high hopes for St. John's and is confident that "we are on the cusp of something powerful, both for St. John's and for what we do." Strong leadership, she says, is vital to help us find our pathway.

IN JANUARY 2006 several parishioners proposed that St. John's become a Partner Church in the Supportive Housing Program of Episcopal Community Services, which provided social services and financial and personal support to help families establish secure homes in the community. At the annual meeting, the congregation agreed unanimously to move forward with the program. Twelve parishioners took the training through ECS, namely, Hank Snyder, Sue Cadwell, Robbin Clamons, Cheryl Hanson, Dick Yore, Alden Drew, Gail Markey, Kathy Brown, Sarah Smith, Cheri Wiegand, Don Husband, Cammie Beattie, and Mary Frances Palmer, with Alys Wilson[15] chairing the committee. In March the committee met their partner family and renamed itself Project Kathleen in honor of their "first fearless mother," who with her partner, Andre, had a blended family of four children. The Pohlad Foundation funded a grant that enabled two of the younger children, Shatera and Payton, to attend acting classes at the Steppingstone Theater Summer Camp in August.

Among those who have served as mentors for Project Kathleen families over the years are Heidi Hellekson, Kat Bourque, Elizabeth Plummer, Phyllis Merrill, Alice Johnson, Holly Weinkauf, and Linda Zelig. In 2010 the committee joined with parishioners from St. Mary's Episcopal Church in order to extend service to more families. Project Kathleen, now renamed Hearts to Homes, continues to find long-lasting solutions to homelessness. Ida Barbara Oftelie, the mother of Dorothy Hand Nesbitt, did similar family mentoring from St. John's in the early part of the twentieth century.

A CONGREGATIONAL SURVEY was taken to assess the demographics of the parish and to determine the satisfactions and wants of its membership, and the results were published in February 2007. Noting that sixty percent of the respondents were married, the researchers asked whether the remaining forty percent were adequately served. There were many new people in the parish, with thirty-five percent of the respondents having attended St. John's for five years or less. An astonishing fifty percent of attendees were not raised as Episcopalians. About sixty percent of respondents considered themselves active—a very high percentage—

meaning they participate more than once a week. Among parishioners' wants were programs for members in their twenties and thirties, and for young families and seniors. Some wanted programs for the neighborhood and for small groups, such as Bible study. Others sought gay and lesbian connections, greater orthodoxy, or a more contemporary approach to theology. Some wanted a more conservative option for worship while others wanted more contemporary options.

THE STIPULATION THAT HE WOULD have a sabbatical after seven years was written into Mr. Wilson's contract when he began his tenure at St. John's in 2000. He assured the vestry that he would return to St. John's after his sabbatical and that he would not be a candidate for bishop. He and Alys left early in May 2007, spending part of their time at the Chautauqua Institution, and returned toward the end of July, well refreshed. Located on Chautauqua Lake in southwestern New York State, the Chautauqua is a not-for-profit community that explores the important religious, social, and political issues of our times and promotes excellence and creativity in the arts. Frank repeatedly referred to the sabbatical not as his alone, but as the parish's as well, meaning that his time away would be healthy for everyone concerned. The Rev. Margaret Fell supplied on Sunday mornings during the rector's absence.

In the summer of 2007 parishioner Julia Ferguson began looking into the needs of the parking lot, where the deterioration of the surface had become a serious safety concern. The Property Commission, the Building Commission, and the Garden Circle (formed in the summer of 2004 for a gardening project for the north courtyard) were asked to devise a plan for improved safety and beautification. Julia obtained estimates from various contractors who would complete the work in October 2008, and the following summer saw a much-improved parking lot, replete with lighting, a new paved surface, and handsome landscaping.

St. John's is fortunate in its setting with its numerous opportunities for small and larger gardening projects. In 2010 teenager Charles Lim Olsen led his scout troop 408 in planting circular flowerbeds around the two saplings in the north garden as part of the larger plan for that area. Charlie was earning his Eagle Scout badge, the highest advancement rank in scouting, which was awarded to him in December in the company of his fellow scouts, and his family and friends, including a fair representation from St. John's that ranged from about the eldest in the parish to some of the youngest—from Bob Binger to Meredith Hansen.

Gary Gleason, then a resident of Northfield and a college student at Hamline University, was hired to serve as assistant advisor to the Episcopal Young Churchmen at St. John's in 1970. Years later he was brought into the diocesan hierarchy by Bishop James Jelinek to serve as canon to the ordinary, the chief pastoral assistant to the bishop, providing him counsel and support, and working with parishes, clergy, wardens, and vestries, especially in times of conflict, crisis or transition. Mr. Gleason completed his mission after seventeen years in the post in September 2008, and St. John's hosted a diocesan celebration of his service, when he was honored by Bishop Jelinek with the awarding of the Bishop Whipple Cross.

The silver cross worn by Bishop Whipple until his death in 1902 has been worn by each of his eight successors. Bishop Robert Anderson instituted the practice of bestowing a replica of the cross on those who have made significant contributions to the life and enhancement of the diocese. Mr. Gleason's sterling silver cross was made from a wax molding of the original, and is stamped on the back with the Roman numeral X, indicating the tenth of its type. He wears it when serving as a lay assistant during the Eucharist at St. John's.

Whipple Cross.

Boy Scout Charles Olsen completed a garden for St. John's for his Eagle Scout project in 2010. He is surrounded by a happy gathering of parishioners who supported him and attended his Eagle Scout ceremony.

A part of the Olsen Garden upon completion.

A section of St. John's North Garden.

IN THE YEAR 2000 THE UNITED NATIONS established eight Millennium Development Goals to encourage the improvement of social and economic conditions in the world's poorest countries, intending by the year 2015 to reduce by half the number of people living in extreme poverty. In response, Episcopal Relief and Development, the international agency of the Episcopal Church, adopted the goals as a framework to guide its own efforts.

In 2008 St. John's became involved. Deacon Barbara Mraz and parishioner Jennifer Kinkead took on the task of determining how our parish of three hundred families could best make a difference in the lives of people living on less than a dollar a day, halfway around the world. Despite the fact that this country was experiencing the worst recession in generations, Barbara, Jennifer, and their committee chose an organization called Give Us Wings to guide the parish in the

Boys and girls at St. John's Clinic in Uganda. The girls are wearing dresses made by St. John's parishioners.

building of a medical clinic in Kayoro, Uganda, where there was currently little or no medical care.

Give Us Wings rebuilds villages and restores hope in Kenya and Uganda, working at the grassroots level to support development projects to meet the medical and educational needs of the poorest of the poor. Its founders, Mary Steinert Whelan and her daughter Shawn Whelan, established the organization in 1999 after hearing the women of an African village mourning the loss of the last village man to die of AIDS. The women wanted to grow food, feed and clothe their children, take them off the streets, and send them to school. One villager explained, "It is nice to give us a few shillings once in a while, but we need information and education. That would give us wings."

Barbara Mraz persuaded the congregation that, despite the financial distress, they could accomplish "One Good Thing" in the lives of people on the other side of the world. In the end, the congregation raised not only the $75,000 required to build the clinic, but another $20,000 to support additional needs. The children of St. John's sold a cookie mix to help raise funds, parishioner Ray Frisby created and sold Christmas cards with his sketch of the future clinic, and many members of St. John's made donations to the clinic in lieu of giving Christmas gifts. A video was produced in which St. John's parishioners explained why the building of the clinic was important to them. A number of parishioners also painted tiles to be affixed to the inside walls of the clinic, and some members of the parish sewed dresses and shirts for the children of the village. And the clinic was built.

In January 2011, four parishioners—Jennifer Kinkead, Cammie Beattie, Shirley Sailors, and Bob Horn—traveled to Kayoro to see the clinic firsthand and to meet some of the people it was serving. The four returned with stories of some of their memorable experiences. While on their way to purchase adhesives for the tiles, for instance, Jennifer Kinkead and Bob Horn passed an Anglican Church and deciding to drop in, discovered

Cammie Beattie, Jennifer Kinkead, Bob Horn, and Shirley Sailors hang a framed image of St. John's Church in the clinic in Kayoro, Uganda, 2011.

St. John's Clinic in Uganda on the day of its dedication.

the congregation giving thanks for the new clinic. Cammie Beattie, a physical therapist, also gave some training to the community health care workers. Perhaps most remarkable of all, the foursome held a "health camp day," attracting about 750 people without any advanced publicity. St. John's Clinic is now serving a critical need in a distant part of God's creation.

In October 2008, Frank Wilson announced that Keely Franke, who was attending Luther Seminary in pursuit of holy orders, would be a seminary intern at St. John's for two years, having already graduated from the Seminary of the Southwest in Austin, Texas. The Rev. Franke remained at St. John's after her ordinations to the diaconate and the priesthood, preaching and presiding at Sunday services, and working primarily with youth and new members. In 2010 she introduced a contemplative service in the gymnasium on Thursday evenings that led the following year to the introduction of sung Compline in the choir stalls, with incense, on the second Thursday of the month.

AFTER NINETEEN YEARS AS CO-CHAIRS of the Altar Guild, Dusty Mairs and Dorothy MacDonald decided in January 2009 that it was time for new blood. Dorothy Griffith MacDonald was a long-time treasurer of the Women of St. John's and also handled the Huge Sale funds for several years. She also served a three-year term on the vestry. Dorothy's American mother was born of English settlers, married Englishman Herbert Griffith, and moved with him to England. Dorothy and her parents lived near London during the first year of World War II and experienced a lot of the bombing. But her father was soon named British vice-counsel in St. Paul. Because her mother had dual nationality, she and her husband and young Dorothy, and her brother Cecil, were allowed to enter the U.S. as refugees, which meant they could bring no money with them.

The Griffiths sailed out of Liverpool on a ship with seven hundred children in August 1940, a convoy seeing them into the St. Lawrence River where they landed at Montreal and took the train to St. Paul. The family became involved at St. John's, her father singing in the choir, Dorothy singing in the St. Cecilia Choir, Cecil serving as an acolyte, and her mother doing "lots of things!" Dorothy proudly remembers that her grandfather was the first science master at the prestigious Harrow School outside London where one of his students was Winston Churchill. When Dorothy and Dusty retired from the Altar Guild, they were followed by Diane Power and Cheryl Hanson.

About this same time, in early 2009, St. John's was also helping Holy Apostles Church on the east side of St. Paul, a mission congregation that since 2005 had experienced an influx of seventy-eight Hmong families, all former Roman Catholics. Despite a diocesan grant of $37,500 for each of the past two years, the mission had needed to cut its vicar's work to three-quarter time and the associate priest to half time. In February the Rev. Letha Wilson-Barnard, the new vicar of the parish, was invited to meet with the vestry to share with them the joys and challenges of the mission congregation, which had incorporated Hmong culture and traditions in its worship while still retaining non-Hmong congregants.

Come summer, in June, Frank Wilson, Barbara Mraz, senior warden Becky Garthofner, junior warden Jay Debertin,[16] Karen Dingle, and youth director Jean Hansen met with leaders from Holy Apostles to discuss a possible partnership by which both congregations could share knowledge, culture, ideas, and programming. People from both congregations began meeting periodically to discuss the nature of the arrangement. In August 2009 Jean Hansen and the Rev. Letha Wilson-Barnard submitted a proposal for a $10,000 grant from the Bishop's Circle Fund to support a joint youth program, including stipends for two youth leaders, a joint confirmation program, a combined mission trip, and a youth band at Holy Apostles.

THE GRANT WAS AWARDED in September and Ms. Wilson-Barnard and Ms. Hansen co-taught a combined two-year confirmation class for their youth. The two congregations worked together to sew dresses for children in Kayoro, Uganda, and learned to make egg rolls. They exchanged visits to St. John's Christmas party and to the Hmong New Year celebration at Holy Apostles, worked on fundraisers together, and enjoyed a summer picnic and joint service in August 2011 at Como Park. Letha Wilson-Barnard and Keely Franke also did a pulpit exchange.

The Rev. Wilson-Barnard wrote:

Youth Group from Holy Apostles Parish, with leaders Jean Hansen (back row, center); Longkee Vang (to the left of Jean); and the Rev. Letha Wilson-Barnard (back row, far right).

The most important aspect of the partnership . . . is building relationships. We have been most successful with this in the area of youth ministry. Jean [Hansen] has gotten to know Holy Apostles youth and families and is mentoring Longkee Vang, our volunteer youth minister, and has even hired him as an assistant at St. John's. Longkee has been an important bridge between the two youth groups. St. John's has been generous with financial support and allowed us to use the church facility for retreats and conferences. As the only paid clergy and staff member at Holy Apostles, I find enormous support in having colleagues in ministry—clergy and lay—at St. John's.

A sign of the vitality of the faith of the Holy Apostles community: one of its members, Toua Vang, attended Virginia Theological Seminary, the first Hmong person to enter an Episcopal seminary.

In recent years, St. John's has hosted the Big Net, an all-volunteer effort under the direction of parishioner Claire Eckley. The Big Net was conceived to support the many people who were losing their employment during the downturn in the economy. Five other Christian and Jewish congregations served on the coordinating committee. The Big Net included a weekly Job Seeker Support Group that provided assistance and support to persons searching for jobs. It also included seminars that met twice monthly, led by parishioners Judy Southwick and Bob Horn, which discussed effective job searching. The Big Net, which now has its own website, has served over 150 people since its inception. It is now housed at Dayton Avenue Presbyterian Church.

FOUR OF ST. JOHN'S CLERGY have enjoyed summer vacations on MacMahon Island off the coast of Maine over the years. The Rev. William Mead, rector in the early 1960s, first went to the island for two summers, serving as chaplain at the quaint, shingled Chapel of St. Cuthbert and residing in the rectory, known as Eastcot. Mr. Mead and his wife Kate were so enamored of the island—accessible only by boat and absent a grocery store—that they later purchased one of its thirty-

INTERNATIONALLY KNOWN AUTHOR, storyteller, and humorist Garrison Keillor began attending St. John's during Mr. Wilson's rectorship. At six feet, three inches in height, an easily recognizable Minnesota icon, Keillor is host of the Minnesota Public Radio show *A Prairie Home Companion*, which is also broadcast in the United Kingdom, Ireland, Australia, and New Zealand. Born in Anoka, Minnesota, one of six children, he belonged as a youth to the Plymouth Brethren, a fundamentalist Christian denomination. More recently he attended a Lutheran church in New York before turning to the Episcopal Church. A member of the American Academy of Arts and Letters and a staunch Democrat, Mr. Keillor's Sunday op-ed column in the *Minneapolis Star Tribune* often considers current events of political import. His numerous books include *Lake Wobegon Days*, *The Book of Guys*, *Love Me* and *Homegrown Democrat*. He and his wife, Jenny Lind Nilsson, live with their daughter, Maia Grace, on St. Paul's Summit Avenue, in a house once home to lumber baron Frederick K. Weyerhaeuser. Keillor and Nilsson also have a home on the Upper West Side in New York City.

Fond of the ritual of the Episcopal Church, Mr. Keillor wrote of the experience of exchanging the peace that befell him one Sunday in 2009 at St. John's, proving that the peace is not always peaceful:

One morning, during the exchange, the lady in front of me, turning to embrace me, lost her corsage. It fell at my feet and I looked down for it and accidentally kicked it and then went to retrieve it and stepped past the plump lady, and the old coot turned, horror-stricken, to see me coming. He tried to retreat but was blocked by other worshippers. My hair was a little long at the time and maybe he expected me to plant a major peace on him—and then he saw me bend down and pick up the flower. He looked disgusted. It was what they call a transforming moment. I had always looked down on the guy and here he was, upset, because he thought I was going to love him up. He stuck out his hand to fend me off and I shook it.

seven houses for themselves. It was through the Meads that their friends and parishioners John and Betty Myers, in 1962, purchased an island home of their own.

Over time the Myers invited three other clergy from St. John's to join them for summer jaunts to Maine while serving as chaplains. The Rev. Joseph Clark, assistant to the Rev. Grayson Clary, went one summer with his wife and surprised his hosts by taking their boat out for a spin, only to capsize it. The Clarys themselves came later for a visit, but they had no better luck on the boat when they went sailing one day in foggy, miserable weather and promptly got lost, discouraging them from ever returning to Maine. The Rev. Frank and Alys Wilson came for two summers. But perhaps wary of clergy luck, they opted not to take the Myers' boat out on their own and instead went sailing with Cammie and Rob Beattie, who summered in nearby Boothbay Harbor.

THE RT. REV. JAMES L. JELINEK, a resident of nearby Lincoln Avenue with his wife Marilyn, made St. John's his home parish for several years after he retired as eighth bishop of the Diocese of Minnesota, in February 2010. Ordained bishop in 1993 at St. John's Abbey in Collegeville, Minnesota, he announced in the statement of his resignation that the diocese had joined together to carry out "the long-standing legacy of what it means to be Episcopalians in Minnesota: we have warmly welcomed all people through our red doors, we have fed the hungry, spoken for those who have no opportunity to speak, stood with the oppressed and given hope to the hopeless." Among his various activities at St. John's, the bishop cooked up some of his specialty soups for the 2011 Lenten suppers on Wednesday evenings, and hosted the reception following that year's Easter Vigil.

In May 2010 the parish lost revered parishioner George Mairs III, husband of Dusty Platt Mairs. George was employed at Mairs and Power, Inc. for fifty-eight years, providing investment counsel to thousands of shareholders across the country. He was the long-time chairman and CEO of the company and for twenty-five years was the lead manager of the nationally acclaimed Mairs and Power Growth Fund.

On January 16, 1995, *The Pioneer Press* ran an article titled "Plain Vanilla Firm Finds Limelight," a tribute to Mairs and Power, noting that it was nationally recognized by *Forbes*, *Fortune*, and *Kiplinger's Personal Finance* as "a little gem of a firm which has steadily out-performed almost everyone else in the field." The article observed that the real strength of the company and its managers was "steady moderate growth over a 60-year period."

A "regular" at the Men's Breakfasts on the second Saturday of each month at St. John's, Mairs had also been an adjunct faculty member in the University of Minnesota Department of Finance, a past trustee of Macalester College, and a board member of Presbyterian Homes and the Ramsey County Historical Society. He was also past president of the St. Paul Chamber Orchestra, and the St. Paul Academy and Summit School Alumni Association, and an active supporter of Episcopal Homes.

Another pillar of the parish was St. John's historian and archivist W. Frederick Myers II who was part of the Myers heritage. His paternal grandparents were parishioners Walter

Frederick Myers and the former Mary Frances Hovey. Walter Myers served on the vestry from 1895 to 1910 and also served as clerk and parish treasurer. The couple had six offspring, including Paul Noxon Myers, whose wife was the former Reine Humbird, and Donald Myers, who married the former Mary Irene Wyman. Paul and Reine had three children: Paul Jr.; John Humbird Myers, who married the former Betty Blodgett; and Elizabeth "Zib" Myers, who married John Parish. Parishioner Judy Parish Diedrich is the daughter of Zib and John.

FRED MYERS, the son of Donald and Mary Myers, grew up in the choir of men and boys and attended many years of choir camp. He majored in history and foreign languages at Macalester College, and in the 1970s as a member of the Property Committee, he was in charge of peeling paint and falling plaster. Fred also taught in the Church School. He worked at the St. Paul Companies from 1951 until his retirement in 1984, serving as supervisor for forms control. He prided himself on being St. John's lovable curmudgeon.

The family of Walter Frederick Myers, 1928. Seated, front row, left to right: Ellen Lee White Wyman, Mary Frances Hovey Myers, Walter Frederick Myers, unidentified. Seated, second row: Zib Myers, Paul Noxon Myers Jr. Standing, back row, left to right: Paul Noxon Myers, Margaret Myers Wyman, Reine (Mrs. Paul) Myers, Mary Irene Wyman Myers, Donald Myers, Cornelia Lake Abbott.

Six women from St. John's have held the prestigious post of president of the Schubert Club of St. Paul: Mrs. Charles A. (Esther Jones) Guyer (1930–1933), Mrs. Julian S. Gilman (1943–1948), Shirley Kartarik Michienzi (1969–1971), Dee Ann Crossley (1999–2001), Mary Probst Morrison (2006–2009), and Lucy Rosenberry Jones, who became the president in 2010. Parishioner Jill Greene Thompson served as vice-president for marketing and development. The historic Schubert Club was founded in 1882, during St. John's second year, by Marion Ramsey Furness, daughter of Governor Alexander Ramsey, along with some music-loving friends, as an outpost of classical music. While the first meetings were merely social gatherings for women, the group soon began to present concerts, lectures, and study groups. Now over 130 years old, and one of the longest surviving arts organizations in the country, the club has brought virtually all of the world's great recitalists to the St. Paul stage.

During Frank Wilson's rectorship, the parish developed a conspicuously welcoming demeanor in the reception of newcomers, modeled after Frank's own deep-felt openness to the stranger, the outsider, and the marginalized. While at various times parishioners have been appointed official greeters to welcome visitors at the door on Sunday mornings, there have probably always been unofficial greeters as well, people doing their best to help newcomers feel like they belong to St. John's. Among the earliest of these was Eleanor Hartman, who would write notes to visitors and newcomers. Another was Ralph Klosterman, who happily gave new ladies a peck on the cheek. When Jim Johnson took over after Ralph, the pecking came to a end.

Jim Johnson is known to most parishioners as the treasurer, and he credits his mentors William Plummer Sr. and Bob Martin who preceded him in the post. But his deeper passion is for evangelism and his unofficial ministry as greeter is where his heart lies. Jim was baptized at an Episcopal church by his grandfather, a pastor in the Norwegian Lutheran church. There were no Norwegian Lutheran churches nearby (only German) and his mother was an Episcopalian. Though he has wondered if his baptism was valid, Jim has been an Episcopalian ever since.

In college he was a member of the Canterbury Club, the student organization for Episcopalians. After graduation from Carleton College, in 1964, he went to work for Minnesota Mutual in St. Paul where he spent his entire career.

After a stint in the U.S. Navy following college, Jim found himself at St. John's Episcopal Church in Chevy Chase, Maryland, where he was impressed by the success of small groups at incorporating new members into the congregation. So successful were they, in fact, that Jim was enlisted to teach junior high youth in the Sunday School. Returning to St. Paul in 1968, Mr. Johnson had no affiliation with a church until 1975 when he attended the eight o'clock service at St. John's. Although he liked the Rev. Grayson Clary, the parish had no method of incorporation that compared with St. John's in Chevy Chase. Indeed, for the stewardship campaign that first year, Jim had to ask for a pledge card. Apart from Sunday worship, he had no involvement with the parish until Mr. Clary invited him to attend Cursillo under his sponsorship, which he did, and enjoyed it very much. He subsequently became involved with Cursillo renewal along with a group of seven other men from St. John's who met in participants' homes on Monday mornings at 6:30. It became a tight group of committed friends, a model of the small group experience.

James Johnson and Lucy Jones were married at St. John's on November 20, 2010.

Along with Jim Johnson and Don Husband, Ray and Phyllis Frisby became unofficial greeters not long after they themselves arrived as newcomers, in 2006. In July of that year the Frisbys inaugurated their search for a loving faith community broad enough to welcome their friends. St. John's was the second church they visited, and after trying five or six other parishes, returned here and in October decided to stay. In April 2008 Ray began baking loaves of bread for first-time visitors to the parish, delivering them to their homes on Sunday afternoons.

After a rectorship of nearly ten years, the Rev. Frank E. Wilson addressed a letter to the congregation on November 17, 2009, to announce his retirement:

> This is a very exciting time at Saint John's, as many of the dreams the parish had when we came have come into being, and many more dreams are now part of the life of this great parish church. Saint John's has strong lay leadership and a gifted staff. When our new bishop arrives he will find here a healthy, growing congregation.

Frank retired on February 1, 2010. He modestly declined a farewell gathering, and instead the parish feted him and Alys at the Annual Meeting at the end of January. In return, Frank and Alys made a contribution to the Saint John's Clinic in Kayoro, Uganda.

If it appears to the reader that Mr. Wilson's name occurs only rarely in this history of his rectorship, the reason is that one of the greatest of Frank's many fine attributes was his deep respect for lay ministry, such that the support he lent both to the professional staff and the congregation provided a spiritual impetus for the innovative programs undertaken by them during his years in the parish. In the best sense of the word, his legacy was the invigoration and empowerment of those with whom he served. Even before he arrived at St. John's, in fact, Mr. Wilson sent a letter to then senior warden Ella Slade noting that "Ours is a shared ministry, and the most important part of Christ's ministry is always done by lay people." Frank was true to his own theology and his own greatest strength was that he enabled the ministry of others.

DON HUSBAND is an unofficial greeter who in recent years has especially enjoyed his work in fellowship—helping to plan social events for members and new members, so as to build their attachment to the church. He has also served several times on the vestry and various other committees, and was junior warden and a delegate to Diocesan Convention.

After college, where he majored in economics, Don and his late wife Merrily moved to St. Paul from Rochester, Minnesota, when he embarked upon a forty-year banking career as a lending officer with the First National Bank of St. Paul, assigned to real estate and commercial lending, and then moved to Norwest Mortgage where he was a real estate loan officer, and thence to Wells Fargo. He found it rewarding to help customers fulfill their financial needs. It was only after Don and Merrily started attending St. John's that his mother told him that he had been baptized there as a child, while living only a half block away on Portland Avenue. Over the years Don has enjoyed a growing sense of community within the church: "It is one of the focal points of my life."

Phyllis and Ray Frisby.

It has been said of Frank that another of his endearing qualities was that he knew how to treat people. He took a totally self-effacing approach to others. He was adaptable, and he knew the value of compromise. He had a caring and compassionate soul, sincere to the core. At all times accessible, he had well-honed pastoral skills and was prompt to visit parishioners ailing or in need, whether at home or in the hospital, sometimes taking flowers. He was fully attentive to groups and to the people he counseled, coming to them as a voice of peace. He was an excellent administrator and when he was forced by circumstance to terminate a staff member—a secretary, a church school director, or a musician—he did so with keen respect and personal regard, and with a deep, personal anguish. If Frank Wilson was a close friend of God, he was certainly also a friend of all the people who encountered him at St. John's, including Fred Myers who would tease him about his penmanship, asking, "What medical school did you attend?"

Don Postema and Phyllis Goff chaired the search committee for a new rector, and on May 1, 2011, some fifteen months following Mr. Wilson's department, senior warden Jay Debertin announced to the congregation that the vestry had extended a call to the Rev. Jered Weber-Johnson. Mr. Weber-Johnson, soon-to-be St. John's sixteenth rector, moved with his wife Erin Weber-Johnson and their twenty-one-month-old son, Jude, to St. Paul in June, and Mr. Weber-Johnson began work in the parish on July 12.

Jason Engquist.

Jayson Engquist joined the St. John's staff in August, 2013, as Director of Music and organist. He is a Minnesota native and came to St. John's from the Greenwich area of Connecticut where he served congregations in the Episcopal Church, United Church of Christ and Jewish traditions. He graduated from St. Olaf College in Northfield, Minnesota. His graduate studies were at the Yale University School of Music. He is also an accomplished singer and has performed with the Dale Warland Singers, Yale Camarata and Repertory Chorus and the St. Thomas Choir of Men and Boys in New York City.

Katharine Bradtmiller.

The Rev. Katharine Bradtmiller joined St. John's as Associate Rector in September 2013. Kate graduated from Wellesley College and Episcopal Divinity School in Cambridge, Massachusetts. She was an assistant rector at St. Barnabas Episcopal Church in Falmouth, Massachusetts, before moving to Minnesota in 2009. She served as staff chaplain at both Fairview South Hospital and Hennepin County Medical Center before joining St. John's staff.

This, then, is an account of the first 130 years of the parish of St. John the Evangelist Episcopal Church, and many of its saints. Seven of its clergy served as deans or rectors of cathedrals elsewhere, either before or after serving at St. John's, namely, the Rev. Henry Kittson, the Rev. Y. Peyton Morgan, the Rev. Dr. Dudley Ward Rhodes, the Rev. Julius A. Schaad, the Rev. Bernard N. Lovgren, the Rev. Dr. Lloyd R. Gillmett, and the Rev. William H. Mead.[17] And six of its clergy were later consecrated bishops, four of them former rectors, namely, the Rev. John Hazen White, the Rev. Edward Makin Cross, the Rev. Conrad Herbert Gesner, and the Rev. William Henry Mead, and two of them former assistant priests, namely, the Rev. Frederick G. Budlong and the Rev. Thomas Greenwood.

Mr. Wilson had proposed in April 2001, early in his tenure, that the congregation plan to double its membership by Pentecost of 2011. He left St. John's too early to see that dream come true, but by the time of his departure the congregation was welcoming so many new members that the dream was on the verge of reality.

The conspicuous contributions of its lay members to the broader community, thanks to its countless leaders in business, industry, the arts, and civil society, and the many more who have labored elsewhere in the vineyard, have all given St. John's a name to be emulated among churches.

We part here with the words
of the dismissal that the Rev.
Barbara Mraz often uses at
the end of the service:

*Life is short and we do not
have much time to gladden
the hearts of those who journey with us along the way.*

*Be quick to love.
Make haste to be kind.
And the God of compassion
will go with us.*

RECTORS OF THE PARISH OF ST. JOHN THE EVANGELIST, AND THEIR TENURES

1881-1884	Rev. Henry W. Kittson
1884-1888	Rev. Eleutheros Jay Cooke
1889-1891	Rev. John Hazen White
1892-1895	Rev. Yelverton Peyton Morgan
1896-1900	Rev. Dudley Ward Rhodes
1900-1911	Rev. Theodore Sedgwick
1911-1916	Rev. Julius Augustus Schaad
1916-1924	Rev. Edward Makin Cross
1925-1933	Rev. Frederick Dunton Butler
1933-1945	Rev. Conrad Herbert Gesner
1946-1959	Rev. Lloyd Russell Gillmett
1959-1964	Rev. William Henry Mead
1964-1986	Rev. Sidney Grayson Clary
1988-1996	Rev. Richard B. Lampert
2000-2010	Rev. Frank E. Wilson
from 2011	Rev. Jered Weber-Johnson

ORGANISTS, CHOIRMASTERS, AND DIRECTORS OF MUSIC

from 1883	Robert A. Bethune
1885-1886	James Blaikie
until 1889	Miss Hyde
1889-1889	Charles Tarbox
1889-1892	Fletcher H. Wheeler
1892-1895	Emil Oberhoffer
1895-1896	James Blaikie
1901-1943	George Fairclough
1943-1972	C. Wesley Andersen
1972-1983	Robert Kendall
1983-1988	Gregory Larsen
1988-1992	William Stump
1992-1997	Larry H. Blackburn
1997-2004	Roderick Kettlewell (choir director)
1998-2004	Howard Don Small (organist)
2004-2013	James E. Frazier
from 2013	Jason Engquist

WARDENS OF THE PARISH OF ST. JOHN THE EVANGELIST

YEAR	SENIOR WARDEN	JUNIOR WARDEN
prior to 1882	Jacob Schefers	W. H. Conver
1882-1883	Jacob Schefers	Albert Matheson Eddy
1883-1884	Jacob Schefers	V. D. Simar
For unstated reasons, a second election took place on May 23:		
1883-1884	V. D. Simar	J. F. McLaren
1884-1885	George W. Dellinger	J. F. McLaren
1885-1886	J. F. McLaren	Maj. George Q. White
After the resignation of J. F. McLaren:		
1885-1886	E. C. Bowen	Maj. George Q. White
1886-1887	J. W. White	Joseph McKey
After the resignation of Joseph McKey:		
1886-1887	J. W. White	John H. Ames
1887-1888	George W. Dellinger	John H. Ames
1888-1892	George W. Dellinger	John H. Ames
1892-1894	George W. Dellinger	Theodore L. Schurmeier
1894-1897	Thomas Irvine	Theodore L. Schurmeier
1897-1899	Thomas Irvine	Victor M. Watkins
After the resignation of Thomas Irvine:		
1899-1901	Victor M. Watkins	John H. Ames
After the departure of John H. Ames:		
1902	Victor M. Watkins	Emerson W. Peet
After the death of Emerson W. Peet:		
1902-1911	Victor M. Watkins	Richards Gordon
1911-1914	Victor M. Watkins	Obed P. Lanpher
1914-1915	Victor M. Watkins	George A. Goodell
1915-1922	Victor M. Watkins	Paul N. Myers
1922-1927	Paul N. Myers	James D. Denegre
1927-1929	Paul N. Myers	Jule M. Hannaford, Jr.
1929-1939	Jule M. Hannaford, Jr.	Benjamin W. Scandrett
1940-1942	Benjamin G. Griggs	Frederick Wigginton
1943-1944	Benjamin G. Griggs	Julian S. Gilman
1945-1948	John W. Thompson	Julian S. Gilman
1949-1950	William E. Ward	William Plummer
1951	William E. Ward	Reynolds Guyer, Sr.
1952-1953	Augustus W. Clapp, Jr.	Reynolds Guyer, Sr.
1954	Augustus W. Clapp, Jr.	Nathaniel P. Langford, Jr.
1955	Nathaniel P. Langford, Jr.	Russell M. Moffitt
After the resignation of Russell M. Moffitt:		
1955	Nathaniel P. Langford, Jr.	Charles Alden
After the resignation of Charles Alden:		
1955	Nathaniel P. Langford, Jr.	James L. Benepe
1956	Nathaniel P. Langford, Jr.	Charles Alden
1957	Nathaniel P. Langford, Jr.	James L. Benepe
1958-1959	Reynolds Guyer, Sr.	James L. Benepe
1960	Reynolds Guyer, Sr.	Cole Oehler, Jr.
1961-1962	James E. Stevenson	Cole Oehler, Jr.
1963	James E. Stevenson	Clarke A. Chambers
1964-1965	John C. Parish	Clarke A. Chambers
1966	John C. Parish	Robert Andrews
1967-1968	Reynolds Guyer, Sr.	Robert Andrews
1969	Reynolds Guyer, Sr.	Frank Wiecher, Jr.
1970-1971	Robert Andrews	Frank Wiecher, Jr.
1972	Robert Andrews	Dorothy Drew
1973-1974	Lyman Heitmiller	Dorothy Drew
1975	Lyman Heitmiller	Edward Johnson, Jr.
1976-1977	John Myers	Edward Johnson, Jr.
1978	John Myers	Mary S. Platt
1979-1980	Thaddeus Ingersoll, Sr.	Mary S. Platt
1981	Thaddeus Ingersoll, Sr.	Ralph Klosterman
1982-1983	Ralph Klosterman	Lola Ferguson
After the death of Ralph Klosterman:		
1983-1984	Lola Ferguson	C. Robert Beattie
1985	James E. Johnson	C. Robert Beattie
1986-1987	James E. Johnson	Edward H. Cook
1988-1990	C. Robert Beattie	Nancy Martin
1991	John B. Edgerton, Jr.	Shirley Sailors
1992-1993	Shirley Sailors	James E. Johnson
1994-1995	James E. Johnson	Mary Probst Halvorson
1996	Mary Probst Halvorson	Ella Slade
1997-1998	Ella Slade	Donald Husband
1999	Ella Slade	Daniel Rooney
2000-2001	Bradley G. Clary	Alden Drew
2002-2003	Alden Drew	Cammie Beattie
2004-2005	Cammie Beattie	Jeffrey Olsen
2006-2007	Jeffrey Olsen	Becky Garthofner
2008-2009	Becky Garthofner	Jay Debertin
2010-2011	Jay Debertin	Elizabeth Snelson
2012-2013	Elizabeth Snelson	Donald Postema

afterword

The Reverend Jered Weber-Johnson.

JERED WEBER-JOHNSON, St. John's present rector, was born near Walker, Minnesota, and grew up in Alaska. He graduated with a degree in mass communication and religious studies from Greenville College, a school in Greenville, Illinois, associated with the Free Methodist Church. It was there that he met his wife, Erin. The couple moved to Seattle after college and worked as paralegals in the plaintiffs' office for the Exxon Valdez settlement. An Episcopal church in the Seattle area became their spiritual home, but they were not sure ministry was their calling. They then moved to Taipei, Taiwan, where they worked as missionaries with the Episcopal Church's Young Adult Service Corps. Returning to the United States, Jered enrolled at General Theological Seminary in New York City. While completing his divinity degree, he was also a grants consultant at Trinity Wall Street, the Episcopal parish nearest Ground Zero, where the twin towers of the World Trade Center stood until the terrorist attacks of September 11, 2001.

After leaving general seminary, Mr. Weber-Johnson became the assistant rector at St. Alban's Episcopal Church in Washington, D.C., located on the grounds of the Washington Cathedral, where he had primary responsibility for the youth program and for programs focusing on young adults, hospitality, and communications. He initiated a parish "Green Team," which partnered with community groups on solar and weatherization projects. Described as having "wisdom beyond his years," both old and young benefited from his pastoral care, and he took a collaborative approach to his work with parishioners, discerning their gifts and encouraging them to be involved where they could best realize God's presence in their lives.

Erin Weber-Johnson has also been active in ministry. At the time of her move to St. Paul, she was a capital campaign consultant for the Episcopal Church Foundation, a national commission that aids churches in fundraising and endowment efforts, and a grants program partner at Trinity Wall Street. She was able to continue her service with both organizations after moving to the Midwest, functioning as a telecommuter and as part of the mobile work force. As evidence of her continuing concern for faith in action, Ms. Weber-Johnson was also involved with Episcopalians for Global Reconciliation, and was a member of the Standing Commission on World Mission for the Episcopal Church.

In the first years of Mr. Weber-Johnson's tenure, several significant events have taken place that bode well for the future. On All Saints Day in 2011, following evensong, the adult choir sang a bluegrass mass titled *The World Beloved*, authored by Twin Cities composer Carol Barnett and accompanied by the local but internationally renowned bluegrass band, Monroe Crossing. As a result of that performance the choir was invited to reprise the work at

Choir members from St. John's sang the Blue Grass Mass at Carnegie Hall with seven other choirs from around the world, including one from Ireland. Several parishioners accompanied the choir to New York, among them Betty Myers who wrote: "I was there and it was quite exciting!"

Carnegie Hall in New York City in a massed choir of three hundred singers, again accompanied by Monroe Crossing. Nearly half of St. John's choir participated, on Presidents Day in 2013.

Two other events have helped to raise awareness of St. John's commitment to the community. Beginning in the summer of 2012 the parish embarked upon a collaboration with Holy Apostles parish to bring a Farmers Market to the Summit Avenue parking lot on Sunday mornings and Wednesday evenings. The produce grown by Hmong farmers is sold to St. John's parishioners and neighbors to benefit local food shelves. And late in the summer of 2013 several small architectural conversions were made in the education

wing, whose cost nevertheless nearly doomed the effort, and in the fall the Crocus Hill Pre-School, involving about fifty area families, was relocated to St. John's Memorial Parish House from its earlier accommodations at the school of St. Thomas More parish, formerly St. Luke's, at the corner of Summit and Lexington.

In sum, Mr. Weber-Johnson has successfully won the hearts of his new congregation at St. John's, displaying administrative astuteness, confident executive skills, liturgical and musical breadth, theological acuity, a thirst for outreach, a passion for ministry, and a winning susceptibility to laughter. We extend to him our very best wishes for a fruitful ministry in the years ahead.

NOTES

NOTE: The principal documents used in the preparation of this text are found in the archives of St. John the Evangelist Church. They include the following items: (1) a sketchy handwritten history, from 1881 to 1894, whose author is unknown; (2) the minutes of vestry meetings from 1882 to the present; (3) a few parochial reports to the diocese, required by canon law, from 1893; (4) the *Yearbooks* (narrative annual reports, with photographs) from 1892, and from 1900 through 1916; (5) the parish newsletter (known originally as *The St. John's Evangelist*, but bearing other names as time went on), from 1906 to the present; and (6) Annual Reports, from 1917 to the present. While most of the above series of documents are complete, there are some lacunae.

The archives also contain a large number of photographs, many of them printed here, along with the valuable architectural plans for the building projects of 1895, 1902, 1919, and 1956. The Ramsey County Historical Society holds building permits for a number of our parish structures, helping to describe the buildings erected by the congregation, the first of which no longer exists. The Minnesota Historical Society holds in its collections four books and pamphlets published by St. John's as well as a great many relevant photographs, not to mention its wealth of other useful books, microfilm, and institutional and personal documents and ephemera, some from the Diocese of Minnesota that have been immensely useful in the preparation of this text.

Chapter 1

1. The present Richardsonian brownstone building, designed by Cass Gilbert and James Knox Taylor, was erected in 1885-1886.

2. Nearly a quarter century later, a letter from Kittson was published in *The St. John's Evangelist* (December 15, 1906) in which he relates that the lot cost $1,000 and the chapel $2,500.

3. *Minnesota Missionary and Church Record* 9:10 (October 1890): 105.

4. An unnamed author indicated that St. John's was "a free church" until 1886. "The Church of St. John the Evangelist, St. Paul," *The Church Record* 28 (May 1902): 138.

5. The original Articles of Incorporation named the institution "St. John the Evangelist." Because of subsequent legal complications, the official name was changed in 1914 to "The Parish of St. John the Evangelist," a title it has retained ever since.

6. Although the term "communicant" is variously used, it technically refers to one who receives communion regularly, supports the parish financially, and is otherwise in good standing with the parish. Even from its earliest years there were probably contributors to the parish who were not technically communicants.

7. Letter from Henry Kittson to C. W. Rife, August 13, 1924. (Minnesota Historical Society. Manuscripts Notebooks. p. 939: Kittson, Norman W.).

8. Henry A. Castle, *History of St. Paul and Vicinity: A Chronicle of Progress and a Narrative Account of the Industries, Institutions and People of the City and its Tributary Territory* (Chicago: The Lewis Publishing Co., 1912): 114-115.

Chapter 2

1. The park lies about ten miles southwest of Duluth.

2. Letter from the Rev. E. Jay Cooke to the Rev. George C. Tanner, March 23, 1891. (Minnesota Historical Society. Episcopal Church, Diocese of Minnesota. Diocesan Correspondence and Miscellaneous Papers, 1891.)

3. The words of the Rev. Theodore Sedgwick, *The St. John's Evangelist* 3:2 (December 5, 1908)

4. Letter affixed to the vestry minutes of July 28, 1887.

5. Letter from Arrowsmith to Albert M. Eddy, August 4, 1887, affixed to the vestry minutes of August 6, 1887.

6. Paul Clifford Larson, *St. Paul Academy and Summit School, 1900-2000* (St. Paul, MN: St. Paul Academy and Summit School, 2000): 11-12.

7. Promotional pamphlet from the Barnard School for the 1888-1889 academic year.

8. Larson, *St. Paul Academy*, 12.

9. Alfred S. Kittson was a student at the school.

10. Larson, *St. Paul Academy*, 12.

11. Ibid.

12. Ibid.

13. Ibid.

14. The documents do not always provide the starting dates of Blaikie's employment.

15. After Sadie and Gale divorced, she married John Patterson, the son of Myron Fayette Patterson who was a member of the parish in 1893 and founder of the M. F. Patterson Co., currently known as Patterson Dental Supply.

16. A later source indicates that the society was established even earlier, in 1881.

Chapter 3

1. This quotation, and other biographical details, are found in the newsclipping, "Sketch of the Rev. John Hazen White, M.A., Bishop-Elect of Indiana," *Church Worker* 11:12 (March, 1895): 1-2. (Minnesota Historical Society. Protestant Episcopal Church. Diocese of Minnesota. Correspondence and Miscellaneous Papers. 1895-1896.)

2. "Sketch of John Hazen White," 1.

3. In 1892, Farrand and Votey purchased the pipe organ business of Hilborn and Frank Roosevelt. Hilborn Roosevelt was the cousin of President Theodore Roosevelt. With this purchase, Farrand and Votey gained control of important patents, and in 1893 they built an organ for the Columbian Exposition in Chicago and eventually provided instruments for many grand residences of the gilded age.

4. Anne Beiser Allen, *And the Wilderness Shall Blossom: Henry Benjamin Whipple, Churchman, Educator, Advocate for the Indians* (Afton, MN: Afton Historical Society Press, 2008): 175-176.

5. Allen, *Wilderness Shall Blossom*, 175. See also Catherine Relf Carlsen, "Faith, Dedication and Strength of Purpose: The Story of Sister Annette," forwarded to the author in an e-mail from Diane Grossman, March 11, 2011.

6. Mary Carlsen Lilja, e-mails to the author, March 31 and April 5, 2011. Lilja is the daughter of Catherine Relf Carlsen and the great-great-great-niece of Sister Annette.

7. Charles Schultz, the cartoonist of the fabled *Peanuts* comic strip, attended the school.

8. John Wann was the great-grandfather of parishioner Betty Wann Binger.

9. Letter affixed to the vestry minutes for June 25, 1891.

10. Letter from the vestry to the Rev. Mr. White, June 26, 1891, affixed to p. 141 in the vestry minutes.

11. "Sketch of John Hazen White." No other information available.

12. In 1933 Seabury Divinity School merged with Western Theological Seminary in Chicago and today Seabury-Western Theological Seminary is located in Evanston, Illinois.

Chapter 4

1. Information from http://itech.dickinson.edu/archives/inquiries/yelverton-peyton-morgan-class-1875, accessed on November 8, 2010.

2. At the Diocesan Convention in Duluth, on June 22-23, 1892, Mr. Peet was elected a delegate to General Convention to take place in Baltimore.

3. Report from the annual meeting on April 3, 1893.

4. *Minnesota Missionary and Church Record* 11:6 (June 1892): 13.

5. Founded in 1839, Christ Church became the cathedral of the Diocese of Texas in 1949.

6. Donald Empson, *The Street Where You Live: A Guide to the Street Names of St. Paul* (St. Paul: Witsend Press, 1975): 81.

7. Howard Burba, "100 Years of Episcopal Church in Dayton," *Dayton Daily News* (October 12, 1930).

8. *The Marietta Daily Leader* 5:247 (October 18, 1899).

Chapter 5
1. Some of the biographical details of Dr. Rhodes are taken from *History of Cincinnati and Hamilton County, Ohio* (Cincinnati: S. B. Nelson and Co., 1894): 749-750.

2. Published by Peter G. Thomson in Cincinnati, in 1879, the book contains eight sermons with the following titles: "The Story of the Tradesmen's Books;" "Food Corrupters; The Story of the Auditor's Books;" "Street Car Life in Cincinnati;" "The Betrayal of a City;" "The Curse of Tenement Houses;" "Church and Theater;" and "Common Sense in Funerals." In 2011 one online bookseller was offering the book for $250.

3. Philadelphia: J. P. Lippincott and Co., 1880.

4. Philadelphia: J. P. Lippincott and Co., 1880. Available from online booksellers.

5. Cincinnati: S. B. Nelson and Co., 1894.

6. Quoted in Simon J. Bronner, ed., *Lafcadio Hearn's America: Ethnographic Sketches and Editorials* (Lexington: University Press of Kentucky, 2002): 10.

7. Ibid.

8. Samuel Haber, *The Quest For Authority And Honor in the American Professions, 1750-1900* (Chicago: The University of Chicago Press, 1991): 177.

9. Ibid.

10. Ibid.

11. Letter from Dudley W. Rhodes to Theodore Sedgwick, November 30, 1906, printed in *The St. John's Evangelist* 1:3 (December 15 1906): 3.

12. The Rev. Lewis Morris and his wife Ruth had a son named the Rev. Frederick Morris who was dean of St. Mark's Cathedral in Minneapolis from 1948 to 1955.

13. In 1902 Miss Catherine Gordon donated sufficient butcher's linen to furnish the choir with new cottas.

14. Another source indicates that an endowment fund had been started on December 27, 1892, with an offering of $73.40.

15. An Army Private George Q. White lost his right hand and suffered wounds to his face during the Battle of Belmont in the Civil War. He won third prize in a left-hand penmanship competition by soldiers and sailors who lost the use of their right arms by amputation or permanent disability during the war. It has not been possible to confirm that Maj. White and Pvt White were the same person.

16. The organization, which still exists, was founded in Philadelphia in 1865 to protect the republic amid rumors of a plot to destroy the government after the assassination of Abraham Lincoln.

17. Another source gives the initial year as 1901.

18. A "crèche" (British) is a nursery where babies and young children are cared for during the work day.

19. By 1910 the vestry had raised the rector's salary to $4,200, of which $600 was for rental allowance in lieu of a rectory.

20. Letter dated June 9, 1900, is affixed to the record book, after the vestry minutes of June 4, 1900.

21. Letter from Sedgwick to Senior Warden Victor M. Watkins, June 18, 1900, affixed to the vestry minutes of June 4, 1900.

22. Burial record from Spring Grove Cemetery in Cincinnati, Ohio. Courtesy of Dennis Harrell, cathedral archivist in the Diocese of Southern Ohio.

23. The building was demolished in 1937 and Christ Church is presently the cathedral of the Diocese of Southern Ohio.

Chapter 6
1. This account appeared in *The Minnesota Missionary* and was reprinted in *The St. John's Evangelist* on August 12, 1950.

2. Slater's felt is an asphaltic paper used as an underlayer for slate roofing. Cabot's quilt is an insulating material consisting of dried eelgrass held between layers of cloth or paper, once used as thermal insulation.

3. Raffaello Romanelli is represented in the United States by his 1903 monument to John Wister in Philadelphia; a 1927 bust of Dante Alighieri on Belle Isle Park in Detroit; the bronze *Fountain Angel* in the Missouri Botanical Garden (originally installed at the 1904 World's Fair); and by several works in Romanelli Gardens, a residential district of Kansas City, Missouri.

4. Information about Amherst Wilder, his wife and daughter, and the Wilder charities is taken from the website of the Amherst H. Wilder Foundation.

5. The Archdiocese of St. Paul and Minneapolis used the Wilder mansion for forty-one years to house the archbishop's residence and the chancery offices. Archbishop John Gregory Murray eventually refused to live there any longer, thinking it too ostentatious, and it was demolished in 1959.

6. For ten months prior to Fairclough's arrival, parishioner Alexander A. McKechnie played the organ and conducted the choir on an interim basis.

7. Anton Lang later produced a similar wood carving of the *Last Supper* in Good Shepherd Episcopal Church in Lexington, Kentucky. John Wright included St. John's altar and reredos in his book *Some Notable Altars in the Church of England and the American Episcopal Church* (New York: Macmillan, 1908): 378-379, identifying it as one of the more beautiful altars in this country. Wright indicates that the work was designed and built by the American Seating Company in their shops in Manitowoc, Wisconsin.

8. In later years the camp took place at Russell Beach on Chisago Lake, and at Camp Lawton, an Episcopal camp at St. Croix Falls, Wisconsin, among other locations.

9. The Girls Choir made their debut in their new vestments—scarlet student gowns and black-velvet caps—in the church on Christmas Eve 1907.

10. Mr. Peet was buried from Christ Church rather than from St. John's.

11. Robert B. C. Bement lived at 27 Summit Court, was on the vestry at St. John's, served as its clerk and was a generous supporter of the parish.

12. Chicago: Century Publishing and Engraving Company, 1900.

13. Designed by Cass Gilbert, the townhouse was one of the best known residences in the city, and has appeared in many architectural treatises on St. Paul structures. Later residents of that address include parishioners Robert and Priscilla Farnham, the long-time executive director of the Ramsey County Historical Society; and present residents architect Gar Hargens and his wife, Missy Staples Thompson. Gar Hargens is the sole owner of the architectural firm Close Associates.

14. See Grace Flandrau's *Memoirs of Grace Flandrau*, edited by Georgia Ray (St. Paul: Knochaloe Beg Press, 2003).

15. Wharton's 1935 review of Fitzgerald's *Taps at Reveille*, one of his stories about Basil Duke Lee, appeared in *The New York Times*. The stories were inspired by Fitzgerald's adolescence and the family's social circle among St. Paul's Summit Avenue elite.

16. The publication changed names several times. Known briefly as *The Newsletter*, it later became *The Evangelist*.

17. Newell Park, comprising ten acres at 900 N. Fairview Ave., was dedicated in 1908, making it one of the oldest parks in St. Paul. It is named after Stanford Newel, but is spelled with two l's.

18. No relation to today's parishioner Bill Plummer.

19. Susan Trevor Knapp, "The Deaconess and Church Training School," paper read at the Woman's Auxiliary meeting of the Missionary Council at Washington, 1903.

20. The name sometimes appears as Evenson.

21. A letter from F. Scott Fitzgerald to Elizabeth Clarkson, dated Sept. 26, 1913, contains Fitzgerald's self-portrait as a collegian (courtesy of Bruce Binger, the son of Robert Binger).

22. Frederick Wigginton to Gertrude Livock, February 20, 1910.

23. John L. Relf, *The Man Whose Dream Came True: A Biography of A. B. Stickney* (John L. Relf, Dellwood, Minnesota, 1991): 9. The house was razed in 1930.

24. *The Church Record* 34:12 (December 1910): 7.

25. The American novelist Edith Wharton used Calvary, the church of the Roosevelt family, as the setting for her novel *The Age of Innocence*.

26. "Rev. Theodore Sedgwick and Family Will Leave for New Home in East Side of New York," newsclipping dated April 18, 1911. Newspaper unidentified. (Minnesota Historical Society. Protestant Episcopal Church. Diocese of Minnesota. Correspondence & Miscellaneous Papers, September 1910-December 1911. P1035.)

Chapter 7

1. William E. Lusk, ed., *Visions of Missouri Bishops or Readings in the History of a Diocese* (Kansas City, Missouri: Diocese of West Missouri, 1998): 83. This information courtesy of Randal Loy, in an e-mail to the author, January 16, 2011. Mr. Loy was working on his *The Glorious Masterworks of Grace and Holy Trinity Cathedral, Kansas City, Missouri*, and doing research on the Rev. Mr. Schaad at the same time as this author.

2. It has been conjectured that Mr. Schaad's nemesis in Kansas City, William R. Nelson, was the source of the rumors.

3. No author, "One of the Old Guard" (*American Lumberman*, August 12, 1911): 54 [?]-55.

4. This is the very site where the 1956 parish house and classrooms now stand.

5. The yellow-brick building is extant but is no longer used by the academy.

6. Unidentified and undated newsclipping from Diane Power and George C. Power III.

7. George C. Power (b. 1889) was the grandfather of current parishioner George C. Power III.

8. *The Church Record* 40:2 (February 1916): 15.

9. Some of the following details are taken from the obituary of Mr. Schaad that appeared in *The Quincy Herald-Whig* (October 25, 1938).

10. E-mail to the author from Marshall Carter of Trinity Church, Bay City, Michigan, February 3, 2011.

11. It was at this church that the Rev. Chauncey Williams was rector when he was offered the rectorship of St. John's in 1891, an invitation that he declined.

12. *The New York Times* (August 27, 1928).

13. Published by the National Council of the Protestant Episcopal Church. In 2011 a rare copy of this book was available from an online bookseller for $125.

14. Published in Kansas City, Missouri, by M. C. Long, 1910.

15. The spelling of this name is uncertain.

Chapter 8

1. The town became famous for its annual motorcycle rallies in August, begun in 1938.

2. Some sources erroneously identify the parish as St. John's.

3. Undated newsclipping affixed to the vestry minutes of May 8, 1916.

4. *Time* (March 11, 1929).

5. First published in 1916 by Sheridan Printing Co. (elsewhere dated 1921), and later published in a hard-cover photocopy edition by Kessinger Publishing, the book is today available from online booksellers.

6. Parishioners Mr. and Mrs. W. H. S. Wright owned the home before the Chamberlins.

7. E-mail from Angela Ford to the author, December 29, 2010. Ms. Ford is a granddaughter of Bishop Edward and Angela Cross.

8. Ibid.

9. From the 1928 *Book of Common Prayer*, p. 225. In the 1979 *Book of Common Prayer* the "Stir-Up" collect is assigned to the Third Sunday of Advent, but its text is different.

10. Hill had been leading the services at the chapel in Lilydale. He later became dean of Trinity Cathedral in Duluth, after the establishment of the Diocese of Duluth.

11. The source of this quote is identified only as "one of the men on our Service Roll."

12. E-mail from Angela Ford. Further reference will be made later to Paul Noxon Myers.

13. Ibid.

14. The book is available from online booksellers.

15. Windows are referred to as being on the right or left as one faces the altar.

16. Vestry minutes of November 27, 1918.

17. The rood screen was not constructed.

18. Letter to the wardens and vestry of St. Mark's Cathedral, Seattle, October 29, 1919, copied with the vestry minutes of December 16, 1919.

19. Mrs. Backus' School for girls, whose curriculum included equestrian training, was located at 580, 586, and 590 Holly Avenue, the buildings of the Oak Hall School. One of the fifteen-year-old F. Scott Fitzgerald's four plays for Elizabeth Magoffin's Elizabethan Dramatic Club, *The Captured Shadow*, his first full-length play, was presented at Mrs. Backus' School on August 23, 1912, for which the author cast himself as the shadow, a gentleman crook. The Oak Hall School, St. Paul's oldest elite school for girls, and the successor to Mrs. Baldwin's Seminary for Girls, also held its baccalaureate in St. John's Church during these years. Scott Fitzgerald attended many dances at Oak Hall. Parishioner Royal A. Moore was principal of the school, a member of the vestry, and superintendent of the Church School. Oak Hall's three buildings were later converted into an apartment complex.

20. Anne Watkins Wilder was the wife of Lieutenant-Colonel W. T. Wilder, no relation to the Amherst Wilder family.

21. There were several editions of *Reliable Recipes*. The 1925 edition allowed that "Non-alcoholic substitutes for the liquors called for in these pre-prohibition recipes can be secured at any first-class grocery." Contributors to the book were the Misses Maud Borup, Cecelia Kalman, and Adele Lanpher, and Mesdames C. M. Bend, D. S. Culver, H. L. Donahower, Roscoe Finch, M. W. Griggs, E. B. Holbert, H. H. Irvine, P. J. Kalman, W. F. McCurdy, J. L. Mitchell, W. C. Motter, Samuel G. Ordway, Frederick Ritzinger, Bruce Sanborn, M. S. Stringer, and Edwin White.

22. There is no clear evidence that the resolution was actually sent to the House of Bishops, nor, if it was, do the parish records contain any reply from that body.

23. A diocesan summer camp for youth, located at Lake Coeur d'Alene in northern Idaho (but part of the Spokane Diocese) is named Camp Cross in honor of Bishop Cross. It also functions as a conference center.

Chapter 9

1. Details concerning Crawford Livingston are taken from John L. Lindley, "Crawford Livingston, Chauncey Griggs and Their Roles in St. Paul History," *Ramsey County History* 34:3 (Fall, 1999): 4-30.

2. Mr. Marston later became the founding rector of St. Stephen the Martyr, in Edina. He contracted polio during the 1946 epidemic and died suddenly.

3. Brown's ordination to the diaconate on October 10, 1926, was believed to be the first such ordination that had ever taken place at St. John's.

4. It is for this reason that the American *Book of Common Prayer* still follows the general shape of the Scottish prayer book, rather than that of the English prayer book.

5. The new lectern replaced the original brass eagle lectern, which had been given in memory of Louis Coyne Kittson, evidently a relative of the Rev. Henry Kittson. The vestry made an unsuccessful attempt to find an heir of Mr. Kittson to obtain permission to dispose of it.

Chapter 10

1. There is no direct lineage between Samuel Mairs and the later parishioner George Mairs.

2. Ethelyn Kempe, the daughter of Mr. and Mrs. Frank A. Kempe, married Lt. Richard F. Rupp in 1943 at St. John's, who was the son of Mr. and Mrs. F. C. Rupp of St. Paul. Their son John has restored, refurbished, and owns several historic properties in St. Paul, including the W. A. Frost restaurant on Selby Avenue, the University Club on Summit Avenue, and the Athletic Club downtown. Ethelyn Kempe Rupp is still a member of St. John's.

3. Weed was ordained to the priesthood at the Cathedral of St. John the Divine in New York City, in 1935, and was a monk of the Order of the Holy Cross, with the motherhouse in West Park, New York.

4. King was a nephew of Bishop Edward M. Cross and was ordained at St. John's on June 11, 1942.

5. Wigginton was the son of vestryman and junior warden Frederick Wigginton, and had been a member of the boychoir, the Acolyte's Guild, the Church School, and Boy Scout Troop no. 2.

6. William Millikan, *A Union Against Unions: The Minneapolis Citizens Alliance and Its Fight Against Organized Labor, 1903-1947* (St. Paul: Minnesota Historical Society Press, 2001). Millikan's account is based on the papers of Frank P. Leslie, treasurer of the Republican State Central Committee, at the Minnesota Historical Society, and on an interview of Totten P. Heffelfinger by Charles Walker (C. Walker Papers at the Minnesota Historical Society).

7. Letter from Richard Lyman to the author, August 3, 2011.

8. After graduating from Breck School in 1949, Moore was killed in a boating accident in White Bear Lake in 1951. He was the brother of parishioners Sara Allen and James Moore.

9. Today the station is WWTC (1280 AM), known as The Patriot.

10. Ingersoll died of pneumonia in Seattle, in December 1942.

11. Garet Garrett, "The Youth Document," *Saturday Evening Post* (Nov. 7, 1936): 8. The *Post* did not identify the site as St. John's.

12. The WPA was the largest and most ambitious project of the New Deal, employing millions of unskilled workers in carrying out public works projects. Artists and writers were also employed for WPA arts projects.

13. When she was thirteen years old Clotilde Irvine, known as Coco, kept a diary for a year. It was published in 2011 under the title *Through No Fault of My Own: A Girl's Diary of Life on Summit Avenue in the Jazz Age*, introduction by Peg Meier (Minneapolis: University of Minnesota Press).

14. Paul Clifford Larson, *Icy Pleasures: Minnesota Celebrates Winter*, (Afton, MN: Afton Historical Society Press, 1998).

15. Many of the following details come from Elizabeth Burns, ed., *The Legacy Project: Remembering Louis W. Hill, Jr. Through Oral Histories* (St. Paul: Grotto Foundation, Inc., 1998).

16. It was impossible to verify the identity of the man in question, with some St. Paul residents certain that it was Hill, while others equally certain that it was Fitzgerald.

17. Dick and Nancy Nicholson are the current residents.

18. The names of the donors appear nowhere in the vestry minutes or *The St. John's Evangelist*.

19. Sheppard, Edward Lee, *Second Fifty Years: The Diocese of Minnesota and the Diocese of Duluth from 1907 to 1957*, p. 79.

20. St. Mark's Church became the cathedral of the Diocese of Minnesota in 1941.

21. Lt. Kay Todd's remains were reburied in Sunset Memorial Park on April 27, 1949, in a service read privately by Mr. Gillmett.

22. Donnie Radcliffe, "The Love Story of Barbara and George Bush," *Good Housekeeping* 209:5 (November 1989): 261. Article courtesy of Caroline Jaffray.

23. For unknown reasons, Klein's name is not included on the bronze plaque in the rear of the church or in the list of those commemorated in the memorial service. Lt. William M. Shepard is listed on the plaque but not in the bulletin for the memorial service.

24. Dorothy subsequently married William Fobes.

25. Printed in The CUB, 1948, and available at www.indiana-military.org (accessed on September 10, 2011).

26. The Rev. Michael Coleman was later elected Bishop of the Diocese of Qu'Appelle in Canada. He returned to the Twin Cities in March 1956 to give an address at the Magna Carta Day service at St. Mark's Cathedral and to preach at St. John's.

27. Charles M. Power was the brother of the George C. Power who was the great-grandfather of parishioner George C. Power III.

28. Much of the following information is taken from "The Rev. Conrad Herbert Gesner Accepts Election as Bishop Coadjutor of the Missionary District of South Dakota," *The Minnesota Missionary* 68:2 (February 1945): 8; and from "Consecration of Bishop Gesner," *The Minnesota Missionary* 68:5 (May 1945): 6.

Chapter 11

1. Mr. and Mrs. Arthur Gross were the parents of Ginny Edgerton.

2. Ellerbe and Co. were architects for the St. Paul City Hall and the Ramsey County Courthouse, built in the art deco style, and for the St. Paul Auditorium Arena and a structure for the Minnesota Mining and Manufacturing Company.

3. Its predecessor at the new site was a house of ill repute.

4. In January 1957 *The St. John's Evangelist* reported that more than $323,000 had been spent in the construction of the Parish House. In February 1958, the full indebtedness was given as $321,396.45.

5. The United Thank Offering is received nationally every three years, at the time of General Convention. In the 1960s the offering went to the nationally appointed women missionaries of the Episcopal Church, to provide them with needed supplies for their work, and to supplement their pension system. Today the offering supports the mission and ministry of the church.

6. As headmaster at Breck, the Rev. Henderson reintroduced female students to the lower grades, undertook aggressive fundraising, strengthened the school's academics, and worked diligently to attract a diverse student body, all hallmarks of the institution to this day. Henderson retired as headmaster in 1973 but was subsequently appointed to head the Breck Corporation (the school's fundraising entity).

7. Crum died in 2002, in Tennessee, of complications from Parkinsons disease.

8. Now the Minneapolis-St. Paul International Airport.

9. Farnham's grandmother was a member of the storied Humbird family, and the sister of parishioner Reine Humbird Myers. Farnham was elected a trustee of the diocese in 1982.

10. Deceased parishioner Clelia Mulalley was the daughter of John Webster Thompson.

11. Published in New York by Macmillan. The book is available from online booksellers.

12. Mrs. John C. Parish was the former Elizabeth "Zib" Myers, the sister of John H. Myers and the mother of parishioner Judy Parish Diedrich.

13. Bishop Hamilton Hyde Kellogg ordained John Robert Hanson to the priesthood at St. John's on June 11, 1958, at the same time that he ordained Troy Anson Keeling and Allan Robert Clark to the diaconate.

14. Mary's father, Frederick Wigginton, also sang in the opera.

15. E-mail to the author, November 23, 2011. In those years a set of wooden steps led from the floor behind the altar to the platform above the reredos. When the columbarium was constructed, the lower part of the steps was removed, but the careful observer can still see the upper steps, which now ascend from the roof of the columbarium, having no useful purpose.

16. Charles N. Hensel was a surgeon, having studied at Harvard University and the University of Vienna as well as the University of Minnesota. His wife Florence Hensel was general chairman of the parish Rummage Sale in 1956.

17. Mrs. Oehler, the daughter of Benjamin and Bertha Reid Scandrett, who were long-standing members of St. John's, was a great-granddaughter of Bishop Whipple.

18. The organization was St. John's branch of the National Episcopal Church Women, which engages women in worship, prayer, study, service, and fellowship.

19. It was no secret that Art Zache had no musical skills. His title as Assistant Choirmaster was a misnomer, as the job entailed no musical duties.

20. Shirley was previously married to Henry Kartarik, a prolific nature photographer, and together they had two children: Laurel and Mark.

Chapter 12

1. A socially liberal activist, DeWitt later became bishop of Pennsylvania and with two other bishops, in 1974, he ordained the first eleven women to the Episcopal priesthood, a defiant act that the church's bishops later declared "valid but irregular."

2. Mr. Hanson was called to be rector of Grace Church in Everett, Massachusetts.

3. Toward the end of 1949, Lanpher gave a clerestory window in memory of her sister Marion Lanpher.

4. Judge Finehout was buried from St. John's in April 1948.

5. It also represented a seventeen percent increase over the total for 1960.

6. Even so, thirty-two new families came to the parish in 1962.

7. Gladys Benepe was a charter member of the Breck School board and one of the Key Women for the Church Home of Minnesota. She was also president of the Ramsey County Medical Auxiliary.

8. From Minnesota Inventors Hall of Fame, accessed at www.minnesotainventors.org.

9. William McIntosh III, "The Spiritual Journey of St. Philip's Church: 1906-2012." Mr. McIntosh plans to publish his book upon its completion.

10. Heitmiller was Right of Way Agent for the State Highway Department.

11. From the parish *Newsletter* (March 1, 1974).

12. After the death of her husband, Kate Mead was ordained a deacon in the Diocese of Michigan, in 1977, on which occasion St. John's sent her a purse of $403. She was later ordained to the priesthood.

Chapter 13

1. The Rev. John Shelby Spong, a liberal proponent of feminism, gay rights, and racial equality, who was later to become

the controversial bishop of Newark, New Jersey, was rector at Calvary Church in Tarboro from 1957 to 1965.

2. E-mail to the author, October 17, 2011.

3. The celebrated choir of men and boys at St. Thomas Church was for many years under the direction of Gerre Hancock. His successor in the post, since 2004, is John Scott, formerly the master of choristers at St. Paul's Cathedral in London, England.

4. David Benson's daughter, the Rev. Gretchen Pickeral, is the priest for the Total Ministry congregation at St. Bartholomew's Church in Bemidji, Minnesota.

5. The Christian Brothers are a Roman Catholic religious order of men whose principal ministry is teaching and the operation of schools.

6. Langford was a Special Agent with Northwestern Mutual Life Insurance Company.

7. Jack Lightner was the husband of St. John's parishioner Nan Lightner.

8. Mr. Smith was the father of parishioner Sarah K. Smith and the uncle of Dusty Mairs.

9. Benjamin G. Griggs, Jr. and his wife Myra lived with their four children in Sunfish Lake. Mr. Griggs had worked for Northwest Airlines in economics since 1950, except for the two years he was in the Korean War. In 1964 he became vice-president for flight operations and in 1969 he was appointed vice-president and chief financial officer for the airline.

10. The following information is taken from Annie Laurie Baker, "Grenville and Annie McMillan Baker Family" (1991).

11. Mr. Frost is the principal librarian for the Columbus Symphony Orchestra in Ohio.

12. Later to become Mrs. George A. Mairs.

13. Thomas M. Johnson, "St. John's of St. Paul," *The Living Church* 159 (August 10, 1969): 9-10.

14. With the other parishes in Region 7, St. John's co-sponsored in 1981 a Vietnamese family comprising two brothers, a grandmother, one wife, and three children. (The diocese of Minnesota is organized into regions; Region 7 includes the churches in the St. Paul area.)

15. Mr. Klein and his wife, the Hon. Harriet Lansing, live in the former rectory to this day. Lansing is a former judge on the Minnesota Court of Appeals.

16. From 2006 to 2012 the former Blair Hotel housed a garden-level bookstore named Common Good Books owned by parishioner and nationally known humorist Garrison Keillor.

17. The Hmong are an Asian ethnic group from the mountainous regions of China, Laos, Vietnam, and Thailand. Thousands of Hmong have immigrated to St. Paul since the late 1970s.

18. Published by the H. M. Smyth Co., the book is available from online booksellers.

19. The book was launched on March 22, at one of the centennial events. Mr. Baker also wrote two articles that

appeared in *Ramsey County History*, the journal of the Ramsey County Historical Society: "Oakland Cemetery: A Safe and Permanent Resting Place" and "The Minnesota Club: St. Paul's Enterprising Leaders And Their 'Gentlemen's Social Club.'"

20. Two other booklets were printed later, in 1983: *History of the Windows*, by Lucille Guyer, and *Tours of the Church* by Adrian Drew.

21. Oliver Towne, "England Rubbing Off On St. Paul Couple," *The St. Paul Dispatch* (April 13, 1978): 21.

22. Johnson had a degree in speech pathology and psychology, but was a vice-president with Quality Park Products, and later a vice-president of Minnesota Envelope Co.

23. The iron gates at either end of the columbarium were given in memory of Ralph A. Klosterman by his family and friends, and were constructed by the Selby Ornamental Iron Company.

24. Episcopal Community Services operates two similar programs today: Ready for Success, serving low-income women, and the Ready for Success Men's Program, serving low-income men.

25. Young Elizabeth Henry, the daughter of Dusty Mairs, was the first to ask Grayson Clary if girls could be acolytes.

26. One of the finalists was the Rev. Margo Maris of Minneapolis who in 1979 became one of the first women rectors in the country. In 1988 she was a candidate for suffragan bishop of the Diocese of Minnesota, but lost to the Rev. Sanford Hampton.

Chapter 14
1. The Rt. Rev. M. Thomas Shaw is today the fifteenth bishop of the Diocese of Massachusetts. Also known as the Cowley Fathers, the Society of St. John the Evangelist, founded in England in 1866, was the first Anglican monastic community of men established after the English Reformation.

2. Interview with brother and sister Craig and Barbara Lindeke, June 8, 2011.

3. St. John's possesses examples of framed artwork by the Rt. Rev. Steven Keeler, Bishop of Minnesota from 1945 to 1956, that are shown between special exhibits.

4. Artist Nell Hillsley illustrated the cookbook *Sacred Food for Soulful Living*, edited by the Rev. Ward Bauman, for the House of Prayer.

5. Michael Tippett's then wife Krista Weedman Tippett wrote "An Oral history of the House of Prayer: A Report to the Advisory Board and Board of Directors" (May 2001).

6. Gail Rosenblum, "Artists Join Forces to Support Global Force For Peace," *Minneapolis StarTribune* (October 13, 2011).

7. It is a remarkable fact of liturgical history that the new prayer book nowhere specifies whether the priest should face the liturgical East—the actual North at St. John's—or the congregation.

8. The school was founded by the Rev. Mother Ruth, who also established the Community of the Holy Spirit, the Episcopal order for women that staffed the school. A bi-

racial nun from Harlem, she wished to create an environment in which children of all races, creeds, and cultures would come together to study academic subjects and learn about each other. "I hope," said Mother Ruth, "that an Episcopalian who attends our school becomes a better Episcopalian, a Jewish child a better Jew, and an agnostic a better agnostic."

9. The Accessibility Committee eventually morphed into what is now the Building Committee.

10. Paula Karl, "Nigerian Pastor to Return to Brainerd for One Service, *Brainerd Dispatch* (May 30, 2003).

11. A hymnal supplement titled *Come Celebrate* was introduced to the congregation in September 1991. The books no longer exist.

12. Michael Tippett is remotely related to Sir Michael Tippett, the British composer and pacifist who served a prison sentence as a conscientious objector during the Second World War. The composer of operas, symphonies, and concertos among other works, Sir Michael is generally acknowledged as one of the most important British composers of the twentieth century. One of the first openly gay composers to explore issues of sexuality in his work, he was a second cousin to the Rev. Michael Tippett's father.

13. Michael and Krista divorced after they left St. John's.

14. Penguin Publishing, 2008.

15. Penguin Publishing, 2010.

16. After a long career as an executive at Dain Bosworth Inc., Robert Martin was named chairman and CEO of the regional brokerage firm John G. Kinnard and Company.

17. Lloyd Johnson was chairman and CEO of Northwestern Banco, now Wells Fargo.

18. After leaving St. John's, the Rev. Michael Tippett became associate rector at Gethsemane in downtown Minneapolis. He is currently the rector of St. Paul's Church in Owatonna.

Chapter 15
1. In 2004 they bought a home in Lakeland that was built in 1848, before the Civil War and before Minnesota became a state.

2. The vestry reelected Mr.Johnson until his retirement in March 2012.

3. The Rev. Mariann Budde was consecrated the ninth bishop of the Diocese of Washington, D.C., and its first female bishop, in November 2011.

4. The Apollo Center is now one of the more than forty programs of People Incorporated in the Twin Cities metro area. The latter organization was founded in 1969 by Pastor Harry Maghakian of Dayton Avenue Presbyterian Church in response to the needs of men with mental illness who lived in the neighborhood. St. John's parishioner Alden Drew is president of the board of People Incorporated.

5. E-mail to the author, December 9, 2011.

6. The Property Committee is responsible for the ongoing maintenance and repair of the church building, while the

Building Committee is in charge of capital improvements, including artwork additions and building use changes.

7. The Rev. Patrick Markie was deacon at Holy Apostles before being transferred by the bishop to St. Anne's, Sunfish Lake.

8. Jay Clark and his wife Lisa met at 3M where he worked in project engineering and she was supervisor of a laboratory. Mr. Clark's mother is a priest.

9. Bishop Robert M. Anderson, the brother-in-law of parishioner Edward (Tom) Evans, died in May 2011.

10. Wendy Audette Johnson later ended her pursuit of holy orders.

11. Elsa Cumming died at the Episcopal Church Home in July 2008, at age 42, and was buried from St. John's in August.

12. Safe Church Policy in the Diocese of Minnesota provides policies for the protection of children and youth from abuse, and for the protection of adults from sexual misconduct.

13. Mr. Small died in July 2007.

14. Mr. Baxter is a direct descendent of the brother of Thomas Cranmer (1489-1556), the leader of the English Reformation and Archbishop of Canterbury during the reigns of Henry VIII, Edward VI and, for a brief time, Mary I. Cranmer established the doctrinal and liturgical structures of the reformed Church of England.

15. Alys Wilson also served as vice-chair of the Episcopal Church Home Board. She and Frank were generous supporters of Episcopal Homes.

16. Jay Debertin is executive vice-president and chief operating officer for CHS Inc., the nation's leading cooperative, owned by farmers, ranchers, and co-ops across the United States, with headquarters in Inver Grove Heights. He also serves on the boards of Horizon Milling and Ventura Foods.

17. The Rev. William H. Mead was dean of the cathedral in St. Louis, Missouri, before his election as Bishop of Delaware. The Rev. Frank Wilson was sub-dean and canon pastor of St. Mark's Cathedral in Shreveport, Louisiana.

Amherst H. Wilder Foundation, St. Paul, Minnesota
p. 63 (top right), Amherst H. Wilder; p. 63 (bottom left), Fanny Spencer Wilder; p. 63 (bottom right), Cornelia Day Wilder Appleby.

Aimee Richcreek Baxter, St. Paul, Minnesota
p. 2, baptismal font; p. 23 (bottom), stone school; p. 96 (bottom), rectory; p. 104, *Te Deum* window; p. 105 (top and bottom), stained glass windows; p. 212 (top), brass rubbing; p. 261, Helen Boyer; p. 260, Habit for Humanity house; p. 262 (top right), Joan Potter; p. 263, chasubles; p. 265, the Baxter family; p. 268 (top), Rose window; p. 269 (top left), Annunciation window; p. 269 (top right), World War II Memorial window; p. 269 (bottom), Women of St. John's Memorial windows; p. 270 (top), stained glass; p. 271, stained glass; p. 272, stained glass; p. 273 (bottom), Helen Boyer and stained glass; p. 287, church exterior.

Corbis Images
p. 118, United States Senators at Signing of Kellogg-Briand Pact, 1928. Copyright: Underwood & Underwood/CORBIS; p. 127 (bottom left), U.S. Secretary of State Frank Kellogg with President Calvin Coolidge. Copyright: Bettmann/CORBIS.

Cram & Ferguson Architects, LLC, Concord, Massachusetts
p. 40, Cram architectural rendering; p. 102, Cram architectural rendering; p. 111, Ralph Adams Cram.

Encyclopedia of Biography of Minnesota
p. 38 (right), Theodore Schurmeier; p. 44, David Chauncey Shepard; p. 46, Charles W. Bunn.

Episcopal Diocese of Minnesota, Minneapolis, Minnesota
p. 276, Bishop Whipple's pectoral cross, photographer: Marilyn Jelinek.

Episcopal Homes, St. Paul, Minnesota
p. 36, Sister Annette Relf.

Jorge Zegarra León Photography, Minneapolis, Minnesota
p. 79 (right), Capitol rotunda.

Landmark Center, St. Paul, Minnesota
p. 195 (top and bottom), Betty and John Musser.

Kevin Matthews, Dexter, Oregon
p. 172 (right), Christmastime at St. John's; p. 194, Hill medallion; p. 212 (bottom), columbarium; p. 245, church entry; p. 270 (bottom), stained glass; p. 273 (top), stained glass; p. 288, church interior; p. 297, church exterior; p. 299, church door; p. 309, church interior; p. 312, baptismal font.

Maud Borup, Inc., Minneapolis, Minnesota
p. 90, advertisement photograph.

Minneapolis Institute of Arts, Minneapolis, Minnesota
p. 185 (left), *Madonna*. Italian, Florence, 15th century. Polychromed wood. Minneapolis Institute of Arts, Bequest of Mrs. Gertrude Hill Gavin 61.19.

Minnesota Historical Society, St. Paul, Minnesota
p. 12; Dayton Avenue Presbyterian Church; p. 13 (far left), Bishop Henry Whipple; p. 13 (second from left), The Catholic Chapel of St. Paul; p. 13 (second from right), Father Lucien Galtier; p. 13 (far right), James M. Goodhue; p. 14 (left), First Minnesota Regiment, Company D; p. 14 (center), Dacotah House; p. 14 (right), The St. Paul Roller Mill Company; p. 15 (left), Minnesota's first state capitol; p. 15 (center), John Sargent Pillsbury; p. 15 (right), Garfield Memorial Arch; p. 16 (left), William Dawson Sr.; p. 16 (center), Snow blockade; p. 16 (right), West Side St. Paul; p. 17 (far left), Christ Church; p. 17 (second from left), the Rev. Mahlon N. Gilbert; p. 17 (second from right), St. Paul's Episcopal Church; p. 17 (far right), Church of the Good Shepherd; p. 19, the Rev. Henry Kittson; p. 20 (left), the Rev. George

Brayton Whipple; p. 20 (center), Bishop Henry Benjamin Whipple; p. 20 (far right), Bryan Ripley Dorr; p. 21 (top left), Senkler residence; p. 21 (center), Delta Lawn Tennis Club; p. 21 (bottom), Lake Como; p. 21 (top center), Major Charles A. Allen; p. 21 (top right), Albert Matheson Eddy; p. 23, (top left), Kittson residence; p. 23 (top right), Norman Kittson; p. 24, welcoming arch for the Villard party; p. 25, Kittson residence; p. 26, ice palace; p. 30 (top), gate entrance to the ice palace; p. 30 (bottom), Owls Club float; p. 30 (right), George Finch; p. 32, streetcar; p. 35 (top), St. Luke's Hospital; p. 35 (bottom), private room at St. Luke's Hospital; p. 37, Seabury Divinity Hall; p. 38 (left), Richards Gordon; p. 39 (top), Peet residence; p. 39 (bottom), Schurmeier residence; p. 47, Cass Gilbert; p. 48, church and guild house; p. 50, Channing Seabury; p. 54, Grace Memorial Church; p. 55 (top), Victor M. Watkins; p. 55 (bottom); Watkins residence; p. 56 (top left), William A. Frost; p. 56 (top right), bishop's residence; p. 56 (bottom), burial site of Bishop Mahlon N. Gilbert; p. 57 (bottom), funeral of Bishop Mahlon N. Gilbert; p. 58, postcard; p. 60 (top), Clarence Johnston; p. 63 (top left), Wilder residence; p. 68, Charles E. Flandrau; p. 69 (top), Grace Flandrau; p. 69 (bottom), Gov. Johnson; p. 71 (top left), Maud Van Cortlandt Taylor Hill; p. 71 (top right), Louis W. Hill Sr.; p. 71 (bottom), Maud Van Cortlandt Hill, Louis W. Hill Jr., James J. Hill II (Jerome); p. 72, Stanford Newel; p. 76, Major John Kelliher; p. 78, Alpheus Beede Stickney; p. 79 (top left), postcard; p. 79 (bottom left), Minnesota State Capitol board of commissioners; p. 85 (top left), Horace H. Irvine; p. 85 (top right), Clotilde McCollough and her children; p. 85 (bottom), Irvine residence; p. 96 (top), Angela Ware Cross; p. 99, F. Scott and Zelda Fitzgerald; p. 112, Bishop Edward M. Cross with clergy; p. 120 (right), Mrs. Horace (Clotilde) Irvine; p. 121 (left), Burbank-Livingston-Griggs house; p. 121 (center), Mary Livingston Griggs; p. 121 (right), Theodore Wright Griggs; p. 122, Cordenio A. Severance; p. 122, Cedarhurst; p. 125 (bottom), Elliott Dar Marston; p. 127 (top left), Frank Billings Kellogg; p. 127 (top right), Clara May (Cook) Kellogg; p. 127 (bottom right), Kellogg residence; p. 128 (left), Marion Simpson Denegre; p. 128 (center), Senator James D. Denegre; p. 128 (right), Charles Wells Farnham; p. 131, Elizabeth Irvine Fobes; p. 138, Mary S. Goodell Mairs; p. 139 (left), George Harrison Prince; p. 140, Jule M. Hannaford Sr. and James J. Hill, 1915; p. 143 (bottom), ceremony consecrating Bishop Douglas Atwill, 1937; p. 144 (bottom), parade for Harrison (Jimmy) Johnston; p. 145 (left), Louis W. Hill Sr.; p. 145 (right), Louis W. Hill Jr.; p. 146 (top), Dr. Louis M. Benepe Jr.; p. 146 (bottom), Alfred J. Jennings and Ware King; p. 148 (left), Miss Vivian Grace Gibson; p. 153 (left), Benjamin Glyde Griggs; p. 153 (right), Martha Dodgson Baker Griggs, Elizabeth Griggs (Nichols), Mrs. Roger Cudworth, Elizabeth Ottis, and Maud Hill; p. 155 (right), J. George Smith Confectionery; p. 156, St. John's Memorial Parish House; p. 158 (top), Harry S. Given; p. 158 (left bottom), Prom Ballroom exterior; p. 158 (right bottom), Prom Ballroom interior; p. 161 (bottom), construction of the new Memorial Parish House; p. 163, Memorial Parish House; p. 167, C. Wesley Andersen; p. 182, Jerry Buser; p. 187 (bottom right), Clara Mairs; p. 204, Alice Borup.

Private collection
p. 187 (top), Clara and Sam Mairs, ca. 1888.

Rutherford B. Hayes Presidential Center, Fremont, Ohio
p. 27, the Rev. E. Jay Cooke; p. 31, the Rev. E. Jay Cooke and family.

St. Catherine University, St. Paul, Minnesota
p. 187 (left), Clara Mairs, *Ramsey Hill*. Etching, 6.5 x 5.37 in.

St. John the Evangelist Church archives and parishioners, St. Paul, Minnesota
p. 6, stained glass and organ pipes; p. 8 (top), the Rev. Jered Weber-Johnson, Rector; p. 8 (bottom); Organist and Choir Director James E. Frazier; p. 11, book committee;

p. 18, letter; p. 29, William and Margaret Plummer; p. 33, the Rev. John Hazen White; p.42, St. John's choir; p. 49, chapel in guild house; p. 51, the Rev. Dudley Ward Rhodes; p. 57 (top), Bishop Mahlon N. Gilbert; p. 59, the Rev. Theodore Sedgwick; p. 60 (bottom), cornerstone; p. 61, floor plan; p. 64, church interior; p. 65, reredos; p. 66 (top), George Herbert Fairclough; p. 66 (bottom), choir camp; p. 73, sheet music; p. 74, Rev. Sedgwick Fairclough and choir; p. 77, Wigginton family; p. 80, vestrymen; p. 81, the Rev. Julius Augustus Schaad; p. 82, the Rev. Arthur Wadsworth Farnum; p. 83, girls choir; p. 84, Caroline and John Humbird; p. 86, Myers family; p. 87, Church club house exterior and interior; p. 89, Power family wedding; p. 93, Club House staff; p. 94, *Te Deum* window; p. 95, the Rev. Edward Makin Cross; p. 96, the rectory; p. 101, The Parish Aid Society; p. 107, Miss Goddard's School; p. 108, John Newlander; p. 109 (left), Edward Kopper; p. 109 (right), McNeil V. Seymour; p. 110, Rufus Harris; p. 114, St. Barnabas Mission; p. 116, women of St. John's; p. 117, women of St. John's; p. 116, Miss Sarah E. Baldy; p. 116, Mrs. Morton Barrows; p. 116, Mrs. Sylvester M. Cary; p. 116, Mrs. H. W. Fagley; p. 117, Mrs. N. S. Poole; p. 117, Mrs. William H. Merrick; p. 117, Miss Dorothy M. Punderson; p. 117, Mrs. Elma J. Harris; p. 119, the Rev. Frederick Dunton Butler; p. 120 (left), Mrs. Paul J. Kalman; p. 123 (left), Royal A. Moore; p. 123 (right), Julian S. Gilman; p. 125 (top), Crawford Brown; p. 126, Elizabeth Hensel; p. 129, Oehler family; p. 133 (top), boys choir camp members; p. 133 (bottom), boys choir camp members swimming; p. 134, boys choir camp; p. 135, girls choir camp; p. 136, William Gardner White and John (Jack) Hannaford; p. 137, the Rev. Conrad Herbert Gesner; p. 139 (right), C. Arthur Lyman; p. 141 (left), Caroline Rose Schurmeier Hannaford; p. 141 (right), Jule M. Hannaford Jr.; p. 143 (top), confirmation class; p. 144 (top), May and Clarence Johnston; p. 148 (right), Miss Carolyn Punderson; p. 149 (top), Betty and Bob Binger; p. 149 (bottom), Forrest and Nancy Clarkson Daniels; p. 155 (left), J. George Smith; p. 157, the Rev. Lloyd Russell Gillmett; p. 161 (top), one of the houses being moved to make room for the Parish House; p. 162, Dusty Mairs; p. 164, basketball Team; p. 165, Horace Hills Irvine; p. 168, Alden, Adrian, and Bram Drew; p. 169 (left), Jule Murat Hannaford Jr.; p. 169 (right), John Hannaford and Gertrude Hannaford Jaffray; p. 170, Kenneth G. Brill; p. 171, Garrett O. House; p. 172 (left), Christmastime at St. John's; p. 173, Nathaniel "Tan" Langford; p. 174, Arthur F. Zache; p. 175, two images of Shirley Hammergren Kartarik Michienzi; p. 176, Mead family and Peter Myers; p. 177, the Rev. William Henry Mead; p. 178 (top), Katherine Baldwin Lloyd Mead; p. 178 (bottom), pen-and-ink sketch of St. John's by Katherine Mead; p. 179 (left), Gertrude Heitmiller; p. 179 (center), Bob and Jan Andrews; p. 179 (right), Mary and Bayliss Griggs; p. 180, the Rev. David Benson; p. 183, Portell family, Marilyn Olson, and the Rev. Grayson Clary; p. 184, Francis G. Okie; p. 185 (right), John H. Myers family; p. 189, the Rev. William Henry Mead; p. 190, Clary family; p. 191, the Rev. Sidney Grayson Clary; p. 192, Reine Myers; p. 193, confirmation class; p. 197 (top), reading room; p. 197 (bottom), recreation program; p. 198 (top), John and Elizabeth Parish; p. 198 (bottom), confirmation class; p. 199, Annie Laurie Baker and the Rev. Robert Orr Baker; p. 200 (top), Dr. Charles Eastwick Smith Sr., Dr. Charles Eastwick Smith Jr., and Charles Eastwick Smith III; p. 200 (bottom left), Esther Easton McDavitt Smith; p. 200 (bottom right), Mary Guest Smith Platt; p. 202, Robert Kendall; p. 206, Betty and John Myers, the Rt. Rev. John M. Allin, Mrs. Allin, and the Most Rev. Donald Coggan; p. 207, the Very Rev. Robert M. Anderson; p. 208, Judy Diedrich; p. 209 (top), wedding of Mimie Pollard and Alden Drew; p. 209 (bottom), Dorothy MacDonald and Jean Clary; p. 210, former rector Lloyd Gilmett, Bishop Gesner, and rector Grayson Clary; p. 211, baptism of Benjamin G. Clary; p. 213, John Humbird Myers; p. 215, the Rev. Thomas Harries; p. 216, the rector search committee; p. 217, Dusty Mairs; p. 218 choir; p. 219 (top), choir; p. 219 (bottom), the Rev. Thomas Harries; p. 220

(top left), baptism of Robert Humbird Farmham; p. 220 (top right), Larson family; p. 220 (bottom left), Brodeen family; p. 220 (bottom center), Beattie family; p. 220 (bottom right), Bachman family; p. 221 (top left), Bob Yaeger and Justin; p. 221 (top center), Dorothy and Art MacDonald; p. 221 (top right), Kathy Yeager and Bree; p. 221 (center left), Mary Newbold, Jim Johnson, Dagny Gryttenholm; p. 221 (center right), Fred Myers and Elinor Strebel; p. 221 (bottom left), Jill Greene and Mary Lou Brackett; p. 221 (bottom right), Rosemary and Amy Klosterman, and Zola Sailor; p. 222 (top left), Monica and Ed Cook, Adrian and Alex; p. 222 (top right), Sarah Smith and Eloise Teisberg; p. 222 (bottom left), Susan Barker, Sarah Smith, and Mary Johnson; p. 222 (bottom right), Adrian and Dorothy Drew; p. 223 (top row from left to right), Ethelyn Rupp, Ellie Motter, Kathy Myer, Bernice Jensen; p. 223 (center), Lightner family; p. 223 (bottom), Plummer cabin; p. 224 (top left), Winton and Eleanor Hartman; p. 224 (top right), Lucy and Ted Owens; p. 224 (bottom), Sommers wedding; p. 225 (top), Cammie and Rob Beattie; p. 225 (bottom left), Ed and Monica Cook; p. 225 (bottom center), Kristi Yore and Paige Hagstom; p. 225 (bottom right), Dick Yore; pp. 226–27, At the Beach photos; p. 228, wedding of Gabrielle Lawrence and Don Postema; p. 229, the Rev. Richard B. Lampert; p. 230 (top), Lampert family; p. 230 (bottom left), Tom Edman and Kate Briggs with children; p. 230 (bottom right), John Edgerton III; p. 231 (top), Christopher Plummer, William Plummer, and Woodrow Keljik; p. 231 (bottom), Sona Plummer; p. 232 (top), Hillie and Ted Divett; p. 232 (bottom), Hagstrom family; p. 233, Brown family; p. 234 (left), altar; p. 234 (right), bell choir; p. 235, Bill and Margaret Plummer; p. 236, Agbaje family; p. 237 (top), Larry Blackburn; p. 237 (bottom), choir; p. 238, Shirley Sailors; p. 239 (top left), Holly Gross; p. 239 (top right), Eloise Teisberg; p. 239 (bottom), the Rev. Michael Tippett; p. 240 (top), Krista Tippett; p. 240 (bottom), Gertrude Jaffray; p. 241 (top), Margery Jeddeloh; p. 241 (bottom), church tower; p. 244, Mark Baumhover and Dusty Mairs; p. 246 (top), George Mairs, Bob Martin, Ella Slade, and Lucy Fellows; p. 246 (bottom), Howard Don Small; p. 248, John Oldfield; p. 249, Bishop James L. Jelinek; p. 250, Teens Encounter Christ; p. 251, the Rev. Frank E. Wilson; p. 253 (top), Youth Choir; p. 253 (bottom), Children's Choir; p. 254 (top left and right), Christmas pagent; p. 254 (bottom), Nell Hillsley; p. 255, architectural drawing; p. 256 (top), Kent Street entrance; p. 256 (bottom), Jaffray gardens; p. 257 (top); the Rev. Frank Wilson; p. 257 (bottom), undercroft; p. 259 (top), clergy; p. 259 (bottom), Artaria Chamber Music School; p. 262 (bottom), Mark Maronde; p. 263, Mimie Pollard, the Rev. Frank Wilson, the Rev. Barbara Mraz; p. 264 (left), Jim Frazier; p. 264 (right), Bob and Phyllis Merrill; p. 266 (top), cornerstone; p. 266 (bottom), Mary Probst Morrison; p. 267, Dorothy Nesbitt; p. 268 (bottom), window plan; p. 274, Dusty Mairs; p. 277 (top), Charles Olsen; p. 277 (bottom), church gardens; p. 278, St. John's Clinic; p. 279, St. John's Clinic; p. 281, youth group; p. 283, family of Walter F. Myers; p. 284, James Johnson and Lucy Jones; p. 285 (top), Don Husband; p. 285 (bottom), Phyllis and Ray Frisby; p. 286 (left), Jason Engquist; p. 286 (right), Katharine Bradtmiller; p. 290, The Reverend Jered Weber-Johnson; p. 291, Carnegie Hall; pp. 310–11, parishioners.

Stillwater Living, Stillwater, Minnesota
p. 262 (top left), Malcolm and Patricia McDonald.

303rd Bomb Group "Hell's Angels"
p. 151, Benepe Crew.

University of Minnesota Library, Minnesota Orchestra Archives Collection, Minneapolis, Minnesota
p. 41, organist and choirmaster Emil Oberhoffer.

Don F. Wong, Minneapolis, Minnesota
Back cover, Easter Sunday, copyright Don F. Wong.

INDEX

INDEX

INDEX

*Suffer the Little Children
to Come Unto Me. . .*

MARK 10:14

September 11, 2011

This book was designed
with care by

Mary Susan Oleson
NASHVILLE, TENNESSEE